CONTEMPORARY POLITICAL THOUGHT

A Critical Study

THE DORSEY SERIES IN POLITICAL SCIENCE

EDITOR NORTON E. LONG *Brandeis University*

CONTEMPORARY

POLITICAL THOUGHT

A Critical Study

EUGENE J. MEEHAN

Brandeis University

1967

THE DORSEY PRESS • Homewood, Illinois

First printing, June, 1967
Second printing, May, 1967

Library of Congress Catalog Card No. 67–21008

Printed in the United States of America

PREFACE

This volume, like its predecessor *The Theory and Method of Political Analysis,* arose out of a profound dissatisfaction with my own work, or more precisely, with my inability to give good reasons for the work I had been doing. This led, as it must for anyone who raises such questions, into a consideration of the methodology of political science, and resulted in the first volume in this sequence. In a way, the present book is an application of the way of thinking about politics developed in the book on methodology, and that work should probably be read in conjunction with this one by those who have not studied methodology systematically. The next step, logically, is to extend the same point of view into the study of political evaluation, at which point, I suppose, I can go back to the beginning and try correcting the mistakes I have made.

What I am proposing here is a new conception of the study of political thought; I have tried to defend and apply it in the main body of the text. While the book might aptly be titled "An Introduction to the Study of Political Thought," it should not be confused with an introduction to the study of *politics.* The latter would be quite different, for it would have to concern itself with the skills and conceptual structures needed to deal directly with political phenomena. The present volume is concerned with the same problem, of course, but at a level one step removed from direct concern with political data. I am trying to produce a paradigm for the study of the study of politics. It differs from methodology in the degree to which the data of politics form an integral part of the subject matter. The student of political thought has before him at all times, or should have before him at all times, both the phenomena of politics and the things that are said about those phenomena by way of explanation or evaluation. His task, as I see it, is to criticize and correct, to integrate, to disseminate, and thus hopefully, to assist in the cumulation of knowledge of politics.

Given this conception of the nature of political thought, the problem is to decide what kind of training the student of political thought needs to perform his job adequately. It is perfectly clear that he needs, more than anything else, sound training *in the study of politics*. Without such training, he is helpless. This volume presumes that it has gone before. And it is very important to say as emphatically as possible that study of the history of political thought is not and cannot be a substitute for the study of politics. The book is intended for students of politics who are interested in the kinds of problems that arise when we pass beyond direct inquiry to the critical study of explanation and evaluation. It is not an introduction to the study of history.

What the student of political thought must have, in this context, is an adequate grounding in methodology (*not* techniques of inquiry) and a conceptual apparatus that will allow him to deal with political studies as classes rather than as unique cases—otherwise the task would be impossible to perform. The key to the problem, I now believe, is the conceptual framework, the intellectual structure in which students of politics couch their explanations or evaluations. The main body of the text, therefore, is devoted to the study of conceptual frameworks. Perhaps it could have been managed in wholly abstract terms, but it seemed wiser, given the state of the discipline, to deal with concrete cases. I have therefore used contemporary political thought (roughly the last decade) as a base, combining a *way of studying* political thought with the actual study of a particular historical period—one that I consider the most significant in many, though not all, respects.

Throughout the text, the accent is on *criticism,* for learning what is the case without learning how it can be criticized is a poor substitute for education. The result will perhaps annoy those whose works have been dismembered, often very unfairly if we are thinking in terms of the value of the whole. It is more usual, I know, to treat one's colleagues and contemporaries with more tact and consideration. But in all honesty, I have little patience with those who can "find some good in everything," if only a balance is struck or external factors are taken into consideration. On those grounds, a man who violated, mutilated, and then murdered a small child could be excused on the ground that "anyone who likes children cannot be all bad." I construe the student of political thought as primarily a critic, and the critic's task, surely, is to render judgment as fairly and objectively as he can. It is no excuse for a weak explanation to argue that "all explanations are weak"; that may help us to understand why the situation exists, but it has no relevance in critical study. What cannot be done simply cannot be done, and it is no good admitting impossibility and then going ahead with the project. An office in which I once worked contained a sign that read, "The difficult we do immediately; the impossible takes a little longer." I do not find the attitude of mind it expresses in the least admirable, and in academic work it is catastrophic. We might end by believing it!

The text covers a wide range of subjects, and it was highly desirable that representative examples from different sub-branches of the discipline be included, but it is perfectly obvious that no individual could possibly be familiar enough with the mountain of material in political science to make an intelligent selection. I have, therefore, relied heavily on advice. Many of my colleagues were kind enough to enumerate for me the books they felt were most representative of the kind of work for which I was looking. In no way, of course, are they responsible for what has been done to the books. Doubtless, other choices could have been made had my own background, or my choice of advisers, been different.

The bibliographic references are included in the main body of the text where they are related directly to different topics. The result is a "messy" book, in some respects, but I believe it makes a more useful tool for the student. A second footnoting practice that may seem strange is the use of the full title instead of *op. cit.* when the original citation occurs more than a few pages earlier. A full citation is given on the first occasion and the date and publisher are dropped for subsequent citations. Anyone who has experienced the exasperation of tracing down a reference through a maze of *op. cit.*'s will, I believe, be grateful.

Finally, there is the ever pleasant task of acknowledging stimulation, assistance, and forbearance. For stimulation and assistance, I owe more than I can possibly say to my friend and colleague, Norton Long. Thanks for forbearance is due my wife, who has become something of a paragon of academic wifely virtues—to the astonishment of both of us. My gratitude to students, colleagues, and those whose writings have instructed me is great but hardly enumerable.

The responsibility for what I have done I accept cheerfully.

May, 1967   E. J. M.

TABLE OF CONTENTS

ix

PART III. POLITICAL EVALUATION

INDEX

CHAPTER ONE

THE STRUCTURE OF POLITICAL THOUGHT

THE study of political thought, political theory, or political philosophy has long been considered a fundamental part of the study of politics—of political science. Courses in these subjects, defined most commonly in terms of historical time periods, cultural divisions, or the writings of specific persons, are found in every political science curriculum; the field, variously defined, is a basic requirement for an advanced degree in political science at most universities. Yet the traditional way of defining and teaching political thought implies a curious bifurcation of the discipline, a separation of political *thought* and political *science* that is unwarranted and grossly misleading. Political science, in the traditional view, is studied to acquire knowledge of politics; but political thought is studied for other, often unspecified, reasons. That is, those who assert the value of studying political thought seldom do so on the ground that knowledge of politics can be acquired thereby; more commonly, they allude to the "broadening" and "humanizing" influence of the study of the great political philosophers, or they assign to "political philosophy" the study of political valuations, leaving the study of political phenomena to the political scientists. In fact, as political science has become increasingly rigorous and systematic, courses in political thought are often advo-

1

cated on precisely the grounds used to dragoon unwilling science and engineering majors into courses in the arts, letters, and humanities. Great, though unspecified, benefits are presumed to flow from participation in an activity that—by implication, at least—is either unpleasant or irrelevant.

This state of affairs is both dangerous and unnecessary. The implied bifurcation between the study of politics and the study of thought about politics suggests that political thought is not necessarily relevant to politics—a fantastic notion. And the belief that political thought ought properly to be classed with the arts and humanities, or made a branch of history, is unwarranted, pedantic, and dated. Such misconstructions flow from a very serious misconception regarding the nature of thought, derived, I suspect, from traditional philosophy and reinforced by the impulse to compartmentalization so endemic to American academic life. It is a major purpose of this book to challenge that construction of the nature and function of political thought and suggest an alternative that is more accurate and more useful.

WHAT IS POLITICAL THOUGHT?

Political thought is thought about politics. A simple tautology? On the contrary, according to contemporary usage, that simple statement appears as a radical assertion, implying both a new direction for the study of political thought and the rejection of certain academic traditions that have had a very long run indeed in Western universities. Yet the proposition *is* a tautology. Political thought *is* thought about politics. What else could it possibly be and remain "political" thought? And "thought about politics" has a reasonably definite meaning. Political thought is not an intellectual wastebasket that comprises anything one wants to throw into it. To be political thought, sets of propositions must satisfy at least some minimal criteria of acceptability; otherwise, they may be thoughts about nothing whatever.

Part of the difficulty with tradition arises from a fundamental ambiguity in the meaning of "political" that has never been resolved adequately. To have any meaning at all, "politics" must designate concrete phenomena that occur in human society. More specifically, politics is usually taken to mean certain phenomena that occur within organized groups of people, within associations. The ambiguity arises out of the common practice of referring to *certain kinds of actions* within an association as politics and at the same time using the term to designate the activities of *certain kinds of associations*. Either usage is acceptable, of course, provided that it is employed consistently. What is significant for our purposes is that the term must refer to some concrete body of phenomena, some aspect of human observation and experience; otherwise, it has no useful meaning. We cannot bound the political in advance any more than we can bound the phenomena that are comprised by physics. The subject matter of physics includes what physicists seek to explain; the bounds of political science can only be defined in the same way. To argue that particular phenomena are "not part of politics" is to resort to pure Platonism. All we can properly do is insist that there be some phenomena.

At this point the clash with tradition sharpens. Surely, it will be said, the person who studies political phenomena is a political scientist and not a political thinker. How are the two to be separated? The answer, quite simply, is that the separation *cannot* be made. What is more, there is absolutely no reason to try to make it except, perhaps, undue respect for outmoded tradition. The study of political thought *is* the study of politics, and if there is some division of labor within the discipline, that is only a reflection of the complexity of the topic. The criteria used in the study of political thought come from the study of politics, not from a historical or philosophical tradition. The political data employed by the political thinker can only be obtained by observation of politics. And most important of all, the political thinker must produce results that are useful for understanding politics, or he is deceiving himself. Literary masterpieces or philosophic gems may be interesting, but they have little or nothing to do with political thought except accidentally.

Political thought, to put the matter succinctly, necessarily involves a claim to knowledge of politics, though it may go beyond the claim to know and indulge in normative judgment or evaluation. Political thought is studied, by political scientists and others, out of a desire to acquire knowledge of politics, to learn the "how" and "why" of political phenomena and the "how" and "why" of normative evaluation of those phenomena. The criteria to be used in the study of political thought follow from these requirements. First and foremost, political thought must be relevant to some phenomenon, some part of human experience; otherwise, it cannot possibly be "political." Of course, various kinds of questions are relevant *to the study of* politics, though they are not part of political thought—methodological considerations are a good case in point. Since thought may be relevant but mistaken, or relevant and valid but trivial, criteria are also needed to distinguish what is valid and significant from what is mistaken and trivial. At a minimum, we must ask of any work in political thought: (1) Is it relevant? Does it say something about political phenomena? (2) Is it valid? Can we use it with confidence? (3) Is it significant? What are the consequences of accepting it? These questions are deceptively simple, and we must examine them in more detail in due course. For the moment, a brief summation of some of the consequences of adopting this conception of the nature of political thought may suggest something of its value for the discipline.

First, it has the virtue of distinguishing sharply between the study of political thought and the study of the history of political thought. Historical political thought can be studied with profit, of course, but the study of political thought is no more the study of intellectual history than the study of biological thought is the study of the history of biology. Biological thought! The words have a queer sound for it is an oddity of history that only a few branches of study use that nomenclature (political thought, economic thought), and they are for the most part in disrepute. Biological thought, if it means anything at all, means thought about the phenomena that biologists investigate. To suggest that it is in some way separate from the study of biology would be grammatically and traditionally improper. The study of biology produces biological thought, and no other activity could possibly do so. The biologist may be interested in studies made at an earlier time period, in the historical development of terms, concepts, and theories employed in his field, but only as an adjunct to his prime concern—understanding the phenomena. Similarly, the political scientist can find among the political thinkers of the past much that is well worth reading on its own merits, and he can profit from studying the development of concepts and conceptual frameworks within the discipline (which incidentally, is not the way in which the history of the development of political thought is usually taught). But as history, the work of past political thinkers can have no intrinsic interest for him.

Again, the concept of political thought proffered here eliminates the study of "great books" because of some intrinsic virtue they are alleged to possess. If the prime reason for studying any work is to acquire knowledge of politics, then the "masterpieces" are subject to the same criteria of evaluation as any other book. The accumulation of endless data about what certain writers have said about politics is a useless and even a debilitating occupation for political scientists. C. D. Broad makes the same point with reference to philosophy, in typically acrid terms:

The minute study of the works of great philosophers from the historical and philological point of view is an innocent and even praiseworthy occupation for learned men. But it is not philosophy; and, to me at least, it is not interesting. My primary interest . . . is to find out what is true and what is false about ethics and the statements of our authors are important to me only in so far as they suggest possible answers to this question.[1]

Great books, as Broad suggests, should be studied because they throw light on the phenomena because they explain or criticize well or because they suggest explanations and criticisms. To study them "for their own sake," whatever that might mean, would be a sheer waste of time for someone interested in politics. I am uninterested in their value as literature when I read them professionally, though I may of course be delighted to find literary merit in a work that is substantively significant.

Must Plato and Aristotle be abandoned by the contemporary student of politics? Of course not. In fact, no student can afford to ignore them, since they gain rather than lose in stature by being taken seriously. It is an insult to Aristotle's capacity to read him as a piece of dead history. The point is not *what* is read but *how* it is read, in what context it appears. To read the *Politics* without some purpose in mind, some criteria of evaluation (relevance to politics, for example) is a meaningless kind of activity that Aristotle himself would have condemned as mere rote learning. Without purpose, evaluation is impossible; and without evaluation, study becomes memorization. The *Politics* is worth careful study by anyone concerned with political phenomena simply because Aristotle said a great deal about the phenomena of organized social life that is still relevant, valid, and highly significant. The assertion that he was a "great political thinker" is not a justification for enforced reading of his works; but a critical reading of his work will, I believe, lead to the assertion that he was indeed a great political thinker. The difference between the two approaches, though it seems minor, is crucial.

A third useful consequence of changing our conception

---

[1] C. D. Broad, *Five Types of Ethical Theory* (Littlefield, Adams, 1959), p. 2 (original publication, 1930).

of the nature of political thought is the elimination of the scholastic outlook from the discipline. By insisting upon certain criteria of relevance, validity, and significance—empirical, logical, and linguistic criteria, broadly speaking—the study of political thought can be removed from the morass created by traditional emphasis upon *critique de texte*. There is nothing like insistence upon relevance to phenomena for eliminating nonsense. The practice of writing endless glosses on the writings of others without once referring to the phenomena in question ought to be stopped. Too many articles, dissertations, and books are produced each year under the general rubric "The Political Thought of _____," or "A Comparison of the Political Philosophies of X and Y," suitably embellished with endless references to the work of other glossators and no references whatever to the facts of political life.

While the elimination of intellectual debris is a worthy undertaking, I would not care to rest my case in favor of the conception of political thought I am recommending wholly on its negative virtues. In more positive terms, it could make the study of political thought an interesting and exciting discipline. Considered as a subdiscipline of political science, political thought could and should become the consolidating and editing device needed for systematic cumulation of our knowledge of politics. There is no reason why political thought cannot perform the same functions for political science that theoretical physics performs in physical science, and every reason why it should. There is no need to imply a sharp division of labor, with a "lower order" of political scientists collecting data and a "higher order" of theorists concocting theories and explanations. The process simply does not work out that way in any case. But the task of forging connections, of criticizing and consolidating both explanations and evaluations in systematic fashion desperately needs doing. The skills required are in some measure different from those used in direct inquiry into phenomena. At present, political science, and social science generally, is training far too few persons in these skills. I do not mean methodological competence alone or capacity to perform statistical calculations; neither methodologists nor statisticians are political scientists, and the task of theory building and normative criticism of political phenomena can only be performed by political scientists.

Ideally, every student of politics should proceed with his own special interests with some awareness of the needs of the discipline and the kinds of problems associated with the systematic cumulation of knowledge. It would add an important—indeed, an essential—dimension to inquiry. Political thought as presently taught and practiced does not further and may even impede development in that direction. The goal, after all, is increased knowledge—a meaningful "science" of politics, if you like, legitimately and not merely honorifically possessed of the qualifying adjective. Without a firm theoretical foundation, we cannot hope to construct valuational systems that can be defended intelligently. Those who condemn "science" on the ground that it interferes with the philosopher's function of moral criticism overlook the fact that no evaluational scheme is any stronger than the explanatory structure that supports it. Hence the development I am suggesting is essential whatever the view one takes of the end of political thought, that is, whether it is construed in explanatory or normative terms. Granted that we cannot hope to construct a system that will endure through the ages, we do know enough now to make certain essential corrections in our way of conducting inquiry; and, even though the results are unlikely to prove a panacea for the discipline, that is no excuse for failure to improve.

THE CONTENT OF POLITICAL THOUGHT

Analytically, thought about human society comprises three elements: descriptions, explanations, and evaluations. The list is exhaustive. Excluding formal logic, which is not "about" anything in the world of experience, and traditional metaphysics, which also has no empirical referents, thought must be relevant to some concrete phenomenon, some aspect of human experience. Observations may be made directly, or they may be taken from someone else's experiences, but every political thinker must begin with some set of phenomena. He can then choose among three courses of action: (1) he can describe the phenomena or assert what is the case; (2) he can explain the phenomena or tell us how or why things came to be as they are; or (3) he can evaluate or criticize the phenomena, either absolutely or relatively; that is, he may assert that "X is wrong" or "X is less desirable than Y." In practice, descriptions, explanations, and evaluations are combined. A "pure" description is virtually impossible to produce; no explanation is possible without description; evaluation depends on both description and explanation. The analytic separation, however, allows us to differentiate the criteria that are applied to different kinds of thought. A description, for example, is judged quite differently than an explanation or evaluation. Since political thought, like a high-fidelity sound system, is no better than its weakest component, the separation also allows us to focus our efforts and suggests an order of priority for inquiry. A good explanation of an ill-defined phenomenon is no better than a weak explanation of well-defined events, though the latter is perhaps to be preferred as less likely to be misleading and more easily corrected. In the remainder of this chapter, we shall examine some of the problems of description, explanation, and evaluation of political phenomena; the treatment is necessarily brief, and students who lack adequate background in methodological questions should probably begin by consulting one of the available volumes on the subject.[2]

[2]See Eugene J. Meehan, *The Theory and Method of Political Analysis,* (Dorsey Press, 1965); Abraham Kaplan, *The Conduct of Inquiry: Methodology for Behavioral Science* (Chandler Publishing Co., 1964); Quentin Gibson, *The Logic of Social Enquiry* (London: Routledge and Kegan Paul, 1960).

Description

Ordinarily, descriptions of political phenomena are not treated as an integral part of political thought. That is a profound mistake. While a volume that contains nothing but data about politics may not fit the traditional view of political thought, the political thinker may nevertheless have an absolute need for the data—transparent illustrations of the point can be found in election statistics and public opinion surveys. Descriptions provide the starting point for thought; without them, there is nothing to explain or evaluate. It follows that a solid grounding in political information, contemporary and historical, is an essential prerequisite for the study of political thought. Obviously, the data that political thinkers need cannot be fitted into a single, neat volume; but the training of those who plan to specialize in political thought must certainly include familiarization with the current state of knowledge in the discipline. We cannot here deal with the substance of political descriptions, but certain general properties of descriptions provide useful focuses for criticism, and they are worth careful attention.

Given a proposition purporting to describe a political phenomenon, three fundamental questions can be asked of it: (1) Does the proposition meet the minimum criteria of description? Does it provide data? (2) What is the degree of reliability of the data? (3) Finally, what is the conceptual framework in which the data appear? The political scientist, in other words, must concern himself with the fundamentals of epistemology.

1. Few persons today dispute the validity of the empiricist's claim that data must refer to experience in some sense of the term. To ask whether a description is valid is to ask whether or not it can be verified by observation or was produced by observation. Extreme empiricism is philosophically untenable; it leads to solipsism and to various other

undesirable consequences.[3] But the use of empirical observation as a limiting device seems a necessary prerequisite to the cumulation of systematic, reliable knowledge. The claim of the mystic, idealist, or intuitionist cannot be repudiated by empiricism, of course; but it cannot be affirmed, either; and if the purported description cannot, even in principle, be related to some kind of human experience, we are entitled to regard it with extreme suspicion. A description, then, means an empirical description. A firm belief in intuition or insight may satisfy the individual, but it cannot provide for either the transfer or the cumulation of knowledge on any acceptable basis.[4]

Perhaps the most common error found in handling descriptions is a failure to differentiate adequately between fact and concept. Indeed, the confusion of fact and concept may well be a more serious hazard in political science than the widely heralded confusion of fact and value. Strictly speaking, a fact is the sum of an observed set of properties, whereas a concept is a rule for dealing with such observations. Usually, facts are stipulated in terms of space, time, and distance, for even properties like color or texture can ultimately be reduced to such simples. Concepts, on the other hand, cannot be observed. Concepts are inferences, manufactured by humans for their own purposes, and not discoverable in nature. In physics, for example, certain measurable traces on photographic plates, obtained under stipulated circumstances, are the brute facts of nuclear physics. They are related and given meaning by the use of concepts like "particle" or "electron." In politics the facts are limited to subjective or objective aspects of human behavior; the concepts that relate them—"alienation," for example—are also unobservable. When concepts are

---

[3]See Robert Bierstedt, "A Critique of Empiricism in Sociology," *American Sociological Review*, Vol. XIV, No. 5 (October, 1949).

[4]A full treatment of the question can be found in Kaplan, *op. cit.*, chap. v.

used, as they must be, it is essential that some linkage be provided with the brute facts of the empirical universe. If I am to speak of alienation, I must have a set of observable indicators that will enable me to distinguish between a situation where alienation is found and a situation where it does not appear. Too often, social scientists make use of concepts for which there are no adequate indicators, especially in evaluation or normative judgment. Claims made on the basis of such concepts are difficult or even impossible to substantiate. Sidney Hook's plaintive protest against the psychoanalysts, who were unable to supply him with a set of indicators that would differentiate the presence or absence of an Oedipal complex, is only one example of the kinds of difficulties met in dealing with inadequately grounded concepts.

2. The reliability of a description depends upon the kind of observations by which it is produced. The term "observation" covers a variety of procedures and can be applied to a wide range of subject matters; there are, in other words, a number of empiricisms and not just one. A basic distinction can be made between observations made by a plurality of observers (a basic requirement in physical science) and observations made by one observer alone. Observation under controlled conditions is more reliable and precise than observation made under "natural" conditions, other things being equal. Observation of the objective aspects of human behavior differs from observation of subjective states. In general, public data are more reliable than subjective (individual, private) data; controlled data are more precise than data obtained in natural observations. But the distinctions need careful handling. Not all private data are trivial, by any means, and much data that is public is not worth gathering. Further, data obtained under controlled conditions may be grossly misleading—the controversy over the usefulness of data gained by observing rats in mazes against data obtained by ob-

serving animals in their natural habitat provides a case in point. A second distinction can be made between data that are measured and those that are not. Other things being equal, measurement is conducive to precision and verifiability. But again, things that can be measured are often less important than things that cannot be measured. Perhaps the most than can be said in general is that those using data should be aware of the manner in which the data were produced and have some notion of the amount of credence they are prepared to allow them. The belief that all facts are equal may be democratic, but it is not a good basis for inquiry.

3. Without a conceptual framework, description is impossible. The meaning and significance of facts derive from the conceptual structure employed by the observer. The reason is simply that every description is partial and incomplete; total description is impossible. We must, in other words, select and choose. The selection, in turn, depends on the purpose of the observer. That purpose shapes the conceptual framework he employs. It is a commonplace that a botanist and a zoologist see quite different things when they examine the same patch of ground. Facts that are extremely important for one are trivial or irrelevant for the other. Similarly, a political scientist concerned with the behavior of elites may produce quite a different description of a particular segment of political life than a political scientist interested in social stability. The problem of selection cannot be solved by developing a universal conceptual framework in which everything has a place—the observer would retire in despair from an impossible task. Yet, every description depends in some way on the particular conceptual structure in which it is produced. This causes some methodologists a great deal of concern; but in fact, it is not necessary to assume that because it is possible to view the same phenomena in different conceptual terms, each equally "valid," we must despair of "ob-

jectivity." It is one thing to agree that the validity of a description depends on the conceptual framework and another matter to argue that there must be one "correct" framework and hence that all others contain bias. That presupposes an absolute truth, a Platonic form, as a standard. We have no such form. Further, there is no reason why different conceptual frameworks should not be compatible, provided, of course, that one or another of them does not contain a hidden bias, a built-in evaluative scheme. Even then, a certain degree of compatibility can be achieved. In the Marxist scheme of things the owner of a business appears as an "exploiter," and the term is often used pejoratively (though not always by Marx himself), but the descriptions produced by Marxists are readily reconciled with other descriptions once we realize that we ought to read "owner of a business" where the term "exploiter" appears. Marxist *explanations* and *evaluations* will not always be compatible with others, of course; but at the descriptive level, reconciliation is often possible.

Explanation

Isolated facts have no meaning. That is why strict empiricism is impossible. Facts must be related systematically before they acquire significance and usefulness for man. The process by which facts are related we call explanation. It is probably the most important kind of intellectual activity in which human beings engage. When we say that we have knowledge, what we mean, usually, is that we are able to explain things. That is, we can say "why" or "how" things occur. Much of our capacity to explain everyday events is so thoroughly ingrained into our behavior patterns that we rarely think about it—unless it fails to work. One of the prime functions of systematic inquiry is to make explicit the kind of processes involved in our everyday thinking—to get at what is involved in explanation.

If water is placed in an open pan and boiled, the volume of water in the pan decreases. Why does this happen? How does it happen? Such questions are requests for an explanation. The basic principles on which explanations of such phenomena are offered are fairly simple, though their application may be rather complex. An individual event (the change in the volume of water) is explained by referring to certain generalizations which link that event to other events in a way that leads us to expect the event to occur. The expectations must have some justification in experience. For example, when a stone is thrown into the air, we expect it to return to earth. Why? Because we know by experience certain well-established generalizations about the behavior of moving objects at or near the earth's surface that we call the laws of motion and the law of gravity. The caveman may well have entertained similar expectations, but we have proceeded beyond him to the point where we know *why* we have those expectations. We are able to explain the phenomenon. Of course, if we go beyond the moving stone and ask why we expect the law of gravity to operate, we ultimately reach a point where explanation fails. All we can say is that things *do* behave in a certain way, and we can make use of the facts of their behavior even if we are unable to explain why the behavior occurs.

It is important to note that generalizations alone cannot provide us with an explanation; they must in some fashion be linked to the particular event to be explained. There must be some *warrant* for believing that the generalization applies to the case at hand. When the generalizations take a particular form ("All *A* is *B*," what are called *universal* generalizations), the warrant for the inference comes from the rules of formal deductive logic. If *all* objects thrown into the air return to earth, and a stone is an object, then it follows that the stone will also return to the earth. When the generalization takes a different logical form ("Some

A is *B*," or *n* percent of *A* is *B*, what are called *probabilistic* generalizations), no formal logical inference can be made from the generalization to the particular case. The problem of connecting the event to be explained to the generalizations that explain it can be a serious matter, and since in the social sciences there are few if any universal generalizations, the problem is real and immediate. Usually it is solved by relating separate generalizations *through* the phenomenon to be explained, not by deducing the phenomenon from the generalization. An example of the two modes of explanation will serve to illustrate the structure of explanations and suggest the kinds of warrants that can be employed for linking data and generalizations.

A Deductive Explanation. When water is boiled in an open pan, its volume decreases. The phenomenon can be observed by anyone, and careful measurement of its dimensions is a simple matter. How is the phenomenon (loss of volume) to be explained? In grossly simplified terms, we can explain it deductively, first by linking it to a single universal generalization and then by linking it to a set of generalizations that we call molecular theory. Note that an explanation is offered only for a difference or a change, not for a static event. It is useful to ask "Why is that cow brown?" or "Why is that one black?" but pointless to ask "Why is a cow?"

We can explain the loss of volume in boiled water first by referring to the universal generalization (which is well established) that water *always* loses volume when it is boiled in an open pan. The generalization links two classes of events: boiling water and loss of volume. Our phenomenon is a member of one of these two classes; therefore, according to the terms of the generalization, it is also a member of the other. The form of the explanation is simple:

1. If boiling water, then loss of volume—All *A* is *B*.
2. Our phenomenon is boiling water—*X* is *A*.
3. ∴ Loss of volume is to be expected—*X* is *B*.

What we have done, really, is to create a set of expectations on the basis of our past experience with a certain kind of event, boiling water.

If the listener then demands to know why the boiling water always loses volume (he wants an explanation of a generalization rather than an explanation of a particular event), the answer will appear, if it is available, in the form of further generalizations of wider generality or sets of generalizations, linked together deductively. Usually, an explanation of a generalization is called a *theory*, though there is no real agreement on the precise meaning of "theory."

In much simplified form, the explanation of the generalization linking boiling water and volume loss—what is called molecular theory—goes as follows:

1. All substances are composed of tiny particles called molecules. They are in constant motion. The state of the substance (solid, liquid, gas) depends on the cohesion of the molecules. Cohesion, in turn, depends on the speed with which the molecules are moving.
2. The speed of molecular motion depends on the amount of energy the molecules carry. Heating a substance increases molecular speed. As speed increases beyond a critical point, the state of the material changes.
3. Water heated above the boiling point changes from liquid to the gaseous state. Gas molecules diffuse through the atmosphere.
4. Molecules of liquid lost into the atmosphere are subtracted from the sum total of molecules in the pan when heating began. That amount is measurable.

From these statements—phrased more precisely, of course —it can be deduced that any liquid heated beyond a given point will lose volume through molecular diffusion. The connection between the phenomenon to be explained, and the generalization to be explained, and molecular theory is strictly deductive.

A Probabilistic Explanation.   Unfortunately, deductive explanations are rarely if ever possible in political science, for there are few if any established universal generalizations in the field. But an explanation can be offered for political phenomena that makes it *likely* that the phenomenon will occur even though the degree of uncertainty is much greater than is the case in a deductive explanation. The key to the difference lies in the *type* of generalizations established within a given discipline. An example will illustrate the kind of explanation that political science can offer of particular phenomena; we can then return to the examination of the structure of generalizations and hopefully account for the difference in force of the two kinds of explanations.

In recent Presidential elections in the United States, most of the Negro vote in the large northern cities has been cast for the candidate representing the Democratic party. How is this to be explained? We cannot simply refer to a generalization like "All Negroes in the United States vote for the Democratic candidate in Presidential elections," since that generalization is known to be false. But by bringing together a number of generalizations, each related to the phenomenon in some way, we can produce an explanation that makes it *likely* that the vote in Presidential elections will divide in this way.

1. On issues of interest to Negroes as a class, the record of the Democratic party is more favorable to the Negro than the record of the Republican party. (Hidden premise: Minority group members tend to vote for the party that favors legislation beneficial to their group.)
2. The major Negro organizations in the United States usually support the Democratic candidate in Presidential elections. (Hidden premise: Members of minority groups tend to follow the advice of the leaders of their community.)
3. The Democratic party tends to be more favorable than the Republicans to legislation favoring low-income groups. (Hidden premise: Most Negroes are members of low-income groups; Negro voters are influenced by economic matters.)

These propositions, plus a number of others that are relevant to the question of voting preference, lead us to expect the Negro vote to be cast chiefly, but not entirely, for the Democratic candidate in Presidential elections. That conclusion cannot, however, be *deduced* from the generalizations; therefore the warrant for the conclusion is not formal. Every generalization employed makes use of relative terms like "tends to," "usually," and "most," instead of "every" and "all." The use of relative rather than universalistic terms reduces the *force* of the explanation, meaning simply that we would be less surprised if the explanation proved faulty than would be the case if the explanation were deductive in form. Finally, the explanation tells us nothing about the behavior of any particular Negro voter: It is only useful when we deal with Negro voters as a class.

We can leave our "overview" of the process of explanation at this point and return to a closer examination of the fundamental elements in explanations—generalizations and theories.

Generalizations

Formally, a generalization is a proposition that relates two or more classes of events so that some or all of the members of one class are also members of the other. For simplicity's sake, we shall consider only the case in which there are two classes, A and B. The use of symbols is deceptive, since either A or B may designate very complex propositions—for example, "all persons who are born citizens of the United States during a given time period of parents with particular ethnic, religious, and territorial properties." Formally, there are three types or forms of generalizations:

1. Universal. "All A is B." The relation is not reversible. For example, all Negroes are members of a minority group if they live in the United States, but not all members of a

minority group are Negroes. The equivalent proposition
in logic is "Not *B* then not *A*."

2. Probabilistic. "*N* percent of *A* is *B*." Generalizations
in this form can be applied *only* to whole classes, not to individual members of a class. If, for example, we know that
75 percent of the students in American high schools are
white, the generalization tells us nothing about the composition of any particular school, class, or person in the
high school system.

3. Tendency Statements. "Some *A* is *B*," or more precisely, "*A* tends to B, unless something interferes." This is
a form of probabilistic generalization that differs from (2)
in not specifying an arithmetical ratio between *A* and *B*.
Like (2), it is applicable only to whole classes, not to individual members of a class. The strength of the statement
depends on our ability to specify interfering factors.

For the present, political science deals almost entirely
with probabilistic generalizations and tendency statements.
Universal generalizations are rare and perhaps nonexistent.

A clear distinction must be made between a generalization, a classification, and a description. A classification system asserts that all members of a particular class share
certain properties *by definition*. If the class *X* is defined as
all objects with properties *a, b, c, d*, etc., then any phenomenon that has those properties, among others, is automatically a member of the class. A good classification system
is an aid to clarification, and it can be highly suggestive,
but it is not an explanation and it adds nothing to our
store of knowledge. To know that a given phenomenon is
a member of class *X* is to know only that it has the defining
properties of class *X*, whatever they may be. On the other
hand, to know that a phenomenon has the defining properties of class Z is to know only that it is a member of the
class. Classification systems are tautologous. A generalization, on the other hand, is nontautologous; it *connects*
classes. If a generalization links classes *X* and *Y*, then to

know that a phenomenon is a member of class X is to know that it is, or may be, related to Y as well. As an example, suppose that I define a class of objects, $ABBA$, as all objects with six sides. If I then say that X is an $ABBA$, we know that X has six sides; any object that has six sides may be called an $ABBA$. That is not terribly illuminating. However, if I am able to tell you that all $ABBA$'s are extremely powerful structures when employed in architecture, then to know that X is an $ABBA$ is to know *more than* the defining terms of the class. Under some circumstances, that extra bit of knowledge can be valuable.

A generalization also differs significantly from a description. Generalizations are inductions; they go beyond descriptions by making assertions about classes not all of which have been observed. That is the reason why no generalization is absolutely certain. New information may always come along to invalidate the generalization, even though we may consider it unlikely. A classic example is found in the case of the white swans. Until black swans were discovered in Australia, the generalization "All swans are white" was, as far as Europeans knew, valid. The discovery of Australian black swans forced a change in the generalization. "All European swans are white" is still valid, of course, as is "All swans are either black or white," but some of the strength of the older generalization was lost. For political scientists, it is particularly important to distinguish between statistical propositions about the past and generalizations. For example, if it can be shown that in the past 64 percent of all Negroes cast their vote for the Democratic candidate in Presidential elections, that would be *evidence for* a generalization in the form "Most Negroes support the Democratic candidate in Presidential elections"; but the statement is not, as it stands, a generalization. It is a description of past events. A generalization makes an assertion about *all* Presidential elections, past and future; a description refers only to elections held in the past.

How are generalizations produced? That we do not know. But every valid generalization has an independent existence of its own, it must rest on some evidence. The relationship between a generalization and its evidence is a very important matter, and some philosophers of science hold that it is far more important to be able to *disverify* or disprove a generalization than to support it. The difficulty with supporting a generalization is that the evidence is never complete, since generalizations refer to the future as well as the past. But it may be possible, on the basis of available evidence, to show that the generalization *does not* hold. That was the case with the generalization about the swans. When a generalization is universal in form, disverification is relatively simple; only *one* case to the contrary is needed to show that it does not hold. Similarly, when a generalization states a definite arithmetical ratio between classes, that too is easily tested. But what is to be done with tendency statements? How much is "most"? More than half, certainly, but how much more? The least useful generalization we can have tells us that exactly 50 percent of all cases of A are B. Given that information, we can only assume randomness. The statement is virtually noninformative. In the long run, even very weak generalizations can be valuable, and gambling establishments operate quite profitably on generalizations that establish a fairly narrow long-run margin of returns. But if no ratios or percentages are available, the usefulness of a tendency statement is hard to evaluate. We shall return to this problem again. For the moment, we need to emphasize the fact that the kinds of generalizations available to political scientists are independent of the wishes of political scientists; their logical structure depends on the nature of human experiences and nothing else. Hence the problem is to do the best one can with what is available, not to sit back and wait for universal generalizations to appear—or worse, to delude oneself into believing that universal generalizations are available when in fact they are not.

Theories and Quasi Theories

Strictly speaking, a theory is a set of deductively related generalizations that can be used to explain other generalizations. In the strict sense of the term, there are few if any theories in the social sciences. It is therefore a relatively simple matter to examine the work being done by political scientists and proclaim, on the basis of this definition of theory, that there are no theories in the discipline. However, if we leave aside the nomenclature for a moment and ask what functions theories perform in inquiry, it soon becomes apparent that the problem of evaluating the work done in political science is not so simple. Clearly, a theory must be able to explain. But deductively related theories do more than explain; they enable us to make predictions, they suggest areas that need further exploration, they suggest the consequences of altering one or more of the variables in a situation, and so on. Some of these same functions can be performed by conceptual structures that are not deductively related. We shall here use the term "quasi theory" to designate them. Some quasi theories explain perfectly well but cannot predict. Some predict but have no explanatory capacity. Some are highly suggestive, though they neither explain nor predict. The point is that discussion of the question "Is that *really* a theory?" is rather fruitless. To take the instrumentalist point of view, if we get the results we need, then the conceptual structure is useful whether or not it is a deductively related system. In these terms the social sciences may have very few "genuine" theories, but that is far less important than their capacity to explain, predict, and direct inquiry.

A set of generalizations can be bound together in a number of ways. When they are related by the canons of formal logic, the result is a deductive theory, a hierarchy of universal propositions formally deduced from a set of prime axioms. In philosophy of science, such structures are considered the only form properly deserving the title "theory." But since they are virtually nonexistent in the social sciences, we can bypass them here and go on to consider other kinds of relationships. When generalizations are related *through* the phenomenon they are to explain, the result is what Abraham Kaplan calls a *concatenated* theory. The most common example is a factor theory, a structure that explains by stipulating the necessary and/or sufficient conditions for the generation of a particular phenomenon. The generalizations must of course be established independently of the theory. The theory is actually the selection of generalizations employed in the explanation plus any statements that can be made about the interaction of the variables included in the theory. The form of a concatenated theory is relatively straightforward:

Unless $A, B, C,$ and D $\longrightarrow$ no X (necessary conditions)
If A, B, C, D, E $\longrightarrow$ then X (sufficient conditions)

The linkage among the variables can be shown schematically as follows:

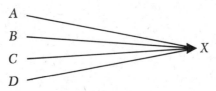

The variables are linked by their common focus on the phenomenon—X.

Theories, or explanations, may be classified according to their logical form or their function. Deductive and concatenated theories are classified by logical form. *Causal* explanations stipulate the necessary and/or sufficient conditions for the appearance of a given phenomenon; *genetic* explanations trace the development of a phenomenon through successive stages; *teleological* explanations make use of the concept of purpose or goal as an explanatory device. We can, for example, explain the appearance of ice by reference to a drop in temperature (causal), explain the existence of the United Nations by tracing a development over the centuries (genetic), or explain the Supreme Court by demonstrating its function in the American political system (teleological).

Most of the conceptual structures found in political science are quasi theories, according to the strict definition of "theory," though there are some factor theories that probably qualify even by philosophy-of-science standards. What is more important, however, is that political scientists have some limited capacity to explain, some ability to predict, and some basis for charting a course through the phenomena, separating what is significant from what is not. Unfortunately, the supply of adequate generalizations is woefully short, and there remain vast areas that have yet to be charted systematically. The problems are severe. Measurement is often difficult. Controlled experiments cannot readily be performed. Even terminology suffers from lack of standardization. The theories political science deploys are weak. We rely heavily upon quasi theories—models, analogies, even metaphors—to relate our data. While quasi theories can generate the same kinds of expectations about the phenomena that theories induce, they are decidedly less trustworthy and more dangerous to use; and of course, they are much less powerful. Too often, we must blast away with a shotgun at long range when it would be much easier and simpler if we had a high-powered rifle with a telescopic sight.

Quasi theories, or conceptual frameworks, consist of sets of generalizations, but of a type different from those found in theories. The generalizations that have been established empirically are likely to be weak. Often, "speculative" rather than empirical generalizations are included; the generalizations are stipulated rather than established. And in the case of models the generalizations may be purely formal and unrelated to any particular empirical phenomenon. However, quasi theories are not usually manufactured out of whole cloth; they are built with some particular purpose in mind, and they are not wholly unrelated to data. They are built by assuming at the outset that a particular set of phenomena behave like the elements in the quasi theory, in the analogy or model. We treat the data "as if" the analogue were a powerful theory. When such speculative structures can be modified and strengthened through application they are a fruitful source of theory. And as a general strategy, in the absence of more powerful resources, the use of such hypothetical structures has much to be said for it. The danger, of course, is that the facts may be forced into a pattern, or that the observer will forget that he is working with a weak analogy and begin treating his results as though he possessed a powerful theory. If the dangers are avoided, quasi theories can be an aid to explanation, prediction, or the conduct of inquiry. A few examples will illustrate their uses and limitations.

Classifications. The simplest possible kind of conceptual framework is a classification, a suggested set of categories for collecting political data. As we have already seen, classification systems have no explanatory capacity, and it follows that they cannot predict, either. Their prime usefulness is for data gathering; they can suggest the lines that research ought to follow. Gabriel A. Almond's proposal that politics be studied in terms of seven "variables" is a typical example of a classification scheme.[5] The four "inputs" to the system are defined as political socialization and recruitment, interest articulation, interest aggregation, and political communication; the three "outputs" are legislation, execution, and adjudication. The classification suggests that information relating to these seven categories should be the prime objects of research, particularly in newly developing countries. This can introduce coherence into research, though it also carries the danger that too many useless data

[5]Gabriel A. Almond and James S. Coleman (eds.), *The Politics of the Developing Areas* (Princeton University Press, 1960), chap. i.

will be collected if the categories are too broad (as Almond's seem to be) and important data may be overlooked if the classification scheme is too narrow. No classification system should be taken too seriously. In all honesty, we simply do not yet know enough about politics to be able to say with assurance that information about category X should be gathered whereas Y can safely be ignored. If the whole profession were to accept Almond's classification, we cannot take it for granted that the results would be desirable. They might equally well be harmful.

The chief use of classification is to aid exploration of a relatively virgin field of inquiry. Even though the ordering proves inadequate, ordered data are easier to handle than randomized information. Other things being equal, a classification ought not to include empty classes, since logically all things are true of them. The defining terms of the system should have empirical relevance. And so far as precision is possible, the more detailed the class descriptions, the more useful the classification. However, there is a limit— the so-called "index number" problem. The more precisely a class is defined, the more limited its membership. The class that includes "all farmers" contains more members than the class of "rich, Protestant, Midwestern farmers," but it is probably possible to say things more precisely and richly about the latter class. Ultimately, classifications reach extremes where it is possible to say almost nothing at all about a very fully defined class or to say a great deal about a class that is so ill-defined as to be useless. Triviality lies at both extremes to trap the unwary.

Classifications must be useful. That is the principal demand that can be placed on them. If a classification does not serve some useful purpose for someone, it is pointless. In extreme cases, it can be argued that the ordering of chaotic data is a sufficient justification for even an inadequate classification, but that condition is rare today. Too often, social scientists propose quite elaborate and complex classification schemes without stipulating how they might be used—without justifying, in other words, the amount of time and energy that would be required to order the data according to the classification. Since there is and can be no universal classification system, no scheme that will serve every purpose, each classification has limited purposes, and those purposes should be made clear when classifications are either proposed or adopted.

Dichotomies. A second form of conceptual framework is the dichotomy, which may take the form of a polarity with two extremes and no middle, or a continuum with intervals that are either scaled or unscaled. Like the classification, the dichotomy is useful for comparison, but it has no explanatory power. Its chief use is to focus observation and suggest further inquiry. The "ideal type" proposed by Max Weber is *not* a dichotomy or a comparative device, at least not in the form in which he used it; it is a model, a system of interacting parts, which can be examined for suggestions about the expected behavior of the phenomena for which it is the model.

The principal difficulty with dichotomies is that they degenerate too easily into evaluational systems. Dichotomies between open and closed societies, between *gemeinschaft* and *gesellschaft* societies, are good cases in point; though they can often bring out quite useful differences among societies, they can—and often do—imply a normative distinction between good and evil, right and wrong, which is very misleading. A second major drawback to the use of dichotomies is that they tend to facilitate improper inferences from observed differences to consequences of differences. Technically, a dichotomy is only a classification scheme, and though it can draw attention to differences between two structures, it provides no warrant for any inference that might be made about the significance of those differences. Inferences require generalizations that can link the differences revealed by the dichotomy to stipulated consequences. Unfortunately, social scientists often seem committed to what might be called the "difference" fallacy— the assumption that *all* differences make a difference. The significance of any difference must be established independently of the conceptual framework that reveals the difference; and the term "make a difference" always demands a referent—the inference must stipulate *for whom* the difference is significant. A common example of this form of abuse is the inferences that are drawn about the consequences for human life of a change from private enterprise to publicly owned productive facilities. There may of course be very important consequences, but few empirical generalizations have actually been established with reference to this point. Until the precise meaning of an inference has been established, and a warrant provided for its acceptance, such claims depend on faith rather than reasoned argument.

Dichotomies, like classifications, must have some purpose. Probably the chief use to which dichotomies are put in social science is evaluative rather than explanatory, and discussion of that use is deferred to Part III. In explanation, their principal use is heuristic—they suggest distinctions that require exploration and may lead to the development of factor theories. Critically, the difficulty with dichotomies is that it is hard to be certain that the comparisons go beyond verbal similarities, that the properties being compared are genuinely comparable. Comparisons of underdeveloped and developed societies in terms of dollar income, for example, may be grossly misleading and evaluative rather than informative. Similarly, comparisons limited to the content of written constitutions, which disregard the implementation of constitutional provisions, are not likely to provide valuable information. These are only "commonsense" limitations, of course, but conceptual frameworks that violate commonsense limitations ought to be regarded very warily.

Analogies. A more complex and more useful kind of quasi theory is the organic or mechanical analogy. By assuming that politics, or some aspect of politics, is analogous to all or part of some living organism or mechanical device, our knowledge of the organism or the machine can be used to further explanation, prediction, or exploration of the phenomena being studied. Analogies between the human body and human society have been common since the earliest days of political speculation; and mechanical analogies are often highly illuminating, even in physical science. So long as it is understood that arguments rest on analogies, much good and little harm can come from their use. In fact, it is probable that political scientists have been overly frightened of organic analogies by the furor in sociology over the work of organicists like Herbert Spencer. The crucial point is the need to demonstrate the similarity of process in the analogue and in the event, and not merely to assume it. We can then transfer knowledge from one field to another in a most effective way. The fact that analogies are readily abused is not an argument against their use; it is only a warning against unthinking or indiscriminate use.

The organic analogy is informal or nonlogical. Mechanical models, on the other hand, are formal and determinate in the sense that the complete operation of the structure can be specified. Formal models can also be borrowed from logic or mathematics, or created for a particular purpose. Characteristically, formal models are completely defined, and the rules for the interaction of the elements in the model are stipulated unambiguously. Chess is a good example of a formal system of this kind; so is geometry. Since formal systems are wholly abstract to begin with, their application requires a demonstration of the relationship between the elements of the model, or its processes, and the phenomenon to which it is applied. The two aspects of formal models need to be kept separate. If it can be shown that the elements in a formal model are precisely the same as a set of elements in the empirical world, it does not follow that the elements in the empirical world behave as they do in the model. *Both* elements and interactions must be considered separately. The kind of parallel that is needed depends on the purpose of the inquiry. If a model is used as an aid to explanation, then the interaction of the elements in the system is prime; if the model is used for prediction, the outcome of dynamic processes in model and empirical world must be similar. A formal model that will predict election outcomes on the basis of partial results, like the "models" used by broadcasting corporations during national elections, may have no explanatory capacity whatever. On the other hand, a model may be used to explain (the use of water-pipe models to demonstrate the properties of electricity, for example) but have little or no predictive capacity. In short, quasi theories of this kind (models and analogies) can be used to create patterns of expectations about the empirical world, both with regard to the past and for the future (explanation and prediction), and they may also serve as useful teaching devices or heuristics.

The warrant for transferring expectations from a model or an analogy to empirical phenomena depends on the degree of congruence between the model and the phenomena. If they are perfectly congruent, expectations can be as confidently held in one area as in the other. However, that never occurs. First, we usually use models and analogies simply *because* our knowledge of phenomena is inadequate; second, a model should be simpler or more amenable to manipulation than the real phenomenon if there is to be any point in using it. Models are always partial and approximate, as are analogies. It follows that there will be properties of observed reality not duplicated in the model, at least potentially, and it is always possible that models have properties that are not duplicated in the empirical world. Furthermore, models and analogies may be useful in creating some expectations with regard to reality (supposing them to have congruence with reality) but may be quite useless and even misleading in other respects. A model may suggest the direction of a change quite accurately, for example, yet prove very misleading with regard to the speed or the scale of change. Finally, models and analogies should not be mistaken for *utopias*. A model or analogy is a *suggestive* device, not an ideal for evaluating reality. The use of models is predicated on the belief that a small, simple system which is congruent to a large and complex system in some respects may suggest characteristics of the larger system that would escape notice if it were examined directly. Now, that is precisely the argument that Plato followed in the beginning of the *Republic*, but Plato did not then proceed to create a model; instead, he created a utopia, a perfect specimen of the type, an ideal, which could be used to *criticize* reality. Methodologically, that procedure is grossly improper.

Models, analogies, and metaphors, then, are useful for suggesting expectations about empirical phenomena. The warrant for actually holding those expectations must come from an examination of the relationships between model or metaphor and the phenomenon. Further, the warrant will only hold good for certain kinds of expectations because of the partiality of the model or analogy. It is sometimes said that the richness and the predictive rigor or the model are among its more important properties, but that does not necessarily follow.[6] Indeed, there may be very good arguments against the use of overcomplex models in social science. What really counts is suggestibility. This may be a function of the model's complexity and richness, but a very complex model may also be less sugges-

[6]For example, Karl W. Deutsch, *The Nerves of Government: Models of Political Communication and Control* (Free Press of Glencoe, Inc., 1963), especially pp. 16–18.

tive than a simpler affair if too much effort is needed to grasp its operation.

The dangers involved in the use of model, analogy, and metaphor have been pointed out so often that it may be superfluous to add to the indictment. The most common errors are (1) to attribute to reality what are only properties of the model; (2) to move carelessly from model to reality and thus create unwarranted expectations; (3) to fail to ascertain the degree of congruence between model and phenomena; and (4) perhaps most important of all, to fail to bear in mind the partially and limited usefulness of any model or analogue. So long as they are treated purely as suggestive devices and all conclusions, expectations, or inferences derived from them are verified carefully by referring to genuine phenomena, models are one of the more useful tools available to social science. Indeed, social scientists can perhaps be chided for failing to create adequate models or make full use of some of the formal logical structures that are now available in mathematics in their explorations of social phenomena.

It is perhaps worth noting that models and analogies have the same logical form as factor theories, for a model or analogy is built upon a set of relationships among prescribed elements. This suggests that the number of points at which an analogy is congruent to empirical phenomena is less significant than the importance of the points of congruence, just as it is more useful to have the crucial factors included in a factor theory than to include factors that have little or no influence on the behavior of the system. In the same vein, "crucial" points are those which define the necessary and sufficient conditions for an event. What is implied here is that the use of models and analogies involves us in a general research strategy of successive approximations, interspersed with testing. Any attempt to apply a model will presumably reveal discrepancies, and they can be used to modify the model; further applications should move the model closer to reality and could change the character of the model to a genuine theory. That is, the generalizations explicitly or implicitly contained in the model would have to be reproduced in empirical reality for the operating conditions of the model to apply; as the two systems move closer together, stipulative generalizations may be replaced by empirical generalizations (which require independent validation), and the model, if successful, is transformed.

Finally, there are conceptual frameworks that serve not as explanatory or predictive devices but as evaluators. That is, there are conceptual structures, or quasi theories, that contain built-in evaluations, and their use produces ready-made value judgments. The classic example, epitomized in the Hollywood "western," is the conflict between good and evil; but the distinction between "we" and "they," between "God" and "Satan," follows the same pattern. The Marxist structure, for all its claim to scientific objectivity, involves a necessary bias, and Freudianism has the same normative characteristics. The distinguishing feature of such evaluative conceptual frameworks is that their use as a frame of reference actually enforces a particular set of values on the user. Ideological systems produce this same "prismatic" effect, so that the meaning of facts and even the facts themselves become contingent on the principles of the ideology. Since these conceptual frameworks much facilitate normative judgment, they are widely employed by social critics, and we shall meet them again in our discussions of the substance of contemporary political evaluation.

EVALUATION

Faced with a set of "political" phenomena, the student of politics may describe, explain, or evaluate. In recent years, political scientists have shunned evaluation, or normative judgment, like the plague, concentrating on description and explanation. Yet there is an undeniably close relationship between government and normative judgment, for to govern is to make normative judgments of exceptional importance. It is therefore somewhat disconcerting to discover how little has been done in political science —or in the whole of social science, for that matter—to develop the criteria and methods that are needed for systematic analysis and evaluation of normative argument. The field of inquiry has gone to others by default, with appalling results. Traditional political philosophy, whose province includes the normative, tends to remain historical, literary, and verbal; it is little influenced by analytic or empirical considerations. Given the importance of the topic, if normative judgments belong to philosophy as a field, then philosophy is perhaps too important to be left to the philosophers. There is no reason why the study of normative judgments cannot be carried on in the same spirit, with the same tools, and by the same people, as political explanation. Indeed, it can be argued that no other group has the necessary equipment. Of course, criteria and methods of inquiry peculiar to the needs of normative analysis are also needed, but current standards of argument could produce an enormous improvement in the quality of the field if they were applied systematically and rigorously. The need for specialization within a discipline is obvious, but if it is carried to the point where students of normative judgment have little substantive knowledge of politics, it becomes self-defeating. Normative inquiry, in other words, needs to be integrated into the study of political thought. Further, it seems reasonably certain that it *can* be made an integral part of the field.

What follows is no more than a beginning, and perhaps only a false start, in that direction. The aim is to produce an analytic framework that will clarify the structure of normative judgments, suggest points in that structure that are particularly significant, and indicate some of the criteria that can be applied to them. The kinds of discussions and arguments presently employed by moral philosophers, particularly in metaethics, are avoided deliberately. Linguistic analysis is certainly useful as a tool for clarifying grammar and syntax, but it is virtually useless when argument depends upon substantive knowledge. The treatment of value judgments suggested here relies heavily on the kind of substantive knowledge of politics that political scientists could be expected to acquire during their training. The object is to suggest the kinds of criticisms that are important for political science and possible for political scientists, and not to produce an essay in moral philosophy.

THE STRUCTURE OF NORMATIVE JUDGMENT

A normative judgment, like a description or an explanation, must refer to some phenomenon, directly or indirectly; otherwise, it is unlikely to be meaningful. The study of normative judgments, then, parallels the study of explanation, for in each case we focus upon the relationship between a set of phenomena and an abstract human creation which relates to those phenomena. One grossly misleading conception of the nature of the problem of evaluating normative judgments can be dismissed summarily, to wit, the view that the logical disjunction between statements of fact and statements of value effectively precludes reasoned discussion of normative argument. Logically, it is true that the relationship between phenomena (expressed as factual propositions) and judgments (expressed as normative statements) cannot be formally deductive; or, to put the point in its more common form, "ought" statements cannot be deduced from premises that contain only "is" statements. But what are the implications of the disjunction? One extreme view concludes that normative criticism is therefore impossible and not worth undertaking. Some social critics, on the other hand, seem to assume that they are somehow thereby excused from any need to concern themselves with the facts. The argument parallels the discussion in explanation of the viability of theories that are not a set of deductively related propositions. Is the search for theory in social science worth pursuing even though we know that social theories are very unlikely to be deductive in form? The reply seems obvious. The logical disjunction between fact and value makes evaluation or explanation more difficult than would otherwise be the case, but if the results are weaker than we might like, they are not altogether useless. Further, if the relationship between fact and value cannot be deductive, formal logic remains a useful tool for criticizing normative judgments. Finally, since normative judgments always refer to something in human experience, "the facts" must be stated correctly if social criticism is to be taken seriously. Normative judgment cannot be reduced to formal logic, but it can certainly be made more responsible and more accurate.

Analytically, a normative judgment consists of four elements: first, a set of phenomena, a "situation," which is the object of evaluation or judgment; second, a set of assumptions about the consequences of particular events or choices for the set of elements in the situation—here called a *technical evaluation;* third, the response or reaction of the evaluator to the situation, which is the normative, ethical, or value judgment proper; fourth, the warrant or justification for the normative judgment, the argument supporting the conclusions. In practice, some of the fundamentals may be omitted, and the analytic distinctions are not always easy to make; but it is worthwhile to specify the properties of normative judgments in terms of these four variables—first, because it serves to clarify the points at issue in normative argument and, second, because it can provide a minimal foundation for criticizing them. The analytic structure provides no "solutions" to the major problems of ethics, but it can serve as a useful tool for political scientists interested in studying political evaluation.

The Phenomena

The point of departure for any criticism of normative judgment is the situation or phenomenon to which the individual reacts. As we noted in our earlier discussion of descriptions, the problem is not simple. The link between bare observation and the definition of the situation that the individual accepts is provided by a conceptual framework that may be extremely difficult to specify. The crucial elements in the situation may be defined either in terms of individual persons or in terms of social groups and associations; for example, a given situation may be held to induce instability into society, or it may be cited as a source of alienation for the individual. When the situation is defined in terms of the individual, the selection of elements of the situation to which the individual responds normatively may be qualities of the environment or subjective states of the person. The same slum, for example, may be defined in terms of physical conditions or viewed as a source of anguish and humiliation for those forced to live in it. Finally, the conceptual framework used to define the situation may or may not contain a normative bias. In the Marxist system, for example, a capitalist appears as an "exploiter" of labor, and it is often hard to distinguish the descriptive from the pejorative use of the term. Each of these four aspects of the definition of the situation can serve as a focus for criticism of normative judgment.

The first question to be asked of any definition of the situation is whether or not it is acceptable, given our knowledge of the phenomena. Clearly, some are more worthy of credence than others, and the validity of a conceptualization has nothing to do with either the strength of the individual's· beliefs or the consistency with which he acts upon them. The paranoid may believe very strongly that he is being persecuted and act on that belief with great consistency; but that does not make the belief reasonable, irrespective of the circumstances. The chief source of difficulty is that any empirical situation can be defined in an infinite number of different ways, all of which may be valid. A given tree may at one and the same time provide a haven from the sun, a source of lumber, a home for a squirrel, a nesting place for birds, etc. It does not, however, follow that all definitions of the situation are equally valid. Not every tree produces syrup, and trees do not suffer pain when their branches are tossed by the winds. We can use our knowledge of the situation, in other words, to separate legitimate propositions about the situation from propositions that are distorted, misleading, or meaningless.

The criteria used to evaluate a definition of the situation are precisely the same as those used to validate any other description. The crucial question, of course, is the relationship between the concepts used in the description and the empirical data obtained by perception of the situation. It is never possible to achieve perfect linkage between concept and data; indeed, it is not desirable to do so, since the looseness of fit gives power to the concept. On the other hand, if concepts cannot be linked to phenomena at least well enough to permit falsification in principle of propositions containing the concepts, the results are useless and even meaningless. It ought to be possible to substitute statements about empirical phenomena for the concept in question without altering the sense of the proposition that embodies the concept. To reuse an example, those who assert that given members of society are "alienated" as a factual proposition must provide indicators that link the concept "alienation" to some kind of human behavior. At the very least, the observer is entitled to ask what kind of evidence would justify the assertion that members of a particular group were *not* alienated. To be positively useful, the indicators used to define the concept must permit the observer to verify the assertion that alienation can indeed be found in a given society. In either case, it is clear that knowledge of the subject matter being discussed or evaluated is a definite prerequisite for an adequate evaluation of the conceptual framework employed in normative judgment.

The second aspect of a definition of the situation that merits close scrutiny is the extent to which it includes normative bias. Powerful ideologies always contain such built-in evaluations, usually by implication, but sometimes quite explicitly. The practice of disguising evaluations as self-evident facts is commonplace. The key to bias is the choice of terms used to define the situation. When they have evocative or pejorative connotations in the culture, it is almost impossible to avoid slipping from description to evaluation, inadvertently or deliberately.

Finally, definitions of the situation may focus on different aspects of the situation, with differentiated normative consequences. First, the focus may lie with either the individual or the collectivity. Any situation can be defined in a way that emphasizes the consequences of the situation for the collectivity or for the individual, and the distinction is important simply because it seems possible to produce two internally consistent but mutually incompatible sets of valuations, depending on the choice, and no satisfactory basis for choosing between them has yet been discovered. Those who accept social stability and order as the prime goals of mankind (Hobbes, for example) order their values quite differently from those who begin with the individual and seek to maximize his opportunities for personal development and satisfaction (the existentialists, among others). Second, the focus of attention may be directed either to the subjective aspects of the individual or to the environment in which he lives, again with quite different consequences. The distinction is nicely illustrated by a comparison of Freudian and "neo-Freudian" psychology; Freud is overwhelmingly concerned with the subjective, whereas the neo-Freudians place their emphasis on social interaction. Evaluations made within the contexts supplied by the two conceptual structures differ quite fundamentally.

It is convenient to consider the definition of the situation as a consequence of the choice of the conceptual framework. Normative judgments in contemporary political thought can then be discussed systematically in terms of the frame of reference they employ. Although this is by no means the only point of view that can be employed, it has the great virtue of introducing some measure of system into a body of otherwise unmanageable data. Further, the choice of frame of reference or explanatory system does seem to have important consequences for the kinds of evaluations that are made, as should be clear from the remainder of this chapter. In each case the same four fundamental points need examination: (1) Is the situation defined in acceptable terms? (2) Does the conceptual framework contain a normative bias? (3) Does the evaluation begin with the individual or the collectivity? (4) If evaluation begins with the individual, does it focus on the environment or on the subjective aspects of the situation? The first of these questions requires general knowledge of the state of the discipline; the others are answered from inspection of the application of the conceptual framework.

Technical Evaluation

Every normative judgment consists of two analytically separable elements: first, statements about the relations between actions and consequences or goals and the choice of means—what are here called *technical evaluations;* second, normative or value judgments proper, statements about the goodness or desirability of means, ends, total situations, etc. The separation of the two kinds of evaluation is essential to critical analysis, since they are subject to two quite different sets of criteria of adequacy. In general, the tools needed to criticize technical evaluations are already available; no

"general solution" to the problem of "pure" normative judgment has been found.

A technical evaluation will usually take the form "To
achieve X, do A." It is only a special kind of explanation,
and it can be evaluated by the same criteria as any other
explanation. In government, for example, when political
goals have been set, the choice among alternative courses of
action is only a technical evaluation—we seek the "best"
means for achieving the goal. Interestingly enough, technical evaluations require a very strong form of explanation,
for it must be capable of predicting and of specifying the
interaction of variables that justifies the prediction. Predictive capacity alone is not enough. The quality of a technical
evaluation, like the quality of any other explanation, depends on empirical evidence, on the state of knowledge in
the field. No element of normative judgment is involved.

The point that is significant for our purposes is that such
technical evaluations are an integral part of every normative
judgment.[7] Normative judgments depend on technical evaluations in all cases where the normative response is directed
to some *consequence* of a given situation. Logically, the
normative and the technical are distinct; dislike or disapproval of situations that result in gross human misery may
be discussed apart from the question whether or not such
situations occur. But normative judgments of social and
political phenomena are not exercises in moral philosophy;
they are applications of moral philosophy, and they must
deal with meaningful, concrete situations. Without agreeing
with John Dewey that meaningful discussion of normative

[7]The clearest exposition available of the point being made here can be
found in Charles L. Stevenson, *Ethics and Language* (Yale University
Press, 1944), especially chap. i. In Stevenson's terms, normative judgments
depend on questions of belief (factual questions) as well as questions of
attitude (normative questions). Stevenson, who belongs to the "emotive"
school of ethical theorists, holds that the second component of a normative
judgment is an emotional response, and on this point moral philosophers
are not agreed. But there is little dispute about the bifurcation of ethical
judgments into a factual and an evaluative component.

questions can take place *only* within a given social context, it is clear that the application of moral principles necessarily involves reference to concréte phenomena and is therefore necessarily contingent upon some form of technical evaluation of that situation. Empirical knowledge is highly relevant even though it may be logically discrete, for the logical disjunction asserts only the absence of any *logical* connection between the two. Fact and value can be brought together—indeed, must be brought together—when social evaluations are being made.

Further, normative judgments directed at the intrinsic properties of concrete situations rather than their consequences are subject to the same restriction. At the very least, normative judgment necessarily implies the possibility of change. To hold that "X is good" or "X is bad" is to imply that X is neither necessary nor impossible, since neither necessity nor impossibility are open to normative judgment. It would be merely absurd to assert that "Osmosis is a good thing" or "All hurricanes are intrinsically evil." But what is necessary or impossible is an empirical and not a normative question, and empirical knowledge defines the limits or constraints under which normative judgments are made.

Normative Judgments*

Narrowly defined, a normative judgment is a response or a reaction to a given situation expressed in propositions that make use of normative terms like "good," "right," "wrong," etc. The meaning of the normative terms will be left undefined, and questions like "Is X *really* good or bad?" will be

---

*The student of politics with an interest in moral philosophy will find a staggering collection of material in almost any college library. Journal articles tend to be specialized, though moral philosophers, like political scientists, publish collections that are often quite useful. Two good examples are Henry D. Aiken's *Reason and Conduct: New Bearings in Moral Philosophy* (Alfred A. Knopf, Inc., 1962); and Charles L. Stevenson, *Facts and Values: Studies in Ethical Analysis* (Yale University Press, 1963).

Of the general texts in ethics, the most useful is probably John Hospers, *Human Conduct: An Introduction to the Problem of Ethics* (Harcourt,

left unanswered. The reason is simply that normative philosophers have been unable to agree on the proper use of value terms. Some hold that they are merely ejaculations or conditioned reflexes; others believe they are emotional responses; still others assert that they are individual perceptions of intrinsic properties of situations which defy "naturalistic" specification. It is at least possible that their "meaning" is different for different persons. Happily, it is not necessary to solve the problem here. Normative judgments *are* made, and they can be taken as given. Our problem is, given an empirical situation and an evaluation of that situation, how can the two be related usefully?

By looking at normative judgments in this way, the meaning of value terms is bypassed, thus eliminating the problem of evaluating normative judgments qua normative judgments. If, for example, a normative judgment is defined as a perception of some intrinsic property of a situation, then a normative judgment based upon an emotional response is

---

Brace & World, Inc., 1961); but see also Luther J. Binkley, *Contemporary Ethical Theories* (Citadel Press, 1961); William K. Frankena, *Ethics* (Prentice-Hall, Inc., 1963); A. I. Melden, *Ethical Theories* (Prentice-Hall, Inc., 1955); and P. H. Nowell-Smith, *Ethics* (Penguin Books, Inc., 1954).

Various "classics" in ethical writing are essential if the main arguments in contemporary moral philosophy are to be understood. At a minimum, Aristotle's *Ethics* (various editions), David Hume's *Inquiry concerning the Principles of Morals,* Immanuel Kant's *Lectures on Ethics,* F. H. Bradley's *Ethical Studies,* and John Stuart Mill's *Utilitarianism* should be familiar to the student. Among 20th-century writers, G. E. Moore's *Principia Ethica* (Cambridge University Press, 1960) is essential, since it provides a point of departure for much subsequent work. A. J. Ayer's *Language, Truth, and Logic* (Dover Publications, Inc., n.d.), first edition, is an example of the extreme logical-positivist approach to ethics; the Preface to the second edition contains a very useful statement of Ayer's reasons for departing from the extreme view. Moritz Schlick, *Problems of Ethics* (Dover Publications, Inc., 1962), provides a useful contrast. E. M. Adams, *Ethical Naturalism and the Modern World View* (North Carolina University Press, 1960), and A. N. Prior, *Logic and the Basis of Ethics* (Oxford University Press, 1949), both take issue with Moore's conception of the "naturalistic fallacy." Abraham Edel, *Method in Ethical Theory* (Bobbs-Merrill Co., Inc., 1963), attacks contemporary ethical theory from yet another point of view, one extremely useful for social scientists. Finally, Stephen Toulmin's *Place of Reason in Ethics* (Cambridge University Press, 1960) should

not a "true" normative judgment at all. By taking all normative judgments as statements of fact about an individual's reaction to a situation, endless argument about the "real" meaning of normative terms is avoided. If Jones asserts that he reacts negatively to a particular situation, he is only stating a fact about his own attitudes. To agree with him is to state another fact about another person's response to the same situation. So long as the discussion remains at that level, there is nothing to do beyond reporting the facts—if they seem particularly important.

The possibility of criticism arises *only* when some attempt is made to justify the normative judgment. If Jones, after reporting his reaction, goes on to give reasons why others should react in the same way to the same situation, the adequacy of those reasons can be examined. If Jones refuses to argue his position, he is beyond attack. Of course, if Jones refuses to argue or justify his reaction, it remains merely *his* reaction and can be valued accordingly. We can only evaluate justifications, not normative judgments. The reason

---

be included in any minimal reading list on contemporary ethical writing. A good summary of the classics can be obtained from C. D. Broad, *Five Types of Ethical Theory* (Littlefield, Adams & Co., 1959).

Contemporary ethical writings of particular interest to social scientists tend to be disappointing. Glenn Negley's *Political Authority and Moral Judgment* (Duke University Press, 1965) is traditional and legalistic. Harry K. Girvetz, *Contemporary Moral Issues* (Wadsworth Publishing Co., Inc., 1963), contains some interesting but overly brief items, particularly those dealing with the ethics of business society. Henry Margenau's *Ethics and Science* (D. Van Nostrand Co., Inc., 1964) is worth reading, as is Henry Hazlitt's somewhat idiosyncratic *Foundations of Morality* (D. Van Nostrand Co., Inc., 1964). T. D. Weldon's *States and Morals* (John Murray, 1946) is disappointing and overly concerned with wartime problems. Bertrand Russell's *Human Society in Ethics and Politics* (Simon and Schuster, Inc., 1955) is an interesting but not particularly systematic statement of the humanist position. E. F. Carritt's *Ethical and Political Thinking* (Oxford University Press, 1947) is traditional, literary, and verbal and not particularly useful. Walter Lippmann's *Preface to Morals* (Macmillan Co., 1929) is relevant but not particularly profound. Simone de Beauvoir's *Ethics of Ambiguity*, trans. Bernard Frechtman (Citadel Press, 1962), is almost the only statement of the existentialist position available in English. Virtually all of these works fall into the "classic" political philosophy tradition and are of little use for the kind of analysis undertaken here.

is quite simple. In order to evaluate a normative judgment intrinsically, some standard would be required; we would have to distinguish between "genuine" and spurious normative judgments; and that, for the moment, we cannot do.

Justification

So long as normative judgments remain strictly personal affairs, no justification is needed. But moral discourse seldom remains at this level very long; it tends to be prescriptive. What I consider good becomes, by extension, what you too should consider good. If I believe this very strongly, I must try to convince you that it is indeed good. Again, there are no ultimate standards of goodness to which appeal can be made; that would again require a solution to the problem of the meaning of normative terms. Nevertheless, systematic examination of the kinds of justification offered for particular normative judgments can be quite fruitful. Usually, the course of argument will lead back to first principles that are beyond argument; but at the very least, it is worth making explicit the content of these fundamental assumptions. Further, the reasons offered for a normative judgment often serve to separate and distinguish normative judgments that are superficially similar—that is, arrive at the same conclusions for quite different reasons. Finally, we may be able to distinguish between legitimate and improper forms of argumentation.

It is worth emphasizing at the outset that we are here concerned with particular value judgments of concrete situations. Hence the first general rule for dealing with evaluations must be: No justification or argument, no evaluation. That is, it is a valid criticism of a normative judgment to assert that it lacks warrant or justification. Normative judgments obtained through the search of one's viscera are no more worthy of credence and serious consideration than "auspices" obtained by scrutiny of the entrails of a dead chicken, though both may lead to interesting and suggestive results. When the end result is stated without argument, the critic must himself supply all of the intervening variables. In view of the enormous number of evaluations made available to the reading public, it would be impossible to examine them all. And in any case, if all of the argument must be supplied by the critic, why not spend the time and energy dealing with valuations generated by the critic himself? There are, perhaps, some few persons whose opinions we value so highly that we believe it worth the time and effort to work out the reasoning that lies behind them, but in most cases it seems a gross waste of time.

Similarly, arguments that lead to decision rules or maxims of behavior depend qualitatively on the clarity and meaningfulness of the rule—its applicability. Question-begging rules for decision are commonplace. Immanuel Kant's famous categorical imperative seems such a rule: You should act, according to Kant, as if the maxim of your action were to become by your will a universal law of nature. But what are the criteria by which we decide whether or not a principle of action should be willed a universal law of nature? Kant tries to provide them and fails. We are told to treat men as ends rather than means, to avoid exempting the self from moral rules, and to accept a good will as the only intrinsic good. However useful they may be, such rules are not decisive. Ultimately, Kant himself was driven to a form of utilitarianism; and utilitarianism, whether in Jeremy Bentham's original form or with John Stuart Mill's modifications, has proved unable to stipulate an unambiguous rule for choosing among alternative courses of action.

Ultimately, every justification of a normative argument, like every explanation, leads to first principles that cannot be "proved" or justified. While such first principles cannot be faulted or defended except, perhaps, by their consequences, the chain of reasoning that leads from the particular judgment to the general rule is open to inspection. In some cases the connection may be formal and logical; more often, the connection is tenuous. For that reason, it is often possible for two persons to agree on a general principle but to differ seriously on its application. In other cases the rule and the particular application may be logically incompatible. Clarification of these and other properties of moral judgments can be one very useful outcome of systematic criticism.

Finally, by moving beyond a single normative judgment to consider sets and sequences of valuations, it is possible to examine the internal consistency of an ethical system as a whole. It is not unusual to find the same person supporting mutually incompatible principles, and no one has yet produced a wholly consistent ethic. The classic case of inconsistency, of course, is the double standard: the application of different standards to the same activity, depending upon the properties of the persons engaged in the activity to differentiate the standard applied. The identification of gaps in the consistency of an ethical system is important, if only because an inconsistent ethic is by definition incapable of realization.

PART I

Methodology

CHAPTER TWO

SCIENCE: MINOTAUR OR MESSIAH?

METHODOLOGICAL questions, problems in the conduct of inquiry, serve a focus for some of the more interesting and significant disputes in contemporary social and political thought. Everyone agrees, of course, that the aim of inquiry is the acquisition of knowledge. But what constitutes an adequate claim to know? What kind of evidence should be accepted in argument? How does the nature of the subject matter influence the conduct of inquiry? Social scientists and philosophers are still a long way from agreement on many of these questions. Their importance is undeniable. Every social scientist—indeed, every serious student—must somehow come to terms with methodology, knowingly or not. Methodological criticism is one of the mainstays of informed study of political thought. This chapter will serve as a brief introduction to some of the basic problems in the methodology of political science and to the manner in which those problems have been resolved by leading contemporary thinkers. It hardly needs saying that one brief chapter is no substitute for concentrated study in an extremely important and complex area of intellectual endeavor.

Differences of opinion over methodological questions have existed for a very long time, sometimes, it seems, without much improvement in the quality of argument. Many of Aristotle's criticisms of Plato are methodological rather than substantive; and both the Platonic errors, if such they be, and the Aristotelian criticisms remain very much in evidence. The contemporary phase of methodological controversy begins with the fragmentation of *mater scientia* at the beginning of the modern era. The resulting proliferation of disciplines and the spectacular success of the physical sciences raised the old methodological questions in a new and challenging context. The achievements of science, more than any other single factor, provided the impetus to methodological discussion in other fields of inquiry and at the same time defined the framework in which the discussion took place. The crucial point is that the expansion of scientific knowledge in modern times, which is beyond cavil, followed a revolutionary break with the canons of inquiry hitherto taken for granted by the Western intellectual community. Deductive reasoning from a priori first principles and the appeal to authority and orthodoxy were replaced by a process usually called inductive reasoning from empirical observations.

Success breeds emulation, and not in the business community alone. Enterprising academics were soon found suggesting that the social sciences, and even the humanities, would benefit greatly by following the physical sciences in methodological matters. Others replied that the distinctions between the two enterprises are so deep and immutable that the social sciences constitute an autonomous branch of inquiry with its own rules and standards. "Scientific" or "not scientific"? Two centuries of argument has failed to answer the question to everyone's satisfaction. Of course, the division between the two points of view is not absolute, and the protagonists are not polarized completely. It is probably more accurate to think in terms of a continuum with those favoring a "scientific" mode of inquiry in social science at one extreme and those unalterably opposed to emulation of science at the other. The region between the poles is populated by moderates of both inclinations.

The consequences of discussing the methodology of the social sciences in terms of the possibility or desirability of emulating the physical sciences have usually been deplorable. "Science" is a most ambiguous term. It cannot be defined in terms of its objects or its methods, and it is unlikely that the necessary and sufficient conditions for a science could be agreed upon, even among scientists. The notion of *the* scientific method, widely disseminated by simplistic and inaccurate textbooks, is a chimera pure and simple. At best, we can stipulate certain fundamentals common to all of the sciences and considered necessary for acceptable scientific investigation. Beyond that point, argument over the question "Is political science a science?" is a fruitless exercise in semantics inspired, usually, by a desire for the accumulation of honorifics rather than by any genuine understanding of scientific inquiry.[1]

The use of "scientific" as a focus for methodological discussion has been further complicated by the fact that the physical sciences themselves underwent a conceptual revolution early in the 20th century, a revolution whose full implications are as yet far from understood. The introduction of relativity theory and quantum mechanics into physics forced scientists to abandon the Newtonian conception of science. The mechanistic and deterministic construction of the universe that Newton had inaugurated was discarded. Absolute relationships were replaced by probabilistic relationships in certain crucial areas in scientific investigation. Werner Heisenberg added to the philosophic confusion by demonstrating, apparently, that determinism was forever ruled out of microphysics because the physicist could not specify accurately both the position and the velocity of a particle; the more accurately the position was stipulated, the less accurate the measurement of velocity became. There is no need here to become involved in the dispute over de-

---

[1]See Eugene J. Meehan, *The Theory and Method of Political Analysis* (The Dorsey Press, Inc., 1965), chap. ii.

terminism in science; the point that matters is that the scientist's conception of his own work changed radically in a relatively short period of time, and we are still a long way from adjusting our thinking to these changes. As Nobel-Prize-winning physicist Max Born put it:

In 1921, I believed—and I shared this belief with most of my contemporary physicists—that science produced an objective knowledge of the world, which is governed by deterministic laws. The scientific method seemed to me superior to other, more subjective ways of forming a picture of the world. . . .

    In 1951, I believed none of these things. The border between object and subject had been blurred, deterministic laws had been replaced by statistical ones. . . .[2]

Born's point is crucial for understanding the contemporary conception of science and evaluating contemporary criticisms of "scientific" inquiry.

So long as science was conceived in Newtonian terms, the task of the scientist was analogous to the investigation of a gigantic and complex piece of machinery—the aim was discovery, uncovering what was "already there." The scientist looked for the principles on which "reality" was organized, using astronomy as a paradigm, and seeking the equivalent of the Newtonian laws of motion. This conception of science accounts for many of the crudities and dogmatisms of the 19th-century positivists. It led the French sociologist Emile Durkheim to assert that there was no need for comparative studies, since a well-designed investigation would reveal the operation of the basic machinery and any principles discovered in this way were then universally applicable. The search for "laws of society" was construed in Newtonian terms. Durkheim's conception of the task of inquiry could not survive the "relativity" unveiled by comparative anthropology any more than Newtonian physics could survive the introduction of the relativity concept into

[2]Max Born, *Physics in My Generation* (Pergamon Press, Inc., 1956), p. vii.

the theoretical structure of science. The mechanical analogy failed, and with it went Newtonian determinism. To be brutally brief, Newtonian science was abandoned and replaced by a different intellectual structure. One of the great intellectual revolutions of modern times took place with little fanfare and even less effect on the general public. Yet, in the long run, the consequences of that revolution for human thinking, in the social sciences and the humanities as well as in the physical sciences, may well exceed anything that has yet occurred in man's history.

The implications of the scientific revolution have been explored with considerable rigor and precision by exponents of a recently established discipline—philosophy of science. For the social scientist concerned with methodological questions, two points of crucial importance have emerged thus far from that investigation. First, it is now clear that science is not and has never been concerned with the nature of physical reality. Science says nothing, and can say nothing, about "reality"; instead, science is now conceived as a process for systematically ordering and relating the elements of human experience so that further experiences can be anticipated (under stipulated conditions) and past experiences can be explained, made to seem reasonable in the light of relationships already established. While the scientist usually believes that there is some connection between his finding and whatever lies "out there," he has no need to concern himself with the question. He can only judge his achievements in terms of his own experience and the experiences of other men. Even if the sciences should ever be able to explain "everything," they would not know that the goal had been reached. Science, in brief, has become a distinctly human enterprise. Its needs and accomplishments can only be measured relative to man; its modes of inquiry are determined by human interests and the limits of human capacity. Science is simply what man can do for man, using man's own experience as a guide. The method is fundamentally comparative; man learns how to anticipate future experiences or explain past experiences by comparing his own and other people's experiences. There is nothing else he can do.

A second point that is important for the social sciences, which is corollary to the first, is that all scientific propositions, since they relate solely to human experience and not to objective reality, are conditional and not absolute—statements of probability and not statements of absolutely invariant relations. Scientific practice is deceptive here, for the scientist commonly employs language that masks the conditional nature of scientific statements. Many well-established scientific laws have a probability that approaches unity, but the logical structure of every scientific law remains conditional and not absolute. The reason is simply that scientific laws, like any other general statements about human experience that go beyond tabulation or description, refer to classes of behavior that have not been completely observed—they are inductions rather than deductions or descriptions. No inductive generalization can be absolute. It might be possible to make inductions absolute by postulating an absolute underlying reality, and that is what the Newtonians in fact assumed, but scientists now realize that the assumption is gratuitous and unwarranted.[3]

A lengthy discussion of a rather technical point in the philosophy of science may seem out of place in a book that purports to deal with social and political thought, but it is essential that a clear distinction be made between the concept of science accepted in the 19th century and the concept of science employed at the present time. When the early positivists like Auguste Comte demanded an extension of the methodological principles of physical science to the social sciences, they were thinking in Newtonian terms; and this

---

[3]A good, nontechnical discussion of the point can be found in Stephen Toulmin, *Introduction to the Philosophy of Science* (Harper & Bros., 1960).

accounts for their search for "laws of society" analogous to
the laws of motion, their use of mechanistic analogies, and
the rigid determinism of their conceptual structures. By
present-day standards, John Stuart Mill, the elite theorists
(Gaetano Mosca, Roberto Michels, and Vilfredo Pareto), or
sociologists like Emile Durkheim and Bronislaw Malinowski
simply entertained an inadequate notion of "science." Of
course, the conception of science presently accepted in
philosophy of science is also open to change, but that cannot be controlled; and since no claim to absolute validity
is implied in the present explanatory system used in science,
conceptual changes will simply lead to changes in the explanatory structure.

Much of the work of the earlier positivists, then, has no
more than historical interest for the present. Of course, their
insistence on the use of empirical data, their concern with
measurement and experiment, and their rejection of metaphysical claims remain a valid part of the methodological
assumptions of science. The point that is crucial here is that
it would be a serious mistake to attack contemporary efforts
to lead the social sciences along the path taken by the physical sciences using examples taken from these earlier writers,
for reasons that should by now be obvious. Yet it must be
said that the error occurs all too frequently among those
violently opposed to "scientific" social science. And in all
fairness, it is necessary to add that those who seek to follow
the physical sciences in methodological matters often commit the equally grave error of adopting a conception of
science that resembles the Newtonian model far more than
the probabilistic model of contemporary science.

THE METHODOLOGICAL ASSUMPTIONS OF SCIENCE

A brief summary of the criteria of inquiry generally considered essential prerequisites to scientific inquiry will serve
as a framework for considering the arguments for and

against the use of similar criteria in the social sciences. Again, the reader is warned not to accept a sketchy account as an adequate substitute for detailed inquiry. In the sciences the criteria used to evaluate claims to knowledge are fairly rigorous and precise in application, a point that sometimes leads social scientists to suggest that they are not appropriate to their respective disciplines. However, it is essential that we distinguish here between declarations of principle and questions of application. In principle, the physical sciences require very precise measurement of phenomena; and in practice, this is achieved remarkably often, though not in every case. Measurement obviously entails observation. Consideration of these criteria must take place at several levels. If it is difficult to measure accurately in the social sciences, that may be admitted cheerfully (or tearfully) while still maintaining that, *in principle*, measurement is highly desirable. One may deny that measurement is necessary or possible, moreover, and still maintain that observation is essential. A distinction must be made, in other words, between what is possible and what is desirable. What is possible is an empirical matter, in most cases, whereas desirability depends on methodological criteria. A further distinction must be made between what is possible in principle and what is possible in practice. One can hold that it is possible in principle to explain all group phenomena in terms of individual actions, for example, and at the same time assert that it is impossible to do so in practice. But if it is impossible in principle to explain group phenomena in individual terms, that automatically implies that it cannot be done in practice. These distinctions are of considerable importance, for many of the arguments about the applicability of scientific methodology in social science hinge on a failure to make them properly.

The physical scientist seeks knowledge that is reliable, communicable, and corrigible. Knowledge must be self-conscious, and it must be public. There is no need to deny that men may have knowledge which they cannot communicate to others, but such knowledge cannot be considered scientific; and more important, it is not useful in argument unless we are prepared to accept argument from authority. The experienced hunter, for example, may be able to anticipate events in the milieu in which he is well versed without realizing that he possesses knowledge and without being able to communicate it to others—this is the distinction between "knowing how to do" and "knowing how it is done." The scientist would not deny that the hunter possesses knowledge, and he might well depend on it if the hunter were taking him through the forests. But the hunter does not have *scientific* knowledge. And, the scientist might add, the world is somewhat the worse off because that is the case. Non-communicable personal knowledge usually dies with the person. Science, which depends fundamentally on cumulation, is forced to insist that knowledge be public and communicable.

Scientific knowledge is defined exclusively in terms of human experience and perception, not in terms of "reality" or absolutes. It is relative to man. And the scientists insist that claims to knowledge refer to concrete human experiences, so that verification is possible. Science, in other words, is empirical. The whole structure of science is built on a solid foundation of human perceptions. Furthermore, "experience" is defined rather rigorously in science. Personal or subjective experience is not considered part of scientific data, and this may well be one point where the physical and social sciences cannot accept the same criteria. For the physical scientist, experience must be public, observations must be made by a plurality of observers; or at the very least, they must in principle be open to plural observation. I may taste "sweetness," and you may have the same taste, but science cannot deal in concepts such as these. Usually, though not always, observations must be quantified, but that requirement is not vital. The advantages of quantification, in terms of precision and manageability, are obvious, and scientists are usually unhappy if they cannot somehow produce measured indexes of their observations.

The basic goal of science is the explanation of observed phenomena—the organization of previous observations and experiences into general propositions and theories whose effect is to lead us to expect particular phenomena to occur in given circumstances. Ideally, the scientist is able to predict the occurrence of a given phenomena, under stipulated conditions, with considerable accuracy; but prediction is *not*, contrary to supposition, an absolutely essential prerequisite for scientific inquiry. The kinds of predictions that astronomers make—and astronomy is usually considered the paradigm for reasons that are probably historical rather than analytic—are actually rare in many other branches of science. Explanation, which we have already met in the previous chapter, depends fundamentally on the capacity to stipulate relationships or linkages, on the availability of generalizations. In principle, science requires of its general statements that they be open to confirmation by observation; but as explanatory structures grow increasingly complex and sophisticated, there may be many intervening layers of generalizations between the brute facts of observation and the propositions that scientists assert, and confirmation or validation becomes a difficult matter. Furthermore, theoretical structures in science contain terms that are not defined solely in terms of observable data—so-called "theoretical" terms like "gravity." There is, in other words, a loose fit between scientific theories or concepts and the hard data of observation, and the structure is far less rigid and precise than the layman might think. It follows that validation of scientific theories is often an extremely difficult process and not a simple matter of deducing singular propositions from general theorems and then checking the deductions against observations.

Finally, the methodological assumptions of science preclude the assertion of certain kinds of evaluative propositions by the scientist: Science is "value-free." The phrase is misleading, for it only excludes *certain kinds* of valuations from science; and it does not, in any case, imply that there are or can be no human values, nor that the scientist, as a man, is not interested in such values. The point is simply that some kinds of propositions would be wholly out of place in the scientific frame of reference: Imagine a scientist asserting that "Osmosis is good, but photosynthesis is bad." Such statements would be meaningless. What is excluded from science, in other words, is the kinds of moral evaluations that we normally apply to human actions. For the remainder the scientist must make the same kinds of valuations as any other scholar. He must assume—for he cannot prove—that truth is to be preferred to falsehood, that knowledge is desirable, and that some phenomena are "more important" than others. These "discipline-centered" valuations are quite different from moral judgments like "Killing is wrong" or "You ought not to treat living creatures in a cruel manner." The scientist, qua scientist, simply has no use for propositions of the latter sort.

Science, then, relies upon empiricism, abstraction, generalization, and explanation; its methods include analysis, experimentation, observation, and measurement; it avoids moral valuations. These fairly straightforward principles may appear little more than generalized common sense, useful in any field of inquiry; and that, essentially, is the attitude taken by those who suggest that social science ought to follow physical science within the limits of its own subject matter. Yet the use of these principles in social inquiry has been seriously questioned or even roundly condemned, in principle and in application. That is, some critics assert that it is not merely impossible to make use of these criteria, but that it is undesirable to do so. Both views will be examined below; but, as is probably clear from the terms of the previous chapter, what follows is written from a point of view favorable to the extension of scientific methodology into the social disciplines.

SCIENCE AS MINOTAUR

Science, it is often said, is "positivistic." Claims to knowledge in science must be supported by evidence; they cannot be accepted simply because evidence is lacking. Metaphysics, on the other hand, deals with questions about which there is no evidence, at least no evidence of the kind that science will accept. The internal consistency of metaphysical arguments can be examined, of course, but it is always possible to build a speculative system that is internally consistent, provided that the axioms of the structure remain unexamined. Science, as we have noted, insists that adequate criticism of thought must go beyond internal consistency and discuss the relations between concept and concrete phenomena. By so doing, it is led to reject or to refuse to credit certain philosophic positions that have had a very long history and still retain a number of highly influential practitioners—idealism and Christianity, for example. It is very important to note that science cannot, according to its own rules, *deny* the validity of the idealist claim to distinguish essences or the Christian claim to discern the hand of God in the history of man. But in the framework that science accepts, such claims cannot be accepted, either, since they cannot even in principle be verified. Similarly, the claims of the mystic or intuitionist to discern a higher form of knowledge must be left with the Scotch verdict—not proven. The idealist and subjectivist therefore argues, reasonably enough from his point of view, that scientific inquiry is far too restrictive, that it omits or overlooks what is essential in human life. The scientist must admit that this is a possibility—his mode of inquiry cannot refute it—but the scientific commitment to cumulative, verifiable knowledge precludes acceptance or support for such claims.

Does the scientific mode of inquiry really entail an impoverishment of the social sciences because it eliminates crucial insights from argument on methodological grounds?

Those who argue that methodological principles ought to be the same for all forms of inquiry, since man is man and inquiry is evaluated according to human capacity, must disagree, though they would doubtless agree that the criteria that science employs can be applied only much less rigorously to the study of society. The one question that might seriously be raised against the scientific attitude is its divorce from normative or moral judgments. But here, it is important to note that the scientist does not make such judgments because there is no need for him to do so. Would the scientist make moral judgments if his subject matter required it? This is an unanswerable question. Again, it should be clear that my own judgment on this matter tends to favor the expansion of social inquiry to include normative questions (along with, and not in lieu of, ordinary scientific inquiry), but there are those who argue very strongly against that point of view.

The argument against the scientific attitude seems to me largely misdirected. Science does not, for example, as is often claimed, eliminate all forms on intuition and insight from inquiry, thereby stifling imagination and creativity. Indeed, scientists are rarely concerned with the way in which propositions are generated. Instead, they concentrate on the quality of what has been produced, on the reliability and usefulness of what is proposed. Presumably, if an idiot managed to produce a profound scientific insight, the scientist would employ it cheerfully and thankfully. What is eliminated from science is not insight but propositions whose implications do not accord with experience and, of course, propositions that have no implications whatever. The rules of inquiry prohibit what Karl R. Popper has called methodological essentialism, the attempt to discover the "true nature" of things, their hidden essence or reality. Science accepts instead what Popper calls methodological nominalism, which aims at "describing how a thing behaves in various circumstances."[4] That is, science rejects attempts to find Plato's ideal forms, or the Aristotelian essences of things; it asserts that the meaning of any universal term is defined by the attributes of the class to which it is applied. Science must also reject the kind of teleological reasoning that occurs in Aristotle and Hegel, or in Christian thought; if history is indeed the product of a divine will or world spirit, science would have no way of determining that this was the case, nor is the conception defeasible. Propositions that can be neither demonstrated nor disproved are simply ignored.

The neo-Platonists, the Aristotelians, the Thomists, and the Hegelian idealists are, of course, major sources of radical criticism of scientific methodology. This may seem an inappropriate grouping, but Hegel himself was very much aware of the similarities between his own position and that of Christian orthodoxy: "The truth that a Providence, that is to say, a divine Providence, presides over the events of the world corresponds to our principle; for divine Providence is wisdom endowed with infinite power which realizes its own aim, that is, the absolute, rational, final purpose of the world. Reason is Thought determining itself in absolute freedom."[5]

While it may be objected that Thomism is Aristotelian, the fact is, I believe, that Thomism really combines Aristotelianism and Platonism. It is certainly not pure Aristotle. It resembles the neoclassicism of those like Leo Strauss, who combine Aristotelian teleology. with some form of Platonic idealism as they seek the essences of political action.

A second major source of antiscientific sentiment in contemporary thought is existentialism, religious and secular.

[4]Karl R. Popper, *The Open Society and Its Enemies* (2 vols.; 4th ed.; Princeton University Press, 1963), Vol. I, pp. 31–32. See also Karl R. Popper, *The Poverty of Historicism* (Harper & Bros., 1964), where Popper claims to have *proved* that it is logically impossible to predict the future course of history while human knowledge is growing.

[5]G. W. F. Hegel, *Reason in History: A General Introduction to the Philosophy of History*, trans. Robert S. Hartman (Liberal Arts Press, Inc., 1953), p. 15.

In practice, existentialism has close connections with phenomenology, particularly Edmund Husserl's attempt to analyze experience as a basic mode of philosophy, and with irrational vitalism as it appears in the works of Henri Bergson and perhaps William James. They have in common the denial of meaning to objective and observable reality and the postulation of an essential inner meaning, knowable only through the actual process of experiencing existence. The external world is considered "absurd" and meaningless; the inner world is held to be beyond the reach of scientific analysis. Even Freudian analysis, which is usually considered too "soft" to be classified as "scientific," has been denounced as overly deterministic by Jean-Paul Sartre.[6]

Literary figures have taken an even more extreme attitude toward the importance of the subjective aspect of human existence, coming, in many cases, very close to nihilism. The works of Franz Kafka are perhaps best known in this genre, but the position of the Dadaist movement in the late 1920's, which involved a renunciation of all rational communication, is still more extreme. And mystics like Simone Weil have found the restrictions of language an insuperable barrier to the communication of important thoughts (though a cynic might point out that Weil apparently wrote down very carefully a quite substantial volume of material). Hannah Arendt, in a typical passage, has drawn a sharp contrast between logical inquiry and the kind of thinking needed to deal adequately with consciousness and experience: "[This] kind of thinking is different from such mental processes as deducing, inducing, and drawing conclusions whose logical rules of non-contradiction and inner consistency can be learned once for all and then applied."[7] Various other authors —Ernest Hemingway, for example—have expressed distaste

---

[6]Jean-Paul Sartre, *Existential Psychoanalysis*, trans. Hazel Barnes (Henry Regnery Co., 1953). This is part of Sartre's main philosophical work, *L'être et le néant*.

[7]Hannah Arendt, *Between Past and Future: Six Exercises in Political Thought* (World Publishing Co., 1963), p. 14.

for "abstract" thought, preferring to place their trust in "feeling," in physical activity. The subjectivist believes that experience defies systematization, that it can only be understood by actually experiencing. To know, in these terms, implies doing. Arendt and others who take the same position have, it seems, substituted "action in thought" for the "action in the environment" that Sartre proposes as a means of escape from the absurdity of existence.

The extreme, minority attitude toward scientific inquiry construes it as a positive evil and not merely a mistaken strategy of investigation. Rationalism, abstraction, empiricism, and systematic explanation are regarded as dangers to morality, practices that drain human life of its mystery, passion, and grandeur. Why? Primarily because the scientific attitude results in a sharp separation of factual propositions and evaluations and tends to inhibit the latter. The charge is an old one. Thomas Carlyle attacked science in much these terms in the 19th century; it was degrading and dangerous, tending to lead man away from the search for the natural laws of the universe, the laws of God. Søren Kierkegaard complained bitterly about the absence of passion and moral commitment in his age, and argued that the tendency to rationalism and the excessive concern for abstraction that came from the sciences were keeping men from their proper concern with religion and values. In his *Concluding Unscientific Postscript,* Kierkegaard asserts unequivocally that all essential knowledge is concerned with existence, that truth is what man believes subjectively and passionately and not what appears as objectively correct. Science, in this context, can only be a distraction.

Gabriel Marcel's strictures against mass society (an outgrowth of scientism and technocracy) provide a good illustration of the same pessimistic attitude toward science. The tone is apocalyptic. There is a crisis in values, a degradation and despiritualization of man, an increase in fanaticism; all these consequences, he holds, are aftereffects of the spirit of abstraction, of the tendency to deal only with material, concrete things:

One might in fact be tempted to suppose that the concrete is what is given at first, is what our thinking must start from. But nothing could be more false than such a supposition; and here Bergson is at one with Hegel. What is given to us to start is a sort of unnamed and unnameable confusion where abstractions not yet elaborated are like so many little still unseparated clots of matter. It is only by going through and beyond the process of scientific abstraction that the concrete can be regrasped and reconquered.[8]

The solution? Marcel asserts the unconditional need for absolute, essentially religious values:

In reality, unless we have recourse to an act of faith perfectly legitimate in itself, and from a religious point of view even requisite, but quite foreign to the spirit of the man of mere technique, we should have to say that the malady from which mankind today appears to be suffering is perhaps mortal, and that there is nothing, at the purely human level, which insures our race against that risk of collective suicide of which I spoke. . . .[9]

An equally astringent criticism of science is produced by Leo Strauss. The attempt to create a scientific social science has led, in his view, to a full-blown philosophical crisis. The crux of the argument is that scientifically oriented philosophy cannot deal with an intelligibly ordered cosmos. Strauss is basically an Aristotelian teleologist and Platonist who favors a return to classic Greek philosophy. Given his premise, that is, that the universe is intelligently and intelligibly ordered, the goal of political philosophy is to discern in the universe the kinds of rules and values that society ought to embody—a search for natural laws:

Political philosophy will then be the attempt to replace opinion

[8]Gabriel Marcel, *Man against Mass Society*, trans. G. S. Fraser (Henry Regnery Co., 1962; first published in 1952), pp. 159-60.
[9]*Ibid.*, p. 88. See also p. 173, where Marcel's views on essences are clearly stated.

about the nature of political things by knowledge of the nature of things political. Political things are by their nature subject to approval and disapproval, to choice and rejection, to praise and blame. It is of their essence not to be neutral but to raise a claim to men's obedience, allegiance, decision, or judgment. One does not understand them as what they are, as political things, if one does not take seriously their explicit or implicit claim to be judged in terms of goodness or badness, justice or injustice, e.g., if one does not measure them by some standard of goodness or justice. To judge soundly, one must know the true standards. Political philosophy is the attempt truly to know both the nature of political things and the right, or the good, political order.[10]

Strauss also insists that fact and value are a unity and hence that science has produced an unfortunate and misleading separation of the two. The "new science," he goes on, rests on dogmatic atheism because it denies the possibility that religion rests ultimately on the possibility that God has revealed himself to man directly.[11] Unfortunately, Strauss *asserts;* he does not argue. At best, he quotes Aristotle as authority. It is readily demonstrated, for example, that evaluation is different from description, that evaluation must be *about* something; and it follows that evaluation is separate—in some respects, at least—from fact. Evaluation refers to fact, and facts must be established independently of evaluation. The scientifically minded assert that careful and impartial study of phenomena, making use of scientific methodology as far as possible, is more likely to produce a reliable stipulation of the facts than any other course open to man. But the issue is really not resolvable. The discussion goes on between two quite dissimilar and fundamentally incompatible frames of reference.

Illustrations of the same attitude of mind could be multiplied, but no useful purpose would be served by it. Some mention may be in order, however, of the outburst of anti-scientific sentiment in the United States that appeared in

---

[10]Leo Strauss, *What Is Political Philosophy?* (Free Press, 1959), p. 13.
[11]Herbert J. Storing (ed.), *Essays on the Scientific Study of Politics* (Holt, Rinehart & Winston, Inc., 1962), "Epilogue," p. 322.

the early 1950's. Neoconservatism, which began with the publication of Francis Wilson's *The Case for Conservatism* in 1951, burgeoned swiftly. A succession of widely read volumes followed from such men as Russell Kirk, Clinton Rossiter, Peter Viereck, John Hallowell, Eric Vogelin, and Wilmoor Kendall. In varying degree, they attacked or denigrated the value of rational, empirical inquiry, extolling the merits of traditional and moral behavior. There was a powerful revival of interest in the work of irrationalists like Kierkegaard; existentialism became quite the vogue; T. S. Eliot's erudite Catholicism found a wide audience in the theater and in print. Minor religious figures like Billy Graham and Norman Vincent Peale fulminated against the decline of contemporary morality and blamed relativism and abstraction for the woeful state of affairs to which society had sunk. For the most part, these attacks on science were conducted in such emotional terms that they are almost impossible to evaluate. Doubtless, some of the vigor of the criticism was due to naïve and excessive claims made by those in the vanguard of the new "behavioral" approach to the study of society. Doubtless, too, the critics were seeking stability and control in an era where rapid change seemed endemic, and they hastened to seize upon the most obvious source of antitraditional belief as a whipping boy. The writings tended to a pessimistic and even apocalyptic outlook, conservative and in some cases reactionary in politics. The revival seems to have been transistory, however; by the mid-1960's, much of the early support for these movements seemed to have dissipated. The American protest movements of the 1960's were once again radical in politics and for the most part centered around the civil rights movement and social reform.

The Dualists

A more moderate group of critics of science, though quite willing to grant science a meed of praise for its utility in certain kinds of inquiry, insist at the same time that other spheres of human behavior are exempt from scientific investigation. By adopting a dualistic attitude toward scientific inquiry, the critics are relieved of the need to deny the obvious efficacy of science, yet free to insist on the need for transscientific knowledge in certain domains of human action. The existentialist theologian Karl Jaspers, for example, has produced a typical dichotomized structure of this sort. Without condemning science in general, Jaspers divides human existence into separate zones (empirical existence, consciousness as such, and spirit), each with its own appropriate "truth." Science and philosophy occupy separate zones, and each is appropriate only for its own sphere, though they are able to remain in touch with one another. Jaspers maintained that science and philosophy are so intrinsically different that they require different criteria of knowledge and different methods of investigation.[12]

The dualistic solution to the problem of dealing with scientific inquiry is even more pronounced in the work of Jacques Maritain, an eminent Thomist with a leaning toward existentialism. The value of positive science in its own sphere of reference Maritain not only admits but argues most strongly; he accepts with virtually no qualification the positivist notion that empirical verification is an essential feature of the validation of scientific claims to knowledge:

[The] principle of the necessity of logico-experimental verification is true in regard to the function of judgment in the *empiriological* sciences; but it is true *only in this domain*. A philosophy which generalizes this principle and extends it to the entire field of knowledge, seeing in it an exigency of the nature of all judgments truly valuable for knowledge—such a philosophy thus destroys itself.[13]

[12]See Karl Jaspers, *Reason and Existenz*, trans. William Earle (Farrar, Straus & Cudahy, Inc., 1955), especially pp. 83 *et seq.;* also Karl Jaspers, *Way to Wisdom*, trans. Ralph Mannheim (Yale University Press, 1954), especially pp. 157 *et seq.*

[13]Jacques Maritain, *Scholasticism and Politics*, trans. Mortimer J. Adler (Doubleday & Co., Inc., 1960), pp. 45–46 (italics in original).

In ontological discussion, Maritain continues, knowledge does not depend upon observation and verification; knowledge is acquired by inner perception that is quite different from empiricism but entirely appropriate to its own sphere. Maritain quotes with approval Saint Thomas Aquinas' condemnation of those who seek to use the same means of investigation in domains of speculative knowledge that are typically different. Since there is no specification of the nature of these differences, the claim cannot be evaluated.

In a similar vein, José Ortega y Gasset says:

The human element escapes physico-mathematical reason as water runs from a sieve.

Human life, it would appear then, is not a thing, has not a nature, and in consequence we must make up our minds to think of it in terms of categories and concepts that will be *radically* different from such as shed light on the phenomena of matter.

Man is no thing but a drama—his life, a pure and universal happening which happens to each of us. . . .[14]

Perhaps the best illustration of all can be found in the writings of Reinhold Niebuhr, a most influential Protestant theologian. Niebuhr is a dualist, though he is so much concerned with the conflict between good and evil, which he takes as the central organizing feature of human history, that he appears consistently pessimistic. Niebuhr offers reasons why the scientific study of society is unlikely to produce substantial results. Since we shall deal with these arguments, among others, in the remainder of this chapter, they need only be listed briefly here. He claims, first, that since men are intrinsically part of the societies they study, no inquiry into social science can be wholly free of evaluation (which does not, of course, condemn the *attempt* to keep free of value judgments). He uses the argument from uniqueness, the assertion that history never

[14]José Ortega y Gasset, "History as System," in Raymond Klibansky and H. J. Paton (eds.), *Philosophy and History: The Ernst Cassirer Festschrift* (Harper & Bros., 1963), especially pp. 294–95, 303.

repeats itself, as a defense against the possibility of explanation through generalization. He employs, as a theologian might be expected to do, the "free will" argument, namely, since men are free to choose, their behavior is essentially unpredictable. Finally, there is the argument from complexity; to wit, the factors that influence human behavior are so numerous and complex that no amount of study of past behavior makes possible predictions for the future (which ignores the fact that if the number of *possible* factors is very large, the number of actual operating factors in a particular case may be quite small and manageable, but more of that later). Niebuhr is careful to stress the fact that he does not deny the need for men to observe and interpret as honestly as possible; the social sciences are not wholly invalid, and induction is a very useful process. But, and it is a vital "but": "The more the whole panorama of history is brought into view, the more obvious it becomes that the meaning which is given to the whole is derived from an act of faith in the sense that the concept of meaning is derived from ultimate propositions about the character of time and eternity, which are not the fruit of detailed analyses of historical events."[15] From the scientific point of view, Niebuhr has created a pseudoproblem, for it is quite impossible to attribute "meaning" to the whole of human history—explanation must refer to particular events or classes of events that can be stipulated fairly precisely. Niebuhr has committed the same fallacy as the man who proposes a "theory of politics" or a "theory of physics"; he assumes that "politics" or "physics" or "the whole of human history" can be considered as a "thing." Having posed his problem, Niebuhr produces a theological solution, substituting faith for knowledge as a basis for belief: "A sane life requires that we have some clues to the mystery so that the realm

[15]Harry R. Davis and Robert C. Good (eds.), *Reinhold Niebuhr on Politics* (Charles Scribner's Sons, 1960), p. 53. Chapter v of this invaluable collection is relevant to the question under discussion here.

of meaning is not simply reduced to the comprehensible processes of nature." The argument cannot be reconciled with the scientific outlook, for the conceptual frameworks simply do not intersect.

The effect of the dualist position is to remove from scientific criticism a broad range of social and material phenomena. When it is argued that the world is directed, that there is some purpose immanent in human history, or that there are essences of things and the task of inquiry is to discover the nature of those essences, such "arguments" do not involve the kinds of "reasons" that scientific inquiry can either mediate or evaluate. We can neither reject nor assent, since to do either would be to commit the fallacy of arguing from ignorance. The only attitude compatible with scientific standards of inquiry is to withhold judgment. To argue that such claims should be accepted on faith in the absence of contrary evidence is merely to restate the problem in different terms. To judge claims solely by their internal coherence is to abdicate reasoned judgment, since *any* argument can be made internally consistent if the initial premises are beyond challenge.

Sympathy and Understanding

The essentialist and teleologist, who cannot reconcile scientific inquiry with what he considers fundamental knowledge of the universe, rejects it completely. The "dualist" accepts the validity of scientific inquiry but restricts its range to certain classes of phenomena. A third point of view, usually referred to as *verstehende Soziologie*, rejects scientific inquiry as inappropriate to the study of social phenomena and argues for an alternative mode of inquiry— the search for "understanding." At one extreme, this outlook merges into pure intuitionism and essentialism, as in Henri Bergson's *Introduction to Metaphysics*, where it is claimed that men who rely solely on observation can only "move around" an object, whereas "intellectual sympathy" makes it possible to "get within" an object and understand it or "grasp its essence." The concept of *verstehen* that was employed by Wilhelm Dilthey in history and Max Weber in sociology and economic history is substantially different. Dilthey, for example, held that there was a fundamental difference in the relationship among people and the relationship among inanimate objects; in social relations, there was a quality that he called "meaningful"—there was a subjective aspect to the relationship on the part of the participants. To grasp this "meaningful" relationship, one did not merely specify relationships by referring to general statements; instead, the investigator made reference to his own "humanness," to the experiences he shared with other human beings; and on the basis of these, he came to "understand" what was happening. "Understanding," in this context, was a consequence of the "inside view" of human nature that is common to mankind. Dilthey was careful to point out that he did not mean that understanding was a substitute for careful study nor that it was in some manner infallible. But he did insist that historical explanation, explanation of human affairs, had nothing to do with the production of generalizations and the establishing of relationships.[16] Nor was he concerned with the verification procedures needed to handle conclusions.

In the writings of Max Weber, there are both similarities with and differences from Dilthey's use of *verstehen*. For Dilthey, understanding was the *end* of inquiry; for Weber, understanding was still subject to empirical verification. In practice, Weber was close to the position taken by Karl R. Popper, for Popper claims that it is wrong to argue about the validity of the inductive process; instead, science should be concerned with the validation of prop-

[16]Wilhelm Dilthey, *Pattern and Meaning in History: Thoughts on History and Society*, ed. H. P. Rickman (Harper & Bros., 1962), pp. 37–43. See also William H. Dray, *Philosophy of History* (Prentice-Hall Inc., 1964), chap. ii.

ositions. Popper's argument is now widely accepted, since it seems to accord well with scientific usage and it is factually the case that the problem of induction is today no closer to solution than it was in David Hume's time.[17] In this context, it would appear that Weber is using *verstehen* to mean nothing more than that men who are deeply involved with a particular subject often come to conclusions about that topic without being able to stipulate the chain of reasoning by which the conclusion was reached. But Weber is not precisely at one with Popper, for there is implied in Weber's usage the notion that understanding means understanding *motives,* or "grasping the relationship between ends and means," and to that Popper would object. When he uses *verstehen* in this way, Weber is far closer to Dilthey than to Popper.

The comparison illustrates what may be the crux of the argument over "understanding" or *verstehen:* It is almost impossible to find a definition of the concept that will cover all of the uses to which it has been and is being put. In the simplest sense, it implies no more than an unspecifiable insight into social relationships, and nearly everyone would agree that such insights do occur and that they can be extremely valuable. In another sense, which is perhaps the most common meaning of the term in sociology, *verstehen* refers to an understanding of motives; that is, it implies that human behavior is never understood until motivation is made clear and, further, that motivation cannot be inferred from observation. This involves a denial of the possibility that human action can be explained by referring to empirical generalizations in any form, since the generalizations would always be limited to observables; and from these, nothing could be inferred about motivation. Further, this view readily becomes psychological reduc-

[17]Karl R. Popper, *The Logic of Scientific Discovery* (Science Editions, 1961), pp. 27-30.

tionism, the belief that the explanation of human behavior always requires references to psychological principles rather than generalizations about observables. That proposition will be considered below; for the moment, it will suffice to say that there seems no good reason to accept psychological reductionism. Finally, *verstehen* or understanding, particularly as it appears in anthropological writing, becomes a matter of having "inside knowledge" gained through actual participation in events—knowing by doing. The mystique that sometimes develops around discussions of the value of fieldwork in anthropology often implies that conclusion. Again, it can readily be granted that living with an aboriginal tribe provides the anthropologist with an exceptionally favorable position for making observations of social behavior; but it does not follow, surely, that in these circumstances the scholar can always in some manner bring to bear his "human sympathies" and through empathetic understanding gain a more accurate or "deeper" understanding of the mode of life of the tribe.

Such ambiguities in the meaning of "understanding" account for the quite different reasons that are offered for the need to make use of the conception in the explanation of historical and social phenomena. One person argues that the uniqueness of social phenomena forces the sociologist to seek understanding rather than search for relationships. A second claims that social phenomena are "all of one piece"; hence, analytic methods fail, and the sociologist is therefore driven to seek understanding. Still others claim that the decisive element in human behavior is free choice or will—a derivative of a conceptual framework associated historically with writers like Friedrich Nietzsche, Arthur Schopenhauer, and William James; hence, generalizations cannot account for particular acts of behavior, for only by understanding the motivation that leads to particular choices can the student of society be said to "explain" the phenomena. These claims, if they can be maintained, would certainly make it futile, if not impossible, to apply scientific methods to social phenomena. Even a summary examination of the objections, however, is enough to show that they do not have that effect.

1. *Uniqueness.* No two events in human history are exactly alike. Therefore, it is claimed, no event in human history can be explained by the use of generalizations, since generalizations depend upon our capacity to express relationships between two or more classes of events.[18] The claim, if true, would certainly invalidate the use of the scientific mode of explanation in history. However, it depends upon the precise sense in which the term "uniqueness" is employed or applied. In a very strict sense, no two phenomena are ever alike, whether they are social or physical; even two successive swings of a pendulum involve some differences. What is involved, therefore, is not exact duplication but degree of similarity. It may be said that two swings of a pendulum share far more common properties than two human actions, and that would have to be granted. But it is not therefore implied that no two human actions share *any* properties at all. The argument is therefore a matter of degree. Are human actions in such degree unique that we cannot generalize about them successfully? We have now a question to which an answer can be given with some confidence, for generalizations have been made about human behavior and they have proved very useful indeed. Generalization in social science could only be rejected in principle if it were the case that human actions were *in no way* similar, but that is observably not the case.

The possibility remains, however, that human actions are so dissimilar that the application of generalizations is either very risky or quite useless because of the large number of exceptions that have to be made, which is another

[18]For example, Michael Oakeshott, *Experience and Its Modes* (Cambridge University Press, 1933), pp. 143, 154; also R. G. Collingwood, *The Idea of History* (Oxford University Press, 1956).

way of saying that there are few well-established generalizations that can be applied to human society. Again,
it is clearly the case that social science has far fewer
reliable generalizations at its disposal than physics or chemistry or even meteorology; but it is not hopelessly bank-
rupt, and the gains made in the last few years have been
substantial. To the extent that those who base their mistrust of generalization on the uniqueness of human actions
thereby call attention to the difficulty of generalizing in
social science, their emphasis is beneficial. But when it is
claimed that dissimilarities in human behavior are so radical that some process other than explanation by reference
to generalizations must be employed, the claim will not
hold. For one thing, it is reasonably certain that no one
can explain anything without referring to general rules
of some sort. It would be impossible to review the enormous body of writing that has accumulated on the subject
in a brief space, but the argument produced by Carl G.
Hempel and those who support him seems, with minor
modifications, decisive. Hempel argues that explanation is
impossible unless connections can be established among
data, and that cannot be done without general statements.
The suggested alternative—complete description of events—
is a physical impossibility, and even if it were possible,
the result would be neither logically nor psychologically
satisfactory.[19] Furthermore, the problem cannot be avoided
by using the notion of a "continuous series" of events to
fill the gaps between phenomena and thus produce a genetic explanation, since the existence of a series itself implies a stipulated relationship and that, in turn, requires
generalizations—otherwise, there is no series but merely a
sequence of discrete events that remain unconnected.

[19]Carl G. Hempel, *Aspects of Scientific Explanation and Other Essays
in the Philosophy of Science* (Free Press of Glencoe, Inc., 1965), "The
Function of General Laws in History," pp. 231–43. I would myself substitute the weaker term "generalization" for the universal laws that Hempel claims are needed for explanation, but the impossibility of explaining
without *any* general statement seems to me clearly established.

2. *Holism.* The argument here is that social phenomena are unified, nonanalyzable entities and hence that the analytic method on which science so much depends cannot be applied to them without destroying some of their essential properties. The analogy, clearly enough, is to the study of the living cell, where any investigation is difficult so long as the cell is alive and functioning, and where detailed analytic investigation is possible only by killing the cell. Unless it is handled with care, this argument degenerates into simple vitalism; and even in moderate form, it cannot weigh very heavily against scientific methodology. As Quentin Gibson points out, the argument depends on a failure to distinguish between the *parts* of an entity and the *features* of an entity.[20] Analysis by feature does not involve the observer in the loss of qualities of the whole, for the features include the relations among the parts. A wheel, a gear, and a spring may be parts of a watch, for example, and no amount of detailed study of the parts of a watch would reveal its time-telling function; that is a logical impossibility. But if the features of the watch, rather than its parts, are studied, then the various actions and interactions that are products of the total mechanism are also an object of study, and the logical block is avoided. The dilemmas encountered in the study of living cells, stated in these terms, stem from the fact that it is exceptionally difficult to discern the features of a cell, though the various parts of elements have been identified quite accurately. There may, certainly, be difficulties about discerning essential features of human behavior; that is the problem raised by the subjectivists and those who are concerned with freedom of the will and its effect on explanation; but that is not an insoluble problem in principle, either.

[20]Quentin Gibson, *The Logic of Social Enquiry* (Routledge and Kegan Paul, 1960), pp. 10–11. Part I of Gibson's book is a detailed critique of the various scientific objections to the application of scientific methodological principles in the study of social science, and I have relied upon arguments taken from his work directly or modified to fit the context in various parts of this chapter.

3. *Subjectivism and Free Will.* The argument here depends on certain fundamental assumptions. Every human action consists of two parts—one public and observable, and the other private or subjective and not open to observation. An adequate explanation of human behavior necessarily involves reference to both the public and the private aspects of the human act. Furthermore, generalizations about human behavior refer not only to behavior in the past but to future behavior as well, since generalizations are inductions and not merely descriptions; all generalizations are predictions of a sort. But given the capacity of man to learn and to choose according to what he has learned, any prediction of behavior must take into account learning; and since learning is unpredictable, generalization is also ruled out. This, essentially, is the case against scientific inquiry made by the subjectivist. R. G. Collingwood, for example, argues that the freedom of action of the human agent precludes explanation by observation completely and forces the historian to rely upon imaginative reenaction of history, thinking himself into a situation and thus coming to understand it. The argument for free will is usually associated with or bolstered by references to the extreme complexity of social phenomena (which multiplies the difficulties of observation), the rapidity of social change (which influences the validity of generalizations), and the need to grasp the motivation behind an action before the action is really understood.

Let us begin with the question of motivation. Does an explanation of a human action *necessarily* depend on knowledge of motivation? Clearly, it is often desirable, and when we ask questions like "Why on earth would he do that?" we are really asking, "What could his motive possibly have been?" But explanation by reference to motivation is not essential in all cases; and in some circumstances, it would be considered rather odd to inquire into motives—catching a train, throwing a baseball, and so on. Motive questions are important when it is assumed that the desire or intention of the actor was the dominant factor in an action. Is it *always* necessary to refer to motives in order to explain human behavior? Clearly not. An adequate explanation of a great many human actions can be made with no reference at all to motives, particularly when the individual is acting in a highly structured social situation—the usual case in much of politics. That is, when the rules of society and external pressures on the individual are the dominant influences on his behavior, the need for reference to motives declines; indeed, reference to motives may be positively misleading. Consider the behavior of a player in organized sports contests. We need only think of the number of actions we perform that can be considered absolutely free of all external influences, including, presumably, the external influences that have been "internalized" by the socialization process, to see the very limited class of activities in which simple motivational explanations are possible. Perhaps it is true that these few cases are crucial, but it is very easy indeed to overestimate the influence of personal motives on one's actions.

Moreover, even if the search for motives is taken as the goal of inquiry, it is still possible to obtain evidence about motivation only by observation; even personal reports must, after all, be "observed" by someone. Furthermore, explanation by reference to motives involves precisely the same logical requirements as explanation by any other means. A particular motive is imputed to the actor, and a generalization about the behavior of persons entertaining that motive in those circumstances must then be cited to make the connection between motivation and action. And the methodological requirements for these propositions will again be the same as those placed on any other form of assertion. As Ernest Nagel states the point: "[The] crucial point is that logical canons employed by responsible social scientists in assessing the objective evidence for the imputation of psychological states do not appear to differ essentially (though they may be applied less rigorously) from the canons employed for analogous purposes by responsible students in other areas of inquiry."[21]

Finally, it is worth noting that sound methodology requires any discipline to maximize the importance of observable data in its explanations, and heavy reliance upon motivation could lead to the same kinds of abuses that occurred in psychology when behavior was being attributed to an apparently endless variety of innate human "instincts." Revulsion from instinct theories led the early behaviorists like John B. Watson to try to produce a discipline that totally excluded reference to mental states, just as it led Emile Durkheim to the same conclusion, and it is worth noting that some psychologists still believe that such references are unnecessary and misleading.

The argument about "free will" seems to hinge upon a gross misunderstanding of the nature of general propositions, for the fact that a human actor may choose a course of action different from his previous acts does not invalidate generalizations made on the basis of those previous actions. All inductive generalizations are conditional in form and in some degree restricted in application. The argument for free will may reduce the applicability of the generalization, but it cannot invalidate it. The generalization, being conditional in form, always includes a *ceteris paribus* clause, explicitly or implicitly, and the learning process that led to changed behavior would be a change in the stipulated conditions; there would be reason to expect the generalization not to hold. Human knowledge is simply one more variable in the collection of factors that influence behavior.

Does the rate of increase in human knowledge lead to behavior that changes so rapidly that generalization over time is impossible? That is an empirical rather than a logical

21Ernest Nagel, *The Structure of Science*, p. 484.

question, to be answered by observation. The answer seems to be that it does not. Human behavior in most, though not all, cases is remarkably stable over time even in a period when society is changing very rapidly. Furthermore, the form in which generalizations are stated can take such change into account by stipulating relations between environment and behavior rather than specifying the actual act of behavior that will occur. To assert that children will usually adopt the political preference of the parent, for example, says nothing about whether the choice will be Republican, Democratic, socialist or communist, for example; yet it is a quite valuable generalization about political behavior.

Antiscience: A Summation

To this point, the discussion has dealt with arguments that purport to demonstrate the inapplicability in principle of scientific rules of inquiry to the study of social science. Often, there has not been time to lay out in detail the kinds of precise distinctions that must be drawn in order to judge the efficacy of an argument. The crucial point, however, is that the burden of proof lies with those who argue that the principles of scientific inquiry cannot be applied to social science, and the aim has been to show that the claim is too strong and cannot be defended. That does not mean that science reigns supreme and all is well with the world. There is no reason in principle that social and physical science may not employ the same canons of inquiry, though they will be much harder to apply rigorously in the social sciences. There are good reasons for supposing that it is worth trying. That is to say, it is essential that social scientists understand that social science cannot be studied with the same precision and accuracy as physics or chemistry; it is also essential that they try very hard to do precisely that, knowing they will fail. Otherwise, the discipline will founder in a morass, for it contains much that is wise and perceptive along with much dross and it needs a basis for separating the two. The great merit of the scientific attitude is its demonstrated capacity for separating intellectual wheat from chaff. The contention that in the process of separating, too much wheat is thrown out in an effort to reduce the amount of chaff that remains seems untenable, though no one would complain against being reminded of the possibility from time to time. Remove all rules of inquiry, and the result is not "creative freedom" but common slavery.[22]

Even if scientific methodology is accepted as a basic strategy for the social sciences, and the unity of rules of inquiry between social and physical science is accepted, not all of the outstanding issues are so easily settled. A substantial argument has been waged, for example, between those who believe that since social science is concerned with the behavior of individuals, all explanations of social phenomena must eventually be defined in terms of individuals and not in collective terms (methodological individualism). This argument, put forward most strongly by Karl R. Popper and F. A. Hayek, has no great practical significance, though it has some interesting philosophic consequences—which may account for the vehemence with which Popper and Hayek state their claims. The most sensible position on the question seems to be that taken by Abraham Kaplan, who deals very briefly with the whole topic. Since explanations require the use of theoretical terms, he says, and since collective terms themselves are of various kinds and not a single type, it is unlikely that every collective term could be defined strictly in terms of individual actions, and some terms cannot be defined strictly in any terms. Hence, if methodological individualism is to be defensible, it can mean little more than the commonly accepted proposition that in the last analysis all explanations of

[22]A contrary view of the desirability of the scientific attitude can be found in Hans Morgenthau, *Scientific Man versus Power Politics* (University of Chicago Press, 1946).

social phenomena depend upon observations of the behavior of single persons.[23]

A second question that has much exercised social scientists in this century has been the relation between psychology and political science. Is political science, as Horace Kallen once declared, nothing but psychology? Can all political explanations be reduced to psychological explanations? Or on the contrary, can political explanations be made with no references whatever to psychology? The argument has an interesting history. Emile Durkheim, in his famous treatise on methodology, argued for the strict exclusion of psychology from sociological explanations, and many of his followers (like A. R. Radcliffe-Brown) took the same line. Karl R. Popper is opposed to psychological explanation, despite his attitude on methodological individualism; F. A. Hayek, on the other hand, argues for psychological explanations. The most plausible position seems that taken by Quentin Gibson, who argues that in principle it is impossible to reduce *all* social explanations to psychological explanations, whereas in practice it is very convenient indeed to be able to give psychological explanations—in many cases, they are essential. The use of psychiatric, particularly Freudian, conceptualizations for the explanation of social phenomena raises still other interesting problems which will be explored in another chapter.[24]

---

[23]Popper, *The Open Society and Its Enemies* and *The Poverty of Historicism.* Note that Popper tends to *assert* and not argue the position for methodological individualism. See also F. A. Hayek, *The Counterrevolution of Science* (Free Press, 1955), especially chaps. iii and v. Compare Nagel, *op. cit.*, pp. 535–46, where the conclusion accepted above is argued very forcibly. Gibson, *op. cit.*, takes the opposite view (pp. 102–6), but to my mind less cogently.

[24]The best treatment of the question can be found in Gibson, *op. cit.*, chap. ix. See also Emile Durkheim, *The Rules of Sociological Method,* trans. Sarah A. Solovay and John H. Mueller; ed. George E. G. Catlin (Free Press of Glencoe, Inc., 1964); A. R. Radcliffe-Brown, *A Natural Science of Society* (Free Press, 1957); Popper, *The Open Society and Its Enemies,* Vol. II, p. 91; Hayek, *op. cit.*, chaps. iii, v.

Beyond these two general questions, there are endless points on which there is no real agreement about the methodology of the social sciences. What is the use and importance of models in explanation? What methods are appropriate for the investigation of social phenomena? The list could be extended almost indefinitely. But such specific questions are best left for the methodologist.

Social Criticism

The introduction of scientific methodology into the social sciences could be expected to arouse the hostility of the established interests and traditions; and so, of course, it did. But it has also encountered a substantial amount of opposition from those who find it quite inadequate as a total strategy for social science—those we may refer to here as the "social critics." The points at issue are somewhat murky, and the whole discussion has suffered from dogmatism on both sides. The "pro science" wing of political science, particularly those who claim, for different reasons, the label "behavioralist," has often appeared to argue as if (1) all those who opposed them were denying common sense or (2) all that was needed in the social sciences was increasing methodological stringency. The opposition seems at times to believe that all those committed to scientific methodology are either (1) wholly indifferent to the role of values in human life or (2) wholly ignorant of the limits of scientific empiricism. Doubtless, some spokesmen for each side are guilty of each of these errors; but for the most part, each side has set up its straw men to attack, which is not a tactic that illuminates. It seems beyond argument that there is much to be gained in terms of reliability, precision, and grounds for adjudication of argument by the application of scientific methodology; it is equally clear that specific scientific criteria of inquiry cannot serve as absolute limits on inquiry within the total framework of the social sciences and that those who insist on the right or even the obligation of the social scientist to evaluate the phenomena he observes and explains can do so without violating any canons of scientific inquiry so long as they do not insist (1) that scientific explanation is wholly irrelevant to evaluation or (2) that the evaluation is itself in some way "scientific."

To repeat what has already been implied in the previous chapter, social evaluation cannot proceed without explanation, and the methodological principles of science offer criteria of explanation that permit adjudication between competing claims to knowledge. To that extent, scientific methodology seems indispensable. On the other hand, empiricism pursued to the nth degree leads to complete skepticism or to idealism, and that is self-defeating. We are left with Stephen Runciman's suggestion that when the social scientist is either explaining or evaluating, he ought to *try* to be a positivist, knowing that he cannot be. And even if he could succeed, a social science that did no more than explain phenomena in the sense that a physicist explains the phenomena would be a poor and barren land to till. Social phenomena *do* require evaluation, by someone. Surely the burden of proof lies on those who claim that such evaluation ought not to be done by the trained political scientist or sociologist. The fact that argument about values cannot be supported through logical relationships with factual propositions is irrelevant. Nor is it significant that one or another social scientist may prefer *not* to indulge in evaluations. That cannot preclude the argument that systematic discussion of social evaluations, and evaluative discussions of society, are a necessary part of the social sciences.

An example of the kind of "bogie" that has crept into the discussion may clarify the point. The social critic objects strenuously to propositions of the following kind:

The scientific aim is to establish generalizations about human behavior that are supported by empirical evidence collected in an impersonal and objective way. The evidence must be capable of verification by other interested scholars and the procedures must be completely open to review and replication.

The ultimate end is to understand, explain, and predict human behavior in the same sense in which scientists understand, explain, and predict the behavior of physical forces or biological factors, or, closer home, the behavior of goods and prices in the economic market.[25]

Taken as an absolute statement of the scope of social science, this clearly will not do. But Berelson *does not intend that it be taken that way,* and that is the crucial point. Further along in the Introduction, he makes the point explicit: "There are many paths to understanding—common observation, philosophical reflection, artistic expression, intuition. All I need urge here is that the scientific approach is another way, and that for many purposes, especially those in which establishing the facts is important, it is a particularly good way."[26] To take the first point as universal, and ignore the second, is to distort the argument.

At the other extreme, we find C. Wright Mills, in his treatment of "abstracted empiricism," indulging in equally excessive and distorted parodies—for example, his attack on specialists in method in sociology: "Theirs is not a proposal for any scheme of topical specialization according to 'intelligible fields of study' or a conception of problems of social structure. It is a proposed specialization based solely on the use of The Method, regardless of content, problem, or area."[27] Mills's argument is also aimed at a straw man, for if it is the case that such idiocies occur in the social sciences, it is still improper to condemn an entire class on the basis of the behavior of a small segment of the whole. No one with the least bit of methodological sophistication would de-

[25]Bernard Berelson, "Introduction to the Behavioral Sciences," in Bernard Berelson (ed.), *The Behavioral Sciences Today* (Harper & Bros., 1963), p. 3.

[26]*Ibid.,* p. 5.

[27]C. Wright Mills, *The Sociological Imagination* (Oxford University Press, 1959), p. 59.

fend the practice Mills is attacking or engage in it. If the intent is to slay dragons, then the first rule must be to "find a dragon"—not a paper tiger.

The substance of the criticism aimed at contemporary society by the social critics will be examined in due course. For the moment, we can examine some of the methodological implications of the kinds of arguments they deploy. It would be easier, of course, if the methodology were explicitly stated, but few of the social critics discuss methodological questions explicitly or even to the extent that such discussion can be found in C. Wright Mills. Furthermore, the term "social criticism" covers a variety of persons and points of view; hence, not every one of the implications that concern us here are to be found in every writer who falls into the classification. There is, however, broad agreement on some few critical principles; or, perhaps more accurately, certain critical principles are contained implicitly in the work of most of these writers; and it is these fundamentals that I would like to examine briefly.

The chief intellectual influences operating among the social critics are (1) Marxism, and particularly the recent doctrines that have come to be known as "Marxist humanism," derived from certain early Marxist writings that dealt with such problems as the "alienation" of the worker from his product; (2) psychiatric theory, more commonly that modification of Freud which is known as "neo-Freudianism"— a gross misnomer, since it quite literally inverts the social teachings that appear in Freud's own writings; and (3) Hegel. As a whole, the social critics dislike "science" except as it appears in Marx and Freud; and they tend to regard the contemporary effort to introduce scientific methodology into the social sciences as an effort to "stifle creativity" or "imaginative freedom," or, worse still, as an invidious plot to defend the status quo against all criticism. They tend to be relativists, in Karl Mannheim's sense of the relativity of all knowledge, and make frequent use of the accusative mode that Marx, Freud, and Mannheim so much facilitate. They are, for the most part, devoted to the view that the human being must be "committed" or "engaged," that knowledge is obtained by participation; and in this, they much resemble the Sartrian branch of the existentialist movement. All of which tends to place emphasis on the *source* of knowledge rather than the validity of the content of claims to knowledge—the argument is *ad hominem*.

Most of the methodological questions raised by this group can be found in the works of Karl Mannheim, and particularly in his *Ideology and Utopia*. Although Mannheim's prescriptions are not necessarily those the others would agree to, Mannheim provided a methodological base from which social criticism could proceed more or less unhindered by the requirements of scientific cogency. The arguments on which he based his position bear close examination.[28] Three points are of prime significance: (1) the claim that all knowledge is relative to social position, and particularly class status; (2) the tendency to concentrate on the source of knowledge or means of acquiring knowledge rather than verification procedures; and (3) the close relationship that is assumed between social criticism and active participation in social life.

Mannheim's major methodological point, which he took from Karl Marx and modified slightly, is that the social observer is always and necessarily a participant in the process he observes. There can therefore be no "pure theory"; collective points of view underlie every conception men employ: "The great revelation it affords is that every form of historical and political thought is essentially conditioned

---

[28]Typical examples of social criticism are Barrington Moore, Jr., *Political Power and Social Theory* (Harper & Bros., 1962); Irving Louis Horowitz (ed.), *The New Sociology* (Oxford University Press, 1964); Maurice Stein and Arthur Vidich (eds.), *Sociology on Trial* (Prentice-Hall, Inc., 1963); Erich Fromm, *The Sane Society* (Holt, Rinehart & Winston, Inc., 1955); and works by David Riesman, Norman O. Brown, Herbert Marcuse, and various others.

by the life situation of the thinker and his groups."[29] From this assumption, Mannheim goes on to assert that theory arises out of a social impulse and serves to clarify the situation in which the impulse arose; in the process of clarifying, theory serves to change the situation; out of the change emerges a requirement for a new theory. This is the Hegelian dialectic once again, put to an interesting use. For it implies that a theory is something like John Dewey's attempt to deal with a concrete social situation by learning how to modify the theory in the act of applying it; Dewey was, of course, under precisely the same general influence as Mannheim in this case. Theory cannot be separated from action, on this view, because *acting* on or with a theory is a necessary element in the production of theory: "Indeed, political thought cannot be carried on by speculating about it from the outside. Rather thought becomes illuminated when a concrete situation is penetrated, not merely through acting and doing, but also through the thinking which must go with them."[30] Or in another context: "Only through acting in the situation do we address questions to it, and the answer we derive is always in the form of the success or failure of the action. Theory is not torn from its essential connection with action, and action is the clarifying medium in which all theory is tested and develops."[31] This view appears to lead to pure relativism and committed activism as methodological essentials for social science. Mannheim tries valiantly to eliminate the total relativism of the argument by using the "uprooted" intellectuals, presumably those with loose class affiliations, as an ideal—they will be least influenced by the ideology of their groups and hence, presumably, will make the best sociologists. Although they will

[29]Karl Mannheim, *Ideology and Utopia: An Introduction to the Sociology of Knowledge,* trans. Louis Wirth and Edward Shils (Harper & Bros., first published in 1936), p. 125.

[30]*Ibid.,* p. 128.

[31]*Ibid.,* p. 133.

not be entirely free of bias, they can be relatively free of it; hence, they are the most valuable potential source of knowledge. That escape route tends to break down when the defining terms of the intellectual class are specified.

What kind of knowledge of politics can be attained, even under ideal circumstances? Mannheim claims that knowledge is possible but that it will take "quite a different form" from what is customarily conceived as knowledge. Again, the acquisition of knowledge is linked to action, knowing to doing, to use a phrase from Dewey: "[In] teaching as well as in politics it is precisely in the course of actual conduct that specific and relevant knowledge is attainable in increasing measure, and under certain conditions communicable."[32] The mode of modern mathematical-natural science cannot be regarded as appropriate to knowledge as a whole. Scientific knowledge takes the form of universally valid statements of the necessary conditions for an event to occur— a requirement that is, of course, far more rigid than any of the present-day sciences could endure. Furthermore, by insisting on verification or validation, the sciences sever the "organic connection" between man as member of society and man thinking about society—or acting. Formal knowledge is accessible to everyone; other kinds of knowledge are accessible "only to certain subjects or in certain historical periods . . . which becomes apparent through the social purposes of individuals," particularly knowledge of others gained by actually living with them. In politics, "where thought is not contemplation from the point of view of the spectator, but rather the active participation and reshaping of the process itself, a new type of knowledge seems to emerge, namely, that in which decision and standpoint are inseparably bound up together."[33] The evaluative point of view is inseparable from observation in political matters

[32]*Ibid.*, p. 164.
[33]*Ibid.*, p. 170.

because acting involves choosing, and choosing implies evaluation.

Mannheim's methodology is perhaps more important for what it omits than for what it includes. Certainly it provides the investigator with freedom to use his imagination, and it accepts commitment as a necessary part of social inquiry. Evaluation is taken for granted—indeed, forced by the nature of the subject matter—much as it is forced in the thinking of Leo Strauss. What Mannheim does not provide, however, is criteria for evaluating claims to knowledge or normative judgments. He opens the door for endless argument about the social bias underlying particular explanations of political phenomena, much as Sigmund Freud's doctrine of "resistance" made his theories wholly irrefragable. And perhaps most attractive of all, Mannheim provided a rationale for the "alienation" of the intellectual in modern society. Methodologically, it simply will not do, and I can provide no better illustration of the limits of Mannheim's approach to politics than to quote the reasonable and sympathetic comments of Anatol Rapoport on the work of C. Wright Mills:

Much as I applaud Mills' insistence that imagination and commitment ought to be recognized as indispensable components of the sociologist's toolbox, I cannot minimize the importance of other tools whose very use is incomprehensible except to a specialist. The acquisition of relevant knowledge is not only a matter of being attuned, motivated, sensitive, and emancipated, it is also a matter of being sophisticated in evaluating the reliability of what one observes and deduces.

Science, with its attitude of detachment, is the only mode of cognition we know which can make showdowns between incompatible views productive and which can reveal the degree of incompatibility between views. Hence logical analysis, extension of concepts, tests of hypotheses, and the rest cannot be avoided if we wish the clashes between serious thinkers to generate light as well as heat.[34]

[34]Anatol Rapoport, "The Scientific Relevance of C. Wright Mills," in Horowitz, *op. cit.*, p. 107.

PART II

Explanations

THE GOAL of systematic inquiry, in political science as in any other discipline, is explanation. Even those who wish to concentrate on political evaluation must attend to the problems of explanation, since the quality of normative judgments is directly and necessarily contingent upon the quality of the explanations they presume. It follows that one of the two principal focuses for the study of political thought is the explanations that political scientists currently offer for the phenomena they find interesting and significant. In the three chapters that comprise Part II of this book, we examine the principal forms of explanation in current use in political science, both in principle and in application. Part II is thus a summary of the "state of theory" in the discipline. It concentrates on those efforts at explanation or theory construction that seem to represent the principal thrust of the discipline at the present time and that seem likely to retain their significance for the immediate future.

If explanations are to be studied systematically, if they are to become one of the objects of the study of political thought, they must be organized or classified on some useful principle. There are various ways in which classifications can be made, none completely satisfactory. The logical form of an explanation, which is heavily emphasized in philosophy of science, is not a good indicator in political science because virtually all of the explanations that political scientists offer for their phenomena are probabilistic rather than deductive and logic cannot differentiate adequately among probabilistic explanations. Explanations cannot be classified by their objects; the phenomena are too diverse, and in any event the quality of the explanation is independent of the properties of the objects explained. The question "What direction is political science presently taking?" is therefore extremely difficult to answer with confidence, and the direction itself can change with astonishing speed. To be useful, the answer must be given in terms of analytic rather than empirical distinctions. In the conduct of inquiry, description, explanation, and evaluation tend to merge; principle and application are barely separable. Furthermore, it is not enough just to have some system for classifying explanations. Somehow, the main channels of inquiry must be separated from the incidental; the fads that ripple the surface of the discipline must be distinguished from the persistent currents that flow beneath.

The classification scheme employed here is not a perfect solution to the problem, but it is both useful and manageable—and it produces significant results. Attempts at explanation are divided according to the *conceptual framework* they employ—the family of concepts, theories, quasi theories, and other explanatory instruments used in inquiry. Although the conceptual frameworks can be defined very broadly, they remain amenable to criticism in principle, and that is the important factor for the student of political thought. It would be impossible to try to examine critically every explanation offered in political science. If, however, explanations can be criticized as members of a family, the task is much facilitated. The particular explanation must still be examined, of course, and the more broadly the family is defined, the less useful is criticism based on family characteristics. But it is possible and worthwhile to examine a conceptual framework like functionalism, divide it if necessary into two or more subspecies, and produce a generalized criticism of the family and/or the subspecies.

Each of the three chapters that follows deals with one major conceptual framework in contemporary political science: functionalism, the family of psychological explanations, and formalism (the use of formal or logical models, simulations, and mathematical systems in political inquiry). The selection is not exhaustive, and that can arouse criticism, for to choose one approach is to reject others, and those busily engaged in research that depends upon one of the omitted approaches do not care to be told, even by implication, that they are flogging a dead or even a dying horse. That is not my intention. No one can say in advance that a particular conceptual framework will certainly produce valuable results, though it may be possible to give reasons why it seems unlikely. The selection of conceptual frameworks made here can, moreover, be defended in terms that leave the value of the approaches omitted from consideration an open question. First, time and space are limited. Since I have no wish to produce an encyclopedia, it seemed better to deal with a few conceptual structures critically and in depth rather than to cover a wider range more descriptively or superficially. Second, there are "style leaders" in political science as elsewhere, and the mode of inquiry they are currently using is a valuable indication of trends within the discipline. These trends seem to me to support the selection I have made. Most important of all, however, there are good critical grounds for assuming that the conceptual frameworks considered here are likely to prove useful and viable for a reasonable period of time. New conceptual structures may be developed in the next decade or so; but it seems very unlikely that functionalism, psychological explanations, and formalism will disappear from political science in that time period.

Functionalism, or "systems analysis," is the predominant conceptual framework in contemporary political science. In the decade from 1955 to 1965, its influence spread with extraordinary rapidity into political research and teaching; by 1965, it stood preeminent in the field. There are a number of subspecies in the functionalist family, and some have proved more useful than others. It is not yet the ideal conceptual framework by any means. There remain serious conceptual problems, methodological inadequacies, and difficulties of application. The conceptual framework is open to serious abuse, and has been abused. But no conceptual framework has a monopoly on nonsense or incompetence, and the drawbacks to the functional approach to politics are more than offset by its virtues—great flexibility, abstractness, capacity to handle phenomena over a wide range of magnitudes, capacity to absorb explanations formulated in terms of other conceptual frameworks, etc. As we shall see in the chapter that follows, functionalism has distinct advantages for the political scientist, and it appears as the most promising of the conceptual frameworks presently employed in the study of politics. For that reason, it deserves careful attention from students of political thought.

The role of psychological conceptual frameworks (in a variety of forms) in contemporary political science has grown steadily since the end of World War II. The relation between psychology and political science remains a tendentious question, but political scientists seem to have lost the fear of "mentalism" that dominated American social science for most of the first half of the 20th century. The influence of Emile Durkheim, Arthur Bentley, John Dewey, and the rigorous (or rigid) positivists has declined, perhaps because psychology itself has become more eclectic and—in the United States, at least—considerably less committed to the strict empiricism inherited from John B. Wat-

son and his followers. There remain, of course, political
scientists who refuse to entertain *any* kind of psychological
explanation and, for that matter, psychologists who insist
that psychology remain rigorously empirical—B. F. Skinner
is a good example—but they are no longer the dominant
influence in either discipline. On the other hand, few political scientists accept the view that political science is only
a special branch of social psychology. The most general attitude on the question seems to be tolerance. It may be
possible to eliminate psychology from political explanations,
but it would be uncommonly difficult to do so, and it is not
necessary. Some social phenomena are most readily explained in terms of psychic theories, but there are also
phenomena that are not particularly amenable to psychological explanation or that are more readily explained in
other terms—behavior that takes place in highly structured
role situations, for example. It would be silly to seek a psychological explanation of a baseball player's reflexive actions
during the course of play; they are determined mainly by
the rules of the game. All of which suggests the not particularly helpful principle that psychology should be used
where it is useful and avoided where it is redundant. In any
event, the use of psychological theories and concepts in political science is widespread and influential, and the student of political thought is going to have to cope with explanations that employ a variety of psychological constructs.
A detailed examination of the major conceptual frameworks
available in psychology, and their application to political
phenomena, is therefore a necessary part of any adequate
study of contemporary political thought.

The third class of conceptual frameworks to be considered
in detail below—*formalism*, defined as the use of models,
mathematics, and simulations—has had a much less spectacular career in contemporary political science than either
functionalism or psychology. Development during the 1950's
and 1960's has been steady; but the results, measured in

terms of volume of interest and square foot of publications, have been modest. Yet formalism is rich in promise. The models presently available, particularly in mathematics, are not especially well suited to the kinds of problems political scientists face; new models have been slow to develop. But the principles that suggest the use of models as an aid to exploration, prediction, and explanation are sound; and a more strenuous attempt to use formal models, analogies, and simulations seems bound to be made. One great virtue of models is that they facilitate the transfer of knowledge from one area to another; to apply a model is, in effect, to try to use what is known about the model to explain or predict behavior in an area to which the model is isomorphic. Formalism also facilitates experimentation, particularly through simulations, and contributes indirectly to the rigor of the discipline by forcing attention to the precise meaning of terms and the precise nature of interactions. For these and other reasons, a full chapter is devoted to the problems and possibilities of formalism. What has already been done is perhaps not a sufficient justification for the choice; what is potentially possible more than justifies it. Hopefully, the chapter may contribute to the realization of that potential by stimulating further interest in the field among political scientists.

Functionalism, psychology, and formalism, then, serve as a focus for the discussion of explanation in political science that follows. Many other conceptual frameworks could be included in the selection, certainly; and some of the omissions may seem strange, particularly to those who have been working in political science for some time. Why formalism, for example, but no detailed discussion of elites, or groups, or the concept of power? The answer to that question provides an interesting insight into the manner in which academic inquiry develops. Had this book appeared 10 or 15 years earlier, the central concepts in the book would certainly have been power, elites, and groups.

Functionalism, formalism, and psychology could at that time be considered no more than peripheral. Yet, by the mid-1960's, it was clear that groups, elites, and power did not provide an adequate conceptual basis for political science. In general, the concepts themselves remain as part of the commonplace technical terminology of the discipline, but the claim to inclusiveness made by their supporters has been rejected. That the group is one of the prime phenomena in political life, for example, few would argue; but the major effort to explain political life in terms of group phenomena that flourished in the 1950's has largely been abandoned. It is a very long way, intellectually speaking, from Arthur Bentley's view that the whole of politics is no more than the interaction of groups ("When the groups are adequately stated, everything is stated. When I say everything, I mean everything.") to contemporary studies of group dynamics where the group appears as the primary environment for individual actors rather than as the primary actor in a wider social environment.*

"Elite theory," or the concept of elites, has had a "cycle of influence" within political science. A powerful effort to construct an adequate political science on the basis of elite

---

*Compare Arthur Bentley, *The Process of Government: A Study of Social Pressures* (new ed.; Principia Press of Illinois, 1935; 1st ed., 1908), with Dorwin Cartwright and Alvin Zander (eds.), *Group Dynamics: Research and Theory* (2d ed.; Harper and Row, 1960). Bentley is not even listed in the index to Cartwright and Zander. Actually, Bentley's "group theory" has had an interesting history in political science. Published in 1908, it created little stir until the 1930's, when it was taken up by an older generation of political scientists (Pendleton Herring, Peter Odegard, etc.). Late in the 1940's, there was another revival, lasting through most of the following decade. It produced, among other works, David B. Truman's *Governmental Process: Political Interests and Public Opinion* (Alfred A. Knopf, Inc., 1951); Bertram Gross's *Legislative Struggle* (McGraw-Hill Book Co., Inc., 1953); Earl Latham's *Group Basis of Politics* (Cornell University Press, 1952); these volumes were and, indeed, are still very widely read. By the late 1950's and early 1960's, however, criticism began to increase, and the influence of functionalism spread rapidly. For a good example of the critics' position, see Roy C. Macridis, "Groups and Group Theory," *Journal of Politics*, February, 1961.

concepts ultimately failed, leaving political science with a useful, even essential, concept but no central conceptual framework. And the efforts of political scientists to build an adequate theory of power would require almost a history of political science to recount. In the broad sense of the term, political science is intimately concerned with the study of power. But every attempt that has been made to narrow the concept has proved unsuccessful, and the claims of the more extreme proponents of power analysis—Hans Morgenthau, for example—have usually been disallowed. The concept of power is now mainly the property of the social critics, and the vagueness and ambiguity that prove such a handicap in explanation are sometimes an advantage in social criticism.*

*The most recent major effort to base a central conceptual framework for political science on the concept of power was made by Harold D. Lasswell and Abraham Kaplan in *Power and Society: A Framework for Political Inquiry* (Yale University Press, 1950). Chapters iv and v indicate the conceptual difficulties involved in the use of power as an organizing principle. A less systematic conception of the use of power in political science can be found in Hans Morgenthau, "Power as a Political Concept," *Review of Politics*, Vol. XVII (October, 1955).

For the study of elites, see Renzo Sereno, *The Rulers* (Frederick A. Praeger, Inc., 1962); and S. F. Nadel, "The Concept of Social Elites," *International Social Science Bulletin*, Vols. VII–VIII (UNESCO, 1956). An extensive bibliography, indicative of interest in elite theory among political scientists, can be found in Harold D. Lasswell, Daniel Lerner, and C. Easton Rothwell, *The Comparative Study of Elites* (Stanford University Press, 1952). For critical comments, see Suzanne Keller, *Beyond the Ruling Class: Strategic Elites in Modern Society* (Random House, 1963); and James H. Meisel, *The Myth of the Ruling Class: Gaetano Mosca and the Elite* (University of Michigan Press, 1948).

For a critique of the theoretical basis of postwar elite studies, see Robert A. Dahl, *Who Governs?* (Yale University Press, 1961); and Nelson W. Polsby, *Community Power and Political Theory* (Yale University Press, 1963). Polsby, in particular, demolishes the "stratification principle" on which classic elite studies rest.

For the use that has been made of the concept of power by social critics, see Gerhard Lenski, *Power and Privilege: A Theory of Social Stratification* (McGraw-Hill Book Co., Inc., 1966), especially chap. iii; Barrington Moore, Jr., *Political Power and Social Theory* (Harper & Bros., 1958), especially Essay 1; Robert A. Nisbet, *Community and Power* (Oxford University Press, 1953); or C. Wright Mills, *The Power Elite* (Oxford University Press, 1956). The relation between power, elites, and groups is here clearly discernible.

It is not surprising that elite theory, group theory, and power theory declined more or less together, for they are intimately related. In the last analysis, all three are concerned with power. As Renzo Sereno points out, the theory of elites (particularly in its early form) reduces the study of politics to the study of power relations; and as Roy C. Macridis says of group analysis, "group analysis is . . . a crude form of determinism. Interest is the primary propelling force and every action is based upon sharing of interest. Power configuration is basically the configuration of competing and struggling interests organized into groups."[1] Without an adequate conceptual basis for studying power, group theory and elite theory lose their usefulness. And power has proved to be an exceptionally difficult concept to tie down. Without attempting a comprehensive review of the writing on the subject, it is fairly easy to point out the source of the difficulty.[2] The "power theorist" wishes to state causal relations between or among elements in a social or political system. If he tries to use power as a concept analogous to the role of money in the economy, he runs immediately into empirical difficulties, for the power to do one thing does not necessarily imply the power to do another—military forces are often quite useless for civil tasks. Power, in other words, must somehow be defined in terms of the realm in which it operates and of the kinds of effects it can produce. The Pandora's box is then opened to discussion of legitimacy, consent, and a whole host of related problems. The best illustrative analogy known to me is between the concept of power and the concept of intelligence. In each case the intention has been to explain certain kinds

[1] Roy C. Macridis and Bernard E. Brown, *Comparative Politics: Notes and Readings* (rev. ed.; The Dorsey Press, Inc., 1964), p. 139.

[2] Two attempts to deal with the concept of power that are well worth reading are Robert A. Dahl's "The Concept of Power," *Behavioral Science*, July, 1957, and Herbert A. Simon's "Notes on the Observation and Measurement of Political Power," *Journal of Politics*, 1953, both reprinted in S. Sidney Ulmer (ed.), *Introductory Readings in Political Behavior* (Rand McNally & Co., 1961).

of human actions in terms of the operation of an abstract conception. David Hume's problem of explaining the causal relationship between two billiard balls is magnified by replacing one of the billiard balls by an abstraction. Unless it can be shown that a given effect is a consequence of a particular abstraction and not some other factor, the explanation is, in principle, beyond challenge. Power theorists have been unable to devise ways of meeting this criticism. It is suggestive, perhaps, to note that psychologists, too, have come to agree that the concept of "intelligence" is not particularly helpful, though "intelligence tests" have pragmatic usefulness.

At a still more fundamental level, conceptual frameworks such as power theory, elite theory, and group theory rested on a serious misconception of the problem facing political science. They require, implicitly, the assumption that the substantive content of "politics" can be defined and identified. Historically, they are closely associated with the search for a "theory of politics," which necessarily implies the capacity to stipulate the meaning of "political" unambiguously. The conceptual error comes from mistaking politics for a phenomenon, which it is not. The term "politics" is used to designate a wide range of activities, none of which is a logical derivative from some "essential meaning" of politics. No discipline can be defined by its objects, whether it is politics or physics, and to ask for a theory of politics is as meaningless as to ask for a theory of physics. The only question that has meaning in this sense is "What kinds of theories do political scientists (or physicists) need to explain the phenomena they consider significant?" To take an example of the search for an overarching framework from the "power theorists": "By making power its central concept, a theory of politics does not presume that none but power relations control political action . . . . A central concept, such as power, . . . provides a kind of rational outline of politics, a map of the political scene."[3] Leaving aside the fact that in context Morgenthau clearly intended his "theory of politics" to serve both normative and explanatory purposes, it is obvious that the concept of the "political" has been reified and politics is treated as a phenomenon, and that is exactly what cannot be done.

From the instrumentalist point of view, a theory is simply a part of an explanation, and it is not always easy to identify one. But a theory cannot be a phenomenon, and one phenomenon cannot provide an explanation for another; an explanation depends on statements of relationships among phenomena. Elites and groups are descriptive concepts, and very useful ones, but they are not conceptual frameworks that can serve as explanatory systems. To make an explanatory structure of the concept of groups, it would be necessary to follow Arthur Bentley and argue that the concept is so pervasive that once it is fully defined, everything is known. But we know that is not the case; exhaustive description is inconceivable, and it is always possible to invent another conceptual structure that reveals relations not hitherto suspected. To take a parallel case, interactions among individuals can easily be conceptualized, and it makes good sense to seek a theory of interactions, but an "interaction theory of politics" is only a meaningless phrase. If our problem were only a matter of terminology, it would not be worth debating; the real issue lies at the conceptual level. Behind the difference in usage lies a genuine and serious error in conceptualization that needs to be rectified. Hopefully, this volume may contribute to a clarification of the point.

Evaluation of Explanations

The treatment of explanations in the three chapters that

[3] Hans Morgenthau, "Power as a Political Concept," in Roland Young (ed.), *Approaches to the Study of Politics* (Northwestern University Press, 1958).

follow concentrates heavily upon the quality, consistency, and limitations of the conceptual frameworks that political scientists employ or recommend. In part, that emphasis is due to the fact that political scientists have often been more concerned to develop an adequate conceptual framework than to apply it to concrete phenomena. In part, it is due to the need for general standards of criticism rather than familiarity with particular applications of a conceptual structure. From the standpoint of political thought, it is extremely important to be able to aggregate large numbers of explanations and treat them critically as a unit. For that purpose, it is better to concentrate on the conceptual framework rather than the details of a particular phenomenon.

Of course, the actual use of conceptual frameworks is ultimately decisive. We need to examine the explanations that are produced with their assistance, the predictions they generate, the discoveries they facilitate. The evaluation of the conceptual framework follows from its applications. If the attempt is well made but the results are inferior, the conceptual framework may be held culpable. If the application is bungled but, like Rostand's Cyrano de Bergerac, we can expiate at some length on what might have been accomplished had the affair been better managed, then the fault may lie with the agent and not the conceptual structure. Always, however, full evaluation of an explanation includes both a conceptual framework and a body of phenomena, and never the one alone. No phenomena, no evaluation! That is the first rule of criticism. Beyond that, it may be useful to summarize briefly the kinds of questions that can be asked about the general applicability and usefulness of the conceptual frameworks considered in the remainder of Part II.

The first point that must be noted is the purpose of the inquiry, which may be explanation, prediction, exploration, clarification, etc. In general, we know that classification systems, models, and analogies cannot provide explanations, though they may suggest them. It is useful, therefore, to separate attempts at explanation from other kinds of inquiry. Explanations, as we have already noted, must begin with a concrete set of phenomena; there can be no "general explanation" or "general theory." Has the phenomenon been explained adequately? That is perhaps the most difficult question in social inquiry. If an explanation is deductive, the question asks no more than whether there is a deductive relationship between the phenomenon to be explained and the generalizations used to explain it. But when explanations are not made in the deductive pattern, as is true in most cases in social science, the problem is not so easily solved. In general, we are asking whether the generalizations produced in the explanation "account for" the phenomena. Since there are no formal rules for deciding whether or not they do, the decision must rest on other grounds. Somehow, we need to "make a case for" or provide a warrant for the inferences required for explanation. The validity of the warrant is field-dependent; it requires a judgment based on knowledge of the phenomena and of relevant explanations in related areas. Some of the points that need to be considered are:

1. Relation to Previous Experience. Although statistical indices of the number of times a phenomenon has occurred in the past in particular circumstances can be misleading, compatibility with past experience is an important factor in judging the validity of an explanation. Men have no other guide than the past when they seek to deal with the present and anticipate the future.

2. Compatibility with Other Explanations. The extent to which an explanation meshes with other explanations in related fields is another significant index to its validity. Of course, a new theory will not be compatible with the theory it replaces; otherwise, there would be no replacement; but it must be compatible with at least *some* other theories, or it is unacceptable.

3. Logical Properties. An explanation may not be deductively related, but it must not be internally inconsistent, or it cannot be accepted. A theory that contains incompatible elements may of course be highly suggestive and useful, but it cannot produce valid explanations.

4. Testability. An explanation must be capable of being tested in principle, at the very least, to be acceptable; ideally, of course, it should be testable in practice. An explanation that explains *everything*, that cannot under any circumstances be controverted, is valueless. There must be potentially exceptionable cases, even though they do not appear. We must, in other words, be able to state the conditions under which the explanation would *not* be valid. A classic illustration of the condition to be avoided at all costs is found in some formulations of Sigmund Freud's Oedipus complex. Presumably, the Oedipus complex appears in every male child; for example, the child is attracted to the mother and resents the father. But in some formulations the male child that is not attracted to the mother, or favors the father, has simply "sublimated" the Oedipal complex; the evidence is discounted, and the explanation then lies wholly beyond refutation.

5. Psychic Satisfaction. One test of the value of an explanation that ought not to be overlooked, though it needs to be treated with care, is the psychic satisfaction it affords to experts in the field. Whether the response is intellectual, sensual, or esthetic, we cannot say, but it remains a fact that persons with wide experience in a given field can often "spot" difficulties that they cannot stipulate in precise terms. Mathematicians, for example, complain about the "lack of elegance" of a formulation when they are displeased with a particular solution to a problem. Such subjective judgments, taken alone, may not be worth much; but when a number of authorities complain about a particular explanation, it ought at the very least to be subjected to close examination before it is accepted.

6. Predictions. Although prediction without explanation is common, most explanations imply some form of prediction; and some, though not all, explanations generate predictions that can be used to test the validity of the explanation. Prediction alone cannot provide an adequate basis for judgment, for predictions may be made by conceptual structures that have no explanatory power whatever. But if predictions can be made from an explanation, and they are taken in conjunction with other aspects of the explanation, they are useful indicators of reliability.

In sum, the evaluation of an explanation in political science is a complex affair with a large margin of uncertainty. In virtually every case a number of factors must be weighed, and the result can only be a judgment of reliability or usefulness; explanations are never true or false. Beyond that point, we need to ask whether the phenomena explained are significant, for it is pointless to expend time and energy explaining trivia. Significance, of course, depends on a frame of reference, and we have already noted that political science does not have a "general" frame of reference that can be used to make such evaluations. The problem has not been explored very thoroughly, and the suggestions offered here are only tentative, but it is at least possible that the traditions of the discipline provide our best criteria for the assessment of significance, however fallible they may be. In one sense, there is no other source to which political scientists might turn. The study of politics does not and cannot begin in a vacuum; we always cut into an ongoing enterprise, and the educational process is designed (when it is carried out properly) to familiarize the student with the kinds of assessment of significance that have been made in the past and are being made, and with the procedures for making them. There is almost always some measure of cumulated experience that can be applied to the case in hand, so long as it is not used dogmatically. It would be a serious error, of course, to assume that everything important had already been discovered or conceptualized; but it would be an equally serious mistake to assume that tradition is worthless and that each discipline, or even every inquirer, must begin with a *tabula rasa*. Both errors are common. Common sense suggests that we "begin with tradition and revise it by experience," and if that provides us with no neat and logically unassailable solution to the problem of significance, it is a working strategy that is worth serious consideration.

Although we are here concerned mainly with attempts at explanation, legitimate political inquiry can pursue other aims that are quite important and relevant. The models and mathematical structures examined in Chapter 5, for example, do not provide explanations, but they can *suggest* explanations. One of the principal reasons for including them in this survey is that such models may well prove one of the more significant intermediary steps between speculation and theory construction or explanation. Similarly, there are certain obvious cases in which political scientists, or government officials, need predictors, whether or not they are capable of explanation—a requirement that is also common in economics. Here the criterion of adequacy or validity is obviously the capacity of the structure to predict; value is measured by success in prediction. Finally, there are some conceptual frameworks that have not been used extensively in the explanation of political phenomena but hold promise of doing so in the future. Although it would be impossible to produce an exhaustive survey of such potential sources of explanation, certain obvious cases—"field theory" in psychology, for example—have been included in the three chapters that follow.

CHAPTER THREE

FUNCTIONALISM

 HE most striking shift in conceptual emphasis in social science to occur since the end of World War II has been the spread of the "functionalist" approach to explanation—identified variously as "functionalism," "structural functionalism," "systems analysis," or "general systems theory." Functionalism originated in sociology, implicitly in the work of Emile Durkheim and explicitly in the writings of A. R. Radcliffe-Brown and Bronislaw Malinowski. Early in the 1950's, a virtual flood of functionalist writings appeared in the social sciences, earliest in anthropology and sociology, but shortly afterward in psychology (group dynamics, for example) and then in political science. By the mid-1960's, functionalism was the dominant mode of inquiry or mode of explanation in political science, hailed by some very influential members of the discipline as "the best posible approach to the development of theory" in the field.*

---

*For early functionalism, see Bronislaw Malinowski, *The Dynamics of Cultural Change* (Yale University Press, 1945), and *A Scientific Theory of Culture* (Oxford University Press, 1945); A. R. Radcliffe-Brown, *Structure and Function in Primitive Society* (Free Press, 1956), and *A Natural Science of Society* (Free Press, 1957). Radcliffe-Brown's classic essay, "On the Concept of Function in Social Science," *American Anthropologist*, Vol. XXXVII (1935), should also be read. Don Martindale, *The Nature and Types of Sociological Theory* (Houghton Mifflin Co., 1960), Part IV, is useful. (Continued on page 112)

What is functionalism? Unfortunately, as almost everyone who writes about the subject points out, the term is highly ambiguous. Ernest Nagel identifies six basic meanings of the term "function," each with quite different implications for inquiry.[1] A brief review of the range of meanings attached to the term will suggest the nature of the functionalist's problem. (1) In mathematics, the concept of function (x is a function of y) is no more than a statement about the interdependence of two variables. In this sense, function is a part of every explanation and not a distinctive characteristic of one approach to social science. (2) "Function" can be used to denote a set of processes within a system without specifying the effects of those processes on the system—a list of

---

The postwar "flood" of functionalism begins with Robert K. Merton's *Social Theory and Social Structure* (Free Press, 1949; rev. and enlarged ed., 1957). Talcott Parsons, a fugitive from positivism and behaviorism, followed with *The Social System* (Free Press, 1951); *Toward a General Theory of Action* (Harvard University Press, 1951), with Edward Shils; and *Working Papers in the Theory of Action* (Free Press, 1953), with Robert F. Bales and Edward Shils. The impact of functionalism on Parson's thought is best seen in his collection of shorter works: *Essays in Sociological Theory* (rev. ed.; Free Press, 1954); and *Social Structure and Personality* (Free Press of Glencoe, Inc., 1964). Parsons himself credits Merton with much of the stimulation to explore functionalism. Two other highly influential pieces of functionalist writing are Marion J. Levy, Jr., *The Structure of Society* (Princeton University Press, 1952), an attempt to synthesize Parsons and Merton; and George C. Homans, *The Human Group* (Harcourt, Brace & Co., 1950).

In political science, David Easton's *Political System* (Alfred A. Knopf, Inc., 1953), is a landmark, though the functionalism is latent rather than manifest. Ten years later, in *A Framework for Political Analysis* (Prentice-Hall, Inc., 1965), and *A Systems Analysis of Political Life* (John Wiley & Sons, Inc., 1965), the commitment to functionalism is much clearer. Others soon followed. David Apter's *Gold Coast in Transition* (Princeton University Press, 1955); William C. Mitchell's *American Polity* (Free Press of Glencoe, Inc., 1962); Morton Kaplan's *System and Process in International Politics* (John Wiley & Sons, Inc., 1957) are typical. A good brief summary of the pros and cons of functionalism was produced by the American Academy of Political and Social Science in 1965—*Functionalism in the Social Sciences,* edited by Don Martindale. The list could be extended almost indefinitely.

[1] Ernest Nagel, *The Structure of Science: Problems in the Logic of Scientific Explanation* (Harcourt, Brace & World, Inc., 1961), chap. xiv, pp. 520-35.

the functions performed in a large business office would be an example of this usage. (3) The term is used to designate common use of an object—the "function" of an ax is to cut wood. (4) Function often refers to processes that go on within living organisms and are essential or vital for maintenance of life. (5) Function can designate the consequences of an element in a system for the system as a whole—the functions of the heart include transmission of food to body cells and of waste from the cells to the environment. (6) Finally, function may refer to the contribution of some element in a system to the maintenance of the system in a given state. The sixth of these uses of "function" is what is most commonly meant by functionalists in the social sciences when they use the term. We can add to Nagel's list the use of "functionalism" to designate a particular form of explanation or a particular mode of inquiry, which is common in political science; and it is also worth noting that "function" is sometimes used as a synonym for "effect"—a serious mistake.

There is no "correct" definition of "function," of course; the purpose of the list is to draw attention to the shades of meaning that can be attached to the term and thus facilitate criticism of the conceptual frameworks that the major functionalists have produced. It is dangerously easy, when technical terms have a number of everyday connotations, to slip from one shade of meaning to another in the course of argument, and a minor change in meaning can produce a major change in the validity of an argument.

The basic principle in functional explanation is the relation of a particular phenomenon, usually a recurrent pattern of social behavior, to the system in which the phenomenon occurs. The explanation consists of a set of propositions that stipulate the consequences of the phenomenon for the system. A functional explanation of the liver in the human body, for example, would stipulate the effects of the liver's activity on the circulatory system, the digestive system, etc. At an absolute minimum, functional explanations require (1) a phenomenon to be explained, (2) a system in which the phenomenon occurs, and (3) a stipulation of the consequences of the phenomenon for the total system. Functional explanations are always causal, and they are factorial in form. A complete functional explanation which included every consequence of a particular phenomenon for a given system would be deductive. Needless to say, social scientists have rarely, if ever, achieved that degree of completeness.

The same phenomenon can occur in an infinite number of different systems, since every system is defined analytically and not empirically. For that reason, careful stipulation of the system being examined is absolutely essential. An explanation of the function of the heart couched in terms of the circulatory system would be quite different from an explanation of the function of the heart which used the whole body as the basic system. Both may be important, of course, and the choice depends on the purpose of the investigator. Systems, in other words, are not given in nature.[2] Functionalists differ widely in their choice of phenomena, in the scope of the system they choose as a base, and in the rigor and precision with which they define the relations between phenomenon and system. Some depend heavily upon concepts of motivation and personality; others rely more upon sociological data and less upon psychology. Some functionalists are openly teleological; others try to avoid teleology. Finally, there are very important differences among functionalists about the role of theory in explanation and about the best way to generate theories—a point that appears very clearly when we compare the work of Robert K. Merton and Talcott Parsons.

Functionalism, in its earlier forms, was frankly derived from an organic analogy, and it made use of postulates or

[2]David Easton, *A Framework for Political Analysis*, Prentice-Hall, chap. ii, contains a good discussion of "natural" systems.

assumptions that are no longer considered essential. Organicism still colors the work of many sociological functionalists, though not to the degree that it appeared in the work of Radcliffe-Brown or Malinowski. A good illustration of the early conception of functionalism is found in Radcliffe-Brown's *Structure and Function in Primitive Society:*

The concept of function applied to human societies is based on an analogy between social life and organic life. . . . It is through and by the continuity of the functioning that the continuity of the structure is preserved.

"Function" is the contribution which a partial activity makes to the total activity of which it is a part. The function of a particular social usage is the contribution it makes to the total social life as the functioning of the total social system. Such a view implies that a social system (the total social structure of society together with the totality of social usages in which that structure appears and on which it depends for its continued existence) has a certain kind of unity. We may define it as a condition in which all parts of the social system work together with a sufficient degree of harmony or internal consistency, i.e., without producing persistent conflicts which can neither be resolved or regulated.[3]

Three points deserve close attention here: the postulate of "functional unity," the organicism, and the conception of an interlocking social structure in which every element has some positive function to perform and in which there is no redundancy. Organicism has been abandoned in most cases, and all of Radcliffe-Brown's postulates have been denied by Merton, who points out that the postulate of functional unity is untenable on empirical grounds, that the notion of "universal functionalism" is similarly disproved, and that not every item in a culture has a definite function. Merton's treatment of functionalism will be considered in detail below.

Some of the differences between Malinowski and Rad-

[3]A. R. Radcliffe-Brown, *Structure and Function in Primitive Society,* Free Press, pp. 178–79.

cliffe-Brown are instructive, both for the strategy of inquiry and for the evaluation of functionalism as an explanatory structure. Malinowski tended to define functions in terms of the fundamental requirements of all human beings. Men were conceived as creatures with certain basic needs, and Malinowski was interested in the way in which society was conditioned by the means chosen to satisfy these human needs. Usually, he used the social institution as a fundamental unit of analysis. Radcliffe-Brown, on the other hand, was more concerned with the "vital" functions in society, with the activities that had to be performed if society was to continue—in this, he resembles Talcott Parsons—and he devoted a great deal of time to the study of such factors as group solidarity. Thus, Malinowski explained the appearance of magic in society as a means of bridging the gap between human knowledge and the need for men to act in order to satisfy their essential needs. Radcliffe-Brown, on the other hand, explained the existence of ritual by referring to the need for group solidarity if society was to survive and asserting that ritual existed to fulfill this need—an openly teleological explanation. The difference in conceptual emphasis had important consequences for their respective work and, through them, for contemporary functionalism. Radcliffe-Brown, for example, taking orderly social life as a norm, was led to assert that the norm could be maintained only if certain common sentiments were shared by all members of society (consensus), and he was much concerned with the machinery and processes by which such sentiments were transmitted from one generation to the next. The same interest and emphasis, of course, is central to Talcott Parsons' thinking and appears with increasing frequency in contemporary political thought.

ROBERT K. MERTON

Broadly speaking, there are two basic modes of functional analysis in contemporary thought, distinguished primarily by differences in the goals that are set for inquiry and by the strategy used to achieve those goals. One variety of functionalism, best exemplified by Robert K. Merton, concentrates on specific phenomena and seeks limited explanations that are closely related to the facts of social life—what Merton has called "theories of the middle range." The other form of functionalism is concerned with the development of what is called "general theory," an all-encompassing set of categories that can be used to explain *any* set of phenomena. The classic illustration of the "generalist" form of functionalism appears in the work of Talcott Parsons. The distinction does not depend on the scale of the system used in explanation or analysis, for Merton often tries to deal with phenomena that affect whole societies—his treatment of anomie in the United States is a good case in point. Nor does the distinction depend on the contrast between empirical orientation and logical orientation, since Parsons, despite the apparent "formality" of his treatment of theory, is in fact not a logician and seldom makes use of formal deductive inference—the "derivations" found in Parsons' writings are not deductions. Parsons is a "system builder" of the old school, a child of the German philosophers, and what C. Wright Mills has called—pejoratively, of course—a "grand theorist." Merton, in contrast, is acutely conscious of the need to stay in touch with the facts: "[The] objective of consolidating sociological theory and research remains sterile until it is brought down to cases." Merton uses functionalism as an explanatory device, a means of "interpreting" data; Parsons is more concerned with the development of categories and relations that can be used to classify and order data. The distinction is much accentuated by differences in style. Merton is eminently readable and clear; Parsons is tortuous and murky. Merton is easily followed, whereas it is virtually impossible to follow Parsons for any length of time without backtracking constantly to recall the meaning of the ghastly neologisms that litter his writing.

Merton's conception of the meaning of functionalism is

engagingly simple and clear: "The central orientation of functionalism [is] expressed in the practice of interpreting data by establishing their consequences for larger structures in which they are implicated . . . ."[4] Like Radcliffe-Brown and Malinowski, Merton begins with an organic analogy and depends heavily upon biological principles in his construction of the functional method of inquiry. To the older notion of system maintenance as a functional consequence of events in society, Merton adds a number of concepts that are extremely useful, indeed essential. No other functionalist has done so much in the systematic exploration of the problems and possibilities of functional analysis. Even a partial listing of his more significant contributions to clarity and analytic sophistication is impressive.

In the first place, Merton distinguishes clearly between functional and dysfunctional elements in a system; and he recognizes the possibility that a given element may be neither, may be simply redundant. He defines "function" solely in terms of the observer and not in terms of the actor in the situation: "[S]ocial function refers to *observable objective consequences,* and not to *subjective dispositions* (aims, motives, purposes)."[5] He examines—and rejects—the postulates of functional unity in society, universal functionalism, and functional indispensability, chiefly on empirical grounds. That is, he does not assume that every item in a culture has a function and that only the item found in a culture could perform the particular function it allegedly performs. Instead, Merton proposes that social scientists assume that any given item in a culture may have diverse consequences, limited in some degree by the structural characteristics of society, and seek to trace those consequences. This produces the distinction between *manifest* functions (objective consequences contributing to the ad-

[4]Robert K. Merton, *Social Theory and Social Structure* (Free Press, 1949; rev. and enlarged ed., 1957), pp. 46–47 (revised edition cited throughout).

[5]*Ibid.,* p. 24 (italics in original).

justment or adaptation of the system that are recognized and intended by the participants in the system) and *latent* functions, which are neither recognized nor intended by the participants. The distinction, one of the more important made by Merton, avoids confusion of conscious motivation and objective consequences and adds a useful dimension to inquiry by forcing attention to the collateral effects of actions with particular intentions—effects that might easily be overlooked if a linear relation between intention and effect were assumed. From this critique comes a third proposition, the assumption that "persisting cultural forms have a *net balance of functional consequences* either for society as a unit or for subgroups sufficiently powerful to retain these forms intact, by means of direct coercion or indirect persuasion."[6] Finally, there is the principle of functional alternatives, the assumption that any given function may be fulfilled in a number of alternative ways. When Merton has finished, little remains of Malinowski's rather rigid conception of particular actions necessarily performing particular functions in society.

Merton's general approach to functional analysis is set forth in a paradigm which he supplies for the prospective social analyst. Nowhere are Merton's empirical orientation and concern for precise research more clearly evident. The paradigm depends heavily upon the earlier work of functional anthropologists and certain biologists like W. B. Cannon, but it is heavily imprinted with Merton's particular approach to functional analysis. The investigator is given a "checklist," as it were, for the study of society, a list that emphasizes the following points:

1. The item(s) to which functions are imputed. Merton urges the inquirer to begin with sheer description but to indicate, in addition, (a) the principal alternatives excluded from possibility by characteristic patterns for dealing with standardized problems in the particular society being

[6]*Ibid.*, p. 32.

studied; (*b*) the "meaning," in the Weberian sense, of the activity for the members of the society; (*c*) the motives of the actors; and (*d*) associated regularities in behavior. The basic strategy of inquiry is to seek standardized patterns or regularities—social roles, institutions, etc.— rather than concentrate on particular or singular events.

2. The motives of the participants. They must be distinguished carefully from attitudes and beliefs.

3. The objective consequences of the phenomena. Merton considers functional, dysfunctional, and nonfunctional consequences, both latent and manifest. He prefers analysis that establishes multiple consequences, thus allowing the inquirer to strike a "net balance of an aggregate of consequences."

4. Concepts of the unit subserved by the function. That is, Merton assumes that social systems are plural, not singular; hence the consequences of any action need to be considered with respect to each of the systems it may affect.

5. Functional requirements—the conditions that are essential for system maintenance or stability. Merton adds, rightly, that this is probably the most difficult part of functional analysis.

6. Mechanisms through which functions are fulfilled.

7. Functional alternatives or functional equivalents.

8. Structural context. Merton opposes those like Erich Fromm or Karl Marx who fail to see the close relationship between structure and function and who argue, in utopian fashion, that certain elements can be eliminated from a social system without altering its entire structure.

9. Dynamics and principles of change.

10. Problems of validation of inquiry. How can conclusions reached in a study be verified?

11. Ideological implications of analysis—the clarification of bias. Merton denies that functionalism *necessarily* implies a bias to conservatism, as is often argued; but he agrees that functionalism, like other modes of analysis, may lead inadvertently into ideological criticism. This particular rubric is intended to remind the inquirer that he ought to examine his own work, as best he can, for evidence of such ideological bias.[7]

---

[7]*Ibid.*, pp. 50–55. Paraphrased throughout.

Merton's paradigm is an oversimplification, of course, as he fully realizes, but it reveals some important facets of Merton's conception of functional analysis and explanation. The emphasis on fieldwork and concrete inquiry as against attempts to formulate "general" theories is striking. I am much impressed by the way in which conceptualization is tied consistently to observation. Illustrations abound, and examples are plentiful. The concrete studies are beautifully done—Merton's explanation of the function of the political "boss" in American politics is on its way to becoming a classic, as is his study of anomie in America. Theorems and hypotheses, where they appear, are clear and readily subject to empirical test—". . . any attempt to eliminate an existing social structure without providing alternative structures for fulfilling the functions previously fulfilled by the abolished organization is doomed to failure."[8] Disregarding Merton's positive contributions to sociology, his presentation of functionalism remains lucid, suggestive, and readily operationalized—no mean accomplishment in a period when social theories tend to be either trivial or so far removed from social data that they are virtually useless. Merton's functionalism is not above criticism, as we shall see below, but it remains far and away the best statement of the functionalist position in contemporary thought. Surprisingly, Merton has had few "followers," especially in political science, perhaps because what he has to offer is not a functional "theory" but a method of inquiry that is rigorous and demanding and promises nothing. The contrast to Talcott Parsons, to whom we now turn, could hardly be greater.

TALCOTT PARSONS

No reasonable man can begin an exposition of Talcott Parsons' work without warning the reader in advance that the going will be heavy and the outcome tendentious. Par-

[8]*Ibid.*, p. 81.

sons is a controversial figure in social thought, and even the sociologists who follow his work closely debate sharply the meaning and significance of different elements in his conceptual structure. It is virtually impossible to be certain of Parsons' meaning in a number of crucial areas: The writing is turgid (badly translated from the German, as someone put it); the structure is elaborate, interlocking, and very complex; the conceptual framework is not logically elaborated and hence is impossible to formalize; the system is not empirically based, though it purports to be related to the empirical world, and thus is not really open to testing and validation. Finally, Parsons himself confounds his critics and adherents by modifying and altering and amending the system continually; the Parsonian paradigm is an unfinished system, and any attempt to expound it systematically runs the risk of being dated before publication.*

In the treatment of Parsons that follows, I have concentrated on the conceptual framework that first appears in his writings early in the 1950's and on the modifications to that framework produced in the following decade. Criticism of the conceptual structure is integrated into the exposition, for it would place an unbearable burden on the reader to

---

*The Parsonian bibliography is simply enormous, and anyone unfamiliar with his work is readily lost in a sea of articles, books, addresses, and collections. I am concerned primarily with the two major conceptual schemes outlined by Parsons during the 1950's and not with the totality of his work, and for that limited purpose the following order of reading is recommended: *The Structure of Social Action* (McGraw-Hill Book Co., Inc., 1937), reprinted by the Free Press in 1949; "The Prospects of Sociological Theory," written in 1950 and reprinted in *Essays in Sociological Theory* (rev. ed.; Free Press, 1954); Parts I and II of *Toward a General Theory of Action* (Harvard University Press, 1951), with Edward Shils; *The Social System* (Glencoe, Ill.: Free Press, 1951); chaps. ii and iv of *Working Papers in the Theory of Action* (Free Press, 1953), with Robert F. Bales and Edward Shils; *Family, Socialization, and Interaction Process* (Free Press, 1955), with Robert F. Bales, James Olds, Morris Zelditch, and Philip E. Slater; *Economy and Society* (Free Press, 1956), with Neil J. Smelser, especially chaps. i and ii; Part III of *Structure and Process in Modern Societies* (Free Press, 1960); "Pattern Variables Revisited: A Response to Robert Dubin," *American Sociological Review*, Vol. XV, No. 4 (August, 1960); "The Point

withhold comment until the whole structure was outlined. Furthermore, Parsons' system is weakest at its roots, at the level of fundamental assumptions, and criticisms of these points need to be made as they emerge. Like its medieval counterpart, Thomist philosophy, the Parsonian system must be treated as an integrated whole, and there is always the danger of losing the argument in a welter of detail.

General Characteristics

It would take a largish book to treat exhaustively the various influences that Parsons combines in his work, but some general observations about the purposes and characteristics of his thought will provide a setting for the detailed consideration to follow. In the broadest terms possible, Parsons combines, or seeks to combine, the kind of 19th-century positivism found in Vilfredo Pareto, the historical sweep of Max Weber, and the philosophic idealism and subjectivism of the 19th- and 20th-century German historians and sociologists. The aim is nothing less than a model or "ideal type" of whole human societies, ultimately convertible into an axiomatic or deductive explanatory system: "[An] ideal theoretical system . . . should be a deductive propositional

---

of View of the Author," in Max Black (ed.), *The Social Theories of Talcott Parsons* (Prentice-Hall, Inc., 1961).

I do not find Parsons' political writings very useful, but an essay on general sociological theory can be found in Roland Young (ed.), *Approaches to the Study of Politics* (Northwestern University Press, 1958), and another on international affairs in James N. Rosenau (ed.), *International Politics and Foreign Policy* (Free Press of Glencoe, Inc., 1961). The famous, or infamous, "McCarthy article"–"Social Strains in America"–is included in *Structure and Process in Modern Societies;* and an article on voting can be found in Eugene Burdick and Arthur Brodbeck (eds.), *American Voting Behavior* (Free Press, 1959).

Parsons' writings on personality and psychology are ignored here for the most part, but they have been collected in a volume entitled *Social Structure and Personality* (Free Press of Glencoe, Inc., 1964). Parsons' influence among political scientists is based primarily on his sociological rather than his psychological writings.

Regretfully, William C. Mitchell's study of Talcott Parsons' social and political theories (Prentice-Hall, 1967), appeared too late to be used in the chapter.

system in which all propositions of empirical relevance should be strictly deductible from a small number of basic assumptions."[9] Parsons has apparently been wholly immune to the influence of modern analytic philosophy and philosophy of science. Even in mathematics, it has been shown that no finite body of axioms will suffice to generate every possible mathematical system and hence that mathematics cannot be derived from a single set of axioms—that is the meaning of Goedel's proof. Logically, axiomatization of the social sciences, which is implied in Parsons' statement of the theoretical ideal, is equally impossible. Parsons has fallen into what Karl R. Popper calls "historicism," for Popper has shown that no system can predict its own future while new information is being created within its bounds, and since a deductively related hierarchy of propositions is a predictor in Popper's sense, it is theoretically impossible to generate a predictor of that kind in a dynamic society.[10] Parsons' ideal is only applicable, empirically, in a static system.

The point is that Parsons' goal is, in principle, beyond attainment. He has been seduced, apparently, by an early positivist love affair with Newtonian mechanics, from which he draws most of his analogies and metaphors and illustrations. But Newtonian mechanics is no longer the ideal form of "scientific" explanation, and if Pareto is sometimes referred to as the "Newton of the moral world," that only indicates that Pareto is outmoded. Modern philosophy of science has destroyed the notion that Newtonian mechanics is an adequate conceptual framework for science. Parsons' intentions are misplaced or mistaken, and I believe it is very important that the point be clearly stated and emphasized. Misdirected thought can of course have valuable or significant consequences, and that is the case with Parsons. But it

[9]Talcott Parsons, "Recent Trends in Structural-Functional Analysis," in Earl W. Count and T. Bowles (eds.), *Fact and Theory in Social Science* (Syracuse University Press, 1964), p. 140.

[10]Karl R. Popper, *The Poverty of Historicism* (Harper & Bros., 1964), especially the Preface, pp. vi–viii.

is a serious error to suppose that his goal is methodologically acceptable and that the Parsonian system can be judged in terms of progress toward that goal. The reader who turns to Parsons for inspiration—and it is worth doing—must bring his own conceptual framework with him. He may well find that Parsons calls attention to relations or conditions that are extremely important within that framework.

Why did Parsons choose this particular mode of theorizing? That we cannot answer. But its implications for social philosophy are worth considering. Parsons, in effect, parallels the Hegelian solution to the problem of individual freedom. Determinism is rejected in favor of voluntarism, but voluntarism is stripped of its meaning by defining freedom as behavior that accords with the needs of the collective and not the desires of the individual—John Dewey comes close to the same position. Freedom is achieved by internalization of norms that are oriented to collective requirements. Furthermore, if the interactions among persons are taken as dialectic relationships, then the Hegelian synthesis corresponds to Parsons' notion of the "social act," and the underlying historical pattern that in G. W. F. Hegel's system gives meaning to systems of social actions, the progress of spirit through the world in the search of self-realization, defines the pattern of meanings that Parsons is seeking. From these patterns, in both Hegel and Parsons, the meaning of history can be inferred, and stipulated, ultimately in terms of the development of "reason." Parsons' definition of a "moral" issue fits precisely into this framework. He claims, for example, that "There is a moral issue only when the alternatives involve a presumption of relevance to the 'integrity' or the 'solidarity' of an interaction system, when the preservation of that integrity or solidarity is itself a value." Or, in another context, "the Confucian Chinese were above all concerned with morality, namely responsibility for the maintenance of a given social structure as a going concern."[11] The

---

[11]Talcott Parsons, *The Social System* (Free Press, 1951), pp. 97, 111.

point I am making, really, is that it is often useful to translate Parsoniana into idealism if we are trying to get at his intentions and purposes.

Yet Parsons is also deeply indebted to Hobbes. The Parsonian system is directed primarily and almost exclusively to the problem of order or stability. As Parsons himself points out: "It is quite true that the empirical-theoretical problem which was at the focus of my own theoretical 'take-off' was the problem of the bases of social *order*. It was . . . the problem posed long ago by Hobbes."[12] As Lewis Coser has noted, once Parsons focuses on the problem of order, and given his assumption that the prime instruments for maintaining order are the internalized normative structures generated by society, he is led to assume that social conflict —and by implication, social change—are always disruptive or dysfunctional.[13] The charges of "conservatism" often made against Parsons are in large measure due to the bias introduced into inquiry by the choice of focus. That is, Parsons does not ask what effect an observed phenomenon may have on society. Instead, he asks which elements of society contribute to the maintenance of social order and concentrates his analysis on them. The form in which the question is put introduces a clear bias case into the inquiry. Factors that do not influence order will be ignored, though they may, as Merton realized, have effects that are of great importance, particularly for the individual. Like Arthur Bentley's group theory, Parsons' system has the effect of dissolving the individual in sets of relationships with others. The effect of the collectivist bias is accentuated by the unfortunate choice of terms used to formulate the concep-

[12]Talcott Parsons, "The Point of View of the Author," in Max Black (ed.), *The Social Theories of Talcott Parsons* (Prentice-Hall, Inc., 1961), p. 336.

[13]Lewis Coser, *The Functions of Social Conflict* (Free Press, 1956), especially pp. 20–23. Coser gives a cogent account of some of the positive functions that social conflict may perform.

tual framework—they are pejoratively colored in common usage. However, the principal point that needs to be made is that once stability and order are accepted as desiderata, the results of inquiry are biased to a particular kind of evaluation, and the parallel to Parsons' mentor, Thomas Hobbes, is perhaps too obvious to mention.

It should also be noted that Parsons has been deeply involved in the study of economics and economic theory, particularly the work of the German historical school and the neoclassicists (for example, Alfred Marshall). Pareto and Weber, two of the chief influences on his thinking, were primarily economists. Parsons' illustrations often come from economic life, and he seems more at home (clearer, perhaps?) dealing with economic theory than with general social theory. More important, of course, are the conceptual parallels. The Parsonian "act" is very similar to an economic transaction; the Parsonian "actor" resembles more than anything else the demand system of an economic unit in a free market. Human interaction generally seems patterned on market interaction. And the problem of social stability is clearly analogous to the recurring problem of economic stability.

Antecedents and Influences

The phenomena men consider, the kinds of questions they ask, and the answers they are willing to accept tend to be determined by the conceptual apparatus they employ. At times, it is easier to identify the elements in the conceptual apparatus by returning to the sources than by unraveling the synthesis. This is the case with Parsons. A brief summation of the sources of his thought can therefore be very useful, not because it is traditionally offered in courses in political thought but because it is a positive aid to clarification of his ideas.

The basic conceptual structure is taken from Vilfredo

Pareto and, to a lesser extent, Max Weber. The uniqueness of Parsons' thought lies in the selection of concepts and the manner of their combination rather than in originality of conceptualization. That is not a criticism of Parsons, of course; no one originates all of his own conceptions, and few persons contribute so much as a single major conception to a discipline—otherwise, we might be well supplied. What matters is not the degree to which Parsons was or was not dependent on a particular source but the meaning of the concepts in their original framework and their meaning when transposed.

From Max Weber, and particularly from the *Theory of Social and Economic Organization,* which he edited, Parsons took, first of all, the concept of *verstehen* (the view that the "meaning" of any situation can be defined only in terms of the subjective perception of the individual actor) and the very important notion that social behavior consists fundamentally of the orientation of individuals and groups to one another (which became the foundation of the concept of social action). Coupled with Weber's voluntarism, or refutation of determinism, these two fundamentals provided Parsons with a definition of "meaningful social action": an interaction between two or more persons that includes the motivation or intention of all parties and not merely a reflexive action. Parsons held to these concepts with great consistency as he built his "ideal type"—another notion taken from Weber.

Much of the theoretical or relational structure comes from Pareto rather than Weber. The central notion of a "system," defined as a set of functionally interdependent elements, is clearly Paretian, as is the conception of society as an instrument for social adaptation. The goal of inquiry also comes from Pareto, the view that what is needed in social science is a general functional theory that will explain the stability of the social system. Pareto supplies the concept of "functional requisites," the necessary conditions for the continued functioning of society; and in Pareto's concept of "residues," the forces that underlie human conduct, internalized sentiments of valuations, Parsons found the conceptual instrument needed for an explanation of social stability. Various other influences could doubtless be traced to Pareto: the concern with irrational as against reasoned action, the distinction between individual and social utility, the use of analogies and illustrations from Newtonian mechanics, and so on. But the prime concepts taken from Pareto are the concern with order, the belief that order depends on a combination of social mechanisms and internalized sentiments (hence structural functionalism), and a consequent emphasis on the socialization process, located chiefly in the family. Here is the hard core of the Parsonian system.

Parsons often asserts that he has been much influenced by Freud, but that influence is hard to specify precisely, and in one sense the two seem wholly irreconcilable. Freud, after all, concerned himself mainly with the individual; Parsons has concentrated on social interaction and virtually ignored the psychic individual. Harry Stack Sullivan and Karen Horney are much closer to Parsons than is Freud, as we shall see in the next chapter. To the extent that Freud has been influential in the development of personality theory, and to the extent that Parsons makes use of personality theory in his social model, the Freudian influence is clear. But Parsons' interpretation of Freud's later works is strained, for it equates them roughly with the form of ego psychology developed by Anna Freud, Erik H. Erikson, and others after Freud's death.

Although Parsons does make use of a psychological base, particularly in the system outlined in *Toward a General Theory of Action,* that base is not orthodox Freudian by any means.[14] In his treatment of personality, for example, Parsons

[14]See "The Superego and the Theory of Social Systems" and "Social Structure and the Development of Personality," both in Talcott Parsons, *Social Structure and Personality* (Free Press, 1964).

relies on a fairly simple drive-reduction theory defined in functionalist terms:

Thus our conception of the actor's drives is that they are organized in an equilibrating system of relationships to an object world and that this system, if disturbed, will set in motion forces tending either to restore a previous state of equilibrum or to make stable a new state. This conception will underlie all our analysis of learning processes and of the operation of the personality as an on-going system.[15]

This conception of personality can hardly be reconciled with a Freudian system that postulates a quantity-energy theory of action in which energy moves linearly and equilibrates only in the sense that gratification is achieved when energy flows through pleasure-producing channels. Further, where Freud dealt almost exclusively with the factors that led to persistent disturbances in the gratification patterns of individuals, and hence to frustration and psychoses, Parsons is concerned with the factors that lead to adjustment or equilibrium; again, he is much closer to Sullivan or Horney than to Freud. Parsons does make use of Freudian terminology, particularly the adjustment mechanisms—repression, displacement, projection, reaction formation, etc.—but always in a context where order and stability are prime. Since stability, in Parsons' own term, requires "above all, the internalization of value-orientations to a degree that will sufficiently integrate the goals of the person with the goals of the collectivity," Parsons is forced to transpose the Freudian point of view in a way that seems to me to alter significantly Freud's original intentions. In Parsons' later writings the individualistic psychology of *The Social System* is dropped, and he is concerned mainly with the influence of the social structure on the behavior and the stability of the total system rather than with individual personality systems and their effects on the person's orientation to the situation.

[15]Talcott Parsons and Edward Shils (eds.), *Toward a General Theory of Action* (Harvard University Press, 1951), p. 113.

The First Formulation

To return to Parsons' primary goal, the formulation of a "general theory" of society, he produced two distinct, though related solutions to the problem in the decade after his conversion to functionalism. In the first formulation, Parsons began with the individual actor in a concrete situation interacting with the objects in that situation, and sought to elaborate his model out of these basic units. The result, set forth in 1951 in *Toward a General Theory of Action*, was not wholly satisfactory. By 1953, Parsons had taken another tack, apparently because of the influence of Robert F. Bales, then working closely with Parsons at Harvard. Beginning with *Working Papers in the Theory of Action*, and following in *Family, Socialization, and Interaction Process* and *Economy and Society*, all jointly written volumes, Parsons reversed his direction and began approaching society from the top down, as it were, defining the units of the system in terms of the structure of the whole society rather than the converse. The move from unit focus to system focus was accompanied by a gradual reduction of emphasis on psychological factors and increased emphasis on structural and functional requirements—again an illustration of Bales's influence.[16] Concern with values internalized by the individual was replaced by emphasis on institutionalized values—those built into the social structure rather than the person. In general, political scientists have relied chiefly on the second of Parsons' formulations rather than the first, on the "social" model rather than the "individual" model. But Parsons has not disavowed the earlier structure and claims to have absorbed it. In any case, it would be impossible to deal with the second model without considering the first. Much that is contained in the second is derivative, and its meaning

[16]For the direction of Bales's influence, see Robert F. Bales, *Interaction Process Analysis* (Addison-Wesley Publishing Co., Inc., 1950), especially chap. ii.

depends on the context established earlier.[17] Once Parsons is taken seriously, the student is committed to a formidable undertaking, for there is no way to deal with parts of the structure intelligibly without referring to the whole.

The conceptual framework that appears in *Toward a General Theory of Action* and *The Social System* begins with an individual *actor,* which may be an individual or a collective, though in fact Parsons seldom deals with collectives as actors in these early works. The actor has goals and interests and the capacity to perceive the environment and grasp its "meaning"—in the Weberian sense. In particular, the actor is able to think (cognize) and feel emotionally (cathect), a loose and commonsense conceptualization that Parsons relies upon very heavily in his first model. The term "action" is limited strictly to "meaningful" or goal-directed choices made by the individual. The actor must be pursuing some definitive goal in a deliberate manner, or there is no action. The meaning of an action, stated in terms of goals and interests, is referred to as the actor's *orientation* to the situation or, more precisely, to the objects that comprise the situation. This is, of course, far more restrictive than Merton's conception of phenomena, for it seems to rule out unintended consequences and even to leave the observer at the mercy of the verbal statements of the actor unless he can find a way of determining subjective intent by objective evidence.

The situation in which the actor functions consists of objects—the self or *ego,* other persons or *alters,* collectivities, and a variety of physical artifacts. Parsons divides social objects into two major classes: social objects or alters, and nonsocial objects. Of the two, social objects are considered

[17]Robert Dubin makes the distinction in "Parsons' Actor: Continuities in Social Theory," *American Sociological Review,* Vol. XXV, No. 4 (August, 1960). Dubin sharpens the contrast between the two "models" more than is done here, and I disagree fundamentally with his statement that the earlier model offers a more promising base for social analysis than the later one.

far and away the more significant for analysis. The Parsonian actor reacts to the elements in a situation in a variety of ways, performing cognitive discriminations, responding to them emotionally, and evaluating them in terms of their usefulness to the attainment of his objectives or their significance for the maintenance of the collectivity. In the process, actors develop integrated patterns of orientation and motivation to given situations, and that is what Parsons means by the acquisition of *personality*. Pluralities of actors interacting with one another develop common or "integrated" procedures for handling interactions, and that is the meaning of the *social* system. In their interactions, actors make use of systems of symbols, sets of ideas, and patterns of value orientations; and these elements, taken together, comprise the *cultural* system. Personality system, social system, and cultural system are not empirically distinct in Parsons; they are analytic categories made up of the same set of actions but viewed from different perspectives.

Parsons' central focus, then, is the social act or, more exactly, the social interaction. The actor must consciously perceive the objects in his environment and make certain decisions about them and their relationship to him; hence Parsons' insistence upon freedom of choice for the individual. The decisions may, however, be made unconsciously—a qualification that seriously reduces the possibility of defining the relationship accurately, since it greatly increases the complexity of the interaction and in a sense makes it impossible for the observer to infer the relationship from observables; the actor himself may be unaware of the decision. In particular, the actor must select what Parsons calls the "modality" of the objects in the situation, the aspects of the objects to which he will respond. These modalities are then evaluated in terms of the actor's individual interests and motivations. The paradigm raises an interesting question for psychologists, since it is well established that *what* men perceive is learned; hence the motivation of the actor at the time of perception may be less important than the prior learning of the individual unless motivation is defined so broadly as to mean almost anything. How useful Parsons' criterion of meaningful action can be in inquiry, that is, what kinds of behavior it eliminates from consideration in social analysis, is very hard to say, but the criterion is formulated in such general terms that it is unlikely to be helpful. If meaningful action includes actions that are made meaningful by unconscious decision, then the definition of the whole class cannot be made in terms that are empirically relevant.

Given the social action or interaction as a base, Parsons' problem is to find a way of classifying the various aspects of the interaction in a systematic way. That is the function of the famous Parsonian *pattern variables*. They are the central conceptual element in the scheme, and their place in analysis is crucial for Parsons' system. In his own terms:

[The] pattern variables enter the action frame of reference at four different levels. In the first place, they enter at the concrete level as five discrete choices (explicit or implicit) which every actor makes before he can act. In the second place, they enter on the personality level as habits of choice; the person has a set of habits of choosing, ordinarily or relative to certain types of situations, one horn or another from each of these dilemmas. Since this set of habits is usually a bit of internalized culture, we will list it as a component of the actor's value-orientation standards. In the third place, the pattern variables enter on the collectivity level as aspects of role definition; the definition of rights and duties of the members of a collectivity which specify the actions of incumbents of roles, and which often specify that the performer shall exhibit a habit of choosing one side or the other of each of these dilemmas. In the fourth place, the variables enter on the cultural level as aspects of value standards; this is because most value standards are rules or recipes for concrete action and thus specify, among other things, that the actor abiding by the standard shall exhibit a habit of choosing one horn or another of each of the dilemmas.[18]

[18]Parsons and Shils, p. 78.

In the earlier and more psychological model of social action, Parsons enumerates five pattern variables, but that number is changed in later works. The five sets of choices define the actor's range of choice; they may be chosen consciously or unconsciously, implicitly or explicitly. Each pattern variable, according to Parsons, states a genuine dilemma that the individual may face in any situation he encounters. The choice is always "all or nothing," and the list is said to be exhaustive. Of course, not all of the pattern variables are relevant to every decision made by the actor, but Parsons does claim that every decision can be defined fully in terms of *some* combination of the five pattern variables. We shall look first at the content of the pattern variables and then examine the claims that are made for them.

1. Affectivity/Affective Neutrality. Given an actor in a situation, he must choose between immediate gratification of his impulses and self-restraint; he may act immediately and without regard to consequences, or he may stop and calculate the consequences before action. The gratification arm of the dilemma is given the peculiar and misleading name *affectivity;* when the actor chooses to restrain himself, the term *affective neutrality* is used. Thus the actor that seeks immediate gratification is said to choose affectively; when he delays, he acts with affective neutrality. This pattern variable is used to classify the normative patterns in a culture, the need dispositions of the individual, and the role expectations found in social systems. It is hard to operationalize completely, for it is not easy to see how an actor could *choose* to act affectively and still have the choice considered affective, though we may readily imagine the behavior of young children being described in these terms.

2. Self-Orientation/Collectivity Orientation. The second pattern variable, dropped in later versions of the Parsonian scheme, refers to the making of choices in terms of the self or in terms of the needs of the collectivity, between "private permissiveness" and "collective obligation."

Pattern variables (1) and (2) refer to the values that guide the individual in his choice of an action or an attitude. The last three variables deal with the relationship between the actor and the objects that comprise the situation. They are used to structure the definition of the situation to which the actor responds.

3. Universalism/Particularism. Given the objects in a situation, the actor may treat them "in accordance with general norms covering *all* objects in that class," which is designated universalism; or he may deal with them according to their standing "in some particular relationship to him or his collectivity," which is called particularism. One may treat a particular woman, for example, as a married woman (universalism) or as the wife of a friend (particularism).

4. Ascription/Achievement. This variable, also identified as a choice between *quality* and *performance*, is a classification of the qualities or properties of the objects in a situation to which the actor chooses to respond. The terms are based on Ralph Linton's distinction between ascribed status (acquired with no effort, like a family name) and achieved status (acquired through personal activity, like the right to make use of the initials M.D. after the name).

5. Diffuseness/Specificity. The last of the pattern variables is used to describe the "range" of the aspects of an object to which the actor chooses to respond—"how broadly he will allow himself to be involved with the object." Parsons also speaks of the dichotomy in terms of conceding to an object either a strictly defined set of rights or an undefined set of rights. As an empirical criterion, he uses the distinction between placing the burden of proof of the existence of a right on those who claim none exists (diffuse) and on those who claim there is responsibility (specific). I confess that I am unclear about the empirical criterion, but Parsons seems to be distinguishing between a relation that involves a very limited claim by one person on the other and a relation that involves wide and unspecified claims on both sides—marriage, for example.

Parsons makes three major claims for his pattern-variable scheme: first, that the pattern variables are "true polarities" and not elements on a continuum; second, that they are exhaustive, defining all of the possible choices that an actor can make; third, that they are "required" by the rest of the conceptual framework. As Max Black has shown quite clearly, none of these claims is substantiated by Parsons himself, and there are good reasons to suppose that they can in fact be refuted.[19]

The specificity/diffuseness pattern variable, first of all, is certainly *not* a true polarity but can be specified on a continuum. In fact, Parsons himself notes that even though the significance of objects can be defined in diffuse terms, the range of diffuseness cannot be unlimited. Similarly, the quality/performance variable seems unlikely to be an all-or-nothing choice, particularly when the object is a complex of properties like another person or a collectivity. Even for specific purposes, the actor is unlikely to treat another person *entirely* in terms of ascribed or achieved qualities. On the other hand, if the actor's choice is to be described by some neutral observer, it might be possible to strike a balance between the importance of achieved and ascribed qualities in a given actor's evaluation of an object, but that would effectively preclude the use of the pattern variables by the *actor*.

Perhaps it is worth interjecting here a brief note about the fuzziness of Parsons' conception of the kinds of activities that an actor actually performs. It is hard to imagine a human actor "deciding," "choosing," "evaluating," and so on within Parsons' context. In some cases the actor is choosing self-consciously; at other times, decisions are apparently

[19]Max Black, "Some Questions about Parsons' Theories," in Black, *op. cit.*, pp. 283–88.

made unconsciously. Sometimes the action appears as a freely determined choice; in other cases, it is hard to believe that the actor's "choice" is much more than a conditioned reflex or habit—certainly the observer would have no adequate criteria for deciding in any particular case. These problems arise very quickly when we try to give examples of Parsons' points. He himself uses very few examples, and I am left with the suspicion that he finds it just as hard as I do to provide them. The relation between his concepts and the empirical data to which they presumably refer is extremely tenuous.

Parsons' claim that the pattern variables are "exhaustive" is impossible to decide; the meaning of the claim is too ambiguous. If, for example, Parsons means that the list is *logically* exhaustive, then the claim is beyond verification because the system itself is not a set of logically (deductively) related categories; hence, it is impossible to say what is logically necessary or exhaustive. If, on the other hand, the list is supposed to be *empirically* exhaustive, then Parsons is simply wrong. There are any number of ways in which an actor can evaluate the objects in a situation and no logical grounds for choosing one in preference to others. It is possible, of course, that Parsons means no more than that these are the most significant criteria of evaluation for the actor, but that is not what is claimed. In no place have I been able to find the criteria used to select the pattern variables or an argument supporting the claims made for them. The same criticism applies to the claim that the pattern variables are necessitated by the structure of action theory. They cannot be logically necessary, and Parsons provides no rules for "deriving" them from the rest of the system. Furthermore, the pattern variables are not governed by a single organizing principle that would relate them to each other and to the rest of the structure; therefore, that escape from the conceptual dilemma is also closed.

In brief, it seems that, barring further evidence, Parsons

has produced a set of alleged dichotomies, doubtless after considerable thought, that he considers of prime importance in social analysis. Nowhere has he provided a rationale for them or related them specifically to the rest of the analytic scheme. They remain an independent set of criteria, introduced into the conceptual framework according to a set of unstipulated assumptions. To make matters worse, the ambiguity of the terms and the complexity of the language effectively prevent the reader from deriving Parsons' assumptions from a consideration of the use that Parsons makes of the pattern variables in his own analyses.

We can now try to bring together the various elements in Parsons' system and reproduce the first of Parsons' basic models of the social structure, bearing in mind that the social act is no more than a unit of analysis and that the organization of these acts into the social, cultural, and personality systems still remains to be considered. It may help the reader to follow the development of the scheme if he bears in mind the fact that the end result is a gigantic classification system. The model is static and not dynamic, and Parsons has been able to reduce the essential features of the model to a two-dimensional diagram. The problem, in brief, is to classify all of the possible relations between actor and situation.

Given an actor in a situation made up of social and non-social objects, the actor must select the qualities of the objects to which he will respond. Two of the pattern variables serve to classify that choice: (1) the ascription/achievement variable and (2) the specificity/diffuseness variable. The actor, in other words, will respond to either the ascribed or the achieved properties of each object in the situation, and he may treat the objects in either categorical or specific terms. These possibilities may be combined in a matrix of eight cells representing the actor's classification of objects in the situation.

The objects must then be evaluated, and the evaluation

can be represented by another matrix, this time employing all five of the pattern variables. The matrix will therefore consist of 32 cells and will presumably represent an exhaustive classification system for dealing with evaluations.

We now add a third dimension to the analysis, what Parsons calls the actor's *orientation* to the objects of the situation, which may be cognitive, expressive, evaluative, or instrumental. The orientation indicates the aspects of the situation that concern the actor. Orientation may be motivational or evaluative, and by combining them, the actor may produce four basic types of actions:

1. Intellectual activity, in which cognitive interests are dominant and cognitive standards control the action—as in the search for knowledge.
2. Expressive action, in which cathectic or emotional interests are prime and appreciative (esthetic) standards control the action—as in the search for direct gratification (Parsons' example).
3. Responsible or moral action, in which evaluative interests are primary and moral standards control the action—this has a strict meaning in Parsons' system: the integration of individual actions in the interest of the larger system of action—which is Parsons' definition of a moral action.
4. Instrumental action, in which the goal of action is in the future. Cathectic interests and appreciative standards are used to define the goal, but cognitive standards control the means by which the goal is attained. Roughly, this corresponds to what the economist would call "rational" action.[20]

Finally, actions can be classified according to the kinds of objects found in a situation. Since objects can have meaning only to ego or alter or a collectivity, there are three classes of object types, and the four types of actions can be cross-classified on that basis.

That completes the classification scheme that Parsons proposes for defining the relationship between an individual actor and his situation. It is intended to cover *every*

[20]Partly paraphrased from Parsons and Shils, *Toward a General Theory of Action*, p. 75.

eventuality. And well it should. Given a single actor, there are more than 3,000 possible permutations to a single act. Double the number of actors, and the number of permutations jumps into the millions. And that is for *one* interaction. Even when the structure is drastically simplified by eliminating otiose cells in the classification matrix, the number of elements in a classification remains in the thousands. It would be impossible to handle a structure of such complexity even in simple empirical situations. Worse, the scheme still remains defined in very broad terms; the categories are loose. To achieve the kind of precision we manage in everyday speech, the theory or model would have to be still further articulated, with a consequent increase, exponential in form, in the number of cells. Here, I believe, we have a clue to the reason why Parsons abandoned the attempt to build a model from below, beginning with the individual actor and the single act. The result is an astronomical number of boxes, and our capacity to handle them breaks down very quickly.

And there is more to come, for we have thus far done no more than classify a single social act, which is the fundamental analytic unit in the first Parsonian model. Individual acts must still be organized into larger systems. Parsons distinguishes three fundamental systems, each comprised of the same set of social acts but viewed in different perspectives. First, there is the "personality" system of the individual, defined in terms of habitual or persistent patterns of reaction to different types of situations. Second, there is the "social" system; and third, there is a "culture" system. The same actor, or the same set of acts, can be organized in three distinct systems, and a complete model of society would include all three. Parsons and Edward Shils sketch the outlines of the complete structure in *Toward a General Theory of Action*, and Parsons elaborates the social system in a volume bearing that title. The remainder of the structure has not been detailed, and the later writings pursue a slightly different goal. For the most part, Parsons' work after 1953 was directed to the major subsystems of the social system and their interactions: family and kinship in *Family, Socialization, and Interaction Process,* and the economic system in *Economy and Society.* There is no volume on the political system, and both the "personality" system and the "cultural" system remain undeveloped. We can therefore concentrate on the social system, following Parsons' own work, with the understanding that we are concerned with only one part of the total structure.

In the first formulation the social system is made up of a plurality of actors, each motivated to optimization of gratification and all controlled by a common value system. A *society* is defined as a social system that is "empirically self-subsistent" and capable of persisting over time. The central problem is order: How do social systems and societies manage to persist? Order is held to depend on the integration of the motivations of the individual actors with the cultural norms of the social system. That is possible only if the cultural values are internalized by the individual actor. The two functional prerequisites of a social system are derived from this framework: (1) The social structure cannot be radically incompatible with the satisfaction of the requirements of its individual members; and (2) the other systems in society must provide "support" for the social system.[21]

The collectivist bias in Parsons' conceptual scheme is here very apparent, for collective requirements, rather than individual satisfaction, are the ultimate criteria of social adequacy. In fact, he notes that so far as the functioning of the social system is concerned, only a sufficient part of the needs of individuals must be met to provide adequate

[21]For an interesting parallel, see Harry Eckstein, *Division and Cohesion in Democracy: A Study of Norway* (Princeton University Press, 1966), "A Theory of Stable Democracy," Appendix A.

motivation for the performance of the vital system-mainte-
nance functions: "[The] significance of an action or class
of them is to be understood not directly and primarily in
terms of its motivation but of its actual and probable consequences for the system."[22] Parsons may not be indifferent to
individual needs, but his conceptual scheme is so constructed
that it is impossible for him to consider the consequences
of social action for the single individual, or even for all individuals.

Three other characteristic properties of the social system are used as defining terms: (1) The system has a capacity for boundary maintenance, meaning that it is able to
maintain closer relations among the elements within its
boundaries than the relations between elements of the system and units external to the system; (2) the role differentiation within a social system is usually extensive; and (3)
there is a tendency for a social system to return to equilibrium when it is disturbed. This homeostatic principle is,
of course, merely a postulate and not an empirical generalization. The central problems of the social system are
identified as the maintenance of order, the integration of
its members into the cultural value system, and the preservation of the equilibrium of the system. The central theme
of the analysis is that order depends fundamentally on consensus, on institutionalized value standards that entail a
sense of responsibility on the part of individual members
of society for fulfilling their obligations as individuals and
for assisting in the achievement of community goals—they
have what Parsons calls a sense of solidarity.

Having repeated in *The Social System*, with suitable elaborations, what appears more generally in *Toward a General
Theory of Action*, Parsons is left with the problem of specifying the principles on which social systems are organized
(structure) and the rules that control the interactions of
the various subsystems in the social system. Here, it must

[22]Parsons, *The Social System*, p. 29.

be said, *The Social System* is extremely disappointing, and
the difficulties met at this stage in the development of the
model may account for the radical change in approach that
followed within two years of its appearance. Parsons begins
with a fairly simple classification of structural differentiation within social systems—relational institutions, regulative
institutions, cultural institutions, relations-regulative institutions, etc.—which he claims will provide "an adequate description of a concrete social system."[23] What follows, however, is a prolonged and sometimes interesting analysis
of the structure of individual motivation, interspersed with a
case study of the American medical profession. The discussion is directed at the problems of structural classification.
The result, however, is a static classification system that
might be useful for ordering data but could not provide
explanations. If Parsons' model is to explain the principles
of interaction, the dynamic properties of the system must
be added.

Parsons attacks the problem of social dynamics in the
penultimate chapter of *The Social System,* but the results
are far from satisfactory. He assumes, first of all, that stabilized social systems have an innate capacity for maintaining equilibrium—the so-called "law of inertia." Even if that
assumption is granted, Parsons' treatment of dynamics begs
the question. First he asserts, without argument, that structural-functional analysis is able to provide explanations even
if our knowledge of the processes occurring within a social
system is not adequate. That position is qualified, however,
when Parsons denies that the result of his analysis is social
theory, since "a general theory of the processes of change
of social systems is not possible in the present state of
knowledge."[24] In the general discussion that follows, Parsons
makes these points:

[23]Parsons, *The Social System,* pp. 138–39.
[24]*Ibid.,* p. 486.

1. Social change always requires enough impetus to overcome the resistance of vested interests.
2. There are many sources of social change and not merely one—offered, rather pompously, as "the conception of the plurality of the possible origins of change."
3. Change has a variety of repercussions within the social system, some of which may be contrary to the direction of change.
4. Change will tend to move in the direction that will increase rather than decrease the gratification of members of the society.
5. Change tends in the direction of rationality rather than the converse.

The discussion concludes with a denial of the charge of "static" bias in structural-functional analysis and an expression of hope that the reader will see that " . . . there is a certain falsity in the dilemma between 'static' and 'dynamic' emphases. If theory is *good theory*, whichever type of problem it tackles most directly, there is no good reason whatever to believe that it will not be *equally* applicable to the problems of change and those of process within a stabilized system." That final proposition manages to combine *petitio principi* and *argumentum ad ignoratio* in a single sentence.

The fact is that the first Parsonian model *is* purely static and descriptive and it does not—and in fact, cannot—provide explanations. Explanations require statements about relations—the point cannot be repeated too often. Unless a conceptual scheme includes propositions that link sets of concepts to specified conditions in a way that creates expectations about the outcome of interactions over time, explanations cannot be made. Parsons has created a vast taxonomy, but there are few general propositions in his work. And the taxonomy itself is so complex and difficult that it could not possibly be operationalized without long and careful study to eliminate ambiguities and fill lacunae. That time might be better spent looking for adequate explanations of concrete phenomena. As Parsons himself points out, methodical development of the full logical implications of the basic structure would be an almost impossible task, even with the aid of computers. Parsons is riding the tiger implicit in any elaborate system of cross-classifications; a small increase in the number of categories creates an enormous increase in the total number of cells in the matrix produced by the classification principles.

Parsons does at one point suggest that the scope of the structure could be reduced by collating it with established empirical data; but that, too, would be difficult in practice, if only because Parsons is not completely consistent in his method. Parts of the system are formal elaborations of nominal definitions. Other parts are clearly derivatives from established social data—generalized commonsense propositions about human society. Anyone undertaking the task of reconstructing the system and integrating it enough to collate it with empirical data might well conclude that demolition and new construction are a simpler task than renovation. Understandably, the first model has not been widely used, though some few attempts have been made to apply parts of the conceptual scheme to specific social situations.

The Second Formulation

The second formulation of Parsons' system began to appear in his writings a very short time after *The Social System* was published. It incorporates some parts of the earlier structure with only slight modifications (the pattern variables, the concept of social action, and so on); but in fact, Parsons abandons the attempt to build a conceptual system from the ground up by beginning with the elementary social act and starts now from the opposite end of the scale, from the composite whole. The second formulation has attracted considerable interest among political scientists; and parts of it—some concepts, at least—are widely used. Parsons does not explicitly disavow the earlier model or even note that he is changing his perspective. But the connecting links between the two structures are tenuous, and they may not be reconcilable.

Beginning with large-scale social systems, approximately our modern nation-states, Parsons divides them into subsystems that are themselves complex and treats of the relationships among the subsystems, and between subsystems and the overall system. The actor-situation nexus employed in *The Social System* virtually disappears, the emphasis on individual motivation and orientation is sharply reduced, and the role of the pattern variable changes radically. Parsons is now concerned principally with the functional requisites of large-scale social systems, with the interactions between systems and their environment, and with the "exchanges" that occur across the boundaries of systems.[25]

The effect of the change in focus on the conceptual structure is very great, of course; but without going into fine detail, we can sketch the central features of the new scheme and perhaps make an estimate of their usefulness. A few general comments about the new formulation may be useful. First, it is much more manageable. There are fewer parts; the concepts seem clearer and more readily linked to empirical data. Second, the new system offers some hope of circumventing the static bias built into the first model. Third, Parsons seems to have achieved a clearer understanding of his own objectives and of the best means of achieving them: The treatment of social change in *Economy and Society,* for example, could not possibly have appeared in the conceptual framework used in *The Social System.* The framework remains very broad and analytic, of course; but the reduction of detail has sharpened the focus, and the focus itself seems closer to the actual data of society than before—certainly Parsons is easier to fol-

[25]The new construction makes a first appearance in chapters iii and v of Talcott Parsons *et al., Working Papers in the Theory of Action* (Free Press, 1953), and is expanded in Talcott Parsons *et al., Family, Socialization, and Interaction Process* (Free Press, 1955), and in Talcott Parsons and Neil J. Smelser, *Economy and Society* (Free Press, 1956).

low in this second phase and, to my mind at least, is far more suggestive.

The central conceptual focus in the second formulation is a set of four functional imperatives, derived from the work of Robert F. Bales but explicated in terms of Parsons' earlier work. An interaction is now defined primarily in terms of roles, and society is conceived as a network of subsystems that includes all of the roles occurring within the overall system. Social interaction has become the behavior of members of a structured system, and the system is the prime determinant of individual behavior. There is, in brief, much more functionalism and far less social action than before. Instead of the complex multielement classification scheme employed in *The Social System,* Parsons now asserts that social systems can be described *and their processes analyzed* in terms of the four functional imperatives. Furthermore, the aim of analysis is no longer classification, but "to assess the effects of changes in the data of the system, the situation, and the properties of its units, on changes in the state of the system and the states of its component units . . . ."[26] Clearly, there has been a major change in Parson's conceptual outlook.

The four functional imperatives are identified as (1) pattern maintenance and tension management, (2) adaptation, (3) integration, and (4) goal achievement or goal gratification. Each of the imperatives is related to the functioning of one of the major subsystems of society. That is, Parsons assumes that each functional imperative produces a subsystem within society that will fulfill that particular need. The instrument used for relating the functional imperatives to changes within the total system is the pattern variables, modified by the elimination of the self/collectivity orientation. The very important concept of "boundary interchanges," or "inputs" and "outputs" from one system to an-

[26]Parsons and Smelser, p. 18.

other, is introduced. We shall first examine the four functional imperatives in some detail, then consider the subsystems associated with them, and finally consider the relation between the functional imperatives and the pattern
variables.

The Functional Imperatives.   Stability and order in society are a consequence of the value system; that basic
Parsonian assumption remains intact. The first functional
imperative for any social system, then, is to maintain the
integrity of its value system. Whereas the earlier model
relied upon individual socialization for that purpose, the
new formulation stresses the need to maintain the social
institutions in which the value system is embedded. Pressures for changes in those institutions originate in two
sources: cultural pressures which come from outside the
system and motivational tensions operating on individual
members of society. Control of the external pressures is
called *pattern maintenance;* control of individual motivations is called *tension management.* The first imperative is
therefore identified as pattern maintenance and tension management. In Parsonian diagrams, it is labeled the L matrix
or quadrant.

Since every social system functions in an environment,
there will be interchanges between the system and the environment. The environment may serve as a source of gratification, as a source of goals. Parsons limits the goals that
systems may pursue relative to the environment by defining "goal" in a rather special way: "[Goals are] relations
between the system of reference and one or more situational
objects, which . . . maximizes the stability of the system."
Goal gratification, the second functional imperative, which
is labeled G in the diagram, is the pursuit of objects that
contribute to the stability of the social system.

Given goals relative to the environment, achievement of
those goals is possible only if the environment can be controlled in some degree—the system must be *adapted* to the

environment, to use Parsons' term, and the environment adapted to the system. The third functional imperative deals with control over the environment and is called *adaptation*. It is labeled *A*.

Finally, since the elements that make up a social system must also be controlled if the system is to achieve its goals, in the sense that support for goal-striving activity must be obtained and obstruction of goal achievement reduced, the fourth imperative is maintenance of such control, termed *system integration* and labeled *I*, but sometimes referred to as the achievement of "solidarity" in a sense reminiscent of Rousseau.

As in *The Social System*, the primacy of the collective over the individual is clear, and the problem of order remains central. The "conservative" bias, if such it is, remains as before. The crucial point is the special definition of "goals" as things that contribute to the stability of the collective and the corollary definition of subsystem goals as outputs that contribute to the functioning of the larger system.[27]

One major postulate introduced into the second formulation of Parsons' model is a tendency for society to differentiate into major subsystems, each concerned primarily with one of the four functional requisites. The assumption is hard to evaluate. If it means no more than the assertion that certain subsystems are found in every large society, it may be acceptable; if, however, it is meant in causal terms, it would have to be supported by far more evidence than is now available, and it might be desirable to drop the teleological form of the assertion and substitute a causal statement. Of course, the analytic distinction can be made without assuming that society has actually produced an empirical structure corresponding in some way to the social subsystems, but that does not seem to be what Parsons intends. As the system presently stands, goal gratification (G) is

[27]See *Economy and Society,* pp. 21 *et seq.*

taken as the prime concern of the "polity," defined as logically distinct from either government or the state; adaptation (A) is identified with the economy as a whole. Neither the I nor the L subsystem is identified, though the family is placed in the I subsystem and its primary function is defined as "the organization of human motivation," which may sound a little strange to those who romanticize the family but is actually no more than a consequence of the special definition of "goals" that Parsons employs. Similarly, the output of the polity is "control of the situation," and "capacity to command support."

Interaction among subsystems and systems, and social change in general, play a far larger role in the new conceptual framework. In *Economy and Society,* for example, Parsons develops a model of institutional change based on Berle and Means's study of the separation of ownership and management in American corporations. The model is broad and general, but it is operationalizable; and as Parsons notes, it parallels the models of internalization of values in the socialization process outlined in *Family, Socialization, and Interaction Process.* The model is dynamic and not static; that is, it is concerned with change over time and not with classification—a considerable improvement over *The Social System.* The process is defined in terms of seven steps or successive states that take place within the corporation:

1. A combination of "dissatisfaction" (cognitive dissonance?) with the productive achievements of society and a sense of "opportunity" for higher achievement provides the initial impetus to change. This is very close to Schumpeter's treatment of innovation in *Capitalism, Socialism, and Democracy,* perhaps not accidentally.
2. "Symptoms of disturbance" appear within the population. They take the form of negative emotional reactions, or aspirations, and they are considered unrealistic or unwarranted by some parts of the population at the first moment of appearance.
3. There is a "reaction" within the system to these signs of

tension. Covert attempts are made to placate dissidents and recruit support for established value patterns.

4. Support for the dissenters appears among the influential elements of the community.
5. The aspirations of the dissenters are "operationalized," that is, converted into meaningful social goals.
6. "Responsible" persons support the innovations, and they are tried out.
7. Gains made from the innovations are institutionalized.

Granted the treatment of social change is very broad and sweeping, and it would be useful to know whether Parsons intends these propositions as either necessary or sufficient conditions for innovation and change; nevertheless, the model is clear, and it could readily be applied to, say, the development of the civil rights movement in the United States, revolutionary uprisings, or independence movements. It is not surprising, then, that this phase of Parsons' work has proved attractive to political scientists, particularly those concerned with the development of new nations in Africa, Asia, and South America. The lesson, perhaps, is that conceptual frameworks couched in operational terms are much more likely to be influential than exalted and esoteric doctrines that no one can make his own and apply.

There remains the problem in integrating the pattern variables and the functional imperatives—a task undertaken by Parsons in the essay entitled "Pattern Variables Revisited." The self/collectivity variable is set aside, and Parsons confesses that he is uncertain whether there ought to be four or six variables; the integration is based upon four.

Basically, Parsons uses the pattern variables to distinguish between the actor's *orientation* to objects (defined in terms of specificity/diffuseness, and affectivity/affective neutrality) and the *modality* of objects (defined in terms of quality/performance and universalism/particularism). But social action is now conceived to occur within a system that is structured or organized, and the change in emphasis focuses attention on the relations between actions in the organized system and the relations between systems and their environments. That linkage is provided in the following way:

1. Pattern maintenance, the continuation of the value system, depends on the *orientation* of the actors in the systems. Orientations are defined in terms of the pattern variables. The *L* or pattern-maintenance and tension-management subsystems are therefore linked with orientations through the pattern variables.

2. Goal attainment depends on the manner in which the actors view objects, on the *modality* of the objects; and modality is also defined in terms of the pattern variables.

3. The integration subsystem (*I*) can be linked to combinations of orientations and modalities and hence to combinations of the pattern variables. That makes it possible to define the conditions of stability *within* the system as a whole. A separate set of relations, also tied to the pattern variables, defines the conditions of order (integration) for each of the four functional imperatives of a system: **(a)** When society faces an *adaptive* problem, objects must be categorized by the actor in universalistic terms, "with enough specificity to exclude more diffuse considerations of orientation." **(b)** When the problem is *goal attainment,* the actor must be concerned with the performance of the object and regard the object affectively. **(c)** When the problem is *integration,* objects must be categorized particularistically and diffusely. **(d)** When the problem is *pattern maintenance,* objects must be categorized by their qualities and with affective neutrality.[28]

Now, it is extremely important to bear in mind that Parsons is here defining the *minimum conditions for stability and order in a social system.* To take one illustration, he is asserting that if a social system is to achieve its goals, the objects that are relevant to those goals must be considered

---

[28]Talcott Parsons, "Pattern Variables Revisited: A Response to Robert Dubin," *American Sociological Review,* Vol. XXV, No. 4 (August, 1960), p. 474.

according to their performance, in terms of what they actually do and not according to the qualities attributed to them. To take a trite case, choose a man known to be a capable sailor as captain of the ship, not a man who has achieved the rank through family connections, if you wish to reach your destination. The basic question that needs to be asked here is whether such general propositions suffice to define the conditions of stability for an empirical system or whether they are merely inferences that hold *for the model* that Parsons has built. There is not enough information available to answer the question, but it is worth noting that models are always imperfect, and qualities of the model cannot be assumed to hold for the phenomena to which the model is analogous; they must be validated in empirical terms before they can serve as explanatory instruments.

4. Finally, the adaptive subsystem of the social system is linked to the pattern variables by adopting a very odd definition of the mechanisms that link a social system to its environment. Parsons conceives the relation between system and environment in terms of inputs and outputs, but the inputs and outputs are thought of as *meanings*. Interchange between system and environment therefore takes the form of transfer of meanings through symbolic devices like language or money. The adaptive capacity of a system, in these terms, depends on the meaning that is attached to the objects in the external environment. Parsons, in effect, *defines* the external environment as a set of objects that are categorized universally. Anything that is categorized particularistically is part of the social system. Hence the problem of adaptation can be rephrased as the problem of dealing with universalistically categorized objects. Parsons offers the following rules for dealing with them:

a) When the *adaptive* significance of an external object is being symbolized, it must be categorized in terms of performance and oriented to in terms of affective neutrality. This has the effect of maximizing the importance of "objective" understanding of the object and presumably maximizes the rationality or "realism" of the definition of the object. This is given the title "empirical cognitive symbolization." NB: It is worth interjecting here once again that all of these stipulations hold *only* for the case where we wish to maintain stability and order in society. It is easy to forget Parsons' basic purpose in the complexity of the structure.

b) When the significance of an object for *goal attainment* is being symbolized, the object must be defined specifically rather than diffusely, and particularistically rather than universalistically. This is called "expressive symbolization." In effect, Parsons here produces a rule for propagandizing the populace and thus generating support for community goal striving.

c) To symbolize the significance of norms external to the social system, the actor must be involved with them emotionally and hence treat them affectively, and he must be concerned with their qualities rather than their performance. This rule, called "moral evaluative categorization," is another propaganda rule. If you wish your population to maintain a free enterprise economic system, "socialism" must be responded to emotionally and without regard to any actual accomplishments; the population must accept the consequences of socialism that are attributed to it, presumably by the rulers of the social system.

d) Finally, to symbolize the significance of the "sources of normative authority," objects must be defined universalistically and the basis of actor interest in the object must be diffuse. This is called "existential interpretation." That is, the members of a social system must accept a broad range of involvement with the sources of normative authority (system authorities), and here the critical importance of Parsons' original definition of this variable perhaps becomes clear.[29] In a diffuse relation the burden of proof lies with

[29]See p. 136 above.

those who claim that no responsibility exists. A claim to authority on the part of society is considered binding unless it can be shown to be improper. Parsons' rules will certainly provide order, but one may begin to wonder how authoritative the resulting system is likely to be.

The relational aspects of Parsons' second formulation have been compressed very neatly into a hierarchically structured diagram that accompanied the revision of the pattern variables. (See Figure 3–1.) In each column the cells form a "cybernetic system." Each cell categorizes the necessary, but not the sufficient, conditions for the cell above it and controls the processes categorized in the cell below—a sort of hierarchical "democratic centralism." The subsystems are arranged horizontally by function. The structural components of the system are set out in columns 1 and 2, and the processes appear in columns 3 and 4. The A column is particularly interesting because it mediates between the system and the environment, converting "meanings." The effect of the conversions can then be evaluated according to the rules for achieving stability that Parsons has outlined. It would take too long to discuss the full content of the diagram, though it is worth careful study; but if the diagram is examined in conjunction with the set of theoretical propositions that Parsons has suggested for maintaining stability and order, it can be very instructive:

1. The hierarchical ordering of control in the social system indicates that the structure of action systems consists of patterns of normative culture, internalized in personalities and institutionalized in the social and cultural systems.
2. The normative culture must be differentiated relative to functional exigencies, and the parts must be integrated according to the standards set out in the *I* cells of the diagram. Social process, in other words, must conform to the normative order.
3. The "distance" between normative requirements and structural limitations must not be too great. Elements of the normative structure must be incorporated into appropriate units of the social system at every level.

4. Functional exigency implies a temporal ordering of process, shown in the left-right arrangement of the diagram.
5. Changes in process arise from disturbances. Otherwise, the system continues as before (law of inertia). Stress in the system may be eliminated by either changing the standards

FIGURE 3-1. The Action System in Relation to Its Environment

	STRUCTURAL CATEGORIES		CATEGORIES OF PROCESS		
	Units of Orientation to Objects (L) (Properties of Actors)	Integrative Standards (I)	Symbolic Representations of External Objects (A)	Internal Meanings of Objects (G) (Inputs-Outputs)	Outputs to Environment
L	Neut Diff — NORMATIVE COMMITMENTS	Qual Neut — Ground-of-meaning Anchorage PATTERN-MAINTENANCE	Diff Univ — EXISTENTIAL INTERPRETATION	Univ Qual — "RESPECT"	
I	Aff Diff — AFFILIATIONS	Part Diff — Manifold of evaluative selections INTEGRATION Allocative selection	Aff Qual — MORAL-EVALUATION	Part Qual — IDENTIFICATION	Responsible Action
G	Aff Spec — CONSUMMATORY NEEDS	Perf Aff — Range of action-choice GOAL (attainment) SELECTION	Spec Part — EXPRESSIVE SYMBOLIZATION	Perf Part — CATHEXIS	Expressive Action
A	Neut Spec — INSTRUMENTAL CAPACITIES	Univ Spec — Empirical-cognitive field ADAPTATION Means-Selection	Neut Perf — COGNITIVE SYMBOLIZATION	Perf Univ — UTILITY	Instrumental Action

Direction of Control ↑
Direction of Limiting Conditions ↑

Direction of Implementation vis-a-vis Environment →
← Direction of Environmental "Stimulation"

SOURCE: *American Sociological Review*, Vol. XXV, No. 4 (August, 1960), p. 476.

(learning) or altering the structure through "performance processes," leaving the integrating standards undisturbed.
6. Long-run stability in a social system depends on the development of an adaptive relation between environment and social system that is relatively immune to momentary disturbance. The relation between system and environment

must therefore be selective, and only those items that can be controlled adequately should be brought into the system (if it is to remain stable). Parsons claims that a principle of "natural selection" operates to prevent or inhibit gross errors in judgment.

That brief survey of Parsons' work should bring out the essentials of the structure. Despite the complexity and jargon, Parsons is worth careful study—more, in fact, than he has received from political scientists. The treatment of Parsons has been expanded deliberately in order to stimulate more interest in his model and to provide the student with some guidelines for working through the mountain of material.

CRITICISM AND APPLICATIONS

Ardent functionalists or systems theorists sometimes claim that theirs is the only possible approach to the study of society: "It is the thesis of this volume," Morton A. Kaplan avers, "that a scientific politics can develop *only* if the materials of politics are treated in terms of systems of action." Those hostile to functionalism reply that it is not a theory (which is true, though a theory can be stated in functional terms) and that functional explanations are not "really" explanations.[30] Kaplan's claim is ridiculous, since there is no possible reason he could give in support of it. The critics, on the other hand, usually support their argument by defining an explanation as a set of deductively related propositions. That criterion, of course, would eliminate virtually *all* explanations from the social sciences, functionalist or not.

A typical formal criticism of functional explanations has been produced by I. C. Jarvie with reference to anthropology. His definition of an explanation is taken from Karl R.

[30]Morton A. Kaplan, *System and Process in International Politics* (John Wiley & Sons, Inc., 1957), p. 4. Compare Kingsley Davis, "The Myth of Functional Analysis as a Special Method in Sociology and Anthropology," *American Sociological Review*, Vol. XXIV (1959).

Popper: Explanations are deductively related sets of propositions that are not tautologies. He then offers a criticism of functionalist attempts to answer the question "Why do people go to church?" choosing his own premises. He finds that from the particular set of premises he has selected, he can only deduce that "when people go to church they are expressing their social solidarity"; but that, he says, does not explain why people go to church. Instead of concluding that his premises are inadequate (which is *logically* the inference to be drawn from the situation), he concludes that functionalism is incapable of explanation.[31] Now, that will not do at all. Ignoring the point that those who rely so heavily on logic ought not to ask such ambiguous questions as "Why do people go to church?" Jarvie can gain no satisfaction from insisting on the deductive criterion of explanation. To do so is merely to demonstrate that functionalism cannot produce deductive explanations, and that we already know. Given the present state of social science, formal logic cannot differentiate between adequate and inadequate explanations; some other criteria are needed.

Formal logic remains a useful and valuable tool, of course; but it serves mainly as a limit, as a device for eliminating improper inferences from explanations, and not as a warrant for explanations. A good example of the value of formal logic is provided by Carl G. Hempel's analysis of a form of explanation often used by functionalists to account for particular "traits" in society. The form of such explanations is as follows:

1. At a given time (t), a system (S) functions adequately in a specified setting (C).
2. S functions adequately under conditions (C) only if certain necessary conditions (N) are satisfied.
3. A given trait (I) would, if present in S, satisfy conditions (N).
4. Therefore, trait I is present in S at T.

As Hempel rightly points out, conclusion 4 involves the fal-

[31] I. C. Jarvie, "Limits to Functionalism in Anthropology," in Don Martindale, (ed.), *Functionalism in the Social Sciences*, pp. 23–24.

lacy of reaffirming the consequent in regard to the premise. The inference is valid *only* if trait *I*, and no other trait, could produce *N*; but that is not stipulated in the premises, and Merton has argued persuasively that it is a bad assumption—it is wiser to assume functional equivalence; hence, various traits might fulfill the conditions required.[32]

Hempel has shown decisively that a particular kind of functional explanation in unacceptable; he has not shown that *all* functional explanations are improper. Those who have examined the methodological foundations of functionalism agree, usually, that it is peculiarly open to abuse, for reasons to be examined below. But no one has shown that functional explanations are impossible in principle; and if simplistic examples involve Hempel's error or make other objectionable inferences, so do simplistic explanations couched in genetic or causal terms.*

In a functional explanation the phenomenon to be explained is related to the functioning of a "system"; the con-

---

[32]Carl G. Hempel, "The Logic of Functional Analysis," in L. Gross (ed.), *Symposium on Sociological Theory* (Harper and Row, 1959), pp. 283–84. The essay also appears in Carl G. Hempel, *Aspects of Scientific Explanation* (Free Press, 1965).

*For the methodology of functionalism, see Robert Brown, *Explanation in Social Science* (Aldine, 1963), chap. ix; Ernest Nagel, *The Structure of Science: Problems in the Logic of Scientific Explanation* (Harcourt, Brace & World, Inc., 1961), chaps. xii, xiv; Carl G. Hempel, *Aspects of Scientific Explanation and Other Essays in the Philosophy of Science* (Free Press of Glencoe, Inc., 1965), especially "The Logic of Functional Analysis" and "Aspects of Scientific Explanation"; Alvin W. Gouldner, "Reciprocity and Autonomy in Functional Theory," in L. Gross (ed.), *Symposium on Sociological Theory* (Harper and Row, 1959); Don Martindale (ed.), *Functionalism in the Social Sciences* (American Academy of Political and Social Science, 1965); Ernest Nagel, "A Formalization of Functionalism," in *Logic without Metaphysics* (Free Press, 1959); Kingsley Davis, "The Myth of Functional Analysis as a Special Method in Sociology and Anthropology," *American Sociological Review*, Vol. XXIV (1959); R. C. Buck, "On the Logic of General Behavior Systems Theory," in H. Feigl and M. Scriven (eds.), *Minnesota Studies in Philosophy of Science* (University of Minnesota Press, 1956), Vol. I; David Easton, "The Limits of the Equilibrium Model in Social Research," *Behavioral Science*, 1956; Robert K. Merton, *Social Theory and Social Structure* (rev. and enlarged ed.; Free Press, 1957), Part I.

sequences for the system of the phenomenon in question are stipulated in terms of "function." There is no reason in principle why perfectly adequate explanations cannot be couched in functional terms, though certain kinds of explanations may be difficult in practice. A brief survey of the criteria (logical and nonlogical) that can be applied to functional explanation, and of some of the more common errors in functional explanations, will serve as an introduction to the use of functionalism in political science. The criticisms that follow do not flow from a carping attitude nor from a conviction that functionalism is a poor mode of explanation. Since all social explanations are weak, whatever the form of the explanation, it is important to know where the weakness lies in a particular type of explanation, for it may help us avoid unnecessary errors.

Functional explanations require, at a minimum, the concept of a system, a statement of the rules of interaction within that system, definitions of the various "states" of the system, a list of the functional prerequisites of the system, and some knowledge of the mechanisms by which systems function and adjust. The quality of a functional explanation will obviously depend on the degree to which these various requirements can be fulfilled. Functional explanations are usually weak, first, because it is often very difficult to stipulate rules of correspondence between concept and empirical data that are wholly unambiguous and open to test. A second major source of weakness in functional explanation is the ease with which unwarranted assumptions can be introduced into them, implicitly or explicitly. Four are particularly common: (1) the teleological assumption, (2) the assumption of functional unity, (3) the assumption of universal functionalism, and (4) the assumption of functional indispensability. Conceptual obscurity and unwarranted assumptions are the two most important sources of error in functionalism. Other criticisms, some valid and some not, have also been brought against it. Merton and others have dealt with the argument that functionalism necessarily involves a commitment to a conservative ideology quite adequately.[33] Verbal obscurity often occurs in functionalism, of course, but it is not limited to that type of explanation. Finally, the claim that functionalism *necessarily* leads to static analysis remains unproven. Most functional studies *are* static, but so are most institutional studies. There seems no good reason why functional analyses cannot deal with dynamics as well as statics. Functionalism has enough problems unique to itself without assuming the burden of responsibility for every error that can be committed in inquiry. We shall therefore limit ourselves to those aspects of functionalism that are particularly sensitive or dangerous.

Functionalism, it is said, is necessarily ambiguous and obscure because the concepts it employs are impossible to define precisely; it resembles "power theory" explanations in political science in this respect. We have already noted the multiple meanings of "function" in everyday usage. The concept of "system," which is also fundamental, is equally ambiguous. Usually, a system is defined analytically or nominally, rather than in empirical terms, and that is quite acceptable; but it is very easy, in the course of discussion, to move from an analytic definition to a real definition without noticing the change, particularly when concepts are borrowed from another field. Parsons' "functional imperatives," for example, are defined in purely analytic terms; yet they are often used by political scientists as though they were defined in real terms, with rather unfortunate consequences.

It is not enough to define a system as a simple, unified entity. As Merton makes clear, if the analysis of function is confined to the study of the impact of particular events on "the system as a whole," the explanation is necessarily incomplete, and it may be grossly inaccurate. Particular items

[33]Merton, *Social Theory and Social Structure*, pp. 37–46.

in a system may have one effect on some parts of the structure and quite a different effect in another area. The system must be stratified or differentiated enough to allow the inquirer to separate the consequences of an event for different parts of the system. A system, in other words, should not be treated like a simple "black box" if that can possibly be avoided, and functional analyses that treat systems in that way should be used very cautiously.[34]

A second set of problems arises from the fact that a system can be conceptualized in two fundamentally disparate ways—as an organic structure or as a mechanical structure. Robert K. Merton, for example, tends to make functional analyses in terms of interacting sets of variables (groups, cultures, individuals, etc.), and he comes close to eliminating the concept "system" entirely—Merton rarely if ever uses the term, and his functionalism is factorial and mechanical. Parsons, on the other hand, uses a concept of system that is holistic and organic, and most practicing functionalists follow his example, particularly in political science. The mechanistic conception of system, rigorously pursued, tends to produce explanations that are hardly distinguishable from factor theories. The organic conception of system is the chief source of contention, since it forces the analyst to make use of a complex set of postulates, particularly the so-called "functional requisites," which Merton calls, rightly, "one of the cloudiest and empirically most debatable concepts in functional theory." Further, though everyone will probably concede that social life is in some respects analogous to the functioning of an organism, there are points at which the analogy fails. And even within the purely organic domain, functional concepts are not always clear and precise. Concepts like functional prerequisites, equilibrium, or homeostasis were borrowed from biology; but even in biology, it may not be possible to specify precisely the functional

[34]*Ibid.*, pp. 52 *et seq.*

prerequisites for the continuation of a system. How to account for bacteria that survive doses of drugs, for example? And what is to be made of a human carcass in which the blood continues to flow, respiration goes on, but the viscera have been decimated and consciousness has vanished? Is it maintaining itself? It has yet to be shown that the functional requisites of even a simple society can be specified in empirical terms.[35]

Functionalists are invariably faced with a difficult "boundary problem" when they seek to relate a system to empirical data. An unbounded system is not a system; systems exist only by virtue of being distinguished from the environment. Analytically, the boundary problem is readily solved. Empirically, it is very difficult. The early functionalists, who worked with small and more or less isolated primitive communities, were still forced to postulate the functional unity of society (everything is related to everything else), functional indispensability (the item that performs a function, and no other item, is able to perform that function), universal functionalism (every item has a function) in order to get around the boundary problem. Merton has argued that these postulates are unacceptable; on empirical grounds, it can be shown that functional equivalence, incompleteness of integration, and functional indifference and even dysfunctionality of particular cultural items must be accepted. Marion J. Levy, Jr., in his discussion of the point, rightly underlines the danger of adding the teleological fallacy to a functional explanation when seeking a solution to the boundary problem, i.e., equating functional necessity with the conditions of origin of the phenomenon to be explained.[36]

Finally, functionalists must deal with the hazardous prob-

[35]See John Rex, *Key Problems of Sociological Theory* (Routledge and Kegan Paul, 1961), pp. 60–77, for a good discussion of the role of functional requisites in explanation.

[36]Marion J. Levy, Jr., *The Structure of Society* (Princeton University Press, 1952), pp. 52–55.

lem of defining the properties of whole systems, or "states of the system," for a given point in time. Functional explanations *are* impossible if the state of the system cannot be stipulated clearly enough to provide a reference point for demonstrating the consequences of the particular event to be explained. To complicate matters further, functionalism has incorporated into its conceptual apparatus a number of concepts like "stability," "self-regulation," "homeostasis," and so on to such a degree that functional explanations often depend on the meaning attached to them. The difficulty again lies in the need to establish connections between the concept and the empirical data. Cybernetic or homeostatic structures that control individual variables within the social system may be located and defined, just as the homeostats that control body temperature and blood sugar in the human system can be identified. But there is little evidence to show that such regulators operate on the system *as a whole*. If regulating and controlling mechanisms are actually specific variables within a system that influence other variables, then it is improper and misleading to attribute such controls to the whole system—an inversion of the fallacy of composition.

Functionalism, particularly the organic variety, appears as a fairly complex and perhaps even nebulous approach to social explanation, largely, I believe, because it is burdened with ambiguous and misleading concepts derived from the organic analogy. Now, it might seem an easier matter for inquiry to deal with sets of interrelated variables, leaving aside the concept of system—in the way that Merton, for example, handles his explanation. The introduction of "the system" seems gratuitous, a step away from Ockham's razor to Hegelian metaphysics. But that is only the case if the concept is misused. Cautiously applied, the concept of system has the great virtue of forcing our attention to sets of interactions occurring within complex wholes that might otherwise be overlooked, and to properties of wholes that cannot be described in terms of their parts. It is worthwhile to compare two political entities *as systems* and not merely through an item-by-item checklist. Doubtless, a further expansion of the conceptual apparatus of functionalism is needed to designate some of the more important properties of systems as a whole and to facilitate such comparisons.

Historically, functionalism has proved a useful and stimulating approach to the study of society and of politics. In a field where *all* explanations are in some degree imperfect, imperfection cannot be eliminated, though it may be reduced. The value of the results seems to justify the effort. Functionalism has, first of all, called attention forcibly to the interdependence of the elements of society and helped in the search for the rules controlling interaction and interdependence. It serves as a useful counterforce to analytic atomism and extreme individualism. Second, distinctions between latent and manifest functions draw attention to the unintended consequences of social action in a very useful way. Third, there are some senses in which society *is* more like an organism than a machine; and in these areas, functionalism is more realistic and useful than mechanistic analogies. Fourth, functionalism, by concentrating attention on the present, serves to reduce interest in origins—an interest that has been an albatross around the neck of political science for a very long time. Finally, functionalism has contributed to the development of social science indirectly by serving as a target for criticism. To learn what is wrong with functionalism, we must inquire systematically and rigorously into problems of inquiry that have influence far beyond the bounds of functionalism. Perhaps the fairest summary criticism of functionalism is found in Robert Brown's work on explanation:

At present, function-explanations in the social sciences are more often invoked by name than employed in fact. This is because their developed use requires that a number of rather stringent conditions be met, and social scientists are seldom in a position to do so. They are, however, often able to make use of functional statements to construct an undeveloped form of explanation whose usefulness nevertheless is considerable. When an investigator has reason to believe that some sort of self-persisting system is present, he can employ a crude type of function-explanation as a stop-gap. He can use it to summarize his information, to indicate the relative importance of the various causal factors, and to refer obliquely to possible laws. His hope, of course, is that later he will be able to replace this primitive explanation by one in which the set of laws that describe the working of the system are made explicit . . . .[37]

Brown will satisfy neither ardent functionalists nor bitter critics of functionalism, but it seems a reasonable summation of the present position of functionalism, particularly in political science.

FUNCTIONALISM IN POLITICAL SCIENCE

Turning to the application of functionalism to political phenomena and the discussion of functionalism in political science, we find two basic types of works available. First, there are books and articles directed primarily to the development of functionalism as a conceptual framework, illustrating its usefulness rather than seeking an explanation through its use. Second, there are works that assume or sketch briefly the functional conceptual structure and then seek to apply it to particular problems. The latter are a minority. However, our primary interest here is in the kinds of conceptual framework that can be constructed within the confines of functionalism and applied to political phenomena, and I have chosen what I believe to be significant and representative examples: David Easton's formulation of systems analysis, Gabriel A. Almond's widely cited "seven-variable" scheme, and Morton A. Kaplan's application of functional analysis to international affairs. There are many others. Those interested in a general overview of the use

---

[37] Robert Brown, *Explanation in Social Science*, p. 132.

of functionalism or systems analysis in political science can do no better than H. V. Wiseman's recent resume of the field.[38]

David Easton

The most consistent and systematic functionalist in political science has been David Easton, though he might not agree; his "systems approach" to politics is an interesting variant of functionalism that commands a great deal of attention among political scientists. Indeed, Easton might almost be considered the political scientist's Talcott Parsons, for their work is remarkably similar in many respects, though Easton claims that the sources of his thinking lie elsewhere —in what is called "general systems theory," an approach to analysis developed largely at the University of Michigan by a small group of scholars with a strong bias to biology and mathematical analysis. Like Parsons, Easton is searching for a "general" theory, a unified conceptual framework for the analysis of political life. Like Parsons again, he is concerned with stability and order, with the "persistence" of political systems in a world of change and stress. His conception of the meaning of "theory" is Parsonian. Unlike Parsons, Easton's writing is clear, and he is readily understood—hence readily criticized.

In *The Political System,* published in 1953, Easton made a survey of the discipline and produced a first tentative attempt at a consistent approach to the study of politics. Two basic needs occupied most of the nonhistorical discussion in the book: first, the need for a definition of "politics" that would effectively separate political from nonpolitical activity; second, a way of combining the concept of equilibrium and the concept of system. The definition of "political" was, I believe, a failure. Politics, Easton said, is concerned with "the authoritative allocation of values," where "authorita-

[38] H. V. Wiseman, *Political Systems: Some Sociological Approaches* (Routledge and Kegan Paul, 1966).

tive" implies that the members of the society accept an allocation of values as binding. Under the terms of the definition, no distinction can be made between value allocation in the national government and value allocation in a business or a boy's club. The treatment of "system" is brief, more a prelude of things to come than a definitive statement. In *The Political System* the derivation of the concepts from economics is fairly clear from the works cited, including the Henderson study of Pareto which so much influenced Talcott Parsons. Beyond a statement of the principle of interdependence and some hints of the principle of functional unity, the structure of systems analysis remained undeveloped.[39]

More than a decade later, Easton published two volumes almost simultaneously, one setting forth the bare bones of a conceptual framework for systems analysis, the other rather misleadingly entitled *A Systems Analysis of Political Life*—misleading because it is, in fact, not a systems analysis of politics but an extension of the details of the conceptual framework to be used for analysis; Easton remains in the "getting ready to begin" stage. Although the larger work contains only some illustrations, Easton has produced one of the few comprehensive attempts to lay the foundation for systems analysis in political science and provide a "general" functional theory of politics, and it is worth careful attention on that count alone.[40] Since we are here interested in the general properties of the approach rather than the fine details, the discussion relies primarily on the structure outlined in *A Framework for Political Analysis* rather than the larger and more detailed volume.

Easton's goal is ambitious: "to develop a logically inte-

---

[39]David Easton, *The Political System* (Alfred A. Knopf, Inc., 1953). Chapter v deals with the meaning of "political"; chapter xi contains the treatment of "system" and "equilibrium."

[40]David Easton, *A Framework for Political Analysis* (Prentice-Hall, Inc., 1965), and *A Systems Analysis of Political Life* (John Wiley & Sons, Inc., 1965).

grated set of categories, with strong empirical relevance, that will make possible the analysis of political life as a system of behavior." Like Parsons, Easton is concerned with a particular aspect of system behavior: "the basic processes through which the political system regardless of its generic or specific type, is able to persist in a world of either stability or change." The justification for choosing this particular question is not included in the discussion.

The basic elements in the conceptual structure are engagingly simple. There is a *system* operating in an *environment*. There are *inputs* to the system (demand and support) and *outputs* from the system (decisions and actions of authorities). There is *feedback;* a "loop" connects authority and membership so that responses of members are communicated to authority and can generate further action by authorities. The basic unit of analysis is the *interaction,* and more specifically an interaction arising out of the behavior of members of the system when they are acting as members of the system. The concept "system" is defined in purely analytic or nominal terms; the possibility of natural systems is refuted. That is, a system, in Easton's terms, comprises *any* set of interactions that an investigator finds interesting. There need be no empirical connection among them. That is a curious definition, and though Easton justifies the choice by pointing out that it avoids arguments about the "reality" of systems, the argument is actually only delayed rather than settled. The question then arises whether the set of variables chosen by an investigator has any significance for political science, and the answer to that question requires the same set of criteria as the definition of natural systems but differently stated. As Easton himself states, "systems analysis, as I shall conceive it, takes its departure from the notion of political life as a boundary-maintaining set of interactions embedded in and surrounded by other social systems to the influence of which it is constantly exposed."[41]

[41]Easton, A Framework for Political Analysis, p. 25.

It is hard to believe that Easton is not here assuming the existence of a natural or empirical political system that can serve as an object of study.

The political system, obviously, is made up of "political" interactions, and "political" remains to be defined. After a preliminary skirmish, the question is dropped until chapter iv, where a definition taken from *The Political System* is offered as a base: "[W]hat distinguishes political interactions from all other kinds of social interactions is that they are predominantly oriented toward the authoritative allocation of values for society." "Authoritative" again implies that those subject to authority consider it binding; the rules made by authority are "legitimate." But Easton has shifted ground by adding "for society." He now concedes that authoritative allocations occur everywhere in society and hence that a further criterion is needed to distinguish the "political." Nonpolitical systems—or "parapolitical" systems, to use Easton's term—are only "subsystems," whereas the "societal political system" (presumably the national state) covers a wider range and has wider powers, that is, special capacities to mobilize resources and support. The subject matter of political science, as dictated by long tradition, should embrace "the most inclusive political system of a society," for "no society could survive without providing for some process through which authoritative allocations could be made." Hence the term "political system" is reserved for "those roles and interactions relevant to the authoritative allocations for a society as a whole." Easton, it seems, is here committing political science to the study of the sovereign national state. In any case the solution begs the question, and the definition of a "member" of a political system offered in *A Framework for Political Analysis* is definitely circular: "[B]y this I shall mean the most general role of a person in a given society with respect to political life."[42] In the last analysis, "political" remains an undefined term.

[42] *Ibid.*, p. 57.

Now, this may seem an awful bit of nit picking, an excess of interest in a minor point. But that is not the case. If a conceptual framework for politics is to be differentiated from a "social" conceptual framework, then criteria are needed for separating them. Easton could, of course, simply assert that "political" means no more than the phenomena that political scientists investigate; and that, incidentally, is probably all that it can mean. But he would then be forced to deny the possibility of examining "the political system" in empirical terms. Since he obviously believes that "the political system" is a useful conception, some means of separating the "political" system from all others must be found. If he chooses the first horn of the dilemma, his undertaking is fatuous; if he chooses the second, a definition of "political" is essential. The second horn was actually chosen; hence the validity of the definition of "political" is a matter of prime concern.

Easton is, in effect, forced to deal with the thorny conceptual problems that appear in any attempt to create an all-encompassing conceptual framework. The clearest illustration of the nature of those problems can be found in the treatment of the concept "system." Since a system is defined as a set of interactions, it should be possible to substitute the phrase "a set of interactions" wherever the term "system" occurs without altering the meaning of the proposition in which the substitution occurs. But that is patently not the case. To illustrate, "the members of a political system have the opportunity to . . . ,"[43] or again, "a political system has managed to persist . . . ."[44] Clearly, Easton is thinking of a system with human members, not a set of interactions. Further, if a "system" of interactions persisted, that could only mean that the structure remained intact over time, which would identify "system" with "structure." Finally, a "system"

[43]*Ibid.*, p. 78.
[44]*Ibid.*, p. 84.

often appears as an actor in Easton's discussions. "Like human biological systems, political systems may be able to keep themselves intact, at least for brief periods, by isolating themselves from all change."[45] Enough has been said, perhaps, to indicate the kinds of ambiguities that can creep into a discussion of systems unless we are exceptionally wary. It may serve as a warning against careless use of concepts in functional analysis and perhaps suggest some of the kinds of misuse that have to be avoided.

Passing beyond conceptual shortcomings of this kind, one major substantive criticism of Easton's approach to functionalism needs to be made. It has to do with the purpose of inquiry, the goal of theory, as Easton defines it. He suggests that the task of behavioral science is to "put kinds of questions that reveal the way in which the life processes or defining functions of political systems are protected."[46] The elucidation of those questions is far from satisfactory. Politics has been defined as the authoritative allocation of values for a society. Persistence is now defined as the continuation of the capacity of a system to make and execute binding allocations on its members.[47] Stresses, which might put an end to persistence, are defined as activities that threaten the capacity to execute such binding decisions, and since they are difficult to visualize in empirical terms, they are defined in terms of certain "essential variables." The essential variables, in turn, become the capacity of a society to allocate values for its members and assure their acceptance.[48] Easton has created a circle of definitions. But where has it taken us? Unless the circle can be broken by introducing some new conceptual element into the structure, or linking the concepts in the system to empirical rather than nominal definitions, we have not moved at all. Like Parsons, Easton

[45]*Ibid.*, p. 99.
[46]*Ibid.*, p. 78.
[47]*Ibid.*, p. 87.
[48]*Ibid.*, p. 96.

does not think of theory in terms of explanation but in terms of the creation of conceptual frameworks. The result is a highly abstract structure that is logically suspect, conceptually fuzzy, and empirically almost useless. Easton's "political system" turns out to be an abstraction whose relation to empirical politics is virtually impossible to establish. The promise of a conceptual framework with "high empirical relevance" simply has not been fulfilled.

The criticisms of Easton's conceptual framework touched upon above—and they could be multiplied many times but to no good purpose—have to do primarily with the conceptual apparatus he produces. It is instructive that this is the case, for one would really expect that criticism of a conceptual structure would be based largely on its adequacy or inadequacy in relation to the phenomena. And here we meet the crux of the difficulty. Easton has no phenomena! The "political system" which he so busily dissects exists nowhere except in his mind; the closest empirical approximation is probably the sovereign national state. Now, it might be possible to think generally about *any* political system, but then it would not be possible to define "political" in terms of authoritative allocations for a "whole society" because the political system in, say, a small town would be unable to do that. And Easton cannot retreat into the assertion that political systems are analytically defined only, for he himself says: "[It] would be pointless, if not impossible, to push ahead in our analysis and to conceptualize political life as an open and self-regulating system, as I shall, unless it were feasible both analytically and empirically to distinguish a political system from its total environment."[49] Further, it is inconsistent to begin with an interaction as a basic unit of analysis and then go on to speak in terms of individual members of political systems performing given tasks. The conceptual inadequacies of the framework prevent Easton from reaching the goal that he sets for himself and

[49]*Ibid.*, p. 48.

at the same time inhibit the kind of generalized treatment of systems in general that might have been carried out. To do the latter, Easton, like Parsons, would be forced into a careful classification of interactions, and much of what he in fact wrote could not have been written if he had adhered rigorously to his own conceptions.

All of which is not to deny that parts of Easton's two volumes are quite interesting and suggestive. The discussion of "support" in Part III of *A Systems Analysis of Political Life,* for example, brings out aspects of the relation between individual and political authority not, to my knowledge, spelled out anywhere else. It is perhaps worth pointing out that the most valuable parts of the book seem to be those in which Easton departs radically from his own conceptual framework and generalizes about Western politics in more or less everyday terms.

Gabriel A. Almond

Gabriel A. Almond's "functional" approach to comparative politics is representative of the kind of functionalism most often met in political science.[50] It is widely read and cited, despite—or perhaps because of—the fact that it illustrates only too well Robert Brown's point that it is easier to talk functional language than to produce functional explanations or near explanations. Yet Almond takes for himself the same objective as Talcott Parsons or, indirectly, David Easton. He aims at a "functional theory of the polity." Indeed, he seems to believe that the essay contains such a theory: "The functional theory of the polity which we have elaborated above does specify the elements of the polity in such form as may ultimately make possible statistical and perhaps mathematical formulation."[51] Like Easton, Almond is a victim of the search for the political Holy Grail, a "theory of politics." At

[50]Gabriel A. Almond, "A Functional Approach to Comparative Politics," in Gabriel A. Almond and James S. Coleman (eds.), *The Politics of the Developing Areas* (Princeton University Press, 1960).

[51]*Ibid.,* p. 59.

best, what Almond produces is a classification scheme, or perhaps a model, a very imperfect and loose model, that can be used to order political data and perhaps standardize observations of political phenomena. Whether or not it *should* be employed for those purposes depends on empirical demonstration that the bundle of categories that the model suggests are indeed the crucial variables in politics. My own opinion is that they are far too broad to be of much use.

Almond's essay also provides a good illustration of the dangers involved in borrowing conceptions without considering the level of abstraction at which they are employed and their precise meaning in the context from which they are torn. He uses much of the terminology of functionalism, particularly of the Parsonian variety, yet the usage in Almond does not fit the meaning of the terms in the Parsonian system. Almond uses the pattern variables, for example, but not as dichotomies. He uses the concept of "function" but does not refer to a system in which the function has meaning. Systems are defined in Almond as sets of interactions, but neither "system" nor "interaction" is defined. Some of the essential ingredients of functional analysis are wholly absent from Almond's conceptual scheme.

The "political system" is defined as "that system of interactions to be found in all independent societies which performs the functions of integration and adaptation (both internally and vis a vis other societies) by means of the employment, or threat of employment, of more or less legitimate physical compulsion."[52] Almond is nothing if not eclectic. He has, in one ungrammatical sentence, combined Weber's definition of the state, Easton's conception of authoritative allocation, and Parsons' view of the function of the political subsystem in society. The meaning of "independent" remains obscure, and its relation to territory is left open. "System" is defined as a "particular set of properties of these interac-

[52]*Ibid.*, p. 7.

tions," of which three are listed: (1) comprehensiveness, (2) interdependence, and (3) existence of boundaries. The meaning of this curious list, as explicated in the text, is as follows: Comprehensiveness means that all interactions that affect the use or threat of use of physical coercion are included in the political system; interdependence means that a change in one subset produces a change in *all* other subsets (surely a typographical error); boundary implies that there are "points where other systems end and the political system begins." The technical problems associated with the definition of system, on which so many functionalists have foundered, are simply ignored.

Political systems are then invested with certain common properties. (1) Every system has a structure; (2) the same functions are performed in all political systems; (3) all structures perform more than one function; (4) all systems are "mixed," in the sense that they combine "modern" and "primitive" elements. In effect, these are empirical generalizations, offered without supporting evidence, and dependent on the hidden assumption that the conceptual framework being outlined is the only possible framework that can be applied to politics. Otherwise, political functions could surely be defined in a way that would make it unlikely that all of the functions performed by the American political system are performed by an East African tribe.

Finally, political systems are given certain functions to perform, but they are not the functional requisites of ordinary functional analysis; indeed, the concept of "functional requisites" does not appear in Almond's essay. Almond's list, we are told, was compiled by "asking a series of questions based on the distinctive political activities existing in Western complex systems."[53] The result is the famous "seven-variable" list of functional categories. There are four "input" functions: (1) political socialization and recruitment, (2) in-

[53]*Ibid.*, p. 16.

terest articulation, (3) interest aggregation; and (4) political communication. There are also three "output" functions: (1) rule making, (2) rule application, and (3) rule adjudication. These seven functions are then examined seriatim. The analysis is therefore "functional," presumably. A typology of structures is produced for each variable, together with a typology of styles associated with each structure, and all defined in terms of a modified set of Parsons' pattern variables. A brief summary of the treatment of functional "imperatives" will indicate the manner in which this conceptual framework is employed.

Political Socialization and Recruitment. Socialization is defined as the process of "induction into the political culture"; it eventuates in a set of attitudes. Socialization may be carried out by various elements in society and with different styles; it may be manifest (connected to politics) or latent (indirectly related to politics). The "style" may be specific or diffuse, particularistic or universalistic, affective or instrumental. The early stages of socialization are the same in all political systems;[54] the process itself is diffuse, particularistic, ascriptive, and affective. In primitive society, socialization ends early; in modern society, socialization continues throughout life, but the effect of primary socialization remains prime. Political recruitment begins where socialization ends. Recruitment "styles" can be compared in terms of the way in which "ascriptive and particularistic criteria combine with performance and universalistic criteria."[55] Since the pattern variables are conceived as continua and not dichotomies, the outcome of interaction among the variables is indeterminate.

Interest Articulation. This function brings into the political system any action arising in society. Four types of structures are involved: (1) institutional interest groups, which are organized groups with direct political relations;

[54]*Ibid.*, p. 30.
[55]*Ibid.*, p. 32.

(2) nonassociational groups (ethnic, religious); (3) anomic interest groups (spontaneous uprisings); and (4) associational interest groups like unions or business groups. The styles employed may be specific or diffuse, general or particular, instrumental or affective. The "structure and style of interest articulation," we are told, has the function of defining the pattern of boundary maintenance between polity and society. But the meaning of the statement is hard to determine, for the discussion of boundaries goes no further than the assertion that "When we talk about good and bad boundary maintenance, we must use criteria appropriate to the system. In one case diffuseness and intermittency may be appropriate boundary maintenance; in another specialized secular structures are appropriate."[56] What exactly is meant by a "good" boundary maintenance is wholly obscure. By implication, it appears related to system efficiency, but the relation is not spelled out.

Aggregation. Aggregation of interests may be achieved by (1) formulation of general policies that combine interests or (2) recruitment of personnel committed to a particular pattern of policy. (The reader may at this point wish to ponder the enormous conceptual gap between Almond's thinly veiled generalizations about American political practice and Parsons' profound observation that social systems must find a means of aligning system imperatives and the patterns of expectations generated by socialization—expectations that would appear as the objectives sought by interest groups. The gap suggests, I believe, the reason for the difficulty encountered when Almond's essay is read *as an example of functionalism.*) Aggregation of interests can be performed by any agency in society; but in practice, the political party is the prime instrument for that purpose. Party systems are then classified as to organization (authoritarian, dominant nonauthoritarian, competitive two-party, and competitive

[56]*Ibid.*, p. 9.

multiparty) and as to style (secular-pragmatic-bargaining parties; absolute, value-oriented or ideological parties; and particularistic or traditional parties). The relations between the capacity of the party system to aggregate interests and these other factors is not explored.

Communication.   Communication is the medium through which other functions in the political system are performed. Almond develops very nicely the importance of independent communication facilities and then considers communication as a boundary-maintenance function. The meaning of free communication is vague, but it seems connected with the flow of information between political system and society —a concept of boundary maintenance that does not accord with anything found in other functional writings. The performance of the communications media is examined in terms of structure and style, using the language of the pattern variables.

The three outputs of the political system are given short shrift, a practice very much in line with the tradition in American political science. The remainder of the essay is devoted to yet another set of classifications, this time of new states.

Almond's "functionalism" is functional in name only. He has not produced a theory, of course, nor even a well-articulated classification scheme. The taxonomy is incomplete and ambiguous. Yet the essay illustrates two trends in contemporary political science that deserve serious attention. First, Almond, like Easton and Parsons, is searching for "theory" rather than explanations. The second point is that specialists in comparative government have for years taken it for granted that comparisons are always worth making even when there is no specific end in view. Now, inquiry may aim at description, explanation, or evaluation, or all three; and comparative government, as presently conceived, seems primarily concerned with description. But it is pointless to make endless comparisons unless the similarities and differences uncovered by the comparison are explained, and explanation does not necessarily depend on still further comparisons. In fact, it seems more reasonable to expect a phenomenon to be explained best in the context in which it appears. The best use for comparisons, then, seems to be as testing devices, as compensations for the lack of experimental data, and as sources of information about similarities and differences among societies. What comparative government sorely needs is a program for going beyond stilted comparisons on the Baconian model and producing explanations that systematize and relate their phenomena.

Morton A. Kaplan

Of the attempts at functionalism in political science thus far examined, Easton is close to Parsons but uses a different language and a different family of concepts, and Almond is most clearly a political scientist without systematic training in functionalism. Both are "organic" rather than "mechanical" in their conception of systems. Yet another approach to functionalism is found in our last example, taken from international relations. Here, the model is mechanistic rather than organic, the treatment is more formal and precise, the influences come from engineering rather than sociology, the aim is factorial analysis and rigorous model building rather than broad generalizations. Morton A. Kaplan's attempt at functionalism in political science is still seeking a "general" theory, but in a way that differs considerably from the others. He is, if anything, closer to Merton than Parsons, and wholly different in emphasis and intention from either Easton or Almond.[57]

In systems engineering a "system" is defined as a set of variables that can be considered as an entity against a given background. Kaplan makes use of this conception in his study, defining a system as "a set of variables so related, in

----

[57]Kaplan, *System and Process in International Relations;* citations to the paperback edition of 1964.

contradistinction to its environment, that describable be-havioral regularities characterize the internal relationships of the variables to each other and the external relationships of the set of individual variables to combinations of external variables." Systems are described in terms of "states," and a state is nothing more than a full specification of the values of the variables in the system. The behavior of the system is stipulated in terms of changes in the variables which are called *outputs*. Changes in the environment that influence the functioning of the system are called *inputs*. Inputs that lead to radical changes in the system are called step-level functions: They alter the characteristic behavior, and even the structure of the system. Step-level functions are, na-turally, of prime significance in the study of the behavior of systems.

Systems may be related or coupled, the output of one serving as an input for the other; coupling may be unidirec-tional or bidirectional. In the latter case, there is "feedback" between the two systems; feedback may be positive (stim-ulating an increase in the same output) or negative (in-hibiting such outputs).

The two most important "states of the system" are equilib-rium and stability. A system is in equilibrium when the variables remain within specified limits for a given time; systems are stable when the variables remain within speci-fied limits in spite of changes in output within a given range. Some systems are "ultrastable," meaning that they actively seek to adapt to the environment, either by making internal changes or by imposing changes on the environment. Equi-librium and stability are analytically separate, and a system may be in equilibrium but unstable, or stable but not in equilibrium. Further, equilibrium may be either dynamic (a "steady state" of operation) or static (at rest). Political sys-tems, obviously, are dynamic. In the case of such dynamic systems, it is important to know whether changes that occur are reversible or not, whether the system will return to its former state after the environment returns to equilibrium.

The principles governing the effect of equilibrium changes on various kinds of systems are stated in broad terms:

1. A system in equilibrium will remain so unless disturbed. If nothing in the environment is likely to change the state, the system is stable. If the environment contains disturbances but their effect depends on their strength, the system has local stability.
2. A system with local stability will change to a new equilibrium state or disappear entirely if disturbed with sufficient force. Systems capable of sustaining equilibrium change are ultrastable.
3. If the disturbance disappears and nothing else changes and the system fails to return to its earlier state, a "system change" has occurred.

The key to the application of Kaplan's structure, suggested in broad outline above, is the capacity to stipulate the variables and their values and the manner in which the variables interact—for example, to show how a change in the value of one variable induces changes in the others. The extent of the problem, as Kaplan notes, depends on the purpose of the inquiry. For the study of international relations, Kaplan suggests five variables:

1. The essential rules of the system, describing the relationships among the elements of the system or assigning role functions to them.
2. The transformation rules, relating essential rules to given parameter values for the variables in the system. In effect, these are the rules of change for the system, and they must include a reference to the previous state of the system.
3. Actor classificatory variables (an awful phrase) which specify the structural characteristics of the actors or elements in the system.
4. Capability variables, specifying the capacity of an actor to carry out given classes of actions in specified settings.
5. Information variables, including estimates of the actor's capacity and his long-range aspirations. Kaplan implies that it would also be useful to include information about the relation between the actor's beliefs and the objective defi-

nition of the situation. Kaplan's "actor," in this context, is nothing more than the sum of a set of variables.

Some general remarks about Kaplan's model or system may be useful at this point. First, though his international system is made up of a few variables, that simplicity is deceptive, for each of the fundamentals would in fact be defined in terms of a large number of subsystem variables. The more precise the specification, the larger and more complex the total structure. Second, by allowing coupling and feedback among systems, Kaplan is left with a serious boundary problem. If A is coupled to B with feedback, the A and B are part of the same system. Here the difference between social science and engineering may be crucial. The engineer can isolate his system, particularly in electrical engineering, as fully as he wishes. The environmental situation is fully controllable, and inputs can be specified quite accurately. But in social science, "systems" cannot be isolated empirically, and it is unconscionably difficult to stipulate the empirical elements in a system that has been isolated analytically. The effect of coupling is likely to be indeterminate in practice (empirically) simply because the extent of the coupling tends to be unknown.

Kapan's definition of a "political" system is based on the concept of sovereignty—one of the more useful and improperly maligned concepts in the political scientist's lexicon. "The modern political system is distinguished by the fact that its rules specify the areas of jurisdiction for all other decision-making units and proved methods for settling conflicts of jurisdiction." The existence of a government is therefore an unambiguous empirical sign of the existence of a political system. However, where religious institutions perform "governmental functions," the system they govern may also be classed as a political institution—an obvious reference to the Vatican. Clearly, Kaplan is seeking a definition that will differentiate the elements in international relations, not a definition that can be used in the study of domestic politics.

Politics, in Kaplan's terms, is a contest to fill decision-making roles, to choose alternative political objects, or to change the essential rules of the political systems.

Political systems may be either "system-dominant," in which case the central government controls the subsystems in society, or "subsystem-dominant," in which case the subsystems may act freely despite the policies of the central government. Again, the concept is more useful in international relations, and perhaps in the study of federal systems, than in the study of domestic politics. Some of Kaplan's observations about the distribution of dominance (roughly equivalent to sovereign authority) within political systems are quite suggestive and worth further inquiry. And it seems possible to transform a variety of relationships observed in domestic politics into Kaplan's conceptual framework and gain in clarity and precision by so doing.

Leaving aside the question whether Kaplan has specified the variables needed to analyze international affairs adequately (I believe that he has not) and concentrating on his conceptual framework, it is clear that the "engineering" approach to systems analysis is of considerable value when the data relating to the various states of the system can be classified accurately and quantified. Experimental evidence is peculiarly well suited to the requirements of the conceptual structure. The use of the conceptual framework in areas where precision is hard to achieve and quantification is very difficult is more problematic.

Some of the conceptual difficulties encountered in other versions of functionalism are also present in Kaplan's structure. For example, the concept of "essential rules," which seems roughly equivalent to functional requisites, is far from clear. Are the essential rules those that the participants follow, those that the participants believe they ought to follow, or those that can be inferred by an objective observer? In Kaplan's model of a "balance-of-power" system, six essential rules are provided for his actors, and they seem to add up to what is called a "winning strategy" in game theory. That is, they are rules by which the actors choose among alternatives during the course of the interactions. The six rules are:

1. Act to increase capabilities, but negotiate rather than fight.
2. Fight rather than pass up an opportunity to increase capabilities.
3. Stop fighting rather than eliminate an essential actor (one needed to preserve the balance of power).
4. Act to oppose any coalition or single actor that tends to assume a position of predominance with respect to the rest of the system.
5. Act to constrain actors who subscribe to supranational organizing principles.
6. Permit defeated or constrained essential national actors to reenter the system as acceptable role partners or act to bring some previously inessential actor within the essential actor classification. Treat all essential actors as acceptable role partners.

In the context supplied here, Kaplan's "essential rules" are clearly a strategy for playing the international game and not a set of empirical generalizations to be inferred from observed behavior. They create some serious problems for the critic. First of all, their internal logic is faulty. If the first rule is taken literally, then the second rule is not compatible with it; the advice is contradictory. The theoretical difficulty is even more serious. If the "essential rules" for international actors are in fact a winning strategy for playing the complex game of international politics, then it is in practice impossible to provide them for the actors. In game theory, where the structure of interactions is completely formal, it has proved impossible to provide a winning strategy for games more complex than tic-tac-toe. Politics, considered as a game, is far more complex than chess, yet chess is hopelessly beyond our capacity to stipulate an adequate strategy.

Clearly, functionalism is not a panacea for political

science. On the other hand, there is nothing in the functionalist conceptual framework that automatically precludes its use in political explanation. All of the examples considered above proved faulty in some respects at least, though only the best-known and most highly regarded applications among those available were selected. In part, the disappointing showing of functionalism is due to the emphasis of the text. The aim, after all, is to produce a critical base for the student, to demonstrate the points in the functionalist conceptual framework that require careful attention and suggest the kinds of errors found in functional explanations. No effort was made to produce a fair or impartial evaluation of an entire book. None of the errors, however, is endemic to the approach and irremediable. And functionalism produces explanations that are as strong as any others that political science can presently generate.

Two major points emerge from the survey. First, it seems clear that the search for a "general" theory, functionalist or not, or for an all-encompassing model of politics is a false and misleading trail that leads to conceptual difficulties that are virtually insoluble. Pressed too strongly, the search can only lead to a new metaphysics in which a great deal of time is wasted discussing the properties of metaphysical entities like "the system." That problem can be avoided, in functionalism as elsewhere, by beginning with a set of concrete phenomena and by employing concepts that are firmly rooted in empirical evidence. If we seek explanations of real phenomena, and not "theories" with no referents, it is much easier to keep inquiry from straying into unproductive activity. The general rule is simple: No phenomena, no explanation; no phenomena, no suggestiveness; no phenomena, nothing accomplished. Political scientists must be interested in, and prepared to study carefully, some concrete aspect of human behavior.

Of course, success is not guaranteed merely by starting with some well-known phenomenon and seeking a functional explanation for it. Functionalism is one conceptual framework that may be employed in the study of politics, and it seems quite promising, but it is by no means the only way of seeking explanations. Political scientists may choose to produce functional explanations, of course, but the choice should depend on the nature of the phenomena and the kind of data that can be accumulated, not on some arbitrary criterion. To the extent that political science can make use of functionalism, it should be possible to take advantage of some of the work that has been done in other fields and perhaps avoid some of the errors that have taken so long to eradicate from sociology and anthropology. Here, the work of Robert K. Merton is fundamental. There is no better introduction to functionalism than the first part of *Social Theory and Social Structure*, and no better examples of functional explanation than his treatment of anomie and the function of the political "boss" in American politics can be found anywhere. They should be required reading for all prospective students of political thought, and perhaps for all prospective students of politics.

There is also much to be said for examining the conceptual system developed by Talcott Parsons in his later work. Much as I disagree with his search for general theory, his treatment of the relation between socialization and stability, between functional requisites and subsystem development, and between perception of the situation and the decision to act is extremely stimulating. He is perhaps the most fruitful source of ideas and hypotheses in contemporary thought; the extent of his influence is perhaps most easily seen as we move from the study of Parsons to the study of functional analysis in contemporary political science. His writing is exasperating, certainly, but there is more than enough substance behind the rhetoric to justify the work needed to peel away the layers of verbiage.

The second point that needs to be made, even at the risk of losing the union card, is that political scientists must abandon the search for a definition of "political" and begin thinking in terms of the phenomena that they find significant or interesting. We pay an enormous price for the dubious privilege of maintaining separate university departments and an independent set of journals. A simple move from the essentialist to the nominalist conception of the meaning of "politics" would eliminate no end of conceptual misery.

CHAPTER FOUR

PSYCHOLOGICAL EXPLANATIONS

THE explanation of social or political phenomena by reference to conceptual structures based on the psychological attributes of individuals or collectives commends itself as a reasonable and useful enterprise—one with a very long history. Indeed, a general concern with the psychic aspects of human behavior has become so much a part of the content of Western thought that it is almost impossible to discuss politics at any length without in some way involving psychology. Nevertheless, political and other social scientists have made surprisingly little use of psychological theories and systems in their explanations, and those few who have ventured into the field have not fared too well. For the most part, social scientists continue to rely on psychological folklore, on the commonsense psychological principles—too often garbled or grossly oversimplified—embedded in the school curriculum. Psychiatry has provided a wide range of social critics with a framework for attacking the existing order, but that is a separate question, to be considered later. Borrowing for purposes of explanation, which is our prime concern here, has usually been eclectic and unsystematic; various sources have been culled for principles applicable to the case in hand, too often without very much regard for the intellectual integrity of the ensuing mélange.

190

In fairness, it must also be said that borrowing theories from psychology is a risky and confusing enterprise. There are at least four major streams of thought in the field at present—perhaps as many as a dozen if different criteria of classification are employed—and they are not wholly compatible. There are mountains of psychological data, and much of it is precisely quantified. But the significance of the data for social science is often hard to determine because the data are usually produced in support of a particular conceptual framework. The political scientist can in fact find a conceptual framework in psychology that will match fairly closely his own methodological preferences, be they ultraempirical, rigorously hypothetical-deductive, or intuitive. The real dilemma lies between choosing psychological principles that are eminently verifiable but almost completely useless for the study of politics and principles relevant to phenomena that are extremely important in politics (personality, for example) but almost immune to test. Psychological theories that cope well with the phenomenon we call learning turn out to be too weak when we deal with motivation or personality; theories that offer rich insights into personality and character are almost impossible to verify; and some psychological "theories" turn out to be classification systems, incapable of explaining anything.

Nevertheless, political scientists do borrow concepts and theories from psychology and apply them to political phenomena. In fact, recent trends seem to indicate a substantial increase in the use of psychological concepts and theories in the study of politics. Some knowledge of the basic conceptual frameworks available in psychology, particularly those that are used by political scientists, is therefore required of the student of political thought. Fortunately, we can deal mainly with those aspects of psychology that are actually employed in social science. The content of this chapter, therefore, implies nothing about the current state of theory in psychology. In fact, a professional psychologist who chances to read the chapter will probably be struck by the archaic quality of the references and the absence of discussion of those questions he considers particularly urgent. For example, there have been some astonishing developments in neurophysiology since 1950, but they have had little or no discernible influence on thinking in the social sciences. Similarly, psychological progress in the field of human cognition seems almost unknown in the other social sciences, except, perhaps, through the work of Jean Piaget.

Political scientists seem most familiar with a limited range of approaches to psychology: (1) "stimulus-response" psychology, or neobehaviorism; (2) orthodox Freudianism; and (3) the sociologized version of Freud found in the writings of Karen Horney, Erich Fromm, and Harry Stack Sullivan, and most inaptly called "neo-Freudianism." References to the work of Clark L. Hull, B. F. Skinner, Edward C. Tolman, Sigmund Freud, Erich Fromm, or Kurt Lewin occur frequently in political science; only rarely is there any mention of K. Spence, Jerome Bruner, O. H. Mowrer, and others whose work is currently attracting much attention in psychology. This chapter deals with four fundamental conceptual frameworks: stimulus response, "field theory," Freudianism, and "neo-Freudianism." Both field theory and orthodox Freudianism are seldom applied systematically by political scientists, but Freud provides the foundation on which much recent psychology depends, and Lewin's field theory is included in the survey because the conceptual apparatus seems particularly well-suited to the study of certain kinds of political phenomena and a brief survey of the fundamentals of the structure is therefore warranted. With one exception, applications of psychological theory to politics are reserved to the end of the chapter and discussed there as a group.*

*BIBLIOGRAPHICAL NOTE: Some of the books, general and specialized, that I have found useful for this study may be of interest to the reader intending to dig more deeply into the psychological literature.

General texts: Morton Deutsch and Robert M. Krauss, *Theories in*

One word of warning. The "approaches" to psychology that are examined below seldom appear today as "pure types" though they can be identified quite readily in analytic terms. The interaction of behavioral theories, Gestalt psychologies, "field" theories, and psychoanalytic theories in recent years has blurred the distinctions among them to a considerable extent. John Dollard and Neal E. Miller, for example, are usually classified as behaviorists on the basis of their intellectual precursors, for both were much influenced by the work of Clark L. Hull, yet their learning theories incorporate some aspects of Freud's findings. Contemporary psychological theories tend to combine elements from the Gestalt psychologist's studies of perception, from Lewin's conception of organisms operating in a field, from traditional behavioralism, and from Freudian psychoanalysis. Psychology is becoming increasingly eclectic.

BEHAVIORISM

The approach to psychology usually designated "behaviorism" or "connectionism" is typically American, and so

Social Psychology (Basic Books, Inc., 1965); E. E. Hagen, *On the Theory of Social Change* (Dorsey Press, Inc., 1962); Calvin S. Hall and Gardner Lindzey, *Theories of Personality* (John Wiley & Sons, Inc., 1957); Gardner Lindzey (ed.), *Handbook of Social Psychology* (2 vols.; Addison-Wesley Publishing Co., Inc., 1956); K. B. Madsen, *Theories of Motivation* (Munksgaard, 1959); Melvin H. Marx, *Theories in Contemporary Psychology* (Macmillan Co., 1963); Benjamin B. Wolman, *Contemporary Theories and Systems in Psychology* (Harper & Bros., 1960).

Specialized texts: Helen E. Durkin, *The Group in Depth* (International Universities Press, Inc., 1964); Sidney Hook (ed.), *The Dimensions of Mind* (P. F. Collier, Inc., 1961); Melanie Klein, *The Psychoanalysis of Children* (Hogarth Press, 1950); Wolfgang Kohler, *Gestalt Psychology* (Mentor Books, 1947); David C. McClelland, *The Roots of Consciousness* (D. Van Nostrand Co., Inc., 1964); V. H. Mottram, *The Physical Basis of Personality* (Citadel Press, 1963); David Rapaport, *Emotions and Memory* (Science Editions, 1961); Philip Rieff, *The Triumph of the Therapeutic* (Harper and Row, 1966); S. Scheidlinger, *Psychoanalysis and Group Behavior: A Study of Freudian Group Psychology* (W. W. Norton & Co., Inc., 1952); David Stafford-Clark, *Psychiatry Today* (2d ed.; Penguin Books, Inc., 1963); Robert Thompson, *The Psychology of Thinking* (Penguin Books, Inc., 1959); M. D. Vernon, *The Psychology of Perception* (Penguin Books, Inc., 1962).

great has its influence been in this country that American psychology was, until very recently, largely behaviorist in orientation. It originates with Ivan Pavlov's studies of conditioning and with John B. Watson's determined effort to rid psychology of the then prevailing mentalism and use of "instinctual" explanations. Throughout the 20th century, behaviorism has remained radically empirical, oriented to experiment and quantification, and eminently practical—closely tied to the educational system, for example, through its emphasis on learning theory. The aim, originally, was to explain the behavior of the organism in terms of an observable stimulus (S) and an observable response (R); hence the name "stimulus-response" theory. Behaviorists sought rules or laws governing the relations between these two variables, most commonly in terms of the frequency with which S and R were related in the organism's experience or the time lapse between stimulus and response. Behaviorism did not necessarily deny subjectivity, particularly in man, but ignored it. Partly this was a consequence of Watson's methodological assumptions, but partly it can be explained by Watson's reductionism—for example, his belief that the learning process involved the creation of actual physical connections within the neural system, the building of patterns of reflex arcs.

The Watsonian paradigm was parsimonious enough to please the most exacting and rigorous enough to satisfy the most extreme of empiricists. But the behavior of organisms, even the white rats so much favored by psychologists, proved too complex to be handled by the simple S-R relationship. The organism was then granted an innate impetus to action, commonly labeled a "drive" but very close, in many respects, to the older notion of instinct. The effect of behavior on the organism performing the action (simple feedback) was introduced through the notion of reinforcement or reward; the classic illustration is E. L. Thorndike's "law of effect," which holds that the strength of the relationship between S and R depends on the satisfaction or annoyance produced within the organism by the consequences of behavior. Clark L. Hull, the very influential Yale psychologist, went on to postulate an intervening mechanism within the organism that mediated between S and R, though in Hull's case the mediating structure itself operated on strictly mechanical principles. The concept of the organism seeking goals or seeking to avoid certain outcomes was utilized by Edward C. Tolman in a system he called "purposive behaviorism," which added to organismic capacities the ability to produce a cognitive map of experience that could be used as a basis for goal seeking and avoidance. Present perceptions, according to Tolman, served as signs which the organism interpreted in terms of a total complex of experience (gestalt), including remembered objects (to which the organism reacted positively or negatively), thereby producing sets of expectations about the means to be used for attaining given ends.[1]

The behaviorist conceptualization of human behavior remains fairly simple. There is an organism, subject to stimuli and capable of responses or behavior. The organism itself is a kind of empty shell into which behaviorists of different persuasions have fitted various kinds of conceptual machinery in their search for explanations of particular phenomena. Some few radical behaviorists like B. F. Skinner have refused adamantly to postulate anything whatever about the interior of the organism, treating all behavior as an effect of external conditioning and hence explicable in terms of observables.[2] Most behaviorists, however, have

[1]Edward C. Tolman, *Purposive Behavior in Animals and Men* (University of California Press, 1934).

[2]Skinner has provided some very interesting demonstrations of the efficacy of the conditioning or "shaping" procedures he advocates as an explanation of behavior. See B. F. Skinner, *Science and Human Behavior* (Free Press of Glencoe, Inc., 1965). For an interesting treatment of some of the implications of Skinner's psychology for society, see his utopian novel, *Walden Two*.

found it necessary to postulate at least some few capacities within the organism. Neal E. Miller and John Dollard, for example, make use of a drive-reduction structure that is derived largely from Clark L. Hull; it postulates a minimal capacity on the part of the individual to learn and retain relational conceptions which permit the identification of cues in the current situation on which behavior is based. In their now classic formulation, drives are initiated by stimuli, guided by cues, so that they produce responses that are rewarding and lead to a reduction of the drive—a return to balance or homeostasis.[3]

Miller and Dollard, despite the influence of Freud, remain fairly close to Hull, or even Watson. Others propose a much more extensive system of intervening variables within the organism for the explanation of human behavior. Charles E. Osgood, to take a typical example, points out that a single-stage S-R model simply cannot handle problems of perceptual organization, motor skill development, or human response to symbols and signs—all essential components of human acts.[4] While Osgood is rather careful to note that he considers S-R psychology insufficient rather than invalid, he does propose a principle of sensory integration (based on the frequency of pairing of stimuli in experience), a principle of motor integration (again based on pairing frequency in output or behavior), and a major extension of the model to cover symbolic and representational phenomena. Like Hull, he introduces an additional S-R stage within the organism, a "learned, self-stimulating, response-like process," which he believes is sufficient to account for the different behavior elicited by objects and the symbols or signs that represent those objects. Osgood's

[3]John Dollard and Neal E. Miller, *Personality and Psychotherapy: An Analysis in Terms of Learning, Thinking, and Culture* (McGraw-Hill Book Co., 1950).

[4]Charles E. Osgood, "Behavior Theory and the Social Sciences," in Roland Young (ed.), *Approaches to the Study of Politics* (Northwestern University Press, 1958).

structure resembles that of O. H. Mowrer (who was also much influenced by Freud) in that Mowrer suggests that there are two kinds of learning, one based on drive reduction and the other, sign learning, falling into a different class. Both Osgood and Mowrer, however, remain committed to the basic S-R pattern, or perhaps more accurately, the S-O-R, where O equals the hypothetical internal capacities of the organism.

Behaviorist psychology, despite its emphasis on learning theory, has had little to say about human social relations— which is rather surprising, since most human behavior is social and is presumably learned and not innate. Instead, behaviorists have concentrated on the single act of learning and, for the most part, on the single individual. Much of the research conducted within the behaviorist conceptual frame- work has in fact dealt with the behavior of rats and pigeons under artificial laboratory conditions. This led to consid- erable criticism from European "ethologists" like Konrad Lorenz and his followers, who argued that principles of behavior based on data obtained by the use of artificial mazes were systematically misleading. The ethologists sug- gested that animal behavior be studied *in situ*, a suggestion that has recently begun to be followed by American psy- chologists. Clark L. Hull promised a volume on interactions among organisms but did not live to complete it. In his *Behavior System*, only one theorem of 133 deals with social interaction, and it is not very useful: *"Theorem 133: Every voluntary social interaction, in order to be repeated consistently, must result in a substantial reinforcement to the activity of each party to the transaction."*[5] Edward C.

---

[5]Clark L. Hull, *A Behavior System* (Yale University Press, 1952), p. 327. See also his *Principles of Behavior* (Appleton-Century, Inc., 1943), and *Essentials of Behavior* (Yale University Press, 1951). Hull favored the construction of a rigid deductive systém from which theorems and particular statements could be deduced and then verified empirically, or modified to suit empirical findings. The final structure comprised 17 fundamental axioms or postulates and 133 theorems, many with several corollaries. Most

Tolman produced a psychological model which was fitted into Talcott Parsons' structuralist-functionalist approach to social theory, but the model is heuristic rather than explanatory.[6] Some few contemporary social psychologists adopt a frankly behavioristic psychology, but the results have not been very startling. Dollard and Miller, for example, originated a theory of social imitation as a base for interpersonal relations that has been much criticized. Carl I. Hovland and others associated with the Yale research center for the study of communication and attitude formation have carried out some rigorous and fascinating studies.[*] Albert Bandura and Richard H. Walters have done some of the most suggestive recent work by behaviorists in social psychology, but still in the "approach" stage of theory development. As Morton Deutsch and Robert M. Krauss point out, "their research involves less systematic theory and more common sense than meets the eye."[7] Finally, the work

of the axioms and theorems deal with very precisely detailed research findings in maze trials. The "system" or model is wholly beyond application to social phenomena.

[6]Edward C. Tolman, "A Psychological Model," in Talcott Parsons and Edward Shils (eds.), *Toward A General Theory of Action* (Harvard University Press, 1962).

[*]Hovland's work deserves to be known better by political scientists. The studies of the American soldier, Volumes I and II of the *Studies in Social Psychology in World War II* sponsored by the Social Science Research Council, are cited fairly often. But see also Carl I. Hovland, Arthur A. Lumsdaine, and Fred D. Sheffield, *Experiments on Mass Communication* (Princeton University Press, 1949); Carl I. Hovland, Irving L. Janis, and Harold H. Kelley, *Communication and Persuasion: Psychological Studies of Opinion Change* (Yale University Press, 1953); Carl I. Hovland *et al.*, *The Order of Presentation in Persuasion* (Yale University Press, 1957); and Muzafer Sherif and Carl I. Hovland, *Social Judgment: Assimilation and Contrast Effects in Communication and Attitude Change* (Yale University Press, 1961). Other volumes in the series deal with personality and persuasion, and with attitude organization and change. There is no better source of information on what is known of the ways in which people can be induced to change their attitudes.

[7]Albert Bandura and Richard H. Walters, *Social Learning and Personality Development* (Holt, Rinehart & Winston, Inc., 1963). For a good critique of behaviorism and social psychology, see Morton Deutsch and Robert M. Krauss, *Theories in Social Psychology* (Basic Books, 1965), especially chap. iv.

of George C. Homans is at least partly the result of a behavioristic framework, largely because of Homans' methodological commitment to verifiability, and perhaps because
Homans and B. F. Skinner were closely associated for a
number of years. In a manner reminiscent of Hull, Homans
suggests that the empirical data obtained through the study
of groups can be subsumed under five basic postulates which
link behavior to (1) rewards in the past; (2) frequency of rewards; (3) quality of rewards; (4) satisfaction with social
treatment; and (5) what appears as a restatement of the law
of diminishing returns applied to interpersonal relations.[8]
The use of a qualitative concept of value faces Homans
with the same problem that John Stuart Mill encountered
when he introduced qualitative distinctions into utilitarian
thought—some standard unit of measurement is needed, and
none has yet been found.

Critique and Applications

Behaviorist psychology began with a strong commitment
to observation and a powerful bias to laboratory experiment;
even with the addition of intervening variables, those com-
mitments remain. Much of the research carried out under
its aegis has in fact been structured to maximize the observable element in behavior; for example, it has been limited
to the simplest of learning situations and to the simpler animals like the rat or the pigeon, and the variable factors in
the experimental situation have been very carefully controlled. Little experimentation has been done *in situ,* and
only a few behaviorists have worked with man. That seems
more than mere coincidence. For the point that occurs first
when we ask about the value of behaviorist psychology in
the explanation of social or political phenomena is that the
method commonly associated with behaviorism is almost
impossible to apply to the study of man. The variables can-

[8]George C. Homans, *Social Behavior: Its Elementary Forms* (Harcourt,
Brace & World, Inc., 1961).

not be controlled; the behavior is too rich and complex. How, under these conditions, are S and R to be isolated? And if they cannot be isolated, how is a connection to be established between them? Behaviorism, in other words, has—historically, at least—favored a single-factor explanation; and though modern techniques of multivariate analysis may facilitate its application to human affairs, there remain formidable practical difficulties to be overcome before it can acquire much explanatory power.

A second difficulty, this time of principle, is far more serious. How is behaviorist psychology to deal with creative actions? Most of the social psychologists who incline to behaviorism have tried to deal with the problem by focusing on imitation; but there are clearly situations in which human beings, and even the primates, behave in a manner that could not possibly have been learned through imitation. Wolfgang Kohler, for example, cites a case in which one of his apes, which had encountered nothing to parallel the problem in its previous experience, was able to fit together the parts of a stick so that it could be used to obtain food from outside the cage. Men quite often demonstrate such "insights," as Kohler called them, and an adequate psychology will have to deal with them. Osgood's postulate of an integrating mechanism might do the trick, though the functioning of the mechanism could not be spelled out in detail in a brief article, but would it then be compatible with the methodological assumptions on which behaviorism rests?

These two problems alone are formidable. In addition, there are certain practical limitations on the usefulness of behavioral psychology in political science that cannot be ignored. Because social phenomena are very complex, the *ceteris paribus* clause in behavioral explanations of human behavior is extremely broad. In other words, the meaning of "stimulus" and "response" is rarely simple. In most cases, humans perform in a complex environment that is very hard to control. The decision as to what stimulus has actually generated a given action may be very hard to make. To take an example, how can we decide when mass propaganda is effective? Although the propaganda is present in the environment, it is clear that humans are highly selective in their reactions to the environment; a mere statistical juxtaposition does not suffice to demonstrate influence. The response of the person being studied is equally difficult to define in real life. Social psychology may in fact have more use for a theory that will explain the way in which humans discriminate among potential stimuli in the environment than a theory that relates stimuli to behavior.

These problems and limitations can be illustrated quite readily from the few applications of behaviorist psychology to political affairs that are now available. One of the more recent political studies to rely explicitly on a behaviorist formulation of psychology is Lester W. Milbrath's *Political Participation,* and a brief examination of chapter ii, "Political Participation as a Function of Stimuli," will demonstrate some of the practical and theoretical difficulties of that approach.[9] The phenomenon Milbrath wants to explain is political participation, or involvement in politics, defined operationally as voting, discussing politics, wearing a button, petitioning, campaigning, contributing to political funds, seeking office, etc. His conceptual structure is assigned explicitly to the influence of Clark L. Hull and B. F. Skinner.[10] He introduces the concept of "predispositions" into the discussion in a manner that Skinner, and perhaps Hull as well, would probably not have approved, though the term may mean no more than "drive" as it is ordinarily used in psychology. The strength of "more strictly political" predispositions (beliefs and attitudes) he makes dependent on reinforcement or reward. He accepts the implicit hedonistic division between positive and negative valence that behaviorism

[9]Lester W. Milbrath, *Political Participation* (Rand McNally & Co., 1965).
[10]*Ibid.,* p. 29.

in its modern form depends on as a discriminator between attraction and withdrawal. The "model" is incomplete, and no predictive claims are made for it, but Milbrath clearly believes that it is capable of some measure of explanation. Chapter ii seeks to demonstrate the relationship between stimuli and political participation, using data taken mainly from the voting studies and opinion surveys. For purposes of criticism, the data will be assumed correct.

If our criticisms of behaviorism are sound, Milbrath should find it difficult to define his stimulus and his response operationally, and that turns out to be the case. As Milbrath himself notes, political action must be preceded by relevant stimulation before his conceptual framework can function. The possibility that political action may appear without external stimulation is ignored, and no evidence bearing on the point is offered—the position is taken as axiomatic. That can be safely passed by, but the problems met in attempting to define a stimulus are less tractable. A "perceptual screen" is postulated which sifts incoming stimulations (which are obviously of all kinds and quite beyond enumeration); that is, some persons in a given environment pick up the available political stimuli, whereas others shut them out.[11] But what makes a stimulus "political"? Is it "objectively" political in some sense that makes it possible to say that there are political stimuli in a given environment whether or not anyone receives them, or is a stimulus political because the individual who is influenced by it conceives it in political terms? In the first case the author must produce a definition of "political" that will allow him to assert that there are such stimuli present in an environment. That Milbrath has not done. In the second case the quantity of political stimuli in an environment is indeterminate, and no statements about the relationship between stimuli and political participation are possible. That is, either Milbrath cannot discuss

[11]*Ibid.*, p. 44.

the number of political stimuli in an environment; or if the term is considered objectively, the significant variable becomes the "perceptual screen" and not the presence or absence of stimuli.

The discussion in Milbrath's chapter suggests that the second of these choices has been made. Consider the following generalizations:

1. The more stimuli a person receives, the greater the likelihood that he will participate.[12]
2. Persons with a positive attraction to politics are more likely to receive stimuli and participate than other persons.[13]
3. It is a truism that the greater the number of political stimuli available in an environment, the greater the likelihood that an individual will pick them up.

Now, (1) is good behaviorist strategy; Milbrath wants to link behavior to frequency of stimulation. But if (2) is also accepted, then (1) creates circularity, and (3) may be false. Certainly (3) is no truism. If stimuli are defined in terms of the individual's interpretation of them as political, then it is statistically likely that more stimuli will be received in large populations than in small populations, other things being equal, but the number of stimuli cannot possibly be a function of the number of units of potential political stimuli because that is an undefined term. If stimuli are defined objectively, it is still not a truism to assert that the number of stimuli received is a function of the number of stimuli in the environment once a qualitative distinction has been introduced into the population; that is, "People who are attracted to politics (interested, concerned, curious, intense preferences) expose themselves more to stimuli about politics than those not so affected."[14] Given the qualification, the number of stimuli that actually reach their goal may be a function of the distribution of subgroups within the population rather

[12]*Ibid.*, p. 39.
[13]*Ibid.*
[14]*Ibid.*, p. 44.

than a function of the number of stimuli in the environment. One could not argue, for example, that if the number of gamma rays striking the earth were to double, that would increase the likelihood that some individual on earth would perceive them because the human perceptive apparatus is incapable of such perceptions. But the postulation of a perceptive screen introduces precisely the same possibility into the discussion of perception of political stimuli. Because of the extreme difficulty of defining a complex variable adequately, Milbrath finds himself discussing the relation between political dispositions and the reception of political stimuli rather than the relation between political stimuli and political participation.

The effort to establish a relation between stimuli and participation fails, then, on definitional grounds; the crucial factor in the discussion turns out to be the individual's disposition toward political matters, a subjective rather than an objective phenomenon. Is any major investigation of social phenomena likely to lead to this same kind of phenomenon? Can behaviorist psychology handle these phenomena adequately? For the present, the second question can be answered in the negative with some confidence. As Milbrath himself points out, the research data are inadequate for a full discussion of perceptual screens, though he suggests that in terms of his conceptual framework the perceptual screen excludes stimuli as "a way of protecting the personality."[15] But that leads only to deeper and murkier water; behaviorist psychology is notoriously awkward in dealing with personality. Whether explanations of social phenomena always and necessarily involve questions of attitude, personality, and motivation one cannot at present say, though the likelihood is that explanations which do refer to these properties of human behavior will be more satisfying and perhaps more suggestive than those that do not. It is not acci-

15*Ibid.*, p. 45.

dental, surely, that behaviorist theorists like Mowrer and Sears have begun to make use of Freudian insights in their work, and Freud is rich and suggestive in precisely those areas. For the moment, however, the most that can be said is that psychological explanations of social phenomena that rely upon the behaviorist arm of modern psychology have been only moderately successful as compared with field theory or with psychoanalytic psychology.

GESTALT AND FIELD PSYCHOLOGY

Behaviorist psychology is firmly rooted in empiricist methodology; it seeks explanations of the behavior of living organisms in observations of externals. Gestalt psychology and "field theory," on the other hand, begin deliberately with conscious human experience, with the internal or subjective aspect of human behavior. The methodological bias is quite different, and the philosophic sources are diametrically opposed. Behaviorism appeals to the empirical-associationist tradition, to John Stuart Mill, Ernst Mach, and the "scientific" outlook; Gestalt psychology rejects positivism as inappropriate to the study of human behavior and appeals instead to the phenomenologist tradition, to Immanuel Kant and Wilhelm Dilthey, and most important of all, Edmund Husserl. For the most part, Gestalt psychology is found in continental Europe, though Wolfgang Kohler and K. Koffka, the two leading figures in the movement, both moved to the United States, as did Kurt Lewin, the originator of field theory. Neither Gestalt psychology nor Lewin's field theory is used for explanatory purposes; they are not coherent theoretical structures. Strictly speaking, both are approaches rather than theories. But the conceptual framework that emerged from the perception studies of the Gestalt psychologists and Lewin's work with fields and group behavior is perhaps the most influential element in modern social psychology. Both approaches to psychology have proved remarkably fruitful, generating large amounts of research and opening new fields for speculation and inquiry—group structure, leadership, attitudinal change, social conformity, and group affiliation, to mention only a few. We can reasonably expect, therefore, that political scientists will use them with increasing frequency in the future.

Gestalt Psychology

Gestalt psychology sacrifices rigid empiricism in favor of "significant" studies of human behavior. Gestaltists oppose quantification of psychological data as premature, preferring to deal with verbal reports of behavior rather than rigorous observation of details. They observe human behavior directly, avoiding studies of animals in artificial learning situations (though Kohler's famous studies of learning in apes are perhaps exceptions). They have carried out very large numbers of experiments, mainly dealing with human perception, and have done much to clarify our understanding of the way in which man perceives his external environment. Inasmuch as the structure of these studies is fairly readily applicable to the study of man's perception of his social environment as well as his physical environment, social psychologists have taken a great interest in Gestalt methods.

Gestalt psychology starts with the assumption that man must be considered as an entity, that it is a mistake in strategy to try to analyze human behavior into constituent elements after the manner of the behaviorists. Gestaltists dislike the "switchboard" conception of learning developed by the behaviorists, preferring to think of brain action as the development of a complex and interrelated field in constant flux. Furthermore, Gestalt psychology asserts, and it can produce a substantial body of supporting evidence, that man perceives his environment in complex, integrated units—in gestalts or wholes that are structured and organized patterns. A great deal of time and energy has been spent trying to establish the principles on which these gestalts or patterns are constructed. Experiments demonstrated that pattern formation depends on factors like similarity of elements, proximity, common boundaries among elements, common direction among elements, and, of course, past experience. More important is the principle called the rule of "closure," which asserts a tendency on the part of a human observer to close or "round out" partial patterns—much as children complete a drawing by connecting numbered dots. Finally, there is the famous, and somewhat obscure, law of prägnanz, which asserts that humans tend toward the simplest and "best" gestalt pattern available in conscious experiment. This "law" proved, in many ways, the most stimulating of all Gestalt suggestions. The hypothesis states, roughly, that when human beliefs and ideas are not simply and clearly interrelated, tension is generated within the person which leads to activity designed to relieve tension or restore balance—a form of drive reduction. A number of contemporary social psychologists have taken the hypothesis as a point of departure—theories that deal with cognitive balance and cognitive dissonance, for example.

Like behaviorism, Gestalt psychology is hedonistic, assuming that humans react positively or negatively to elements of the environment. It also takes for granted the goal-directedness of behavior. But unlike behaviorism, Gestalt psychology places great emphasis on the integrative operations performed by the brain, on the kind of perceptual reorganization of the elements of experience that is called "insight." There has been much concern among Gestaltists for the way in which humans handle sets of perceptions rather than for the relation between a particular perception and a particular reaction. In effect, this implies a bias toward the study of creative thinking rather than response behavior, and the Gestaltists in fact postulated three kinds of learning (by conditioning, by trial and error, and by the regrouping of experience into an ends-means relationship) and concentrated their research mainly on the third. Although Gestalt psychology provided no overall conceptual framework for explaining all forms of human behavior, its contribution to the study of thought and perception has been highly significant. The results were readily adapted to the study of social relations, they satisfied intuitive judgments about the nature of human behavior better than behaviorist psychology, and the experimental results seemed to justify most of the basic assumptions on which the Gestalt approach to psychology rested. If the results were more ambiguous than those obtained through behaviorist studies, and more difficult to verify, they were also more interesting. Gestalt psychology had an enormous impact on social psychology, though it has not yet been used widely by political scientists.

Field Theory

"[Field] theory can hardly be called a theory in the usual sense . . . .*Field theory is probably best characterized as a method:* namely, a method *of analyzing causal relations and building scientific constructs.*"[16] Kurt Lewin's judgment of the nature of the approach to the social theory he created is precisely correct. Though Lewin borrowed extensively from topological geometry and from vector analysis, the vectors and the topology were not combined in a formal mathematical structure; both were modified to suit Lewin's requirements. That is, the axioms of topological geometry and vector analysis are not satisfied in Lewin's usage; hence the formal transformations possible in those two branches of mathematics cannot be performed with his conceptions. Lewin produced a classification system and not a formal logical structure, and in the strict sense of the term, his constructions are heuristic rather than explanatory. But if our prime criterion for the adequacy of a conceptual frame-

---

[16]Kurt Lewin, *Field Theory in Social Science,* ed. Dorwin Cartwright (Harper & Bros., 1951), p. 45 (italics in original).

work is the amount of research and inquiry that it stimulates, then Lewin has been one of the more successful psychologists in modern times, almost the equal of Freud. Curiously enough, his "field" construct has rarely been applied as a whole, and his work in personality theory is usually considered the best part of his output, but the impetus he provided for the study of group dynamics through his writings and the works of his students, not to mention the Institute for the Study of Group Dynamics that he established at the Massachusetts Institute of Technology, was simply enormous.[17]

Lewin begins, in good Gestalt fashion, with the situation as a whole of the individual, which he calls "life space." The life space is psychological, bounded by the physical environment (with which it interacts), and is defined solely in terms of the present. It is divided into regions or differentiated situational elements that emerge as the human being develops. Here, Lewin's topological concepts enter the picture, for the psychic regions are connected, and there are boundaries between the regions (which may appear as barriers); but as in topology, neither distance nor direction are relevant—topology is a logic of connections among bounded surfaces. Lewin tried to offset the limitations of topology by using "vectors" to indicate psychological locomotion or movement, but the dimensions of the vectors and their direction cannot be stipulated fully within the topological conceptual framework. Each of the regions in the life space has a "valence," a positive or negative attraction for the sentient person, and "movement" by the person toward or away from different regions in the life space is explained in terms of these valences. Personality is treated as a system of regions, and personality differentiation is explained in terms of region changes, changes in the strength of the vectors that propel

[17]The Institute for the Study of Group Dynamics is now located at the University of Michigan at Ann Arbor.

the individual from one region to another, changes in the location and strength of the boundaries among regions, and alterations in the properties of the regions. The qualities of regions and boundaries are dealt with in some detail, and there is some experimental evidence to support the kinds of predictions made possible by Lewin's conceptualization.

Dynamically, field theory, like all other psychological theories that concern themselves with subjective experience, depends on the concept of equilibrium and on tension reduction, though the terms in which tension and tension reduction were stipulated allowed for a much richer conceptualization than strict S-R approaches. Sources of tension may be psychic or environmental, positive or negative. The thought of an ice-cream cone or the sight of an ice-cream truck may create a positive desire in a child. If the child has no money, there is a barrier between desire and goal, and the child will seek to surpass the barrier (unless another desire intervenes with an even stronger valence or attraction), perhaps by trying to borrow money from a playmate or by returning home to seek funds from one of its parents. The child is thought of as creating "paths" through its life space toward the goal of an ice-cream cone, and such paths may be quite ingenious and complex. The "direction" of the activity is toward the goal, but not in the ordinary sense of the word "direction"—the meaning is psychic, not physical. The child may pursue its goal very realistically or quite unrealistically. All of these points can be represented in the diagrams that field theorists commonly use to illustrate their conception of action within a field, using the concepts need, tension, valence, barrier, time, and an unreality-reality dimension. Achieving the goal produces equilibrium. Suppose the child fails to obtain the desired ice cream. In that case the disequilibrium continues until the genesis of another tension leads the child off on another course. The suggestion that persons whose strivings for goal attainment are largely frustrated may end in breakdown or escape into fantasy fits very readily into the conceptual scheme simply by adding concepts such as "substitute" locomotion or "imaginary" locomotion.

No brief summary can do justice to the richness, complexity, and suggestiveness of Lewin's development of his conceptual scheme. It can be used to chart an enormous range of behaviors and to illustrate qualities of behavior that are intuitively important yet very difficult to approach through behaviorist methodological principles. It facilitates the treatment of symbolic manipulation by the individual and provides a framework in which quite complex behavior patterns can be related systematically to particular goals; that is, it leads us to expect patterns of behavior that might otherwise seem wholly unconnected. The child seeking an ice-cream cone may have learned from experience that sulking and pouting at home will produce the desired coin; and in Lewin's terms, that behavior is quite reasonable and realistic. To try to explain the objective aspects of the child's behavior in pure stimulus-response terms, without the mediating process that makes the behavior a means to a further goal, would be exceptionally difficult. Lewin is weak in learning theory, on which he wrote very little; hence, his structure does little to explain changes in the life space and its regions. Furthermore, the life space is defined entirely in terms of the present—Lewin ignores the history of the individual—and in this, he differs sharply from the Freudians and others who feel that the explanation of present behavior lies wholly or partly in the past experience of the person. In sum, Lewin's structure is more suggestive than explanatory; but that is not necessarily a criticism at this stage of psychological development. A brief examination of the work being done in the study of group behavior, which is derived mainly though not entirely from Lewin's work, will illustrate that suggestiveness.

Group Dynamics

The term "group dynamics" has acquired a certain popular currency in recent years, and this has led some academics to regard any study of groups and their properties with a certain amount of suspicion and dislike; William H. Whyte's strictures against group dynamics in *The Organization Man* are a good case in point. The principles of "democratic" management, for example, are sometimes referred to as "group dynamics," as are management training techniques like the "buzz session" or "role playing." In its legitimate academic sense, group dynamics is concerned with the systematic study of the properties of human groups and is justified on the very good grounds that much of the important activity in human life is conducted in groups and more knowledge of the dynamics of these associations is needed. It may well be that a certain amount of nonsense is published under the general rubric of group dynamics; but that field of inquiry has no monopoly on the production of nonsense or trivia, and if some of the work that has been done is not very impressive, some of the experimental data and theoretical constructions are quite relevant to any branch of social inquiry and have in fact been employed as a framework for criticizing traditional conceptualizations of social and political phenomena in a very trenchant manner.[18]

There is no single theoretical structure for dealing with groups that can properly be attributed to group dynamics; in fact, even Kurt Lewin's work did not "set the pattern" for the field, though many of the conceptualizations employed by those engaged in the inquiry have been taken from Lewin and from Gestalt psychology. Like other forms of psychological inquiry, group dynamics has become increasingly eclectic in recent years, and traces of behaviorism, psychoanalysis, and neo-Freudianism are quite evident in the work of some of its practitioners. Certain basic properties of groups have been investigated more or less systemati-

[18]For example, Robert T. Golembiewski, *Behavior and Organization: O & M and the Small Group* (Rand McNally & Co., 1962); or James G. March and Herbert A. Simon, *Organizations* (John Wiley & Sons, Inc., 1958).

cally, and the existence of an Institute for the Study of
Group Dynamics provides for some continuity in research.
Beyond that, group dynamics has developed in a "normal"
academic fashion, except perhaps that it has been rather
better funded than most branches of social inquiry. Dorwin
Cartwright and Alvin Zander, in what is perhaps the best
general survey of work being done in the field, divide their
materials into five broad areas of study—group cohesiveness,
group pressures and group standards, individual motives
and group goals, leadership and group performance, and the
structural properties of groups—and that is probably as fair
an ordering of the material as one could produce at this
time.[19] Some work has been done with "power fields," with
conflict within groups, and with the relationship between
communications within and among groups and other aspects
of group life, but the main line of emphasis has been directed along the terms outlined by Cartwright and Zander.
Most of the studies have sought to relate two or three factors to particular outcomes—for example, social stratification and cohesiveness, authoritarian leadership and uniformity, the effect of interruptions on group activity, and so on.
Obviously, there are sometimes great difficulties with op-
erationalization of conceptions, and the search for meaningful indicators of "cohesiveness" and "conformity" has occupied a good deal of time. Not all of the indicators employed
by group dynamics studies are persuasive, by any means.
The relationship between the number of "I" and the number
of "we" remarks in casual discussion, for example, is at best
a very loose indicator indeed of "social cohesiveness," however the latter is defined. And in many of the experiments
conducted with natural groups, control over variables would

[19]Dorwin Cartwright and Alvin Zander (eds.), *Group Dynamics: Research and Theory* (2d ed.; Harper and Row, 1960). Chapter ii, which
deals with some of the basic issues and assumptions in the field, is an
excellent introduction to the literature. See also Deutsch and Krauss,
op. cit., chap. iii.

hardly satisfy the canons of inquiry of the behaviorist. Nevertheless, by variation in experimental techniques, it has been possible to define problems much more clearly, if not to solve them. For example, it is clear from studies that have been made of group leadership that the position of the leader is crucial in determining group atmosphere and structuring communications movement, though neither the mechanism by which leadership operates to influence these features of group life nor the variables in leadership that determine particular kinds of outcomes can be specified very precisely.

Criticisms and Applications

Gestalt psychology, field theory, and group dynamics enjoy much the same advantages and suffer from the same disabilities so far as their application to social phenomena is concerned. None of the three is a "theory," strictly speaking; each is an approach, a general orientation to the subject matter and not an explanatory device. Within the broad framework provided by these approaches, a variety of specific theories has been developed, particularly in field theory and in group dynamics. In field theory, for example, a number of attempts have been made to deal with human behavior in a general way, viewing it as a consequence of tensions and conflict within the individual's life space.

Leon Festinger's "theory of cognitive dissonance" is perhaps the best-known example of this class of theories.[20] Briefly, Festinger argues that "dissonance" or incompatibility among individual cognitions leads necessarily to individual action designed to reduce the dissonance; essentially, Festinger has applied a drive-reduction conception to cognitions. If the proposition could be demonstrated, it would have rather interesting consequences for our thinking about curiosity, and corollary effects on educational philosophy. For

[20]Leon Festinger, A Theory of Cognitive Dissonance (Row, Peterson & Co., 1957).

example, the introduction of dissonance into the education structure would be an excellent indirect stimulus to individual search for knowledge. However, though Festinger deals with his conceptions systematically, the conceptions themselves are rather vague and hard to relate to empirical data. What is the operational meaning of dissonance or inconsistency? Are there degrees of dissonance? How can they be determined? Such questions are hard to answer from Festinger's treatment of the argument. A review of the experimental literature produced some stringent criticism of both methods and interpretation,[21] and a rebuttal of the critics; and Festinger was led to revise parts of his theory (an excellent illustration of the value of stimulating speculation when freedom of controversy obtains).

An example from field theory illustrates how similar are the strengths and weaknesses of the two approaches—they have great heuristic value but limited verifiability, and they are conceptually obscure. In an effort to formalize a theory of social power, John R. P. French, Jr., has produced a deductive structure dealing with power relations within a group, communications patterns within a group, and the relation among opinions within a group.[22] The formal model, which is quite improperly termed a "theory," consists of three axioms and a number of theorems, some few of which are included in French's short article. The postulates are:

Postulate 1: For any given discrepancy of opinion between A and B, the strength of the resultant force which an inducer, A, can exert on an inducee, B, in the direction of agreeing with A's opinion, is proportional to the strength of the bases of power of A over B. ("Power" is defined as the maximum force A can exert on B less the maximum resistance that B can exert against

---

[21]Natalie P. Chapanis and Alphonse Chapanis, "Cognitive Dissonance: Five Years Later," *Psychological Bulletin,* Vol. LXI. But see also Irwin Silverman, "In Defense of Dissonance Theory," *Psychological Bulletin,* Vol. LXII.

[22]John R. P. French, Jr., "A Formal Theory of Social Power," in Cartwright and Zander, *op. cit.,* pp. 727–43.

A; the basis of power is the "enduring relationship" between A and B which gives rise to power).

Postulate 2: The strength of the force which an inducer, A exerts on an inducee, B, in the direction of agreeing with A's opinion, is proportional to the size of the discrepancy between their opinions.

Postulate 3: In one unit (time required for all members who are being influenced to shift their opinion to the point of equilibrium of all the forces operating at the beginning of the unit), each person who is being influenced will change his opinion until he reaches the equilibrium point where the resultant force is zero.

Typical theorems are:

Theorem 1: For all possible patterns of initial opinion, in a completely connected power structure, the opinions of all members will reach a common equilibrium equal to the arithmetic mean of the initial opinions of all the members, and this final common opinion will be reached in one unit.

Theorem 2: In a weakly connected group the members will not reach common agreement except under special conditions in the distribution of initial opinions.

What are we to make of this model or "theory"? Postulate 3, which is adapted from Lewin, is beyond test; or as French puts it, "this assumption is close to a conceptual definition which cannot be directly tested."[23] Postulate 2 is typically imprecise, for the key terms, "strength of the force" and "discrepancy between their opinions," are exceptionally difficult to operationalize. Postulate 1 suffers from the same handicap, because the "strength of the resultant force" is held proportional to the "strength of the bases of power." Ultimately, we are led back to the crucial difficulty—the meaning of "power" and "force." Until they are operationalized, the model has feet of clay.

As a rule, the shortcomings of formal models are most easily detected at the level of fundamental definitions of

[23]*Ibid.*, p. 733.

terms and relationships. Given a very few basic postulates, most competent logicians can produce a powerful and unassailable system of relations among elements. But so far as the empirical value of models is concerned, if there are no clear rules for linking the elements of the formal system to empirical data and the postulated relational rules are unrealistic, then the superstructure is empirically meaningless, however elaborate it may appear. French has written a short paper, and it is very difficult to spell out all of the details in a brief space; but in view of the great difficulty that others have had in their dealings with the concept of power (Bertrand Russell, Bertrand de Jouvenel, Harold D. Lasswell, and Abraham Kaplan), anyone proposing to use the concept has an obligation to spell out the indicators in some detail so that the validity of the usage, or its meaningfulness, can be judged. It is doubtful, for example, that the *amount* of power a given person can exercise can be specified in anything but very gross terms, yet such comparisons are crucial for French's model. There is another dubious hidden assumption in the model, to wit, that the prime connections among members of a group all lie within the group. The discussion of connectedness tends to ignore the social context. Yet the members of a very loose workman's group may, through religious affinity, find themselves in close agreement on a number of issues which no amount of study of strictly group mores or power structure could explain. Is it reasonable to assume that in most groups it is the group relations that count most heavily? What of the well-known conflicts between teen-age children and the family, when the former import the mores of their peer groups into the family structure?

The application of field theory and group dynamics to social and political phenomena has taken place mainly in the field of organization, though conceptions taken from group dynamics, known more often as "small-group theory," are common in opinion and attitude studies and in some studies of underdevelopment.[24] Sidney Verba has produced an excellent survey of the usefulness and limitations of small-group theories as applied to political science, summarizing the relevant research, commenting on the problems of transplanting theories based on artificial laboratory situations to empirical phenomena, and examining in detail the validity of some of the hypotheses derived from small-group studies, particularly the so-called "participation hypothesis," which asserts that major changes in the behavior of members of small groups require the participation of the members in the decision-making procedure if the changes are to be effected. Verba's conclusions are moderate and reasonable. He points out the limited applicability of the leadership studies that have been made by dynamics psychologists, suggests some of the ways in which research in the laboratory and empirical theory might be related, and indicates in a general way that small-group theory is no panacea, though it may prove extremely useful if used intelligently.

These are judgments with which one can only concur. The importance of the small face-to-face group in human life is patent; its influence on political beliefs and ideologies is too well documented to require further argument. The transfer from experimental findings to empirical phenomena must be made carefully and not dogmatically. The application of small-group theories to political phenomena requires tact and judgment.

Verba's caution in handling small-group concepts can be justified beautifully by an example taken from Robert T. Golembiewski's *Behavior and Organization*. The aim of the

---

[24]See Golembiewski, *op. cit.;* Sidney Verba, *Small Groups and Political Behavior* (Princeton University Press, 1961); Elihu Katz and Paul F. Lazarsfeld, *Personal Influence* (Free Press, 1955); George C. Homans, *The Human Group* (Harcourt, Brace & Co., 1950); Gabriel A. Almond and James S. Coleman (eds.), *The Politics of the Developing Areas* (Princeton University Press, 1960); Gabriel A. Almond and Sidney Verba, *The Civic Culture* (Princeton University Press, 1963).

book is to criticize the application of formal or traditional organization and mangement theory, using principles provided by small-group theorists. The tone of the book is decidedly annoying, and that makes it difficult to avoid bias in evaluation. The point, however, is that Golembiewski is much less sophisticated than Verba about the pitfalls encountered in transferring theories from laboratory to society, and this leads him consistently into overstatement, followed by hedging. For example, in treating the participation hypothesis, Golembiewski first states it quite flatly, as a criterion for evaluating O & M theory: "In any case, the method of selection of supervisors in the Section, while consistent with O & M theory, implied substantial adverse effects on productivity. To explain, students have argued that peer representation, or even self-choice, be utilized in such matters as promotion."[25]

Then follows a discussion of the differences in criteria of evaluation employed by different ranks in organizations, a flat assertion that choice of supervisors by management ignores the desires of the supervisees (which is true only of grossly mismanaged organizations, whatever the theory on which they operate); that culminates in the assertion of a need for structural integration of the organization, to be obtained by using small-group theory, including the principle of self-choice or peer representation in the choice of supervisors. Then come the reservations. First, supervisors chosen by those supervised may have to support norms antithetical to the norms of the organization. The qualification is further qualified, however, to read that use of the participation hypothesis is a good strategy for obtaining maximum organization efficiency. Finally, "[this] coin of self-choice, however, has another side. Self-choice may sometimes—though apparently not often—simply reinforce existing opposition to the formal organization."[26]

[25]Golembiewski, *op. cit.*, p. 189.
[26]*Ibid.*, p. 190.

Golembiewski's difficulty is understandable. Few principles in small-group theory are so well established that they can be asserted confidently and used as critical standards in empirical situations. Small-group theories can call attention to shortcomings in other approaches to organization theory, but their validity must be established in the situation in which they are employed, and not merely in an artificial laboratory situation. And even in the laboratory, the results of experimentation are often far from clear. The moral seems to be that such theoretical structures or principles should be exploited as fully as possible in heuristic terms, but applied explicitly with considerable caution and care.

PSYCHOANALYSIS

Explanations of social phenomena based upon psychoanalytic theory or, more precisely, on the work of Sigmund Freud and those who followed him are frequently met in social science, particularly in normative judgment of social phenomena. Freudian psychology is certainly one of the two most influential modes of thought to appear in Western civilization in the past two centuries—the other, of course, is Marxism—if influence is measured by capacity to attract the attention of scholars and intellectuals with widely ranging interests, to stimulate endless discussion of the validity of constructs, and to generate streams of supporting or conflicting data. The scope of the Freudian impact on contemporary thought is staggering. Yet the precise status and value of psychoanalysis is much disputed. Freud revolutionized psychology, yet today his influence is probably greater in the social sciences and humanities than in psychiatry. Freud enriched the vocabulary of nearly everyone fortunate enough to acquire the rudiments of an education, yet the meaning of the terms he added to the language is often woolly and imprecise. Freud contributed to the conceptual equipment of everyone in the social sciences and humanities, yet it is hard to say whether these disciplines have thereby been advanced or retarded. Freud's collected works fill some 23 volumes, all large, and the stock of derivative writings and criticisms is already sufficient to fill a small library, yet the last word on the subject will probably not be heard for decades. No adequate critique of so monumental a mass of literature could be compressed into a few pages.* Happily, our purposes are adequately served by a fairly concise treatment of the basic structure of Freud's thought; a detailed criticism of the whole corpus of Freud's work is not needed. The question to be answered is simply: "Does Freudian theory provide adequate explanations of significant social and political phenomena?" Freud's value to the arts is irrelevant. The therapeutic worth of his methods of treatment of neurotic patients is also beside the point; witch doctors may succeed with their patients without in any way validating the conceptual framework used to approach the disease. A distinction is needed, in other words, between the influence of a conceptualization or theory and its explanatory value. Paul Samuelson once remarked that Karl Marx will go down in the history of economic thought as a second-rate Ricardian; that judgment is perfectly justified in context, but it says nothing about the extent of Marx's influence. Similarly, the whole of the Freudian apparatus may one day be abandoned as inadequate and misleading, and that seems

---

*The standard edition of Freud's works, translated and edited by James Strachey in collaboration with Anna Freud, is published by the Hogarth Press in London. However, there are so many different editions of Freud now available that a list of the major titles will serve our purpose adequately. They include *Psychopathology of Everyday Life, Introductory Lectures in Psychoanalysis, Totem and Taboo, The Ego and the Id, Beyond the Pleasure Principle, The Future of an Illusion, Group Psychology and the Analysis of the Ego, New Lectures on Psychoanalysis, Moses and Monotheism,* and *Civilization and Its Discontents.* The more useful and important of the secondary sources are Ernest Jones, *The Life and Work of Sigmund Freud,* edited and abridged by Lionel Trilling and Steven Marcus (Anchor Books, 1963); Philip Rieff, *Freud: The Mind of the Moralist* (Anchor Books, 1961); and J. A. C. Brown, *Freud and the Post-Freudians* (Penguin Books, Inc., 1961).

rather likely, without affecting Freud's originality or influence. Freud's place in the history of psychology is assured; his place in working psychology remains to be determined.

General Characteristics

Freud died in 1939 at the age of 83. Though most of the work that will be considered here was written after World War I, Freud was in many ways a product of the 19th rather than the 20th century—his treatment of the female of the species, for example, is purely Victorian. Further, the Freudian system underwent two and perhaps three major revisions as Freud's interests changed; but certain fundamental characteristics remained constant, and it will much facilitate our examination of the conceptual structure if these general properties are explicated first.

Freud's outlook was consistently biological. Early training in physiology and medicine taught him to think in terms of physical organisms; and if he is sometimes called a mechanist, the term is misleading, and "organicist" is more appropriate if taken literally and without metaphysical overtones. More than anyone else in psychology, Freud dealt with a biological organism, a creature dominated by inborn drives and instincts, ignoring the environment or treating it as a matter of secondary importance. Further, he thought in evolutionary or Darwinian terms, though he followed Jean de Lamarck rather than Charles Darwin to the extent that he believed that acquired behavior traits could be transmitted genetically—a principle that seriously detracts from the value of his work in social psychology, since no competent scientist today accepts that possibility. His psychology is quite properly called "instinctual," and it could also be termed "individualistic," for he is concerned primarily with the single person rather than with society. That emphasis has important consequences for the application of Freudian concepts to social phenomena, and it was also responsible for a sharp division within psychology between those who followed Freud and those who believed that he understated the influence of the social environment.

Freud was a determinist—in the 19th-century sense of the term. The assumption is absolutely essential, given Freud's methods and purpose, for he must be able to infer what lies beneath the surface from what appears in consciousness. Every human action, physical or psychic, trivial or traumatic, must be relevant and significant. Dreams and jokes, slips of tongue or pen, movements of the body—all are sources of information about the great sea of urges and desires that lie beneath consciousness. Yet determinism is only an assumption, not an established principle. Can it be upheld? The question is today much disputed in philosophy of science, and the results are inconclusive. We can only note the place of determinism in the Freudian system of thought and move on, though it is perhaps worth emphasizing the particularity and specificity of Freudian determinism, which is peculiarly 19th century in flavor. It can be argued, for example, that dreams are merely a device by which the brain rids itself of cumulated electric charges (a theory advanced quite recently by a group of British scientists), in which case dreams may be construed in deterministic terms but the conclusions inferred from the content of dreams would be extremely limited. Freud, on the other hand, must give specific meaning to each unique phase of each dream; he thinks in terms of a rigorous deterministic relation between overt action and unconscious motivation.

Freud was a physician, dealing regularly with disturbed patients; and his early work, in particular, is shaped by clinical needs. His data were obtained from sustained observation of individual—particularly verbal—behavior during the process that he called "free association." In essence, the patient talked without any particular purpose in mind while Freud listened. Now, data obtained in this manner are referred to by psychoanalysts as *clinical,* and their status in explanation is far from clear. The close and peculiar relation between analyst and patient, particularly after the so-called "transference" has taken place, makes it almost impossible for a third party to evaluate the significance of the conversation, even when recordings and transcriptions are available. The strictly factual element in Freud's reports of his observations (patient X stated *A*) is very small. For the most part, Freud records interpretations rather than observations. That tendency, combined with the literary and dramatic qualities of Freud's writings, the deliberate "speculations" which are so difficult to evaluate, and the frequent resort to what can only be termed "word play" and even puns upon words, accounts for much of the criticism to which Freudianism has been subjected on methodological grounds. When the "meaning" of a number written casually on paper is explained in terms of combinations of numbers representing age, properties of arithmetical series, square roots, house numbers, etc., the contemporary reader is entitled to feel that he is closer to numerology than science, Freud's protestations not to the contrary.

Finally, Freud was raised in the cultural atmosphere of the late 19th-century middle-European Jewish family, and this doubtless influenced his idea of family relations and the development of personality very powerfully—that much can be gathered from Ernest Jones's biography, though the details are not always clear. Certainly there are a number of curious parallels between the theory he produced and his own life history—for example, his relations with his parents, his attitudes toward women, his enormous ambition, his theories of sibling rivalry, and so on. Freud, in other words, generalized the results of prolonged introspection—a commonplace, of course, in any form of intellectual activity—and if that is irrelevant to the evaluation of the validity of the Freudian structure, it does, I believe, explain a great deal of its content.

The Basic Framework

The fairly simple basic structure of the Freudian conception of man is diagrammed in Figure 4–1, and it may be useful to refer to the diagram as the conceptualization is elaborated, for the simplicity of the elements is attained at a considerable cost in ambiguity and imprecision. Freud begins with pure drive energy, innate in man, very much like Henri Bergson's *élan vital*. This energy, first identified as *libido*, is called the *id*, or *Eros* in the post-1923 writings. The id is governed wholly by the "pleasure principle"; that is, it seeks pleasure and is wholly indifferent to morality or even to its own safety. There is some ambiguity here, for it is uncertain whether the id obtains pleasure simply through discharge or from the consequences of discharge. In the former case the id need only be postulated, and no "feedback" connections between id and the outer world are required; if the id receives gratification from the external world, however, the loops bringing the consequences of action back to the brain must pass through the ego/superego system and back to the id. In the first case the actions of the ego will have no effect on the id so long as the id can continue to discharge energy; in the latter case the ego can block energy discharge and actually inflict pain or pleasure on the id. It seems likely that the id receives its pleasure simply from the act of discharging; otherwise, the interrelations become hopelessly complex, and some of the other dynamic principles Freud uses in the explanation of behavior do not make sense. A second problem connected with the concept of the id arises out of Freud's use of basic instincts as drive-direction systems. It is not clear whether the primary energy of the id is already structured into instinctive drives when it first appears or whether there is a secondary structure between the id and the action systems of the body, also innate, which channels the id's energy into particular modes of expression. Presumably, the instinctual structure is superimposed on the id, but that would require some network

FIGURE 4–1

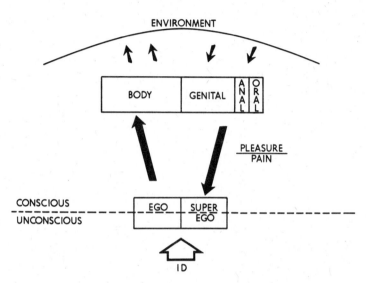

linking the controls of the ego system to the output of the instinctual drive mechanism; and here, as with most of the fundamentals like the learning process, memory, habit formation, etc., Freud is extremely vague.

The *ego* in Freud's structure, which begins to develop in the human infant at about the age of six months, is the structure that mediates between the pure drive of the id and the reality of the external environment. Again, Freud "vitalizes" the concept until it seems to sit like a brooding intelligence, ever alert to stomp on the id if it seeks to escape from its subterranean region in the mind. The ego operates according to the "reality principle," seeking modes of expression that will at least partially gratify the id and at the same time not endanger the total living system.

The *superego,* which develops much later than the ego, is roughly the human conscience, the internalized mores, learned primarily from the family. Both ego and superego lie partly in human consciousness and partly in the unconscious. Freud thought that in males the superego was a remnant of the Oedipus complex (attachment for the parent of opposite sex based on sexual desire) which was eradicated from the male child by fear of castration and by sublimation of the original sexual drive.

After 1923, Freud opted for two instinctual drives in man. The first, *Eros*, was roughly a drive for life and, by implication, fundamentally a sexual drive if the term "sexual" is taken very broadly. The second, *Thanatos*, is a death instinct, an urge in the direction of inanimate matter, appearing as a drive for aggression and destruction. Even orthodox Freudians have not attached too much importance to this particular polarization, preferring to remain with the older notion of libidinal or sexual drive. Freud's disillusionment with the slaughter of World War I (which he had rather naïvely welcomed when it first began) may account for his decidedly pessimistic structuring of instincts in the post-World War I period.

The human body appears in Freud's theories primarily as a container, divided into zones of different erogenous value to the internal structure, and connected with the outside world in a vague and unspecified manner. Freud was little concerned with questions of perception and apparently little influenced by either behaviorism or the work of the Gestalt theorists. The environment is blurred in outline and viewed internally from the standpoint of the organism. Objects in the environment are differentiated, but rarely outside the immediate family. The division of erogenous zones into oral, anal, and genital is used by Freud in his theory of personality and character development. In the very young infant the chief source of pleasure is the oral region. Later, it becomes the anal regions and then, ultimately, the genitalia. The experience of the human being during each of these phases, which occur during the first few years of life, is, in Freudian terms, vital in personality development. Further, the development can be arrested, and even turned back upon itself (regression), so that older persons may return to earlier stages of development, or at least exhibit the traits associated with earlier stages of development, if later life is unsatisfactory or frustrating.

Finally, the total mental apparatus must be divided into an unconscious and a conscious element or, more precisely, a conscious element, a preconscious element that can be recalled at will, and an unconscious element that is beyond the individual's power of recall. Freud's "discovery of the unconscious" has been widely hailed as his principal conceptual achievement, but that seems a dubious proposition. It has long been realized that people often act without a clear understanding of their own motives; indeed, Christian vitalism substituted "Satan" for the person to account for such hidden motives. More important, the function of the unconscious is by no means clearly spelled out in Freud, and it too often seems to serve as a convenient repository for all sorts of inexplicable contradictions and residues. Freud's deliberate subordination of conscious life to the unconscious, though in keeping with the general principle that he shared with David Hume—reason is subordinate to emotion and not the converse—introduces an unnecessary complexity into discussion of human behavior and in fact makes anything like scientific knowledge quite impossible. If there are some classes of statements made by human beings that can and must be taken at face value (a necessary assumption in any science), then Freud's suggestion that overt behavior *always* has a meaning rooted in the unconscious cannot be accepted. Freud is then faced with the problem, presently insoluble, of providing criteria for differentiating those overt actions that contain their own proper meaning and those that require interpretation. Freud avoided the difficulty by claiming that *all* propositions are open to interpretation, but that assertion has too many unacceptable consequences.

Freudian Dynamics

The blind impulse of the id supplies the driving force behind the Freudian system, and the instinctual structure transforms pure energy into directed libidinal energy (in the early theory) or into the quest for life or death. The crucial questions, given the framework that Freud has chosen to use, have to do with the relationship between id, ego, and superego. But there is no logical reason why the relationship between ego and environment might not be chosen as a central focus for inquiry, and that is in fact what both the neo-Freudians and the ego psychologists have done. Freud, however, remained true to the biological base with which he began, subordinating environmental influence to inherited capacity and direction. He also maintained the hedonistic dichotomy between pleasure and pain as the discriminator for the system, ignoring unselfishness and altruism alike.

The id lies wholly within the unconscious, and since all drives and impulses originate in the same area, the meaning of human behavior can only be determined through interpretation. Memory is a faulty guide to meaning, since the decision to retain or reject memories is itself a consequence of actions taken within the unconscious. In *Beyond the Pleasure Principle*, Freud seems to accept the view, which he agrees is speculative, that conscious experience seldom plays an important part in memory, that most of the important experiences stored in memory came from the unconscious. Modern theories suggest, on the contrary, that the content of memory is in fact limited to what has been consciously experienced. In any event, Freud's way of looking at memory literally forced interpretation. Unfortunately, he seldom elaborated very precisely the rules for making interpretations, and the looseness of the Freudian structure is in large measure due to the absence of any systematic principles for interpreting the meaning of acts of behavior. Freud assumed, for example, that dreams are always meaningful—always wish fulfillments, in fact—but that even in dreams the actual content of wishes is disguised. This led to the elaborate and rather fanciful procedures of interpretation outlined in *The Interpretation of Dreams.* The inferences which Freud makes are beyond verification or checking; even the rules by which inferences are made cannot be determined. The analyst's interpretation seems more a creative work of art than a scientific inference. Indeed, Freud on one occasion noted that a patient had managed to dream *without* wish fulfillment in order to fulfill the "secondary wish" that Freud's theories might be proved wrong. There are no possible principles on which an inference of that kind can be drawn from a patient's statements about dream content. Finally, Freud's theory of memory was in part responsible for his extreme emphasis on the formative influence of early childhood and the belief that "repetition compulsion" in effect doomed man to repeat the experiences of those early years. *Because* early experience is easily and usually forgotten, Freud assumed that it must have great importance, the curious doctrine that what is decisive is what cannot be remembered.

The impulses, wishes, or desires stemming from the id, or the basic instinctual drives, may suffice for a newborn infant; but man must live in society with others, and hence his behavior must be accommodated to the wishes and desires of others, lest he find himself destroyed—thus Freud restates the Hobbesian thesis. The task of restraining the fundamental drives, of directing psychic energy toward attainable and acceptable goals and away from self-destruction, falls to the ego, functioning according to the reality principle. The ego, in other words, must adjust drives to reality, presumably using experience as a guide, though in some cases Freud held that there were innate, inherited "archaic memory traces" that guided the ego in its work. Freud usually writes as if the ego were a finite, vitalized element in the mind; but if it is simply considered as a function of the neural mechanism, it makes much more sense. A major part of Freud's work was concerned with the psychic mechanisms, with the devices by which man modified his primary drives.

And Freud's theory of neurosis was couched in terms of the relationship between drives and the limits enforced by the ego and superego. Here, we find Freud's major contribution to psychology, for he identified (as attributes of the ego) a wide range of functions that the nervous system does seem to perform. Ignoring the question of locus of feeling, and the lack of detailed procedures for identifying these functions when they occur, we find a set of concepts of mental activity that have wide currency in contemporary thought.

Repression: Keeping an impulse from entering consciousness, exemplified by the common injunction, "Don't think about it."

Rationalization: Substitution of a suitable for an unsuitable impulse, related to but not identical with common usage, where the term tends to mean a false explanation of motives used to justify failure to achieve the original goal.

Projection: Location of an impulse in another person, though it actually originates in the self.

Introjection: Identification of the self with another person.

Retrogression: Moving backward through the developmental stages (oral, anal, genital).

Reaction formation: A conscious override of an unconscious motive—for example, substitution of love for hate.

Displacement: Relocation of attitude from one object to another—for example, kicking an inanimate object when one really wants to kick one's parents.

To the list we can add guilt feelings, frustration, anxiety, wish fulfillment, defense mechanism, insecurity, and repetition compulsion, all of which were used by Freud in a technical sense and have now largely entered the English language as commonplaces.

Finally, a word is needed about Freud's theory of personality development. The theory concentrates on the first five years of life, dividing it into three stages—oral, anal, and phallic or genital, according to the chief locus of pleasure. In the oral stage, pleasure comes mainly from eating, from "incorporating" things into the body; fear is caused mainly by the absence of the prime protector, the mother. The anal stage begins with toilet training, usually in the second year; pleasure is derived from the expulsion of feces, pain from their retention. Depending on the type of toilet training employed, the child may become expulsive (cruel and destructive) or retentive (stingy and miserly), or even productive and creative (if the mother lauds his efforts to produce). In the phallic stage the sexual organs become the focus of pleasure, and the Oedipus complex—sexual attraction for the parent of the opposite sex and hatred for the parent of the same sex—begins. In the male child, fear of the power and authority of the father, and of the possible loss of genitalia thought castration, usually leads to a repression of sexual desire for the mother and a subsequent identification with the father. The female child, who loves the father, discovers that she has no penis and becomes envious of males and ambivalent toward the father—he becomes a love object as well as an object of envy. Freud's treatment of female development is less incisive than the treatment of males, much to the chagrin of some female analysts like Karen Horney.

Social Psychology

Beginning with *Totem and Taboo* in 1913, Freud produced a number of major works treating social rather than individual themes, but making use of much the same fundamental orientation and conceptualization. Curiously enough, social psychologists have found less that is useful in Freud's social psychology than in his treatment of individual personality development. Partly, that is due to Freud's emphasis on origins—of taboos, totems, religious beliefs—and partly to his reliance on dated anthropological information and untenable genetic principles. Freud, for example, consistently treated primitive society as developed society in embryo, never recognizing it as an autonomous structure with its own functions and goals. Finally, it must be said that Freud produced an aristocratic and even authoritarian conception of human society, pessimistic in outlook, and radically conservative in its implications. This, too, has doubtless tended to limit his influence in the Western democracies, and particularly in the United States, in matters of social psychology.

Freudian man is an atom, an isolated entity, driven by inherited desires toward activity hardly compatible with stable, organized society. The need for society, which Freud recognizes clearly enough, forces man to submit to limitations on his natural urges, but he submits unwillingly and only under constant pressure and threat. Every individual, as Freud put the point in *The Future of an Illusion*, is virtually an enemy of civilization; civilization must defend itself against the natural creature with force, threats, and constant pressure. Civilization is literally built upon human repression, and though Freud is not perfectly clear on the matter, he seemed to believe that a nonrepressive civilization was utterly impossible:

One would think that a reordering of human relationships would be possible, which would remove the sources of dissatisfaction with civilization by renouncing coercion and the suppression of the instincts, so that, undisturbed by internal discord, men might devote themselves to the acquisition of wealth and its enjoyment . . . but it is questionable if such a state of affairs can be realized. It seems rather that every civilization must be built upon coercion and renunciation of instinct; it does not even seem certain that if coercion were to cease the majority of human beings would be prepared to undertake to perform the work necessary for acquiring new wealth.[27]

Further, Freud had no faith whatever in man in the mass, sharing the antagonism to crowds and mobs of Gustav Le Bon, Wilfred Trotter, and others. A group, according to Freud, is a number of persons who identify with a leader,

[27]Sigmund Freud, *The Future of an Illusion* (Doubleday and Co., 1961) pp. 4–5.

who are bound together by a common ego ideal, a common obedience to a father image, and in some degree directed by "unconscious memory traces" inherited from the archaic past. This notion of a collective unconscious, very similar to that used by Carl Jung later, plays an important part in Freud's description of the roots of crowd behavior.

Freud's writings on international affairs, particularly the well-known exchange of letters with Albert Einstein, made use of much the same conceptions. The natural desire of instinctual man is for aggression and domination of others. The basis of law and of society lies in the union of the weak against the strong, the imposition of collective power on everyone. Conflict continues so long as there are inequalities in power and a central authority powerful enough to dominate the whole society is lacking. The only solution to war is the creation of a powerful central authority able to prevent wars forcibly. Here, Freud differs sharply with Marx, for he claims that aggressiveness in man antedates the development of private property and that the abolition of private property would have no effect on human behavior. Men do not fight *over* something, they fight because they must—fighting is a consequence of instinctual drive.

Groups, in Freud's view, appeared simply as a contemporary manifestation of the kind of horde behavior he had described in *Totem and Taboo*. There, Freud had accounted for the existence of totems and taboos in primitive societies by postulating an era long since past when man lived in small hordes, ruled by an authoritarian father who dominated the horde and monopolized the women. Frustrated, the younger men in the horde slew the father and possessed the women. But they were seized with remorse, renounced their rights to the women (incest taboo), and totemized the father, ceremoniously slaying and eating him periodically thereafter (totem). This sequence of experiences "left indestructible traces on the history of human descent" in the form of archaic memory traces, not just for the individual;

"the masses, too, retain an impression of the past in unconscious memory traces."[28] Further, a communal superego developed, much as it develops in the individual, to enforce these limits on behavior. Freud has translated his individual psychology almost literally to a group mind.

Criticism and Applications

Does the Freudian conceptual framework provide adequate explanations of significant political or social phenomena? No. Does it have heuristic value? Yes, but it must be employed cautiously, for it can be highly misleading. Does it have therapeutic value? That is not a question that concerns us here, and the evidence is in any event too obscure for decision. The anachronisms, ethnocentrisms, and temporocentrisms in Freud's thinking can be ignored or eliminated, in some cases, without seriously damaging the structure. The outdated treatment of women, the highly specialized conception of family life that Freud employed, the constant use of dichotomies, the mechanisms, the "energy-quantity" theory of motivation, and the innate conservatism of the outlook—these are relatively trivial matters. Even the "great-man" notion implicit in Freud's thought—Freud, after all, was the *only* person capable of self-analysis—is characteristic of thinkers like Plato, G. W. F. Hegel, Karl Marx, or Karl Mannheim, of thinkers who commit themselves to a special kind of knowledge not available to the common herd. The notion may be distasteful to those who believe in the equal capacity of mankind to acquire knowledge, but it is not thereby falsified. Even the "archaic heritage," the belief that behavior modes acquired by one generation could be transmitted genetically to the next, though it is anathema to modern science, could probably be eliminated without too much difficulty. Freud's tendency to anthropomorphize

---

[28]Sigmund Freud, *Moses and Monotheism*, p. 120; and *Civilization and Its Discontents*, p. 101. Both published by Doubleday and Co.

his concepts, to use *Id* and *Ego,* for example, as though they were vitalistic entities, though annoying to the reader, can be eliminated readily by careful rewriting. But when all that has been done, when all possible concessions have been made, the explanations that the structure provides remain faulty, and the investigations that it suggests are in many important respects misleading.

The first difficulty with the Freudian structure is that it is virtually impossible to refute. In part, this may be due to the notable intolerance of Freud and his disciples. Freud did not, for example, feel that biological evidence against Lamarckian genetics refuted any of his fundamental premises; and that being the case, it is hard to see how *any* evidence could be taken to refute them. More important, however, is a fundamental methodological error in which orthodox Freudians consistently indulge, that is, the belief that consistency with the facts serves as confirmation for theories. One can account for facts without explaining them, or as Donald C. Williams put the point:

[A] hypothesis is not in general confirmed at all by merely being consistent with some facts; almost any hypothesis is consistent with almost any facts. What count are, first, the antecedent probability of the hypothesis in relation to the funded knowledge of mankind, and secondly, the determinateness and probability with which it might actually have predicted those special current facts normally denominated "the" evidence: and what mainly counts about these is not the absolute values of the probabilities but how they compare with the corresponding ones attached to rival or contrary hypotheses.[29]

Leaving aside for the moment the question whether the "clinical" data obtained in psychoanalytic interviews qualifies as factual evidence, the failure of orthodox Freudians, including Freud himself, to seek linkages between psychoanalytic theory and what Williams calls "the funded

[29]Donald C. Williams, "Philosophy and Psychoanalysis," in Sidney Hook (ed.), *Psychoanalysis, Scientific Method and Philosophy* (Grove Press, 1960).

knowledge of mankind" is a serious matter. H. J. Eysenck's criticism of dream interpretation by orthodox analysts provides an excellent illustration of the point. Eysenck examines in some detail the assumption that symbols and other dream mechanisms are used to camouflage unbearable experiences, and demonstrates quite conclusively that the assumption simply is not consistent with the facts. More specifically, he notes that notions expressed symbolically in one dream may be expressed quite directly in another; that the symbols which supposedly hide the content of a dream often are patently transparent; and finally, that there are no good grounds for asserting that the symbolic meaning of a dream rather than its literal meaning is decisive. In the circumstances, no consistent principle for linking dream content to experience seems possible.[30]

Most of the conceptions employed in Freudian explanations of behavior suffer from a similar vagueness; few are defined adequately in observable terms. Sidney Hook, for example, has complained bitterly of his inability to obtain a definite answer from any psychoanalyst of the Freudian persuasion to the question as to "what kind of evidence . . . would lead them to declare in any specific case that a child did not have an Oedipus complex."[31] Hook was not, of course, demanding to "see" an Oedipus complex but was asking for a delineation of the evidence on which one could either affirm or deny the presence of an Oedipus complex. Freud's treatment of the "repetition compulsion" in *Beyond the Pleasure Principle* provides a good example of the kind of conceptual difficulties met in his writing. He begins with what seems a clear assertion that "there really does exist in the human mind a compulsion to

---

[30]H. J. Eysenck, *Sense and Nonsense in Psychology* (Penguin Books, Inc., 1957). Chapter iv, "The Interpretation of Dreams," is excellent. The points cited above are taken from pages 163–67.

[31]Sidney Hook, "Science and Mythology in Psychoanalysis," in Hook, *op. cit.*

repeat which overrides the pleasure principle" but adds shortly that "only in rare instances can we observe the pure effects of the compulsion to repeat, unsupported by other motives." A discussion of the validity of the concept then follows, employing the method of residues, and concluding with the assertion that "enough is left unexplained to justify the hypothesis of a compulsion to repeat." Yet at the end of the paragraph, the proposition is restated in the form of a question, raising doubts whether it was seriously intended in the first place. And to make matters worse, the remainder of the chapter, which deals with the archaic memory traces Freud believed man to possess, uses the repetition compulsion as implied evidence for the validity of the theory of memory.[32] At no point in the discussion does Freud provide the kinds of statements about relationships to observable behavior that would allow another observer to decide independently whether or not a particular act of behavior or sequence of acts did or did not support the hypothesis.

The point can be put in more general terms which may help to clarify the weakness of Freudian attempts at explanation. In an explanation the conceptual framework serves as a linking mechanism; events are related and explained *through* the conceptual framework (Fig. 4–2A). Freud consistently explained phenomena by relating them to theoretical terms which did not provide linkages with other observables. In some cases the theoretical structure served as one terminus of a two-part linkage; when the structure did serve as a connecting device, a connection was made not to other observable events but to other theoretical constructs. Freud's theoretical system, in other words, has no inputs—there are only outputs and sources. The powerful scientific technique of relating inputs to outputs and thus

---

[32]Sigmund Freud, *Beyond the Pleasure Principle*, trans. James Strachey (Bantam Books, Inc., 1959), pp. 43–47.

FIGURE 4-2

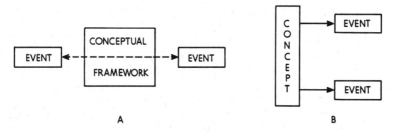

A   B

specifying the internal structure of an unknown system
is not used in Freud's work. Instead, he was forced to infer inner structure solely from performance. Instead of
relational propositions linking inputs and outputs, Freud
produced propositions that link outputs to hypothetical
constructs. The hypothetical constructs do not *connect* the
phenomena, they *account for* them. That is analogous to
making inferences about the intelligence of a human being solely on the basis of general performance, that is,
without using a standardized input as a basis for measuring.
Intelligence testing does not really "test intelligence," of
course, but the tests do provide useful comparative data relating to particular kinds of performance by individuals.

Formally, the Freudian system has two major defects.
First, the concepts are so vague and metaphorical that it is
almost impossible to determine the content of the propositions that contain them and hence virtually impossible to
decide what kind of data would support or refute them. Second, though every theoretical structure contains some terms
that are not fully linked to empirical data, it is absolutely essential that *some* theoretical terms be tied to observation
through a set of rules of correspondence. Otherwise, as
Ernest Nagel points out, the theory can have no determinate consequences for the empirical world.[33] A good illus-

---

[33]Ernest Nagel, "Methodological Issues in Psychoanalytic Theory," in
Hook, *op. cit.*, pp. 39–40.

tration of the problem is found in "The Dynamic Theory of Dream-Formation":

> The motive power for the formation of dreams is not provided by the latent dream-thoughts or the day's residues, but by an unconscious impulse, repressed during the day, with which the day's residues have been able to establish contact and which contrives to make a *wish-fulfillment* for itself out of the material of the latent thoughts. Thus every dream is on the one hand the fulfillment of a wish on the part of the unconscious and on the other hand . . . the fulfillment of the normal wish to sleep . . . . If we disregard the unconscious contribution to the formation of the dream and limit the dream to its latent thoughts, it can represent anything with which waking life has been concerned— a reflection, a warning, an intention, a preparation for the immediate future, or, once again, the satisfaction of an unfulfilled wish. The unrecognizability, strangeness and absurdity of the manifest dream are partly the result of the translation of the thoughts into a different, so to say *archaic,* method of expression, but partly the effect of a restrictive, critically disapproving agency in the mind, which does not entirely cease to function during sleep. . . .[34]

What expectations about human dreams does Freud create here? Every dream is a wish fulfillment, but the wish may be conscious or unconscious. Every dream is disguised, presented in an archaic mode of expression; and it is also modified by the influence of a postulated critical agency in the mind. At least four variables interact, then, in the production of each dream. Three of the four variables are hypothetical—the unconscious, the mechanism for translating conscious thought into an archiac mode, and the mechanism of conscience. What effect does each of these variables have? How do they interact? What indicators can be used for differentiating those influences? None of these questions can be answered from reading Freud, whether it is the brief article cited above or the bulkier works.

[34]Sigmund Freud, "Psychoanalysis," in Philip Rieff (ed.), *Character and Culture,* trans. James Strachey (Collier Books, 1963), pp. 237–38. The article was written in 1922.

Lacking stipulations explicating the interactions among these variables and linking them to observable acts of behavior, there simply is no way of deciding in advance what expectations the "theory" implies; the fact that the structure can be used after the fact to *account for* the phenomena does not mean that it has explanatory power.

From the social scientist's point of view, the substantive criticisms that can be leveled against the Freudian conceptual framework are even more telling than methodological criticisms. The Hobbesian view of man that Freud assumes in all of his later work is today seriously questioned by many social scientists, mainly because of the findings of anthropologists and students of comparative sociology. The Freudian system depends heavily upon the assumption of innate drives, aggressive and insatiable. The discovery of peoples largely lacking in aggressiveness, though known to Freud, was treated with skepticism verging on contempt: "We are told that in certain happy regions on the earth, where nature provides in abundance everything that man requires, there are races whose life is passed in tranquility, and who know neither compulsion nor aggressiveness. I can scarcely believe it, and I should be glad to hear more of these fortunate beings."[35] In general, Freud was little concerned with the influence of society on man or with current experience and its consequences for behavior. Combining his theory of childhood sexuality with a theory of personality development that concentrated on the first four or five years of human life and largely ignored intervening periods, Freud was forced into a conceptualization that omitted precisely those factors that are most interesting to the social scientist.

---

[35] "Why War?" in Rieff, *Character and Culture*, p. 143. Freud goes on to attack the Marxist belief that rearrangement of the economic order can lead to peaceful social existence, thus creating a serious dilemma for those who sought to combine Freudian and Marxian principles into a single instrument for social criticism.

It is no accident that orthodox Freudian theory is rarely if ever used to explain social phenomena and that Freud's own excursions into social explanation are usually ignored. Harold D. Lasswell's widely cited "application" of Freudian theory to politics is in fact nothing of the sort, as Lasswell himself observed, but an attempt to make use of the Freudian *method*. "The *Psychopathology* was the outcome of an attempt to apply and adapt a procedure rather than to propose a formally exhaustive body of applications of a comprehensive system of theory."[36] Where Lasswell *did* seek to derive theoretically useful propositions from the Freudian corpus, he was not very successful. The famous formula—political man displaces private motives upon public objects and rationalizes them in terms of the public interest—tells us nothing, unless we are prepared, as Lasswell was not, to argue that the explanation of political phenomena must always be made in terms of private motivation. This was a notion not without its appeal to American progressivism, or at least that form of progressivism found in the writings of Charles Beard, Thorstein Veblen, and the reformers. But to seek an explanation for the behavior of a political figure like John F. Kennedy solely in terms of private motivation would lead to results that would simply be ludicrous. We are left with the commonsense proposition that it is a profound mistake to ignore the private aspects of the behavior of public figures, a proposition that few significant commentators on politics since Plato have rejected or overlooked. We are also left with a nagging suspicion that it is an error of equal dimensions to ignore the public aspects of the behavior of private persons—as Freud did so systematically.

How, then, to account for the continued vitality of the

---

[36]Harold D. Lasswell, *Psychopathology and Politics* (Viking Press, Inc., 1962), chap. xiii, "Afterthoughts: Thirty Years Later," p. 274. Lasswell, in the postscript, strongly favors the "sociologizing" of the Freudian structure; see p. 288, n.

Freudian system of thought? First of all, it should probably be noted that its vitality is all too often overestimated. There have been few if any major theoretical developments in orthodox Freudianism in the last three decades—the last major revision of the system was completed in the 1920's. The influence· of orthodoxy in the United States is slight, and it is not much greater in Britain; it remains most powerful in continental Europe. The use of psychoanalytic theory in *explanation* has been comparatively slight; mainly, it has been used as a foundation for social criticism.[37] And it can be added that it is precisely those characteristics of Freudian theory that are most criticized when the theory is used to explain that have proved the greatest boon to social critics—vague and indeterminate conceptualizations which permit gross variations in the interpretation of observable phenomena to survive challenge and allow the social critic to attack society in terms that are exceptionally difficult to either validate or refute. Discussion of these points, however, is best left to the following section of the book.

The great value of Freud's speculations lies in their suggestiveness, in the lines of inquiry that he opened or enlarged. In terms much more forcible than those employed by Hume, Freud called attention to the limited scope of rational action in human life and the immense power of emotional or irrational behavior. He pointed out forms of social repression of the individual, and not merely in sexual matters alone, adding an existential dimension to an aspect of the relation between society and the individual that Marx had considered only in terms of the interaction of classes. Further, by insisting on the importance of the

---

[37]Norman O. Brown's *Life against Death: The Psychoanalytical Meaning of History* (Alfred A. Knopf, Inc., 1959), although an "interpretation" of Freud, remains fairly close to orthodoxy; it is a good example of the attempt to reconcile psychoanalytic theory and Christian theology (see, in particular, Part VI, pp. 305–22).

earlier years of life in the formation of character and habits, he linked these factors to child-rearing and educational practices. He forced man to attend to the unconscious element in human behavior, to the hidden motivations and desires lying beneath the superficial gloss of civilized behavior. Finally, by insisting upon the importance of the genetic heritage in human behavior, he provided a useful balance against the environmentalism and extreme empiricism of the behaviorists. Even if all of Freud's theories and concepts prove ephemeral and worthless, he performed an invaluable service to the development of human knowledge by stimulating inquiry into aspects of social life that had hitherto been neglected. Error, after all, may be as stimulating as correctness; the antagonism and hostility that Freud induced in his readers, and the ensuing efforts to dispute or disprove his assumptions, were probably as useful in the long run as a better articulated but less controversial set of theories might have been.

SOCIALIZED PSYCHOANALYSIS

No prophet or system builder has managed to suppress all heresy, though many have tried, and Freud was no exception to the rule. The modification and reinterpretation of the Freudian system began as early as 1911, when Alfred Adler parted with Freud on the question of sexuality and its influence on behavior. Others—Carl Jung, Otto Rank, Wilhelm Stekel—followed. Like all heretics, they were duly denounced by the orthodox, often quite savagely; and in their turn, they attacked orthodoxy, with equal savagery. However, the older generation of psychoanalysts—Adler is the major exception—tended to remain distinctly Freudian; they kept the genetic bias, the biological orientation, the determinism, and much of the conceptual structure that Freud had created, and they tended to ignore the influence of social factors on behavior and personality.

The "socialization" of psychoanalysis began in the 1930's with the work of Karen Horney and Erich Fromm, and particularly with the system developed by the American psychoanalyst, Harry Stack Sullivan. These three figures are often identified as "neo-Freudians," but the term is a gross misnomer. In fact, Horney, Fromm, and Sullivan created a base for psychoanalysis so radically different from the Freudian system that it is a travesty to classify them together. They created, in effect, a new way of approaching the problems that Freud had investigated—Horney's *New Ways in Psychoanalysis* is well titled. Fromm, and perhaps Horney, was profoundly influenced by Karl Marx; and Fromm, at least, is more accurately classified as a Marxist than a Freudian, for it is often difficult to see any connection between his methods and purposes and those of Freud. Horney, on the other hand, is much closer to Adler's individual psychology than to Freud; and she was, in fact, often accused of plagiarism by the Adlerites. Sullivan departs most radically from Freud, since he refused even to discuss individual behavior outside a social context and he minimized the influence of genetic endowment on character formation. This "socialized" or "neo-Freudian" version of psychoanalysis has been enormously influential since World War II, particularly in the United States, but to an increasing degree in Europe as well. The general public has read Fromm and even Horney extensively; and if Fromm is preferred by social critics (for reasons that will be apparent), Sullivan's theories have been adopted by a number of social scientists in recent years as a basis for the exploration of social relations.

Socialized psychoanalysis marks a distinct change, a direct and evident departure from Freudian orthodoxy. Within more orthodox circles, however, revision, interpretation, and modification, in emphasis and in conceptualization, have also occurred, particularly in the years following World War II (Freud's death in 1939 and the experience gained from treatment of neuroses during the war perhaps account for the trend). A number of influential psychologists—Ernest Hilgard, David Rapaport, and Kurt Lewin, for example—have taken an interest in psychoanalytic investigations; and prominent psychoanalysts like Heinz Hartmann, Thomas French, and Erik H. Erikson have adopted an approach to psychoanalysis that is methodologically more acceptable to established academic psychology than the pure Freudian system. No rapprochement has been achieved as yet, certainly, but a considerable intermingling has taken place. Further, Freud's emphasis on the primacy of pure drive or instinct, which he maintained strongly until the end of his life, has been modified greatly by the development of what is called "ego psychology"—notably in the writings of Anna Freud, Wilhelm Stekel, and, more recently, Heinz Hartmann and Erik H. Erikson. The shift in emphasis from id to ego has had the effect of transferring emphasis in psychoanalysis from inherited drives to the social and other external factors that shape the development of ego and superego, or personality and character.

As a consequence of these and other developments, it is today pointless to speak of the use of a "psychoanalytic" theory in the study of social phenomena. Conceptions and theories drawn from psychoanalysis are used in social science by a wide range of persons—Norman O. Brown, Erich Fromm, Herbert Marcuse, Talcott Parsons, David C. Mc-Clelland, Robert Presthus, Nathan Leites, Theodore Adorno, Lucian W. Pye, and a host of others—but the differences among them are sometimes greater than the similarities. In very general terms, we may say that social scientists tend to rely upon one of the two major offspring of orthodox Freudian psychoanalysis—the "sociologized" system developed by Horney, Fromm, and Sullivan, and "ego psychology"—so long as that statement is not construed to mean that either approach to psychoanalysis is a formally complete system or that social scientists borrow conceptual frameworks from the psychoanalysts accurately and completely. As we shall see when we examine some of the applications of post-Freudian theory to social problems, conceptual borrowing tends to be governed by the requirements and predispositions of the borrower rather than by the intentions of those who produced the conceptual framework.

Karen Horney

It is interesting to note that the first steps toward the socialization of Freudian theory were taken by a socialist—Alfred Adler—for socialism is fundamentally incompatible with Freud's Hobbesian view of man, whereas the modifications that Adler introduced, and Fromm, Horney, and Sullivan expanded, conduce readily to the kind of social meliorism that socialists propose. Adler retained many of Freud's concepts, but he inverted some of the more fundamental Freudian relations, producing a system with very different implications. As against Freudian self-interest, Adler postulated an innate social tendency, an inherited propensity to regard the social interest as well as the personal interest. Consciousness, rather than unconscious motivation, occupied the central position in Adler's analysis; present purposes rather than the infantile past were taken as the prime determinants of behavior. Adler began with an individual consciously inferior to his fellowmen, striving for compensation ("will for power" in Adler's earlier writings, "striving for superiority" later). Actually, Adler's individual sought self-perfection rather than domination over others; the emphasis is quite different from Freud or Friedrich Nietzsche. Each person molds his own personality out of the features of his environment, and each personality is quite different and unique (hence Adler's psychology is frequently referred to as "individual"). Further, Adler was much concerned with creativity, with the manner in which man developed his individual life-style, and he introduced the very useful conception of "fictional" goals to explain, in teleological terms, how human behavior was motivated.

Karen Horney's indebtedness to both Freud and Alfred Adler is readily apparent in her major works; the influence of anthropologists like Margaret Mead, Ruth Benedict, and Edward Sapir is equally plain.* While she claims to be a follower of Freud and uses some of Freud's basic conceptions, her writings owe far more to Adler, Fromm, Sullivan, and the anthropologists than to Freud himself. She accepts unconscious motivation, psychic determinism, the importance of dreams, and the various defense mechanisms organized by the ego—repression, reaction formation, displacement, and rationalization. But the context in which these conceptions appear is so different that their significance changes radically.

Horney refuses to accept what most orthodox analysts consider Freud's crucial contributions to psychoanalysis. Geneticism, or instinct theory, is rejected flatly in favor of environmental influences. The importance of sexual motivation is downgraded, and sexual action becomes a consequence of anxieties rather than the converse. The Oedipus complex, the repetition compulsion, libido theory, the death instinct, penis envy in women, and the overriding importance of childhood are all either rejected or explained as consequences of cultural and interpersonal relationships.

In Horney's formulation, the two prime goals of the individual are safety and satisfaction; and in most cases, it appears that the former comes first. In terms reminiscent of

---

*Karen Horney's major works are *The Neurotic Personality of Our Time* (W. W. Norton & Co., Inc., 1937); *New Ways in Psychoanalysis* (W. W. Norton & Co., Inc., 1939); *Our Inner Conflicts* (W. W. Norton & Co., Inc., 1945); and *Neurosis and Human Growth* (W. W. Norton & Co., Inc., 1950). The best general introduction is *New Ways in Psychoanalysis*. Her first book, despite its title, deals with *neuroses* and clinical practice rather than with the relations between neuroses and culture.

Adler, Horney speaks of man striving for power as a means of protecting himself against helplessness, of resolving his own anxieties. The central concept in the structure is anxiety; in fact, Horney postulates *the* basic anxiety, a condition arising out of fear on the part of the individual, fear of uncertainty, loneliness, hostility. Here, according to Horney, is the point of origin of neurosis. And anxiety arises out of human relations, not out of genetic drives. There is a fundamental character mode, formed in childhood, which serves as a matrix for human behavior in adult life; but adult behavior is not, as in Freud, stated in terms of repetition of experiences. Her treatment of the sources of anxiety and the protective devices that individuals employ to shield themselves against its effects is detailed and liberally illustrated. All of these changes have considerable importance for therapeutic treatment, of course, but what is more interesting for the social scientist is the implication for the interaction of culture and neuroses. Unfortunately, the social part of Horney's conceptualization is not spelled out in anything like the detail of the clinical material, but a general outline of the structure can be put together from her writings.

Anxiety is the basic source of neurosis; anxiety, in turn, is culturally induced and not due to genetic attributes of the person. It follows that those aspects of the culture that induce fear and anxiety can be identified and presumably modified. Horney's version of psychoanalysis thus becomes a powerful weapon for social criticism if its precepts are sound. Anxiety begins in childhood. Lack of warmth and parental love is the prime source of anxiety; but it can also be generated by hostility, parental repression, unpredictability, frustration, and jealousy. The environment, in other words, must satisfy the basic needs of the child, and of the adult as well, for security and satisfaction. If it does not, anxiety appears as neurosis, taking the form of a demand for affection, for a partner, for power, for exploitation of others, for prestige, for personal admiration, for achievement, for independence, and for perfection, all in excessive degree. The individual, broadly speaking, may search for affection and submit to authority, rebel against authority and seek power, or withdraw. He may move toward people, away from people, or against people. In all cases the individual is seeking to escape from anxiety, but the mode of escape is determined by character and personality, which, in turn, depend on early life experience.

Horney's treatment of the relation between culture and neurosis is interesting, though brief.[38] When social practices induce feelings of fear, alienation, or hostility in the person, neuroses develop freely; and Horney believes that contemporary American culture is a veritable breeding ground for them. She ascribes these consequences to five aspects of contemporary culture in particular: competition and the resulting hostility and insecurity it breeds; inequities in access to education and the other good things of life; fear of disapproval, much aggravated by parents who deliberately foster guilt feelings in the young; lack of a solid foundation of personal relations from which human personality can develop (*gemeinschaft*); and the conflicts that arise between the fundamental value structure of society and the realities of social existence—for example, incompatibility of the idea of freedom or equality that society endorses and the actual amount of freedom and equality that the person enjoys in real life. Social conditions thus serve as the prime source of individual anxiety, and Horney's treatment of the problem implies that modifications of the social system can reduce the amount of anxiety generated within society. Freud's purely repressive society is abandoned, and Horney suggests some degree of merger of Marxian social criticism and Freudian analysis of neuroses into a single coherent weapon for social criticism, though Erich Fromm exploited that possibility much more thoroughly.

Karen Horney, then, emerges as primarily a clinical psy-

---

[38]The best statement of the point can be found in Horney, *New Ways in Psychoanalysis*, W. W. Norton & Co., Inc., chap. x, "Culture and Neuroses."

chiatrist, concerned with therapeutic questions, seeking to explain individual behavior, particularly abnormal behavior; in this sense, she is close to Freud. But where Freud explained the behavior of the individual almost wholly in terms of internal mechanisms, ignoring the environment, Horney relies very little on Freud's internal mechanisms, preferring to relate behavior to environmental conditions, particularly interpersonal relations, but also the "objective" conditions that obtain in society. Erich Fromm, largely under the influence of Marx, chose to couch his explanations of individual behavior almost wholly in terms of these objective conditions, developing a conception of behavior that makes little or no use of Freud's internal mechanisms and depends comparatively little on the interpersonal relations in which the individual engages during his lifetime. Harry Stack Sullivan, on the other hand, ignored Freud's internal mechanisms completely, paid little attention to the "objective" properties of society, and focused his attention on interpersonal relations, particularly in the early years of life, and their consequences for human personality, character, and behavior. While Horney might reasonably be considered a neo-Freudian, neither Fromm nor Sullivan can be classified in this way without stretching the meaning of the term quite unreasonably.

Erich Fromm

Unlike Horney, Erich Fromm can hardly be considered a clinical psychiatrist; more accurately, he is a trenchant social critic who makes use of psychoanalytic conceptions in his descriptions of the ills of human society but explains those conceptions in historical and essentially Marxist terms.*

*Most of Fromm's basic ideas are contained in three volumes: *Escape from Freedom* (Rinehart & Co., Inc., 1941); *The Sane Society* (Holt, Rinehart & Winston, Inc., 1955); and *Man for Himself* (Holt, Rinehart & Winston, Inc., 1947). The introduction Fromm has written to Marx's philosophic manuscripts (*Marx's Concept of Man* [Frederick Ungar Publishing Co., Inc., 1961]) is interesting, as is *Sigmund Freud's Mission* (Harper &

That is, while Horney is concerned with the effect of the environment on the human psyche, Fromm goes one step further to examine the conditions that generate the kind of environment in which the person is formed. Fromm, like Horney and Freud himself, develops a characterology; but in Fromm, character is environmentally determined, and the environment in turn is shaped primarily by the dynamics of the productive system. Like Marx, Fromm conceives man as a producer, and he concentrates on the satisfaction or lack of satisfaction that men derive from their work rather than on the interpersonal relations in which they engage. Even Fromm's characterology, which is a central part of his conceptual scheme, is rooted in the mode of production employed in the economic system rather than in personal relationships. While this might seem to lead to complete relativism, Fromm in fact attacks relativism by asserting that there is an unchanging human nature, rooted in the human genes, that can be defined in terms of basic human needs and wants. This central conception of human nature is postulated or, as Fromm would prefer, obtained by inference from an examination of the relation between human behavior and social structure and dynamics through time. Fromm finds human nature in an examination of history, not in clinical evidence.

Sensate man, subject to innate drives that are partially but not completely malleable, is the starting point. Human behavior is molded primarily by human character, and character structure is in turn determined mainly by the character of the economic system or mode of production—not, as in Horney or Sullivan, by the relations that obtain in the primary groups in which the individual is raised. Man has certain fundamental needs, which are genetically determined; and the manner in which those needs are frus-

Bros., 1959). The best full-scale critique of Fromm's writings can be found in John H. Schaar, *Escape from Authority: The Perspectives of Erich Fromm* (Basic Books, Inc., 1961).

trated or satisfied, which depends on the productive system in society, determines the social character (the core character traits) of society. There are five fundamental human needs: (1) for relatedness with others; (2) for transcendence over nature, for creativeness; (3) for roots and stability; (4) for an identity; and (5) for a frame of orientation. Since man is not, according to Fromm, infinitely plastic, the social system must in some degree correspond to these needs, or unbearable conflict and frustration will follow and, with it, mass neuroticism. Fromm is quite willing to discuss the properties of "neurotic" and "sane" societies, using his concept of "human nature" as a criterion for classification.

Most of Fromm's work is devoted to the examination of man's need for relatedness with others and the means by which that need can be satisfied in capitalistic society. The principal thesis, which is repeated endlessly in his works, is that modern man is lonely, alienated from his work, unable to enter into fruitful relations with other humans, dissatisfied, neurotic, unhappy. The assumption is taken without evidence. Following R. H. Tawney and Max Weber and, in particular, the early works of Marx, Fromm concludes that the reason for this unpleasant state of affairs is the development of capitalism and of a character structure that is necessary for capitalism but fundamentally incompatible with human nature. Capitalism demands conformity or uniformity, formal rather than personal relationships, punctuality, tidiness and close supervision of behavior, rationalization and large-scale enterprise. For the individual, life in a society dominated by the capitalistic ethic is sterile and unsatisfying. Man's capacity to produce, what Thorstein Veblen called his "instinct for workmanship," is frustrated; hence, man is "alienated" from his labor and production. Instead of productive relations with others based on love and respect, man is driven to nonproductive relations that are positively harmful. Specifically, man can only satisfy his need for relatedness with others by moral masochism or complete submission (which Fromm claims as an explanation of modern totalitarianism), by sadistic efforts to dominate others, by a striving for power and destructiveness, or by automaton conformity. Modern character types in capitalist society are nonproductive; men develop receptive characteristics rather than a capacity for giving, a marketing orientation in which men are conceived as objects with prices upon them rather than sentient creatures with intrinsic value, a hoarding rather than a sharing orientation, a competitive struggle for domination rather than a loving attitude toward others. Few persons in capitalistic society can develop what Fromm calls a productive orientation toward others. Only through "love," which Fromm uses in a slightly technical sense, can man achieve sound relations with others—inner security coupled with due regard for others and an adequate self-regard. Against Freud's pessimism and Hobbesian outlook, Fromm projects a utopian vision of a nonrepressive society in which men are psychically well balanced and able to make the fullest possible use of their innate potential.

Fromm's prescriptions for social ills we shall leave for another chapter. What is to be made of his explanations of social phenomena? First of all, though Fromm seeks explanations of human behavior or, more precisely, human psychic attitudes, and finds them in the broad sweep of historical development, his "phenomena" are in fact mainly postulates rather than empirically grounded events. The claim that man is lonely, isolated, alienated from his work, unhappy, and lacking an "identity" or adequate roots is extremely ambiguous, and Fromm nowhere provides the kinds of indicators that are needed to decide on the validity of his claims. Similarly, Fromm's catalog of basic human needs (in effect, his definition of fundamental human nature) is beyond verification or test. What does it mean precisely to "need" an "identity"? As J. A. C. Brown has noted, the social problems that obtain so much emphasis from Fromm and others like David Riesman or C. Wright Mills are by no means considered to be universal:

The problem of loneliness and social adjustment emphasized by the Neo-Freudians and by Riesman and other American writers may become more important here [in England] as populations become increasingly mobile both geographically and socially; but there is no doubt at all that, so far from being regarded as a problem, loneliness in the sense of not being bothered by neighbors or being unnecessarily spoken to on the train . . . is an important English middle-class ideal, and so far as social adjustment is concerned the English have always cherished their eccentrics, at least in retrospect.[39]

Certainly Fromm cites no firm evidence for his position on these questions, the only references being to the work of C. Wright Mills, who himself takes Fromm's assumptions for granted and does not seek to substantiate them. In strict terms, one is left with the feeling that Fromm is tilting with windmills until such time as he can demonstrate the existence of the phenomena he seeks to explain.

Even if it can be granted, however, that alienation and the need for identity are genuine social phenomena, Fromm's method of explaining them remains far from satisfactory. For example, Fromm's explanation of the phenomenon of political totalitarianism begins with the transition from medieval to modern society, in which process, according to Fromm, man gained freedom at the expense of isolation, powerlessness, and unbearable anxiety. Modern man seeks to escape from an intolerable position, either by submission to others or by self-assertion. Annihilation of self, submersion of the self in the group, is one mode of escape. The "sadomasochistic" character, basically authoritarian in outlook, which includes both the weak and the power-hungry, is temperamentally inclined to this kind of submersion.

[39]J. A. C. Brown, *Freud and the Post-Freudians* (Penguin Books, Inc., 1961), p. 79.

Fromm asserts (without evidence) that "large parts of the lower middle class in Germany and other European countries are sado-masochistic in character." Nazism, which became identified with Germany, with power, with organization and success, offered this character type an outlet for its psychic desires. Hence the growth of totalitarianism in Germany.[40] Q.E.D. Clearly, this will not do at all. Fromm has committed the teleological fallacy of supposing that what has occurred is in fact what has been desired. But that assumes, first of all, that what occurred was clearly foreseen by those who desired it and, second, that the machinery for the transformation of desires into consequences was readily at hand and available for use. It ignores the possibility that social phenomena may well be an outcome that no one desires and everyone seeks to avert—the outcome of the interaction of large aggregates of complex entities is likely to be so complex that foresight is utterly impossible, however fully informed the individual may be. To explain totalitarianism as an outcome of the interaction of character types created by the development of a particular form of economic system is to add very little to our knowledge of totalitarianism, and it comes dangerously close to the type of "instinct theory" that explained human behavior by postulating an instinct mechanism responsible for that particular form of behavior.

Fromm has been widely read in recent years, particularly by the general public, but he has not been too influential in academic circles. That is hardly regrettable. For Fromm is a social critic, not a systematic psychoanalytic theorist, a historicist rather than a historian, a historical sociologist in the German tradition rather than an analytic sociologist. The "phenomena" he purports to explain are at best tendentious; the concepts he employs are vague and ill-defined, and he rarely if ever supplies either the concrete evidence that would justify their use or the rules of transformation that

[40]Erich Fromm, *Escape from Freedom* (Rinehart & Co., Inc., 1941), especially chap. vi.

would link them to such data; his historical data rarely conincide with the facts of recorded history—they are "interpretations," not documentations; his characterology is loosely defined, complex, and impossible to apply meaningfully, since Fromm has not provided any indication of the manner in which combinations of character traits (and character is, according to Fromm, always a combination of traits and not a pure "ideal type") influence behavior. Finally, Fromm is a methodological essentialist, in Karl R. Popper's sense of the term; and certain key conceptions in his thought (the idea of human nature, for example) are treated in an essentialist rather than a nominalist manner, thus removing them irrevocably from all possibility of verification or testing.[41] Whatever the value of Fromm's work as social critic may be, his attempts at explanation are at best too weak to be taken seriously; and at worst, they are grossly misleading and wholly at odds with the facts.

Harry Stack Sullivan

Harry Stack Sullivan, the third major figure usually included in the so-called "neo-Freudians," was a practicing clinical psychiatrist, American-born and American-trained. Though he was "influenced" by Freud in the general sense that any psychiatrist owes a debt to the founder of the psychoanalytic movement, Sullivan was no Freudian: Freud is rarely cited in Sullivan's writings, Freudian terminology is abandoned, few "Freudian" conceptions are found in his theoretical structure. Sullivan created his own concepts for explaining psychic phenomena; and in many respects, his work provides the most fully developed non-Freudian conceptual structure presently available to psychiatry. Primarily, Sullivan was a social psychologist, seeking a bridge between psychology and social science. Like most American psy-

---

[41]See Erich Fromm, *The Sane Society* (Holt, Rinehart & Winston, Inc., 1955), p. 29; and *Man for Himself* (Holt, Rinehart & Winston, Inc., 1947), pp. 88, 97, 102–3, 105.

chologists, he was profoundly influenced by logical empiricism, particularly the "operationalism" of Percy Bridgman, and by the writings of sociologists and anthropologists like George H. Mead, Ruth Benedict, Bronislaw Malinowski, and others. Sullivan was quite eclectic, even incorporating a number of concepts taken from Kurt Lewin's field theory in his construction. Sullivan's use of the concept "experience," for example, is very close to Lewin's notion of "locomotion," and Sullivan's conception of the environment in which men live is stated in terms very similar to those used by Lewin to explain the notion of "life space." Finally, Sullivan was interested in semantic and communication problems and was strongly influenced by the work of Edward Sapir—largely, of course, because communications theory has important consequences for any psychological theory that emphasizes the importance of interpersonal relations. In contrast to Fromm's sweeping historical generalizations, Sulivan's work is cautious, empirically based, and quite rigorous. He was acutely aware of the requirements of adequate explanation, of testability or verification; and his writings are heavily interlarded with data. He concentrated particularly on the study of what he called "dynamisms," defined as "relatively enduring patterns of energy transformations [acts of behavior] which recurrently characterize the organism in its duration as a living organism."[42] Dynamisms are very close to habits, as Sullivan has defined them, indicating clearly his preference for dealing with *regularities* in behavior rather than the unique and nonrepeatable—an essential emphasis for anyone concerned with the development of consistent empirical theory.

In sharp contrast to Fromm or Horney, and more especially Freud, Sullivan begins with an "unperson" rather than a person. The individual as a distinct unit simply does not

[42]Harry Stack Sullivan, *The Interpersonal Theory of Psychiatry,* Helen Ewick Perry and Mary Ladd Gawel (eds.) (W. W. Norton & Co., Inc., 1953), p. 103.

exist so far as Sullivan is concerned; following George H. Mead, he conceives of the individual as the center of a complex set of actions and interactions; and in quite radical terms, he insists that these interactions *are* the person, the unit to be studied, thus making psychiatry a discipline concerned with more or less observable phenomena rather than a study in depth of a psychic organism. The emphasis has led some students to complain that the individual virtually disappears in Sullivan's work, leaving a social matrix in which the individual serves only as a carrier or transmission element rather than an integral and independent unit. Even self-evaluations are made in terms of the reactions of others, as in Mead's theory of self.

From birth, according to Sullivan, the living human organism undergoes three basic types of experience: (1) prototaxic—the undifferentiated raw experiences of the infant; (2) parataxic—the disconnected, atomistic experiences of the child before it learns a language; and (3) syntactic—experiences gained through the manipulation of consensually validated and applied symbols and signs. Types of experience are related to a developmental program based on changing needs in the growing organism. Each of the seven periods in Sullivan's hierarchy ends with the development of a new need on the part of the growing child. Thus the period of *infancy*, commencing a few minutes after birth, lasts until articulate speech begins; *childhood*, which succeeds infancy, endures until the need for playmates arises; the *juvenile* period ends with the need for intimate friendship; *pre-adolescence* ends with the need for relationships with members of the opposite sex; *adolescence* lasts until a behavior pattern has been established for the satisfaction of genital drives; *late adolescence* survives until a stable personality pattern emerges; at that point where the person is capable of establishing love relations with another person in which that person is as significant as the self, he has reached *adulthood*. Sullivan's conception of "love" resembles in some respects the usage adopted by Erich Fromm, but it is much more specific and more clearly defined. Love relations, in Sullivan as in Fromm or Horney, are the principal source of satisfaction in human life.

The dynamic characteristics of Sullivan's structure are quite simple. Tensions within the organism (needs) produce energy transformations, or behavior, aimed at satisfaction of those needs. The organism is essentially a homeostat, moving between the polar extremes (ideal types) of absolute tension, which Sullivan describes as utter terror, and absolute satisfaction, which he calls euphoria. All human behavior, then, is designed to relieve tensions. However, there is another behavior generator in the system—anxiety. Unlike needs, which are specific and can be pursued, anxiety is general, and the organism cannot deliberately seek to eliminate anxiety after the manner in which it pursues its own needs. Anxieties arise from two principal sources: from sudden disturbances in the environment, and from an empathy, which Sullivan cannot explain, between the significant caretaking person, usually the female parent, and the infant. The search for security, which comes with the relaxation of anxiety, cannot be pursued successfully without aid from the external environment. Fulfillment of needs (satisfaction) and relief of anxiety (security) are the two goals that human beings pursue, according to Sullivan—clearly a teleological construction of behavior. Further, since Sullivan's dynamisms are habitual patterns rather than unique behavioral acts, his system is concerned primarily to account for the regular manner in which the individual deals with tensions and with anxieties, defined in terms of the individual's relations with other persons. This leads, clearly enough, to personality theory and characterology as Sullivan seeks to generalize and systematize his data. The central focus is anxiety rather than need satisfaction, since anxiety rather than tension generates the kind of behavior that indicates a need for psychiatric care.

Faced with anxiety, or conscious of anxiety, the individual

can seek to eliminate the source, seek to escape from its influence, neutralize its influence through apathy and attenuation of attentiveness, or ignore the source of anxiety. Sullivan places a great deal of stress on the importance of anxiety in human life, noting that it can literally paralyze the individual and force him to devote all of his energies to attempts to escape from anxiety rather than to constructive and productive projects. And anxiety, in Sullivan's scheme, arises from the external environment; thus, it cannot really be handled by the individual alone (hence the need for psychiatrists?). This places a great deal of responsibility on the maternal person, on whoever mothers the child, since it follows from Sullivan's assumptions that plenty of tender loving care, as the aphorism goes, makes for security in the infant. In fact, he considers this so important that he postulates a special empathy between child and caretaker that induces the parent to care for the child and the child to find relief from anxiety through the ministrations of the parent or caretaker.

Out of its succession of experiences, its feelings of tension and relief from tension, and its feelings of anxiety and modes of dealing with those anxieties, the individual develops a personality, a "relatively enduring pattern of recurrent interpersonal situations which characterize a human life." It also develops a self-system, an organization of past experience that can be used to cope with anxiety, based on self-understanding gained through self-reflection in the behavior of others. These two structures interact to produce the behavior patterns the individual displays in his relations with others. Interpersonal situations, then, may be characterized as the interaction of complex personality and self systems, each of which is in some degree consistent and stable, but each of which is open to influence by current experience. Sullivan postulates some few principles governing these interactions—unattainable objects may be treated as though they did not exist (selective inattention), the self-system may tend to ignore experience that does not fit into previous patterns, or patterns may be substituted when they create discord, thus eliminating tension or anxiety—some very close to those found in Freud; but the emphasis on relations with others and the lack of concern with innate drives set him off from the Freudians almost completely.

Sullivan's characterology or, more precisely, the typology he used to deal with different kinds of orientations toward living begins with the fundamental assumption that the individual's way of behaving in different situations "is derived from consensually validated trial-and-error learning from personal examples, analysis and synthesis of the experience thus obtained, and the remedial disintegration of self-system processes which have survived from the earlier 'education by by anxiety'."[43] A person with a fully integrated personality will have developed behavior patterns which satisfy both his inner needs for satisfaction and security and the external requirements of the community. The latter point is extremely important, for, unlike Freud, Sullivan believed that no person could simply seek inner satisfaction without regard for the consequences of his actions for others—indeed, that is tautologously true in Sullivan's conceptualization simply because the self-system includes necessarily a reflection of the evaluation of self by others. The implied suggestion that psychiatry and sociology or cultural anthropology should be fused would certainly meet with Sullivan's approval.[44] However, Sullivan's typology has only limited usefulness for social scientists. He distinguished, for example, a variety of characters or personalities, but the manner of their development is only sketched or suggested, and the interaction of various personality types in structured situations, which is of most concern to social science, is hardly touched, perhaps

[43]Patrick Mullahy, "The Theories of H. S. Sullivan," in Patrick Mullahy (ed.), *The Contributions of Harry Stack Sullivan* (Hermitage House, 1952), p. 53.

[44]One volume of Sullivan's work is entitled *The Fusion of Psychiatry and Social Science* (W. W. Norton & Co., Inc., 1964).

because Sullivan was fundamentally committed to the therapeutic outlook. In a brief note on the problem of explaining individual-group relationships, for example, he limits the psychiatrist to the study of interpersonal relations in which he is a participant or to other aspects of the interpersonal relations of the patient that have influenced his particular mode of development.[45] Certainly the kinds of personality structures Sullivan identified and used—the self-absorbed, those without social feelings, the hostile, the negativistic, the attention-seeking, the ambition-ridden, the asocial and detached, the homosexual, the chronic adolescent—are more helpful to the therapist than to the social scientist. In this, as in other respects, Sullivan is much closer to Horney than to Fromm.

Interestingly enough, if we move from Sullivan's interpersonal theory of psychology to the work of "ego-psychologists" like Erik H. Erikson (a pupil of Anna Freud), the gross differences in language serve to cover great similarities in conceptualization. Sullivan and Erikson very often say exactly the same thing, even though they use quite different language. Sullivan rarely mentions Freud and does not use the Freudian vocabulary. Erikson's patients are described in Freudian terminology: His little girls discover that they have no penis, his boys have Oedipal complexes, the various pleasure zones of the body are described in erotogenic terms; but what emerges, beneath the cover of language, sounds very much like Sullivan, Horney, or Fromm.

For Erikson, the child is no longer a simple Freudian font of pure libidinal drive. "The human being, thus, is at all times an organism, an ego, and a member of a society and is involved in all three processes of organization. His body is exposed to pain and tension; his ego to anxiety; and, as a member of a society, he is susceptible to the panic emanating

---

[45]Sullivan, "A Note on Formulating the Relationship of the Individual and the Group," *ibid.*

from his group."[46] Even the organism is spoken of as a process for dealing with anxiety, construed in terms very similar to those Sullivan employs. Anxiety is primarily social rather than individual; "there is no individual anxiety which does not reflect a latent concern common to the immediate and extended group." The ego handles anxiety in much the same way that Sullivan's organism seeks security and for the same reasons:

[This] central process [organization of experience in the individual ego] guards the coherence and the individuality of experience by gearing the individual for shock threatening from sudden discontinuities in the organism as well as in the milieu; by enabling it to anticipate inner as well as outer dangers; and by integrating endowment and social opportunities. It thus assures to the individual a sense of coherent individuation and identity; of being one's self, of being all right, and of being on the way to becoming what other people, at their kindest, take one to be.[47]

The simple substitution of "security" for "ego identity" would make this statement completely compatible with Sullivan without any significant change in meaning. Like Fromm, Erikson links the loss of identity (or loss of security, that is, anxiety) to certain aspects of American culture—relations between mother and son, toilet training, failure of political leaders to allow the educated youth of the country some voice in communal affairs (which may well account for Erikson's popularity with the younger generation). Like the "neo-Freudians," he stresses the importance of the early years of life; "therapy and guidance by professionals are doomed to failure where the culture refuses to provide an early basis for an identity and where opportunities for appropriate later adjustments are missing." And his sketch of the development of the child's ego follows closely the pattern set by Sullivan

---

[46]Erik H. Erikson, *Childhood and Society* (2d ed.; W. W. Norton & Co., Inc., 1963), p. 36.
[47]*Ibid.*, p. 35.

in his writings, again provided that "security and satisfaction" are substituted for "sense of ego identity." "The infant's first social achievement, then, is his willingness to let the mother out of sight without undue anxiety or rage, because she has become an inner certainty as well as an outer predictability. Such consistency, continuity, and sameness of experience provide a rudimentary sense of ego identity. . . ."[48] Further, he makes use of Sullivan's notion of empathy between parent and child, though under another term: "Parents . . . must also be able to represent to the child a deep, an almost somatic conviction that there is meaning to what they are doing," that is, a sense of security.

Erikson's developmental scheme, a sequence of "identity crises," shows similar parallels with Sullivan's conceptual structure. The first crisis, occurring in early infancy, determines the basic attitudes of trust or mistrust on the child's part. Sequentially, others determine the dichotomy between autonomy/shame or doubt, initiative/guilt, industry/inferiority, identity/role confusion, intimacy/isolation, generativity/stagnation, ego integrity/despair. Both Erikson and Sullivan define these outcomes in terms of relations with other people, and in both cases the outcomes themselves are a consequence of the behavior of other people. In both cases the ultimate criterion of an integrated personality becomes a capacity for love for others (Sullivan) or genitality (Erikson). Both make use of George H. Mead's view that the self is organized by the individual in terms of its reflection in the opinions of others; "developing youths . . . are now primarily concerned with what they appear to be in the eyes of others as compared with what they feel they are, and with the question of how to connect the roles and skills cultivated earlier with the occupational prototypes of the day."[49] Further, Erikson, like Fromm, is much concerned with the relation between the emergence of modern industrial civilization

[48]*Ibid.*, p. 247.
[49]*Ibid.*, p. 261.

and character development, and even more particularly with the rise of authoritarianism and totalitarianism—hence his studies of Adolf Hitler, Maxim Gorky, and Martin Luther. And finally, Erikson is open to criticism on the same grounds that can be used to attack Fromm and, to some degree, Sullivan. The conceptions employed are loose, the data are often tendentious, the explanations are really interpretations —often very free interpretations indeed. Verification or dis- verification is difficult or even impossible.

Critique and Applications

Horney, Fromm, Erikson, and, to a lesser extent, Sullivan have had an enormous influence on contemporary social thought, particularly on the quality of social criticism. Fromm, Erikson, and, to some degree, Horney have been closely related to what is sometimes called the "culture and personality" school of social inquiry—to those who seek to explain and criticize social phenomena in terms of the way in which culture and personality interact.[50] Those who have sought to explain modern mass society, particularly in the United States, have very often used them as sources. In part, this influence may be due to the fact that Fromm and Erik- son, in particular, have concentrated heavily on explanation and criticism of mass society; hence, they supply ammuni- tion for the critic. In part, it may also be a reflection of the effort to find adequate grounds for social criticisms that are not open to irrational attack as "Marxist" by a nation some- what hagridden by international tensions.

Very briefly, Fromm, Horney, Sullivan, and Erikson all begin with the concept of an individual as an equilibrating

[50]Margaret Mead, Abram Kardiner, Geoffrey Gorer, A. T. Adorno, Erik H. Erikson, Ruth Benedict, and Erich Fromm, among others, are usually considered part of the "culture and personality" set. The development of this line of inquiry is traced in a very interesting way by one of the participants, Margaret Mead, in an article entitled "National Character and the Science of Anthropology," in Seymour M. Lipset and Leo Lowenthal (eds.), *Culture and Social Character: The Work of David Riesman Re- viewed* (Free Press of Glencoe, Inc., 1961).

mechanism fitted out with some few basic operating procedures but organized primarily by principles drawn from experience. They differ in some degree in the emphasis that is placed on the influence of early childhood: Sullivan and Horney tend to give a larger place to subsequent experience than Erikson, who is closer to orthodox Freudianism. Each is concerned with the more or less regular behavior patterns of the individual, with what is called character or personality, including both its conscious and unconscious elements. They discuss, with varying degrees of precision, the manner in which character and personality are formed, and the kinds of influences that count most heavily in their formation. Here, Fromm, who stresses the importance of the objective conditions in society, differs most sharply from Horney, Sullivan, and Erikson, who tend to emphasize interpersonal relations rather than the influence of social institutions and practices. Each develops a typology of character, fairly simple in Fromm and Horney, more complex in Sullivan and Erikson, but in many respects similar for all four systems of thought. Finally, each is concerned with the impact of interpersonal transactions and social conditions on different kinds of character, most prominently in Fromm and least prominently in Sullivan. Horney, Sullivan, and Erickson are strict personalists, perhaps an indication of their clinical bias; Fromm is oriented more to sociological explanation of classes of humans rather than individuals—a distinction that emerges very clearly when we examine the kind of work that Fromm has inspired.

More formally, the "sociological" psychiatrists deal with factorial theories, or factorial models, of a very weak sort. Their character typologies are uniformly ideal types, since in every case they agree that actual working characters are "mixes" of the various "pure" character types. In general, all four writers deal with man in broad and general terms rather than with concise and specific empirical instances; their concepts and terms tend to be vaguely defined, particularly in

Fromm and Erikson and less markedly in Sullivan. None of the typologies they have offered are definitive, since there are significant differences among the four and no means of deciding which should be accepted. Further, the rules governing the interactions among the elements of the typologies are rarely if ever specified; hence, there are no guidelines for dealing with empirical data where the typology is mixed. In general, little concrete evidence is offered to support the conceptual structures used to explain behavior, and there are not enough transformation rules to provide linkages to empirical data that would allow a decision on the validity or applicability of the typology. Finally, though each of the four psychiatrists deals with social phenomena, and even with "social character," no justification is offered for the transition from individual to social terms, despite the serious methodological problems that are raised by the "personification" of social groups implied in discussions of "national character" or "social character." In sum, the conceptual schemes comprised in what we have called "sociological" psychoanalysis are exceedingly difficult to employ in concrete empirical research and, in most cases, almost impossible to test or verify adequately.

These shortcomings, as well as the heuristic usefulness of "sociological" psychoanalysis, are best illustrated by a brief examination of some of the efforts that have been made to use them in the explanation of concrete social phenomena. No "theory" or conceptual framework has value beyond its capacity to link phenomena together or suggest lines of inquiry that are worth pursuing, and the attempt to actually use a theory to deal with genuine phenomena is the acid test. Although "neo-Freudian" psychoanalysis, or preferably "sociological" psychoanalysis, has been more influential than orthodox Freudianism among social scientists, it has not really been applied to *explanation* very frequently; most often, it is used as a basis for social criticism rather than explanation. I can find no clear illustration of an application of Horney's theories to social phenomena, for example; but in the case of Fromm, Sullivan, and Erikson, we are more fortunate. David Riesman's *Lonely Crowd: A Study of the Changing American Character,* one of the most widely read sociological-psychological volumes of the postwar era, is clearly influenced by Fromm. As Riesman himself asserts: "Thus, we ourselves were in the tradition of the neo-Freudians, particularly Erich Fromm, with whom I had studied. Fromm's *Escape from Freedom* and *Man for Himself,* were decisively influential models in the application of a socially oriented psychoanalytic characterology to problems of historical change."[51]

Robert Presthus' *Organizational Society: An Analysis and a Theory* specifically relies upon the work of Harry Stack Sullivan, though in fact Sullivan's conceptions are combined with stimulus-response learning theory, and Presthus is somewhat eclectic in his borrowing.[52] For an illustration of Erikson's influence, we have available a study of Burmese politics by Lucian W. Pye of the Massachusetts Institute of Technology.[53] An examination and comparison of these three studies will indicate better than any generalized argument the kinds of strengths and weaknesses the respective conceptual structures display in use.

Riesman's *Lonely Crowd* is a difficult book to evaluate and an exasperating book to read; in fact, it has been the subject of a whole volume of criticism and evaluation—a compliment to its attraction if not to its clarity.[54] The difficulties

[51]David Riesman, *The Lonely Crowd: A Study of the Changing American Character,* with Nathan Glazer and Reuel Denny (abridged ed.; Yale University Press, 1961), p. xiv.

[52]Robert Presthus, *The Organizational Society: An Analysis and a Theory* (Alfred A. Knopf, Inc., 1962), p. 93.

[53]Lucian W. Pye, *Politics, Personality, and Nation Building: Burma's Search for Identity* (Yale University Press, 1962).

[54]Lipset and Lowenthal, *op. cit.*

arise mainly out of a lack of conceptual clarity (noted by the author but left unremedied), a disparity between announced intentions and accomplishments, and a failure to make explicit the principal theme of the work, to be expected in a student of Fromm, regarding the influence of social institutions and practices on the development of character. That is not to say that the book does not provide some fascinating insights and speculations and criticisms of American society in the mid-20th century, for that is the book's principal attraction. But as an attempt to explain social phenomena, to organize and relate data through a typology of character (a model, actually, constructed of "ideal types"), the book fails miserably.

The conceptual framework that Riesman employs centers around three basic types of social—not individual—character, which he called *tradition-directed, inner-directed,* and *other-directed,* each associated with a particular form of society. Briefly, people in a tradition-directed society are controlled and directed by the traditions of the society in which they live; inner-directed societies are characterized by persons whose behavior is directed by an internalized set of restraints, implanted early in life by the elders, and "directed toward generalized but nonetheless inescapably destined goals"; other-directed character types seek direction from their contemporaries rather than from themselves or from tradition.

There are two difficulties in the characterology. First, the concept of social character is ambiguous and very difficult to link to empirical data, as Riesman realizes:

I do not plan to delay over the many ambiguities of the concept of social character—whether it may properly be ascribed to experience rather than to heredity; whether there is any empirical proof that it really exists; whether it deserves to be regarded as more important than the elements of character and personality that bind all people everywhere in the world together, or those other elements of character and personality that separate each individual from every other, even the closest. The assumption that a social character exists has always been a more or less invisible premise of ordinary parlance and is becoming today a more or less visible premise of the social sciences.[55]

In addition to the cavalier treatment of conceptual clarity, Riesman's scheme is open to the further objection that even in his own terms it is the content of the environment rather than the form of the relationship to the environment that is decisive in the behavior of the character types he formulates. That is, an inner-directed person in a traditional society who occupied the same social position as an other-directed person would, in Riesman's terms, behave in exactly the same way as an individual directed solely by tradition. That being the case, the distinction in environments is crucial, and the difference in the mode of acquisition of behavior patterns is derivative, unless it can be demonstrated that the manner in which conformity is ensured (Riesman's standard) has consequences of its own. If, for example, Riesman were to argue that even if the behavior patterns enforced by society were the same, the consequences of inner direction and other direction for the individual psyche were grossly disparate, then his characterology would be useful, but that is precisely what he does not argue in any detail. Riesman, in other words, has confused or failed to distinguish psychological and sociocultural data; he is not seeking to explain behavioral phenomena in psychological terms but, following Fromm, to relate historical and sociocultural data on a broad scale to very generally defined personality or character types.[56]

The lack of a clearly defined purpose in *The Lonely Crowd* makes it singularly difficult to evaluate its usefulness, since accomplishment is always measured relative to intent or pur-

[55]Riesman, *et al., op. cit.*, p. 4.

[56]See particularly Sheldon L. Messinger and Burton R. Clark, "Individual Character and Social Constraint: A Critique of David Riesman's Theory of Social Conduct"; and Robert Gutman and Dennis Wrong, "David Riesman's Typology of Character," both in Lipset and Lowenthal, *op. cit.*

pose. In particular, it is almost impossible to say what role is intended for the typology of character he has devised. The opening paragraph of the book reflects this indecision:

This is a book about social character and about the differences in social character between men of different regions, eras, and groups. . . . More particularly, it is about the way in which one kind of social character, which dominated America in the nineteenth century, is gradually being replaced by a social character of quite a different sort. Why this happened; how it happened; what are the consequences in some major areas of life: this is the subject of this book.[57]

However, when Seymour M. Lipset objected that the postulated change in American character did not really fit the facts, citing book, chapter and verse, Riesman's reply considerably weakens the case that might be made for designating this the central thesis of the volume: "Reading Lipset's paper, we had the strong feeling that, whatever the testimony of travelers and historians, we had *seen* American character change in our lifetime. Such a sentiment is unscientific but stubborn. Yet we think it amounts to something more than the customary feeling of each generation that it isn't what its fathers were."[58]

A second possible goal of the book is to determine the relation between social character and society. Here, Riesman quotes a suggestion from Erich Fromm to the effect that societies acquire the kinds of characters they need by socializing people to do what is necessary through inner compulsion. Riesman claims that the link between character and society is to be found "in the way in which society ensures some degree of conformity from the individuals who make it up."[59] But he is not going to investigate the nature and operation of the linkage, for he turns immediately to a Frommian discussion of the relationship between "modes of conformity"

[57]Riesman, *et al.*, *op. cit.*, p. 3.
[58]See Seymour M. Lipset, "A Changing American Character?" in Lipset and Lowenthal, *op. cit.*, and David Riesman, with the collaboration of Nathan Glazer, "The Lonely Crowd: A Reconsideration in 1960," *ibid.*, p. 431.
[59]Riesman, *et al.*, *op. cit.*, p. 5.

and the two "great revolutions" in Western civilization—one ending medievalism and the other shifting social emphasis from production to consumption (following a thesis developed by John K. Galbraith in *The Affluent Society*). That, too, is dropped quite abruptly, and Riesman shifts to still another possible focus for the book—the relation between population shifts and trends and the development of social character. Using a demographic conceptualization (since discredited), Riesman then examines in some detail the characteristics of societies marked by "high growth potential," "transitional growth," and "incipient population decline" (terms taken from Frank W. Notestein) and their predominant social characters. A substantial part of one chapter is devoted to this discussion; it seems to be the central focus of explanation in the book. But Riesman has since abandoned the population-character relation as a consequence of the criticisms offered by professional demographers.[60] Hence, if the basic aim of the book is to explore that relation, we need only say that it failed for lack of an adequate demographic base.

In sum, Riesman fails to stipulate clearly and explicitly the way in which his psychological constructions are to be employed in the inquiry he has undertaken; and though the theory is framed in psychological, individual terms, *The Lonely Crowd* actually contains very little data that refer to these matters. Riesman has not produced a book that explains behavior in psychological terms, but a book that contains an implicit historical-sociological explanation of psychological phenomena. Riesman supports this assessment in the Preface to the 1961 edition of *The Lonely Crowd*:

It is our surmise now that the change toward other-direction with a loosening of the sense of personal destiny, is in part a consequence of those forbiddingly powerful and efficient institutions that inner-directed men conceived, organized, and rendered transportable. One of these institutions was the free market,

---

[60]*Ibid.*, pp. xxx–xxxii.

which, in late capitalism, affects not only the market for money and goods but the self-salesmanship of individuals (as Erich Fromm's term in *Man for Himself*, "the marketing orientation," makes clear).[61]

Riesman has followed Fromm extremely well, if not always self-consciously. But he has not produced a psychological explanation of social phenomena, nor has he used his characterology as an explanatory device. Instead, the typology has been used as a framework for the examination and criticism of certain recent developments in American society. There is a serious gap between the stated intentions of the author and the actual content of the book, even if all of Riesman's caveats are taken into consideration. It is much easier to assert that a "psychoanalytic" or "psychological" explanation of certain phenomena will be offered than to produce the explanation.

The fault does not lie entirely with the user, though it seems that a clearer understanding of the nature of explanation might reduce some of the confusion. Nonpsychologists tend to overrate the coherence and explanatory power of psychological theory, and more generally to confuse a systematic approach to the subject matter with a genuine theory. More important still, those who borrow conceptual frameworks from other disciplines—or take them from their own field, for that matter—too often forget that every theory must have a referent; it must be a theory *of* something, some phenomenon. When Robert Presthus asserts that "Sullivan's interpersonal theory of psychiatry is turned to the analysis of individual behavior in big organizations," he is talking utter nonsense—there can be no "theory of psychiatry" any more than there can be a "theory of physics" or a "theory of politics." Theories explain particular phenomena, and if they are to be applied to different phenomena, their relevance to those phenomena must be established. Furthermore, in the

[61]*Ibid.*, p. xxvi.

social sciences and in psychology the theories available for use are rarely able to explain adequately even the limited phenomena for which they were intended. Sullivan and Horney, for example, can explain certain limited kinds of neurotic behavior more or less imperfectly; and those explanations may be preferable, for complex reasons, to the explanations that an orthodox Freudian can offer. A theory that could explain every human action would be a very powerful tool indeed, but the complexity and richness of the phenomena are such that it seems unlikely that such a theory could be applied without stipulating endless limiting conditions. To "explain" human behavior as "anxiety reduction," for example, is a waste of time. It leads to endless discussion of the meaning of "anxiety," the differences in the means chosen for anxiety reduction, and so on. The reason is simply that all explanations must be open to control and modification by the evidence available, and evidence is always particular.

Although Robert Presthus belongs in the same broad tradition as David Riesman, C. Wright Mills, Thorstein Veblen, and other contemporary social critics, his stated intentions in *The Organizational Society: An Analysis and a Theory* are explanatory as well as critical. Specifically, he aims at "a theory of organizational behavior" that will explain the way in which individuals accommodate themselves to the milieu supplied by large-scale organizations. His principal conceptual tool is a typology of personality (he seems unaware of the distinction that is customarily drawn between personality and character) which is his own formulation, though it resembles in many respects the typologies of Fromm, Riesman, and others. The book also pursues a normative goal: criticism of the value structure fostered by large-scale organizations in terms of "the democratic ideals of free expression, individual worth, and spontaneity."[62] Our

[62]Presthus, *op. cit.*, p. 17.

concern here is with the explanatory aspects of the book only.

The model, or "ideal type," of large-scale organization that Presthus employs is characterized by large size, specialization of function, hierarchical ordering of authority, status differentiation, oligarchical rule with co-optation of rulers and rational, efficient operation. This form of social organization is related to three personality types: *upward-mobiles*, defined as those who react favorably to the bureaucratic milieu; *indifferents*, who use work as a means of satisfying off-work desires; and *ambivalents*, who can neither renounce their ambitions within the organization nor accept the discipline and control it requires. Presthus assumes that organizations can be taken as societies in miniature so far as the socialization process is concerned—though it should be noted that no society is so formally and rigidly organized and controlled as a large business firm.

The typology suffers at least one major fault. The types are defined in terms of reaction to bureaucracy, yet that implies that something is brought to the bureaucracy by the person, not created by the bureaucracy. Hence the assumption that the bureaucratic situation serves as a character-or personality-*forming* device cannot be tested against these categories, though that is one of the goals Presthus has set for the inquiry. The tendency for American parents to raise children with personalities suitable to life within large-scale organization is touched upon but not treated in detail; adequately handled, it might provide a bridge between the two sets of conceptualizations. To further complicate the question, Presthus seems to accept the usual psychoanalytic position that the earlier years are decisive in personality formation, even though change continues in later life, for he ascribes to childhood experiences the various personality structures of administrators examined in brief vignettes in the introductory material, presumably as an indication of the operation of the socialization process.

The dynamics of the interaction between personality and social environment is adopted from Harry Stack Sullivan's *Theory of Interpersonal Psychiatry,* though Presthus also claims to employ theoretical constructs from stimulus-response psychology. That is, man is assumed to be predominantly a social product and not a prisoner of his genetic heritage. Personality is defined as "a consistent way of reacting or accommodating to interpersonal situations." Here, there seems to be some departure from Sullivan's conceptualization, for Presthus' definition of personality corresponds most closely to Sullivan's definition of a dynamism—"relatively enduring patterns of energy transformations which recurrently characterize interpersonal relations" —rather than Sullivan's definition of personality—"relatively enduring patterns of recurrent interpersonal *situations* which characterize a human life."[63] Furthermore, Presthus does not make Sullivan's distinction between tensions arising from specific situations and the more generalized anxiety tensions which require outside assistance for dispersal. In view of the importance Sullivan attaches to the distinction, we can expect Presthus to fail to differentiate adequately between Sullivan's generalizations about actions aimed at tension release and those directed specifically to the relief of anxiety; and that, in fact, is the case. Presthus asserts, for example, that "most behavior" is the result of the individual's search for relief from tension (conforming to authority). Sullivan makes no such assertion. First, Sullivan would argue that men seek relief from *anxiety* rather than tension; second, he nowhere claims that the principal mode of releasing tension is conformity to authority. Security,

[63]Sullivan, *The Interpersonal Theory of Psychiatry,* pp. 103 and 110–11. While it can be granted that Sullivan's distinction is not entirely clear, a dynamism is very close to the everyday notion of habit, while personality is defined in terms of the total interpersonal situation, including the "others" in the environment—a peculiar usage, but one consistent with Sullivan's notions that the psychiatrist in an interview is actually "part" of the relational complex, and it is tied to the concept of "personifications," which Presthus does not mention.

which Sullivan defines specifically as relief from *anxiety* (as against satisfaction, which is relief of need tensions), may be sought in various ways, and the principal thesis in Sullivan seems to be that the individual seeks to *avoid* interpersonal situations that are associated with tension or anxiety in the past.

To further complicate the theoretical structure, Presthus makes use of some conceptions drawn from Margaret Mead, Abram Kardiner, and Erich Fromm that are not really compatible with Sullivan's conceptual framework. Mead, for example, claimed that the custom of teasing children in Bali leads to "withdrawn" adults; and Kardiner claims that where both parents reject the child, the result is a suspicious and hostile adult—generalizations that Sullivan would certainly not endorse in that form. Fromm's claim that the German middle class sought to "escape from freedom" into Hitlerian authoritarianism would similarly have violated the methodological principles Sullivan tried to hold to in his work.[64] Furthermore, Presthus' use of the authoritarian personality scale from Adorno's *The Authoritarian Personality* (equating the authoritarian personality with his "upward-mobile" personality) is also incompatible with Sullivan's conceptual scheme. Sullivan's enumeration of character types is much more detailed than Presthus' and oriented more to the needs of the clinical psychiatrist.

In sum, when we ask specifically what Sullivan has added to Presthus' treatment of large-scale organizations or, perhaps more concisely, what difference it would make in Presthus' treatment of his subject matter if Sullivan's influence were eliminated from *The Organizational Society*, the answer must be "Not very much!" Presthus follows Sullivan in

[64]See Abram Kardiner, *The Psychological Frontiers of Society* (Columbia University Press, 1945); and R. E. Money-Kyrle, *Psychoanalysis and Politics* (W. W. Norton & Co., Inc., 1951); or any of Margaret Mead's books for typical examples of this mode of treating character and the formative influences of childhood.

assuming that environmental influences are prime in the formation of personality or character. He deals with the problem of character formation only in passing, preferring to concentrate on the dysfunctional properties of large-scale organizations for the three different personality types he posits. While some of his observations about human interactions within large-scale organizations are interesting and informative, in no sense can the book be considered an application of Harry Stack Sullivan's psychiatric theories to social phenomena. Like Riesman, Presthus seems to have "tacked on" a psychiatric orientation to a work in which it does not really fit. While it is true that many of Presthus' criticisms of society parallel those found in Horney, Sullivan, and Fromm, the criticisms are neither peculiar to psychiatrists nor justified by psychiatric theory; they happen to be couched in terms that are associated with psychiatry and psychology (anomie, alienation, loss of identity), but that does not make them valid psychiatric conceptions.

Lucian W. Pye's study of Burma is an attempt to explore the psychiatric or psychological aspects of what Pye calls "transitional society," using the concept of "ego identity" developed by Erik H. Erikson.[65] The title of the book is misleading, for Pye nowhere discusses personality systematically, does not define it, and does not produce a typology of either character or personality; even the index contains no entry under "personality." Pye seeks an explanation of the apparent failure of the underdeveloped nations to expand and develop as rapidly as might have been expected when nationhood was first achieved. He finds that explanation in the development of certain states of mind among the Burmese through the interaction of the socialization process and social institutions and practices. The bulk of the book, however, consists of a more or less traditional—and extremely well-informed—examination of the political process in tra-

[65]Pye, *op. cit.*, pp. 52–53.

ditional and contemporary Burma. The psychological speculations are, as it were, imposed from without on this body
of material, often quite casually and artificially and without any real integration of conceptual structure and data.

The analytic model of transitional politics offered in chapter ii, for example, is carefully stated in the form of 17 postulates:

1. The political sphere is not sharply differentiated from the
   spheres of social and personal relations.
2. Political parties tend to take on a world view and represent a way of life.
3. There is a prevalence of cliques.
4. The character of political loyalty gives political leaders a
   high degree of freedom in determining policies.
5. Opposition parties and aspiring elites tend to appear as
   revolutionary movements.
6. There is little or no integration among the participants
   due to the lack of a unified communications system.
7. New elements are recruited to political roles at a high
   rate.
8. There are sharp differences in the political orientation of
   the generations.
9. Little consensus exists as to the legitimate ends and means
   of political action.
10. The intensity and prevalence of political discussion bear
    little relationship to political decision making.
11. Roles are highly interchangeable.
12. There are relatively few explicitly organized interest
    groups with functionally specific roles.
13. The national leadership must appeal to an undifferentiated
    public.
14. Leaders are encouraged to adopt more clearly defined
    positions on international issues than on domestic issues.
15. The affective or expressive aspect of politics tends to
    override the problem-solving or public-policy aspect.
16. Charismatic leaders tend to prevail.
17. The political process operates largely without benefit of
    political "brokers."

Curiously enough, there are no propositions included in
the defining model of transitional politics dealing with the

process of socialization, implying by silence that socialization is universal and not subject to cultural variation. The socialization process is defined in three stages: the introduction of the child to society; political socialization; and finally, political recruitment. The treatment is brief, about four pages, yet the generalizations made about socialization are very wide-ranging indeed. In the basic socialization process, involving both manifest and latent experience, the individual "finds his identity as a member of society and achieves coherence as an effective person with a central perspective and direction and with a capacity to preserve his integrity and his essential characteristics."[66] Pye assumes, without specifying in any way, that there is "some" systematic relation among the genetic, experiental, conscious, and unconscious states of the person. He also assumes "that persons experiencing much the same process of socialization will develop roughly similar personalities which constitute the essence of their sense of common cultural identity," citing Kardiner, Mead, and Ralph Linton as authorities. The basic socialization process is followed by political socialization, the development of "awareness of his political world," and political recruitment, in which the individual gains a "deeper and more esoteric understanding of politics" and achieves "a more clearly defined and more institutionalized identity."

The contrast between the conceptualization of transitional society and the treatment of socialization is striking, and it serves to underline the vagueness and imprecision of the latter. "Identity" is nowhere defined. The reader is supplied with no criteria that would allow him to judge for himself whether or not an individual had acquired a "sense" of identity or solved his "identity crisis." Indeed, one is left uncertain exactly how the word ought to be used, for Pye speaks at different times of "individual identity," "social identity,"

[66]*Ibid.*, p. 45.

"sense of identity," "ego identity," "society's sense of identity," "his own identity," and "self-image," apparently using the latter as a synonym for "identity" or "sense of identity." The same strictures can be applied to Pye's use of terms like "loneliness," "isolation," "insecurity," "anxiety," and "guilt." Furthermore, the method by which these judgments were made does not inspire confidence in the results:

> In essence, our approach was to treat seriously what our respondents said, but to try also to find behind their words the logic and patterns of emotion and reasoning which underlay their basic orientations toward life and politics. Thus, for example, *as we listened* to the politician describe why he believed that his group was likely to have success in the coming elections, *we began to get at* his methods of calculating power, his ways of interpreting political justice, his sense of the relevant factors in determining history, his emotions toward the tangled web of political relationships. As the administrator described the development of particular programs, *we could sense* how he interpreted control and command, what he felt to be the relationship between plan and action, between official and civilian, between politician and administrator.[67]

We have here a classic and seemingly unavoidable difficulty met in every attempt to make use of psychiatric concepts in social research; the absence of clearly defined rules for linking the concepts to empirical data makes it almost impossible to evaluate the results. Pye has revived Freud's practice of lay analysis.

The treatment of specific psychic states attributed to individuals in Burmese society raises similar problems. Pye asserts, still without evidence, that there is a "sense of failure" among important elements in Burmese politics,[68] that the Burmese have a compulsive desire to work in a situation in which they have no superiors,[69] that the Burmese

[67]*Ibid.*, p. 160 (emphasis added).
[68]*Ibid.*, p. 130.
[69]*Ibid.*, p. 133.

crave warm and intimate relations with others but feel this cannot be achieved without total submission,[70] that the Burmese are uneasy and unsure in their personal relations. The explanation? The Burmese feeling of uneasiness in human relations may be traced back, first, to the relatively unpredictable emotional basis of the Burmese mother's relation to her child and, second, to the manner in which the acculturation process appears to have threatened the modernizing Burman's sense of identity.[71] The way in which an acculturation process threatens an identity is far from clear; but with reference to the first point, Pye involves himself in something of a dilemma. For if parental training is crucial, then the elaborate treatment of transitional society is pointless; the "anxiety" or absence of a sense of identity in the person is due to childhood training, not to the structure of society—unless, of course, social structure and child training can be linked; but as I have already noted, Pye's list of properties of transitional society includes no propositions about the methods of socialization employed in them.

The treatment of identity, which is taken as "the most basic of human issues," is equally obscure. Lacking a clear definition of its meaning, there is literally no way of evaluating the conclusions that Pye reaches. For example:

[Those] intimately associated with power and politics are most disturbed over their own sense of identity.[72]

.   .   .   .

[70]*Ibid.*, p. 134.

[71]*Ibid.*, p. 138. Pye refers to the "unpredictability of the Burmese mother" in various places to account for the hostility and suspicion that Burmese entertain for one another. See pp. 157, 182, 183, 185, 196, 206. Yet, on page 182, we find that "The Burmese mother displays a high degree of genuine happiness and affection toward her child . . . he is nursed whenever he cries so that feeding occurs frequently and under quite matter-of-fact circumstances. . . . The child is the object of attention by all members of the family, who casually pass him around among themselves while freely fondling, cuddling and playing with him."

[72]*Ibid.*, p. 53.

In a transitional society the politicians must above all struggle with the problem of giving expression to the identity of an entire people.[73]

.   .   .   .

Psychologically, the lack of a stable self-image seems to raise feelings of anxiety and guilt in Burmese politicians, feelings that tend to become particularly strong whenever they have to face the realities of life.[74]

.   .   .   .

[The] search for individual identity hinges on the existence of a national identity, and the latter calls for a coherent and consensus-bound political process; but people cannot fundamentally respect their political spokesmen when they are not sure that they can respect themselves, and so back to the issue of personal integrity and identity.[75]

More precisely still, what is to be made of Pye's explanation of the development of authoritarianism in Burmese society?

More fundamentally, it is a tragedy of the transitional society that the processes of change create profound insecurities in its people which cause them to feel a deep need to be bound to others, and to escape the sense of individual isolation. These psychological needs tend in turn to cause political leaders . . . to delude themselves into believing that their feelings and opinions must be those of the people as a whole. In an atmosphere of personal insecurity it is especially difficult for anyone to admit that he might stand alone or be in a minority. . . . But in the absence of any genuine mobilization of public opinion, self-doubt lingers on, and in an insidious fashion, leaders begin to clutch at the apparent certainties of authoritarian methods.[76]

First of all, the explanation cannot be reconciled with Pye's emphasis on child-rearing practices in Burma; insecurity and anxiety may come from both child-rearing practices and social pressures, of course; but the two are both logically and empirically distinct, and Pye does not make the separation.

[73]*Ibid.*, p. 97.
[74]*Ibid.*, p. 252.
[75]*Ibid.*, p. 4.
[76]*Ibid.*, p. 46.

Second, although Pye claims that stress can also arise from conflict between "conscious teaching and subconscious personality"—indeed, he asserts that these stresses and strains provide much of the dynamic force for evolutionary political change—his explanation omits consideration of that possibility, too. Finally, the explanation is wholly beyond test; that is, even if empirical data were available, there are no grounds on which it could be said that the data either support or conflict with the explanation.

However green the pastures on the psychological side of the academic fence may appear to the political scientist, it is clear that psychological explanations are, for the most part, not much better than political explanations, particularly when the phenomena to be explained are complex patterns of human behavior. Yet the psychologist, like the political scientist, is not completely helpless; *some* things he can explain reasonably well, some less well, some not at all. The tool is useful but imperfect, and that puts more of a strain on the user than might otherwise be the case. He must choose among psychological conceptual frameworks, balancing gains in rigor against costs in applicability, at least until such time as psychologists can, hopefully, supply both. Already there are broad areas in which the political scientist can hardly proceed without drawing upon the resources of the psychologist—the socialization process, opinion formation and opinion change, individual behavior in critically situated small groups in the political process like legislatures or courts, etc. The student of political thought is going to have to cope with such attempts at explanations, and he must be prepared to do so critically. Clearly, the first step is a more general dissemination of information about the conceptual frameworks and theories available in psychology, followed by an exploration of some of their uses and limitations in the explanation of political phenomena. This chapter is intended as a first tentative step in that direction. Happily, there are signs that others are also taking an interest in the subject. A volume in social psychology intended for use in the study of decision-making has been published.[77] It summarizes the data available in the field of small-group study. Others are almost certain to follow. As they are gradually integrated into the study of political thought and political science, it should be possible to strike a productive balance between the two disciplines in which neither is absorbed in the other.

[77]Barry E. Collins and Harold Guetzkow, *A Social Psychology of Group Processes for Decision-Making* (John Wiley & Sons, Inc., 1964).

CHAPTER FIVE

FORMALISM

ONE of the more interesting developments in contemporary political thought has been the increased use of formal models, simulations, and mathematical structures in the study of politics, what is here called formalism. Much more is implied by the term than the use of probability and statistics to handle political data, though such techniques may play a part in a formal structure. Analytically, formalism includes four types of activity: (1) efforts to create models—logical, mathematical, or informal—that can be used to study politics; (2) the application of such models to political phenomena; (3) discussion of the methodological and practical problems involved in the development or application of formal and informal models; and (4) the use of concepts borrowed from formal apparatus—Kurt Lewin's use of topology is a good case in point.[1] These distinctions may blur or merge in inquiry; but they are extremely useful, and even necessary, for the analysis and evaluation of formalism. Inquiry along these lines may serve a variety of purposes, and the

---

[1] The four distinctions made here are roughly equivalent to the "cognitive styles" spelled out in Abraham Kaplan's *The Conduct of Inquiry: Methodology for Behavioral Science* (San Francisco: Chandler Publishing Co., 1964), pp. 259–62. They are derived, however, from the actual work being done by political scientists in the formal mode.

validity of any given use of formalism depends on the purpose of the inquirer. The criteria to be applied in any given case are in some measure contingent on the type of inquiry undertaken and the kind of formal apparatus employed.

Formalism is a recent innovation in political science; its development has been comparatively slow, and the results obtained thus far in political study are not particularly impressive. It is important more for its potential than for its accomplishments. Critics of formalism—and they are numerous—argue that its potential is so limited that it is hardly worth serious attention. They point out that few political scientists are trained to make use of logic and mathematics and that few branches of mathematics have proved useful for the study of politics. It is also relevant to note that much of the basic impetus to formalism comes from economics, where it appears as a logical extension of the use of the concept of rational economic man. Indeed, some of the more significant applications of mathematics to politics have been made by economists rather than political scientists, yet it can be argued that conceptualizations that prove useful to the economist are not prima facie useful in the study of politics. Such criticisms must be balanced against the positive aspects of formalism—the gain in clarity, suggestiveness, and analytic power to be had from its use. As the remainder of this chapter should demonstrate, excessive pessimism seems unwarranted, but the implied warning against indiscriminate enthusiasm is well taken. Formalism, like any other mode of inquiry, must be judged by its results. And if the results are sometimes disappointing to those whose expectations are high, they can also be considered rewarding and fruitful. A brief survey of the uses and limitations of each of the four major aspects of formalism will suggest some of the reasons for both the enthusiasm and the disappointments.

1. The construction of a logical or mathematical system is an exercise in pure mathematics or logic, whether or not

the system is designed for some particular application. Although some few attempts to create formal models have been made by political scientists, most of the work has been carried out by mathematicians and logicians. Indeed, it can be argued that such work is not properly a part of political science; the political scientist who sets out to construct a formal system is working as a mathematician or logician.[2] This raises some very interesting questions about the training of political scientists. If mathematical and logical systems are to prove useful in the study of politics, their axioms must in some sense be relevant to the empirical data of politics, and relevance is a matter best decided by the political scientists. The construction and manipulation of the system, on the other hand, requires mathematical or logical training. Should the political scientist wait on the pure mathematician to develop appropriate systems for him, or should he be provided with the formal competence needed to develop his own? Are the two kinds of training compatible? Is it humanly possible for a single person to achieve competence in two disparate fields of inquiry in an era of intense specialization? In physics, where the importance of mathematics is clear, the physicist obtains some basic training in mathematics, but he is not a mathematician; physicists, with some few exceptions, apply mathematical systems developed by others. Happily for the physicist, much of modern mathematics has proved useful for his purposes. But for the political scientist, that is not the case. Unless competent mathematicians take an interest in the political scientist's problems (and there are some difficulties, since

[2]For examples of formal model construction by social scientists, see Herbert A. Simon, *Models of Man: Social and Rational* (John Wiley & Sons, Inc., 1957); Anthony Downs, *An Economic Theory of Democracy* (Harper & Row, Publishers, 1957); and Ithiel de Sola Pool and Robert Abelson, "The Simulmatics Project," Harold Guetzkow (ed.), *Simulation in Social Science: Readings* (Prentice-Hall, Inc., 1962). Downs is primarily an economist, Simon is formally trained in mathematics. A great many examples of formal models intended to serve limited purposes can be found in the journals, but the absolute volume of model construction remains small.

the kinds of problems social science investigates are not particularly inviting to the mathematician—in the formal sense and without regard to content), he must either develop his own or go without. Some few branches of mathematics seem useful to political scientists, and some few political scientists are receiving some mathematical training (how adequate it may be is hard to say). Whether the two disciplines will integrate successfully remains to be seen.*

Interestingly enough, political science is meeting the same problems when it deals with mathematics that it has met in handling statistics in the past, and it is perhaps worth noting that the question of how best to deal with statistics in political science has not yet been resolved adequately. As statistics moves beyond description, it becomes increasingly complex and requires more and more formal training. The need for political scientists to understand the *meaning* of statistical manipulations can probably be agreed upon by nearly everyone, but the extent to which the political scientist must be able to perform such manipulations is moot. There are very powerful arguments in favor of a division of labor, the political scientist maintaining his interest in political phenomena and the statistician tending to his sta-

---

*There is now a fairly impressive set of volumes available for the political scientist interested in mathematics, some demanding a fairly high level of mathematical competence, namely: Fred Massarik and Philburn Ratoosh, *Mathematical Explorations in Behavioral Science* (Richard D. Irwin, Inc. and Dorsey Press, 1965); Kenneth J. Arrow, Samuel Karlin, and Patrick Suppes, *Mathematical Methods in the Social Sciences* (Stanford University Press, 1960); Paul F. Lazarsfeld and Neil W. Henry, *Readings in Mathematical Social Science* (Science Research Associates, Inc., 1966); James S. Coleman, *Introduction to Mathematical Sociology* (Free Press of Glencoe, Inc., 1964); Paul Horst, *Matrix Algebra for Social Scientists* (Holt, Rinehart & Winston, Inc., 1963); John G. Kemeny and J. Laurie Snell, *Mathematical Models in the Social Sciences* (Ginn & Co., 1962); Joseph L. Bernd (ed.), *Mathematical Applications in Political Science II* (Arnold Foundation, 1966). The lion's share of the material in these volumes is relevant to economics and psychology rather than political science; and in the Bernd volume, which is intended specifically for political scientists, perhaps half of the material deals with statistics rather than formal logic and mathematics.

tistics. Yet, from the political scientist's point of view (not that of the statistician), collaboration is essential. The dilemma is real. The combination of a first-class statistician and a first-class political scientist in the same person seems improbable. But can an individual become a first-class political scientist without being able to employ the more sophisticated statistical techniques now available? The resolution of the dilemma seems to lie in a form of training in the *use* of statistical techniques that is presently not available. The same situation seems to hold for mathematics and logic. Like the physicist, the political scientist should be able to use mathematics without becoming a mathematician.

Strictly speaking, the evaluation of logical or mathematical systems qua logic and mathematics is not a problem in political thought and will not be undertaken here. Since the author is neither mathematician nor logician, the temptation to let matters rest there is quite strong, but to do so would be improper. Any application of mathematics to empirical phenomena involves some reference to the formal validity of the system being applied. For the nonmathematician, there is no reasonable alternative to assuming validity and working on other aspects of the application, and that is what must be done in the remainder of the chapter. But that resolution of the problem is not wholly satisfactory, and the reader should be aware of the possibility that the formal part of a mathematical or logical application may be faulty and perhaps misleading. In a few cases—game theory, for example—the mathematics involved has been discussed quite fully by competent mathematicians; and the basic structure, at least, is acceptable to members of the mathematicians' guild. But even here, there are a variety of special cases (n-person, nonconstant-sum games, for example) where the formal validity of the mathematical structure is less certain. And in those cases where a particular formal model has been constructed, or a general system modified for a particular purpose, there is no alternative to systematic scrutiny by a competent specialist; and in many cases, this has not been done. I can do no less, and unfortunately no more, than warn the reader of the gap in the critical apparatus employed here.

2. In the second mode of formalism, which is most significant for political thought, formal logical or mathematical systems (formal models) are *applied* to concrete phenomena. The model may be a fully articulated structure taken from mathematics or a logical structure constructed for some particular purpose. In either case the crucial point is the meaning of "apply." Simplistic treatments of the use of mathematics in social inquiry sometimes seem to imply that there is no more to the use of formal models than stuffing data into a set of categories defined by the model in order to produce a set of logical relationships among the data. And economists sometimes write as though the sole aim of inquiry was to construct models and manipulate them. Neither simplification will do. The usefulness of a formal model depends on the properties of the model, the nature of the data, and the purpose of inquiry. Further, formal models can be "applied" in various ways, not all of which serve the same purpose equally well.[3]

What is a formal model? In the simplest terms possible, it consists of a set of carefully defined elements and the rules for manipulating them; the whole system is usually reduced to symbolic form—Euclidean geometry is a classic example. From a slightly different point of view, a formal model comprises a set of axioms and all of the postulates of theorems that can be derived from those axioms according to the canons of formal logic. The elements of such formal structures need not be quantified, though the mathematical systems now available for use with quantified elements are

[3]For a general discussion of the use of models in the social sciences, see Kaplan, *op. cit.*, chap. vii; May Brodbeck, "Models, Meaning, and Theories," in L. Gross (ed.), *Symposium on Sociological Theory* (Harper and Row, 1959); Karl W. Deutsch, *The Nerves of Government: Models of Political Communication and Control* (Free Press of Glencoe, Inc., 1963).

more powerful than those that can be applied to nonquanti-
fied symbols. Logic and mathematics are techniques for handling interrelations among specified "things" that behave
in particular ways. The power of the techniques depends on
the precision with which behavior can be specified. In the
language of statistics, when interactions can be specified on
a ratio scale, the tools available for analysts are much more
powerful than those that can be used to handle interactions
specified ordinally or nominally.[4] Mathematics and logic,
in other words, have to do with abstract reasoning about
the interactions of specified symbols where the rules of interaction are fully and carefully specified; the result is a
"model" of the results of such interactions. These formal
models have nothing whatever to do with empirical reality.
They are formal constructions whose meaning is limited
strictly to the nominal definitions from which they are derived. That is, the theorem that "the shortest distance between two points is a straight line" is not an empirical
proposition but a tautology that follows from the axioms of
plane geometry. In fact, it is not universally true of *all* geom-
etries, and the validity of the proposition cannot be assessed
until we know precisely the formal system in which it appears.[5]

Political inquiry may be directed toward explanation

[4]Briefly, a *nominal* scale groups elements according to certain common
attributes; an *ordinal* scale rates the elements along a continuum (higher-
lower, more-less); an *interval* scale specifies the interval between elements
on a scale (as in measurements of weight or distance); and a *ratio* scale
adds a natural zero point (measurements of temperature).

[5]Philosophers of science do not use the term "model" in this way, but
I believe the usage adopted here is preferable, particularly for social scientists. In effect, the philosopher of science asks of a given structure: "Is it
a model?" and his answer depends on the criteria employed in his field to
define models. As the term is used here, any structure that is applied to
social phenomena can be termed a model, and the crucial question becomes: "Is this a good or an appropriate model?" This usage avoids the
dangers of essentialism and leads the social scientist to insist on criteria of
relevance and relative validity. We need to ask whether the model will
serve the purposes we have in mind, and in what degree, not whether it
is or is not a model.

and/or evaluation of political phenomena. Formalism must be evaluated, therefore, in terms of its contribution to either of these goals and their various corollaries. The first point that needs to be made is that formal models, however useful they may be, are not a substitute for theory. Explanation or evaluation may be furthered by the use of models, but models do not explain or evaluate. That is, formal models may have heuristic value, they may suggest ways in which elements interact; but they do not, as models, explain inter-actions—explanation is a function of theory. Models can become theories, of course, but the distinction between them needs to be preserved. A model is an analogue, an approximation, even though it is formal. It is suggestive for both explanation and evaluation, but it cannot perform explanations or evaluations. The distinction is important, for some formal structures like game theory appear to be devices for making value judgments. Strictly speaking, that is impossible. Game theory can choose the "best" course of action when that course or the rules for choosing it have been fully defined. But no set of formal procedures is intrinsically capable of choice. The rules of choice are built into the assumptions on which those procedures are based—they are external to the formal system.

The use of a formal model, then, is justified if it assists us to explain or evaluate, a question that can only be decided by referring to the specific case. There are a number of possible ways in which formalism can benefit the inquirer or the discipline. First, the process of reducing empirical questions to formal logical terms often serves to clarify the problem at hand. Second, formal models can be used for quasi testing of assumptions when experimentation is impossible; the use of simulation in international affairs and elsewhere is a good illustration of this function. Third, formal models can often be used as predictors, even though no explanation of the phenomena being examined is available. In economics, for example, such predictions are common, and they are found occasionally in politics as well—election predictions are a good case in point. On the negative side, excessive dependence on formal models can, as Abraham Kaplan suggests, lead to overemphasis on the importance of symbols, concern for logical form at the expense of content, rigor at the price of meaning, and oversimplification (or undercomplication). Finally, there is the danger of forcing the data to fit the model, particularly when there is an urgent need for some means of justifying decisions—as in military affairs.[6] Those who use formal models can too easily forget that models are not theories—with catastrophic results.

Unfortunately, there are no formal rules for evaluating the usefulness of models in political inquiry. The judgment and experience of the individual must come into play, obviously, but the rules of evaluation have thus far defied formalization. Clearly, our evaluation of the usefulness of a model depends on a firm grasp of both the properties of the model and the empirical conditions to which the model is being applied. Beyond that, the purpose of the inquiry is the prime determinant of the value of any given model. No model can be condemned because there are some purposes which it cannot serve. A selection of variables adequate for the study of coalitions in Congress, for example, may be quite useless for the study of decision making in congressional committees. Policymakers have different needs than academicians; teaching models may be quite different from research models, even though they are directed at the same phenomena; and predictive models will usually differ from models intended to suggest explanations. The purpose of inquiry provides a basis for evaluating the assumptions on which a model functions, whether the model is used for descriptive or for normative ends. Thus, for some purposes, poker can be considered a zero-sum game in which the sum

---

[6]Kaplan, *op. cit.*, pp. 275–85; Anatol Rapoport, *Strategy and Conscience* (Harper & Row, Publishers, 1964), especially chap. x.

of all gains is equal to the sum of all losses; but for other purposes the psychic gain of the players (which makes the game nonzero-sum) must be taken into consideration. Interestingly enough, the complexity and sophistication of the model is often irrelevant to its value in use. The aim of inquiry is not, after all, to build interesting models but to produce sound explanations and defensible evaluations. Models have no intrinsic value except to logicians and mathematicians.

3. A small number of formal models are available for application to political phenomena, and a few more appear each year. Similarly, some few attempts to apply formal models to political phenomena have the status of "classics," and their number is increasing. By way of contrast, there is quite a substantial body of writings dealing with the methodological and practical problems encountered in formalism. Some are quite general, dealing with the use of *any* mathematical structure in political inquiry; others are more specific, concentrating on a particular kind of model—game theory, for example.[7] Discussion of the points raised in such writings is best reserved to a later part of this chapter where the application of particular models to political phenomena is considered in more detail.

4. Finally, we need to be aware of the use of conceptual frameworks that are derived from formal models but are not, strictly speaking, formal systems. They provide a difficult problem of analysis, since they are logically distinct from formal models, yet some are very close, and all may be considered "informal" models of a sort. Of course, some appli-

---

[7] See James C. Charlesworth (ed.), *Mathematics and the Social Sciences* (American Academy of Political and Social Science, 1963); Kenneth J. Arrow, "Mathematical Models in the Social Sciences," in Daniel Lerner and Harold D. Lasswell (eds.), *The Policy Sciences: Recent Developments in Scope and Method* (Stanford University Press, 1951); Carl J. Friedrich (ed.), *Nomos VII: Rational Decision* (Atherton Press, 1964), especially chaps. i–iv; Deutsch, *op. cit.;* Arrow, Karlin, and Suppes, *op. cit.;* Massarik and Ratoosh, *op cit.;* Rapoport, *op. cit.*

cations of models like game theory or decision making are little more than term borrowing, often for what seem like honorific rather than explanatory purposes. But in other cases, it may be very difficult indeed to say whether or not a particular model is formally structured. William H. Riker's *Theory of Political Coalitions,* for example, is an attempt to apply a modified form of *n*-person game theory to coalition formation; it combines formal and empirical considerations into an indissoluble whole that is almost impossible to classify. Models and simulations that have been constructed for particular kinds of inquiry present similar problems. Some simulations rely wholly on computers; others combine the activities of computers and human players; some are purely formal, others purely empirical (gaming); and still others combine formal and empirical elements.[8] Clearly, they are related to the development of formalism in politics even though they are not formal logical systems. The value of such informal models depends entirely on their usefulness in inquiry. In some cases, formal models may provide better results, but there is no reason why formal models should always be preferred. Triviality is not a consequence of formal properties alone.

If all possible sources are considered, a very wide range of models has been used in the study of politics, and even

[8]Compare, for example, Richard C. Snyder, H. W. Bruck, and Burton Sapin, "Decision-Making as an Approach to the Study of International Politics," in Richard C. Snyder, H. W. Bruck, and Burton Sapin (eds.), *Foreign Policy and Decision-Making* (Free Press of Glencoe, Inc., 1962), a classic example of an informal conceptual framework, with Herbert A. Simon, "A Behavioral Model of Rational Choice," in William J. Gore and J. W. Dyson (eds.), *The Making of Decisions* (Free Press of Glencoe, Inc., 1964), or Peter C. Fishburn, *Decision and Value Theory* (John Wiley & Sons, Inc., 1964). Similarly, compare Downs, *op. cit.,* one of the better formal models that has been applied to politics, with works like Herbert A. Simon, *Administrative Behavior* (2d ed.; Free Press, 1945); James G. March and Herbert A. Simon, *Organizations* (John Wiley & Sons, Inc., 1958); Victor A. Thompson, *Modern Organization* (Alfred A. Knopf, Inc., 1961); Thomas C. Schelling, *The Strategy of Conflict* (Oxford University Press, 1963, first published in 1960); and William H. Riker, *The Theory of Political Coalitions* (Yale University Press, 1962).

more often in the study of economics. But certain kinds of models are far more widely employed than others; a few basic types are dominant. The most pervasive of all, certainly, is the theory of games. Communications theory and cybernetics, though a potential source of models, are in fact seldom used. The third "class" of models includes all those constructed for some specific inquiry in political science. They vary greatly in scope and complexity, and they include the formal and informal models known as "simulations," some intended for use with computers and some employing live actors as "simulators."

The remainder of this chapter contains a brief, nontechnical survey of formalism in political science. The aim is to illustrate the basic types of formal structures employed in political inquiry and clarify their uses and limitations where that is possible. It is particularly important to be aware of the distinction between the descriptive and the normative uses of such models. Some models are intended to provide their users with a means of making choices, or selecting strategies, under particular circumstances. They will be referred to as "normative" or choice-making models. Others do no more than provide a scheme of interrelations that can be used to facilitate learning, suggest explanations, channel inquiry, etc. The distinction is significant mainly because the criterion of adequacy or usefulness is likely to be different in the two cases, and some models (game theory, for example) may serve both purposes.

THEORY OF GAMES*

Game theory has had an interesting career in the post-World War II era. Some hold it worthless in social science;

---

*The basic volume in game theory is, of course, John von Neumann and Oskar Morgenstern, *Theory of Games and Economic Behavior* (Princeton University Press, 1944), but the von Neumann–Morgenstern volume is not the best place to begin the study of game theory, even though it is

others feel it may offer solutions to some of our more pressing social and political problems. Like so many other models
now used in political science, it originated in economics as

---

widely cited; its scope is too limited, and it is extremely complex. For the
nonmathematician the best general introduction to game theory can be had
from R. Duncan Luce and Howard Raiffa, *Games and Decisions: Introduction and Critical Survey* (John Wiley & Sons, Inc., 1957), and Anatol Rapoport, *Two-Person Game Theory: The Essential Ideas* (University of Michigan Press, 1966). J. D. Williams, *The Compleat Strategyst: Being a
Primer on the Theory of Games and Strategy* (McGraw-Hill Book Co., Inc.,
1954), is easy reading and interesting but is limited to one narrow segment
of the mathematical structure dealing with games. Much of the important
work in the field has been published in the journals and is accessible only
to the accomplished mathematician. Some of the more general essays are
brought together in the very useful—indeed essential—collection edited by
Martin Shubik, *Game Theory and Related Approaches to Social Behavior*
(John Wiley & Sons, Inc., 1964).

A number of books that are not, strictly speaking, either formal con-
tributions to game theory or applications of game theory are very useful:
Kenneth J. Arrow, *Social Choice and Individual Values* (John Wiley & Sons,
Inc., 1951); Kenneth E. Boulding, *Conflict and Defense: A General Theory*
(Harper & Bros., 1962); Anatol Rapoport, *Fights, Games and Debate* (Uni-
versity of Michigan Press, 1960); Anatol Rapoport, *Strategy and Conscience*
(Harper and Row, 1964); William H. Riker, *The Theory of Political Coalitions* (Yale University Press, 1962); Thomas C. Schelling, *The Strategy of
Conflict* (Oxford University Press, 1963); and Herbert A. Simon, *Models
of Man: Social and Rational* (John Wiley & Sons, Inc., 1957). Rapoport,
Riker, and Schelling discuss applications of game theory to politics; but
they do not, strictly speaking, make such an application themselves. Riker
comes closest to doing so, but he also departs most from the formal mathematics of games.

The problem of finding clearly defined illustrations of the application of
game theory to politics is vexing. Morton A. Kaplan includes a version
of game theory in his *System and Process in International Politics* (John
Wiley & Sons, Inc., 1957), but the book is a taxonomy and not an application. James Buchanan and Gordon Tullock's *Calculus of Consent: Logical
Foundations of Constitutional Democracy* (University of Michigan Press,
1962) includes some use of game theory, but it plays only a small part
in a large and sprawling book. Many political scientists have written to
suggest the uses and limits of game theory, but few use it. Richard C.
Snyder, "Game Theory and the Analysis of Political Behavior," and Karl
W. Deutsch, "Game Theory and Politics; Some Problems of Application,"
both reprinted in S. Sidney Ulmer (ed.), *Introductory Readings in Political
Behavior* (Rand McNally & Co., 1961), are of this sort. Glendon A. Schubert's "The Study of Judicial Decision-Making as an Aspect of Political
Behavior," reprinted in the Ulmer readings, gives two very brief illustrations of the application of game theory to court behavior. Merrill M. Flood
(ed.), "A Symposium on Game Theory," *Behavioral Science*, January, 1962,
also contains some interesting material.

an attempt to deal with the classic problem of defining the behavior of economic man, the "rational" actor. The mathematical apparatus employed in the model was developed by John von Neumann as early as 1928, but interest in its applications really dates to the publication of the von Neumann-Morgenstern basic volume in 1944. Since that time, the mathematical base has been extended, new applications have been sought, and development in corollary fields (statistical decision theory, for example) has been substantial. Game theory has both normative and descriptive uses, though the intent of the originators was fundamentally normative: "[We] wish to find the mathematically complete principles which define 'rational behavior' for the participants in a social economy and to derive from them the general characteristics of that behavior."[9] Whether or not that ambitious goal has been achieved, or can be achieved, remains a moot question.

Game theory is an attempt to develop and apply to social problems a special branch of mathematics. Like any system of applied mathematics, it has two parts: First, there is the formal mathematical apparatus, wholly abstract, symbolic, and without any necessary relationship whatever to the empirical world; second, there is the "theory" or, more precisely, the rules of correspondence that link the elements of the formal model to certain empirical phenomena. Failure to make this basic distinction explicit can introduce endless confusion into discussions of the merits and drawbacks of game theory. Every term used in the discussion, for example, and every general statement or theorem has two distinct meanings, one within the framework of the formal apparatus and another within the empirical framework to which the formal model is applied. A "coalition," for example, is an agreement between two players in a game, empirically

[9]John von Neumann and Oskar Morgenstern, *Theory of Games and Economic Behavior* (2d ed.; Princeton University Press, 1947), p. 31.

speaking; but mathematically, it has to do with the fusion of two matrices. Similarly, a "move" in an empirical game is an action by a player; but in the mathematical part of game theory, it is a row or column of ordered symbols. The general principle to be observed here is to begin always with the formal model, to determine the precise meaning of terms within the framework supplied by the model. Since the calculations involved in the application are always carried out within the mathematical part of the structure, the precise meaning of the outcomes of such calculations is always determined, strictly speaking, by the definitions employed in the formal model.

The formal part of game theory is deceptively simple. The mathematics deals with the properties of matrices consisting of ordered rows and columns of symbols (which may be letters, numbers, or any other form of conventional sign). Figure 5–1 shows two very simple matrices (A and B); each matrix contains two columns (C_1 and C_2) and two rows (R_1 and R_2). Each box in the matrix contains a letter or

FIGURE 5–1

	C_1	C_2
R_1	a	b
R_2	c	d

	C_1	C_2
R_1	1	2
R_2	3	4

number. The mathematician is, of course, wholly unconcerned with the "meaning" of the letters or numbers, the rows or the columns. They do not "stand for" anything in human experience so far as he is concerned. What interests him are the mathematical properties of various kinds of matrices, the results that can be obtained from combining and manipulating them. For the mathematician the important "variables" are the size and number of matrices to be combined or related, and their internal properties, that is, the relations that hold among the symbols within the boxes or cells of the matrix. Certain kinds of problems in mathematics can be "solved"; for example, it can be shown mathematically that given certain properties of matrices, certain other conditions will obtain within and among matrices; other problems are presently beyond solution; still others are in principle insoluble. The size and number of the matrices to be combined or analyzed are obviously matters of prime importance to the mathematician, since they limit his capacity to find adequate solutions to relational problems. The relations that hold among the symbols that populate the cells of the matrices are likewise significant, since they limit the kinds of comparisons and transformations that can be made. For example, two matrices that contain nothing but whole numbers can easily be subjected to a wide range of manipulations, whereas two matrices that contain symbols ordered on an ordinal scale ($a > b > c > d$) are open to a much more limited range of comparisons and require transformations which are far more difficult and cumbersome to make.

The simple elements of the mathematical structure employed in game theory, then, are rows, columns, and the ordered symbols contained in the cells. This may be combined to form one or more matrices. To *apply* or use the mathematical structure, the game theorist must produce a set of "rules of correspondence" that link these elements to empirical phenomena—he must stipulate that each element "stands for" something in the empirical world. Game theory depends on the suggestion made by John von Neumann and Oskar Morgenstern that if rows correspond to the choices made by one person and columns correspond to the choices made by another person (using the term "person" to designate any actor, individual or collective), and the symbols in the matrix cells can be made to correspond to the "utility" of the consequences of each choice (the payoff) for the person making the choice, then the mathematical structure will serve as a formal model of human interaction. To take the simplest case, imagine a situation in which two persons interact in such a way that each must choose between two—and only two—different actions. The children's game in which one person conceals a coin in either the left or the right hand and the second person tries to guess the hand in which the coin is hidden will provide an illustration. Let the columns designate the hider's two choices and the rows designate those of the seeker. We then have the outline of a matrix (see Fig. 5–2). Now the cells of the matrix must be

FIGURE 5–2

HIDER

		LEFT HAND	RIGHT HAND
S E E K E R	LEFT		
	RIGHT		

filled. Each cell represents an interaction that results from two choices, one by the hider and one by the seeker. That outcome must have some explicit significance or utility for each of the two players; its utility for each player must be expressible as a quantity or number. For simplicity's sake, we can assign a utility of one to winning the game—for the seeker, guessing correctly the hand in which the coin is hidden; for the hider a failure on the seeker's part to guess correctly (note carefully that these two alternatives are mutually exclusive; that is, either the hider or the seeker can win, but not both, and the utility of the play to each person, the pleasure gained from playing the game, is strictly excluded from consideration)—and a utility of zero to losing. The outcome of each choice, in terms of winning or losing, is a necessary consequence of the rules of the game. We can therefore exhaust all of the possibilities of the game within a single matrix; indeed, that must be done if the logical rigor of the model is to be maintained. The results are shown in Figure 5–3. If the hider chooses the left hand and the

FIGURE 5–3

HIDER

		LEFT		RIGHT	
			UTILITY		UTILITY
S E E K E R	LEFT	HIDER:	0	HIDER:	1
		SEEKER:	1	SEEKER:	0
			UTILITY		UTILITY
	RIGHT	HIDER:	1	HIDER:	0
		SEEKER:	0	SEEKER:	1

seeker picks the left hand, the outcome has a utility of zero for the hider and a utility of one for the seeker—*with respect to winning the game only,* not with respect to every other conceivable aspect of the interaction—and so on through every possible result that can be obtained within the framework of interaction that has been stipulated.

Certain general characteristics of the structure require special emphasis:

1. The range of choices facing each person involved in the interaction must be finite, and each choice must be specified in clear and unambiguous terms.

2. The consequences of the interaction of each choice with every other choice made by the second participant must also be specifiable, since these are the results to which utilities are attached.

3. The utility of each outcome must be specified for each player in such a manner that utilities can be compared and otherwise manipulated. At a minimum, the following requirements must be met:

   a) The meaning of "utility" must be the same for all participants in the interaction.

   b) The standard unit for measuring utility must be the same for all participants.

   c) Utility measurements must be stated on an interval scale rather than an ordinal scale (for most purposes). That is, it is not enough to say that one outcome is preferred to another; the utilities of two outcomes must be comparable in a way that permits one player to compare the utilities for him of two different outcomes as well as comparing the utility of the same outcome for himself and the other participant.

d) Utilities must be *transitively* ordered (internally consistent) so that if (a) is preferred to (b), and (b) is preferred to (c), then (a) must also be preferred to (c).

e) The scale used to measure utility must remain constant throughout all of the operations involved in any particular application. That is, the value of a given outcome must remain the same for both players whenever and wherever it appears in a game.

These are *mathematical* and not empirical requirements, of course; they are the minimum conditions under which the mathematician can perform logical operations on the material in the matrix. The degree to which these requirements can be met empirically, particularly those that pertain to the measurement of utility, is hotly disputed even among those who feel that game theory has genuine value for the social sciences.

In the simplest possible game, there are two players, each permitted two moves or choices by the rules of the game. The moves are known to both players. Each of the four outcomes has a utility function for each player, and the gains made by one player exactly equal the losses of the other. The game terminates at the end of the second move, and utilities are "paid off" at that point. We have, in the jargon of the game theorists, a two-person, zero-sum game with full information. The matrix in Figure 5–4 shows such a simple game. Alpha must choose between A–1 and A–2; Beta be-

FIGURE 5–4

		ALPHA	
		A–1	A–2
BETA	B–1	4	–1
	B–2	3	2

tween B–1 and B–2. The utilities shown in the cells are those of Alpha (Beta's utilities are the negative of Alpha's utilities). All moves are open or public.

Notice that for Alpha the choice of A–1 rather than A–2 is clearly the course of wisdom, so far as the game is concerned. Since A–1 is a better choice than A–2 for every cell in both columns, we say that A–1 *dominates* A–2. Dominance is a very important factor in choosing a strategy for play, since every choice that is dominated by another can be eliminated from consideration, thus reducing the complexity of the problem. Notice also that if Alpha chooses A–1, he cannot do worse than + 3 in the payoff; and if Beta chooses B–2, he guarantees that he will do no worse than − 3 (this is the "best" of the worst that could happen as a result of either choice). The intersection of A–1 and B–2, therefore, is the best result that either Alpha or Beta can hope for, given full information and a "rational opponent." If Beta chooses B–1, Alpha will naturally choose A–1 and gain + 4; if Beta chooses B–2, Alpha will still choose A–1. Under no circumstances would he choose A–2, since that move is dominated by his other choice. This intersection point, which is both the maximum that Alpha can get and the minimum that Beta can lose, is called a "saddle point." The terms "minmax" or "maxmin" refer to the saddle point or, more precisely, to the choice of a row or column that contains a saddle point. All games of perfect information have at least one saddle point, and some games contain more than one. Others, particularly those with limited information (poker, for example) contain none. The theory of games asserts that in a two-person, zero-sum game which contains a saddle point, the best each player can do is to choose the strategy (row or column) in which the saddle point lies.[10]

[10]Rapoport, *Two-Person Game Theory: The Essential Ideas* (University of Michigan Press, 1966), p. 60.

In our earlier example of hiding the coin, the matrix contains no saddle point. Indeed, it is clear from the matrix that neither the hider nor the seeker can hope to win in the long run—the task is to avoid losing, and one of the great uses of game theory is to make clear the long-run consequences of this kind. For the hider the problem is to avoid choosing in a way that will provide the seeker with some clue that will enable him to gain an advantage; the same problem faces the seeker. For such situations, game theory offers the concept of a "mixed strategy," useful in two-person, zero-sum games without saddle points. The calculations are somewhat lengthy, but it is possible to determine a mixture of choices that will provide a guaranteed minimum gain for each player, so long, of course, as the available moves are known and the payoffs can be calculated. In effect, a maxmin or minmax solution to the two-person, zero-sum game can usually be calculated, even if there are no saddle points in the matrix, and game theorists recommend this strategy or rule of choice for any rational player facing a rational opponent in a game that is truly zero-sum. That does not mean that such games can always be solved in practice. Chess, to take an obvious example, fits the formal requirements but is far too complex for solution.

For the two-person, zero-sum game, then, the mathematical apparatus is already available, and the von Neumann–Morgenstern solution to the problem of strategy (minmax) is widely accepted. But these games find only a very limited application in social science; they are too simple, their assumptions are unrealistic, too much that seems important in human choice is ignored. The player in a two-person, zero-sum game is in effect a robot, without a psychology, a personality, a value structure; he shows no trace of irrationality, no impatience, no aspirations. The concept of pure conflict that is assumed in the simple form of game theory can seldom be satisfied in real life; most human interactions have cooperative possibilities. The search for better models, however, raises some very formidable difficulties.

In the first place, the mathematical structure of game theory begins to fail when the limits of two-person, zero-sum games are transcended. There is no "theory of n-person games," for example; and all of the proposed solutions to nonzero-sum games are open to criticism on various grounds, some mathematical and some empirical.[11] The extensions of two-person, zero-sum game theory that have been most actively used in recent years are, first, an increase in the number of players (the n-person problem); second, a modification of the utility scale to include nonzero-sum outcomes; third, the extension of the theory to risky situations in which the outcomes cannot be specified fully (the matrix is incomplete); and fourth, the introduction of nonmathematical (empirical, psychic) considerations into discussions of the best strategy. A fifth point that might also be mentioned is the search for empirical evidence that could be used to justify some of the assumptions required for the solution of these more complex kinds of games, through procedures like gaming or normal investigation. These extensions are to some degree interlocking, in the sense that an increase in the number of players, and a loosening of the rules to permit negotiation or bargaining, focuses attention on the problems of coalition formation—as von Neumann and Morgenstern pointed out. The critical issue then becomes the need for some theoretical basis for studying cooperative behavior, and particularly negotiations leading to a division of payoffs. The analogy to the behavior of states in international relations, or to legislative behavior, is fairly obvious.

In very general terms, the players in a nonzero-sum game

---

[11]See Martin Shubik (ed.), *Game Theory and Related Approaches to Social Behavior* (John Wiley & Sons, Inc., 1964), pp. 44–57; von Neumann and Morgenstern, *op. cit.*, chap. v and Sec. 56.3, pp. 506–7; Rapoport, *Two-Person Game Theory: The Essential Ideas*, chap. viii; Schelling, *The Strategy of Conflict*, especially Appendix B.

need criteria by which to determine the price of their cooperation, and strategies for maximizing the benefits to
themselves of cooperative action. One suggested solution to
the problem begins with what is called a "security level,"
calculated as the utility that can be gained by each player
in a game through his own efforts alone. No player would be
willing to negotiate payoffs that were less than those provided in the security level; hence, that could be taken as a
beginning point for calculations of the best strategy. Thomas
C. Schelling and others, however, point out that this method
of defining the "zero point" for negotiations implies the impossibility of any communication during the play, tacit or
open, which is not necessarily the case, since "communication" can occur even in strictly competitive situations.[12] Von
Neumann and Morgenstern's solution to the problem relies
upon the concept of "Pareto optimality," the assumption that
in every game a solution exists which no individual can
modify without decreasing the share of another person.
When this point is reached, in a rational population, any attempt to modify it would be resisted by those affected by
the modification. However, as is often pointed out, several
solutions may actually satisfy the rather weak requirements
made by von Neumann and Morgenstern, and there is no
agreed basis for choosing among them.

Another way of attacking the "bargaining problem" is to
make some initial assessment of the power of the participants
in the game and suggest means by which they can exploit
their advantages and thus obtain maximum payoffs. The
famous solution proposed by John Nash, for example, makes
use of this approach, though it does not apply to n-person
games, since it ignores coalition formation within the game.
Nash relies upon the *implied* consequences of carrying out
threats made during the course of play for providing a base
for bargaining. The stronger the threat, in effect, the stronger

[12]Schelling, *op. cit.,* p. 272.

the bargaining position of the player. That is, the point of interaction of the various threat strategies (not actual choices of moves) are first calculated, and the results are used as a basis for defining the payoff to the players. L. S. Shapley follows a similar procedure, beginning with the "security level" of the individual players as a base point. Howard Raiffa offers the useful suggestion that cooperative games be divided into two parts: first, the attempt by the players to maximize the collective payoff; second, the actual division of gains among the players. Raiffa's solution to the problem also makes use of the "threat capacity" of the players as a basis for a "rational" division.

Although the mathematics may become quite difficult, or even in practice impossible, the really serious problem facing the game theorist seeking to extend the compass of the formal structure is not mathematical but conceptual. In the normative mode, game theory seeks a "rational" solution to certain kinds of interaction problems among human players in which there are losses and benefits to everyone involved in the interaction. Extended even moderately, such situations raise some of the more fundamental problems in ethics, value theory, and psychology. It is interesting to note, for example, that solutions to the bargaining problem tend to begin either with a conception of the power of the individual player to force a solution that favors himself through coercion or threats or with some proposal about the meaning of "fair" or "equitable" divisions. Clearly, we have here a restatement of the classic problem of justifying political authority. And game theory has produced already its "Hobbesians" and its "legalists." This may suggest that game theory is moving closer to the traditional interests of political scientists and therefore may imply that it should in the future be of greater use to political inquiry; or it may suggest (to the pessimistic, at any rate) that game theorists who have begun to interest themselves in genuine human problems have at last come face to face with some of the great dilemmas that have baffled students of human society for centuries, dilemmas which are by implication unlikely to yield to the game theorist's tools.

GAME THEORY AND POLITICAL SCIENCE

It should by now be clear that "game theory" covers a wide range of activities and that the field as a whole is incomplete and unevenly developed. Discussion and criticism of game theory are not particularly useful until the specific aspect of the field to be discussed is identified more precisely. In general, the best-developed part of game theory (two-person, zero-sum games) is least useful in the social sciences, whereas the least formalized part of game theory contains most of the really interesting problems and, of course, is most easily criticized, not always on valid grounds.[13] Game theory, perhaps more than most tools of inquiry, can be criticized only within the context in which it appears; that is, unless the purpose of inquiry is stated very clearly, it is quite impossible to say whether or not game theory will prove useful. Furthermore, substantive knowledge, familiarity with the empirical data, becomes increasingly important as the formal apparatus declines in power; and in the ill-developed areas of game theory, arguments quite often hinge on the nature of the evidence rather than on the logical structure.

Despite widespread belief to the contrary, sophisticated game theorists seldom if ever claim that game theory has solved the problem of making decisions or that it is likely to do so in the future. Minmax strategy in zero-sum games would perhaps be defended as rational behavior by most game theorists, but virtually everyone realizes that this form

[13]Anyone interested in fair and unfair criticisms of game theory and game theorists should read Albert Wohlstetter's delightful article, "Sin and Games in America," reprinted in Shubik, *op. cit.*

of game is seldom approximated in real life. It is readily admitted that the assignment of utility functions, which is essential if formal game theory is to be applied, is a difficult and perhaps impossible task. The fact is that there have been very few concrete applications of formal game theory and that game theory has not proved particularly useful in empirical research or even in the exploration of strategic or political alternatives. Without prejudging the future, it can be said that the explanatory and predictive uses of game theory are at present very limited indeed. Nevertheless, a small but articulate and influential segment of the academic community, including some political scientists, continues to explore the potential of game theory, seeking applications, trying to extend the conceptual apparatus, and in the process contributing to the development of game theory itself. The principal justification for this continued interest is usually the conceptual clarification that has already been achieved through the use of game theoretical concepts and methods in important areas of social inquiry like bargaining theory, studies of international and domestic conflict, and the study of power relations.

On the other hand, a considerable amount of experimental work has been carried out in which human subjects reacted in artificial situations to game theoretic problems. Some of the findings, at least, indicate that the rules of choice developed by game theorists have some relevance to actual behavior patterns and that game theoretic findings related to coalition formation and negotiations are often quite perceptive.[14] A major review of experimentation by Anatol Rapoport and C. Orwant suggests that (1) in zero-sum games with saddle points the minmax solution is in fact most often chosen by the players; (2) where no "rational" strategy can be provided (as in the Prisoner's Dilemma game), personality

[14]Anatol Rapoport and C. Orwant, "Experimental Games: A Review," *Behavioral Science*, Vol. 7, No. 1, 1962; reprinted in part in Shubik, *op. cit.*

and motivational factors tend to determine individual choice; (3) members of coalitions tend to split their winnings evenly, rather than according to a formula, except that later adherents to the coalition are penalized by older members; (4) traditional game theory strategies tend to be too conservative, judging by the behavior of experimental subjects, though it may be that the lack of serious danger inherent in experimental situations tends to make players more adventuresome than usual; (5) the predictive capacity of the various solutions to the bargaining problem is weak. Although the evidence is far from decisive, continued experimentation seems more than justified, as is Schelling's view that for the moment it seems essential that game theory be linked deliberately with experimentation and empirical research. It may be noted that simulation projects (model building) seem also to have been most successful to date when they were linked with experimentation and empirical study. As an example of the latter case, we can cite two studies of judicial decision making by Glendon A. Schubert in which the behavior of the justices conformed very closely to the strategic principles that the game model prescribed for the situations that Schubert abstracted.[15] In one case the payoff to one bloc of judges was 92 percent success in rulings when the pure strategy recommended by game theory was followed and only 73 percent success when the justices adopted another strategy.

The point of these few illustrations is that general criticism of the use of game theory in political inquiry, though sometimes quite suggestive, is not really very helpful.[16] Too

[15]Glendon A. Schubert, "The Study of Judicial Decision-Making as an Aspect of Political Behavior," *American Political Science Review*, Vol. LII (1958).

[16]A good example of generalized criticism of game theory that is interesting without being convincing can be found in chapter iv of Deutsch, *The Nerves of Government: Models of Political Communication and Control.* See also his "Game Theory and Politics: Some Problems of Application," in S. Sidney Ulmer (ed.), *Introductory Readings in Political Behavior* (Rand McNally & Co., 1961).

often, general criticism concentrates upon particular forms of game theory or upon dogmatic claims made on behalf of game theory by ill-informed enthusiasts. Most important of all, general criticism usually avoids considering the relation between the purpose for which game theory is used and its accomplishments. It is one thing to recommend game theory as a basis for rational decision by governments and quite another matter to suggest that game theory can lead to a clarification of concepts or suggest ways in which particular phenomena like coalitions might be explained.

Morton A. Kaplan

A good illustration of the dilemmas that appear when game theory is proposed as a normative or decision-making device can be found in Morton A. Kaplan's widely cited volume on international politics.[17] Kaplan is aware of the mathematical shortcomings of game theory, and he warns against misapplication of the theory in politics. On the other hand, he also maintains that "game analysis is the best tool available for the analysis of problems of strategy"[18] and that game theory, properly used, "is likely to increase the expectation of success in policy." Given the state of the field, the two claims are too strong, and a careful reading of the text sustains the objection. Two of the three chapters on strategy contain a summary account of game theory which is acceptable; but the crucial chapter on applications, "Strategy and Statecraft," which presumably should deal with problems of application, turns out to be a technical discussion that is only vaguely linked to empirical decision making. There is no discussion of the problems of measuring utility, predicting outcomes, and otherwise fulfilling the assumptions on which game theory is based. A brief treatment of decision making under uncertainty, following Jacob

---

[17]Morton A. Kaplan, *System and Process in International Politics* (John Wiley & Sons, Inc., 1957), especially chaps. xi–xii.

[18]*Ibid.*, p. 206.

Marschak's generalized solution of the problem of utility scaling under risk, leads only to the conclusion that "an interval scale exists." The question of how the cells in the matrix are to be filled with real numbers is left unsolved: "Utilities are to be assigned, under the von Neumann assumptions, upon the basis of preference among gambles." A lengthy discussion of a particular form of stochastic learning theory concludes the chapter.

It is almost impossible to say, from reading the relevant chapters, whether Kaplan intends the discussion as a guide for policymakers or a suggestion of the ways in which stochastic learning theory might be put to use. There are a number of pithy apothegms for statesmen: "If one has no intention of defending, it is unwise to bluff by making a definite commitment," or "It is also unwise to make statements of intent more definite than the intention to implement warrants"; but the source of these generalizations is unclear, and their status is uncertain. The curious tone of the work and the rather abrupt and disconnected style of writing may account for the difficulty of interpretation. Consider the following:

The utility numbers placed in the matrix boxes are neither more nor less accurate than those social science methods which predict the consequences of interesting moves or than the valuational frameworks that give preference to one physical outcome over another. It would be dangerous if it were forgotten that the numbers represent highly complex entities. They represent projections of physical consequences over time. But such projections are not the simple projections of a single action.[19]

If this is intended as a treatment of the problem of assigning utilities, as seems the case in context, then it is extremely disconcerting. Taken literally, much of it is nonsense: Utilities do not—indeed, cannot—represent "projections of physical consequences over time," though they are contingent on such projections. Taken more metaphorically, the result is

[19]*Ibid.*, p. 240.

still unsatisfactory, since the statement begs the very questions that need to be answered before game theory can be applied.

The summation included in the final chapter of the book provides no enlightenment on questions of application; in fact, it only adds to the confusion. We are told that "The game theory model is important in clarifying the nature of the choice situation" and that it can, in some way, "demonstrate whether a cooperative solution is likely or not" and serve as a "parameter for other social processes." Yet the political scientist is excluded from a very crucial area of policy formation by the assertion that "The theory of strategy primarily must remain within the province of the mathematician, for few political scientists have the mathematical equipment or the time to solve the mathematical problems of strategy."[20] Clearly, Kaplan intends a formal mathematical solution to questions of strategy; hence, he intends the application of game theory in the normative sense, not merely as a device for clarification and analysis. The illustration that is offered of a "specialized problem" that can be "fitted within present game structure" confirms this interpretation of intention: "Consider a situation in which there are three international actors. Assume further that one can order the preferences of the players for various outcomes and that one can predict the consequences of intersecting moves or strategies, at least with certain probabilities. Let the number of moves be finite and known . . . ."[21] Kaplan, to put the point as strongly as possible, burkes the whole issue of applying game theory to political phenomena. This quite extraordinary example raises all of the questions that must be answered before game theory can be applied, but it assumes the very things that need to be questioned!

If formal game theory is to be applied in this way, that

[20]*Ibid.*, p. 248.
[21]*Ibid.*

is, used as a decision-making device, then the axioms of the formal model must be reasonably well satisfied by the empirical data, and the basic problem in application centers on the possibility or impossibility of doing so. Kaplan's basic dilemma is a desire to make use of game theory in a way that simply cannot be justified at present. It is perfectly clear that accurate prediction of all of the possible outcomes in an empirical interaction is rarely if ever possible; very often, they cannot even be specified, let alone predicted accurately. Further, the difficulty, or even impossibility, of satisfying the assumptions behind the utility function is widely agreed. Witness R. Duncan Luce and Howard Raiffa: "There can be no question that it is extremely difficult to determine a person's utility function even under the most ideal and idealized experimental conditions; one can almost say that it has yet to be done";[22] or Martin Shubik: "It is difficult enough to be able to state with certainty that an individual prefers to see Jones as a senator rather than Smith; it is more difficult (and some say impossible) to state by how much he prefers Jones to Smith."[23] Yet it is this latter requirement that must be fulfilled before the theory can be used normatively. Finally, as Anatol Rapoport points out, applied game theory must in some way provide real solutions to real problems; and real problems are exceptionally difficult to handle within the game matrix, since "it is all but humanly impossible to obtain either the matrix representation or the game tree of any parlor game worth playing. In the case of a very simple game like Tic-Tac-Toe, a game tree could conceivably be drawn, but a matrix representation of the strategies remains out of the question."[24]

In brief, the use of game theory *in the way that Kaplan implies* seems at present out of the question and likely to

[22]R. Duncan Luce and Howard Raiffa, *Games and Decisions: Introduction and Critical Survey* (John Wiley & Sons, Inc., 1957), p. 36.
[23]Shubik, *op. cit.*, p. 19.
[24]Rapoport, *Two-Person Game Theory: The Essential Ideas*, p. 193.

remain so. The mathematics of complex games is uncertain, and there is no real agreement on the kinds of assumptions needed for their solution (an empirical as much as a logical problem). The assumptions of the formalized part of game theory simply cannot be matched to the empirical data. Outcomes cannot be predicted with sufficient accuracy or given a reliable probability index. Utilities cannot be scaled. There are good empirical reasons to suppose that the whole concept of "rationality" with respect to utility choices is an error in conceptualization, that is, that better explanations can be had of the choices actually made if they are based on socialization processes, cultural norms, etc. The number of moves in even the simplest of empirical situations is usually unmanageable. Objections of this kind could be multiplied *ad infinitum*. If game theory is to serve political inquiry, it must be directed to other needs and purposes; its value as a normative device is virtually nil. Few game theorists would dispute that judgment.

Thomas C. Schelling

That game theory can in fact serve other purposes, and serve them well, is readily demonstrated from available studies. Two examples may serve to illustrate the point: Schelling's study of conflict, which demonstrates the value of using the conceptual apparatus of game theory (with modifications) as a clarifying device; and Riker's study of coalitions, which shows what can be done when game theory is used as a base for inquiry into empirical phenomena. The examples are, of course, among the best available, but my purpose is to demonstrate what is possible using game theory, not to survey what is available in the field.

Although Schelling is critical of formal game theory, particularly in the zero-sum form, he makes use of a modification of game theory in his study.[25] Indeed, his work is at

[25]Schelling, *The Strategy of Conflict.*

once a substantial contribution to the development of game theory and a good example of the usefulness of what might be called a "game theory approach" to the study of political problems. It is impossible to do justice to a book so rich in insights in a few paragraphs, but if the value of an applied theory can be estimated from its power to find solutions that "elude the practitioners," an Anatol Rapoport suggests, then Schelling's study, with its seemingly paradoxical conclusions, must rank very high indeed in contemporary literature on politics. The lucid and convincing treatment of bargaining, the exposition of the importance of the power to bind the self and of the value of weakness in negotiation are exemplary. The examination of the role of communications in negotiation is carried out in a way that brings forth conclusions that seem startling at first but appear sound upon further reflection—perhaps the highest compliment an idea can receive. Perhaps such insights should not be credited to the influence of game theory, but even if they are ignored (and they should not be, for they are one of the more valuable parts of the book), the reformulation and application of game theory that Schelling undertakes seems uncommonly promising.

What Schelling is seeking, if I read him correctly, is a theory of games that will be more useful to the social scientist, and he is willing to pay for usefulness by relinquishing formal completeness and precision. What he proposes—among other things, of course—is a set of fundamental changes in the typology of games, the typology of moves, and the foundations of strategic thinking. We shall examine each set of proposals separately, ignoring illustrations and examples, though the text is in fact richly furbished with them.

The change in game typology is designed to eliminate the excessive emphasis on pure conflict games characteristic of the mathematician's approach to game theory, substituting an approach which emphasizes game forms that have empirical rather than formal interest. Pure conflict games (zero-sum) and pure coordination games (in which there is complete identity of interests) are to be regarded as the extremes of a continuum. Those games which combine conflict and mutual dependence, which make up the bulk of the empirical population, are to be called "bargaining games" or "mixed-motive" games. Further, Schelling points out that the intellectual processes involved in a choice of moves are quite different in games of pure conflict and games of pure cooperation and hence that it is important to consider the extended or game-tree form of play and not the collapsed or "normal" form of the game. The extended form calls attention to the character of each particular choice in the play of the game and thus underlines the importance of the individual's psychic relationship to the choice, to the "definition of the situation" which the individual maintains—an introduction of psychological considerations that purists among the game theorists tend to deplore, not because it is empirically unsound, but because it tends to complicate their calculations and reduce the precision of their categories.

The next step, obviously, is to replace the wholly formal and abstract concept of "move" by constructions that allow the introduction of the psychic aspects of choice into consideration. Schelling argues, in a most convincing way, that excessive abstraction prevents the full utilization of the rich cumulation of knowledge already available about human behavior, the everyday knowledge that we acquire simply by living together with others. In Schelling's typology of moves, players make threats, give promises, relinquish the initiative, identify friends and enemies (real or potential), delegate authority, accept mediation, communicate, etc. The meaning of these terms incorporates much of the nuance and complexity of everyday speech. The moves are incorporated into the game matrix by the delightfully simple device of viewing them as alterations of the individual's payoffs to himself.

Finally, Schelling attacks the classic assumption of game

theory that the choice of strategy is to be decided by purely formal operations: "[W]henever the facilities for communication are short of perfect, where there is inherent uncertainty about each other's value systems or choices of strategies, and especially when an outcome must be reached by a sequence of moves or maneuvers, . . . some *essential* part of the study of mixed-motive games is necessarily empirical."[26] The aim, once again, seems to be the enrichment of game theory by the introduction of complex human experience into decision procedures. Indeed, Schelling outlines a considerable number of research projects that would contribute to our knowledge of the decision-making process and enable us to generalize the theory of games still further, including, among others, studies of (1) the effect of changes in the amount of information available to the decision makers, (2) the importance of temperament and motivation on choice, (3) the influence of cultural differentiation on the players' definition of the situation, (4) the importance of control over the opening move in a game for later strategy, (5) the classification of cues to which decision makers respond, and (6) the effect of inadequate or conflicting norms on choice.

Schelling's study, which is rounded out by a lucid and perceptive examination of the problem of surprise attack in international relations, is a particularly good example of the use of game theory for clarification of concepts. Schelling has quite literally incorporated the patterns of thought that appear in game theory into his own mode of thinking about politics. A close examination of the book will in fact expose influences that are not obvious at first reading: The kinds of questions that are asked, the types of relationships that are explored, etc., clearly derive in some measure from game theory. Doubtless, it would be wrong to ascribe to game theory the full achievement of the volume; Schelling would,

[26]*Ibid.*, p. 162.

one suspects, write clearly even had he never heard of the theory of games. But as an attempt to use game theory in political study, and in the process modify the theory so as to make it more useful to political scientists, the book stands in a class by itself.

William H. Riker

In the more conventional notion of the way game theory or any other formal system can be used in concrete studies, the formal system is employed as a model, and generalizations drawn from the model are tested against the available empirical evidence in an attempt to produce generalizations that can be employed in other forms of inquiry. A good example of this type of application can be found in William H. Riker's *Theory of Political Coalitions.*[27] The game model is *n*-person zero-sum; that assumes rational players, perfect information, and side payments or bargaining among the players. The concept of rationality is modified slightly to avoid some of the criticisms made of earlier statements: "Given social situations within certain kinds of decision-making institutions (of which parlor games, the market, elections, and warfare are notable examples) and in which exist two alternative courses of action with differing outcomes in money, power, or success, some participants will choose the alternative leading to the larger payoff. Such choice is rational behavior . . . ."[28] The use of zero-sum models, which has been criticized rather sharply by others, is defended on the ground that decisions made by voting or fighting have a "winner-take-all" quality that justifies the assumption. Perfect information is not assumed; instead, the state of information in the system is used as one of the variables in the application. Finally, it is assumed that the

[27]See also William H. Riker, "A New Proof of the Size Principle," in Joseph L. Bernd (ed.), *Mathematical Applications in Political Science II* (Arnold Foundation, 1966).
[28]*Theory of Political Coalitions*, p. 23.

property of the model that is most important in social science is the number of players involved in the game.[29] The aim is to expose some of the general principles that govern the formation of coalitions in groups and associations whose decisions are controlled by coalitions. Three major propositions are developed from the model and applied to empirical or historical data: the "size" principle, the "strategic" principle, and the "disequilibrium" principle.

Given the assumption of the formal model, the following proposition holds good for coalition formation within the model: "In n-person, zero-sum games, where side-payments are permitted, where players are rational, and where they have perfect information, only minimum winning coalitions occur."[30] The analogous statement to be applied to the empirical world is: "In social situations similar to n-person, zero-sum games with side payments, participants create coalitions just as large as they believe will ensure winning and no larger." This is the "size principle." Notice that the "perfect information" requirement has been dropped. This makes verification extremely difficult, as Riker himself points out.

Support for the size principle is obtained from an examination of cases in history where overwhelming majorities have been formed accidentally. These applications require the assumption that "American politics on a national scale, where the stakes are the control of the decisions by the national government, is popularly perceived as zero-sum" and a similar assumption with respect to other situations from which such evidence is obtained. Riker's assertion that the size principle has been "proved" for two classes of cases because the historical evidence shows no exceptions is too strong, but the weaker claim that there is a strong probability that the principle will hold in such cases seems tenable if

[29]*Ibid.*, p. 34.
[30]*Ibid.*, p. 32.

the evidence is accurate. Perhaps the chief difficulty in assessing the claim is the nature of the cases used to support it;
they are broad, drawn from earlier periods of American history, and they involve the attribution of intentions and
motivations to some of the actors in these historical situations in a way that could be challenged as lacking theoretical
justification. Again, Riker is aware of the difficulties, and he
proposes a further set of inquiries that could provide stronger evidence to support his size principle. In particular, he
suggests research into what is called the "information effect,"
a general proposition about coalition formation derived from
the model but not formally demonstrable:

> The greater the degree of imperfection or incompleteness of
> information, the larger will be the coalitions that coalition-makers
> seek to form and the more frequently will winning coalitions
> actually formed be greater than minimum size. Conversely, the
> nearer information approaches perfection and completeness, the
> smaller will be the coalitions that coalition-makers aim at and
> the more frequently will winning coalitions actually formed be
> close to minimum size.[31]

The size principle and its corollary, the information principle, are then employed in the investigation of the coalition
formation process. For that purpose, another model, dynamic
rather than static, is needed.

The dynamic model is less satisfactory and much less precise than one might wish. Coalitions form around leaders,
like the accretions that produce a pearl within an oyster, beginning as "protocoalitions" and evolving through the acquisition of members to whom "side payments" are made. The
development of one protocoalition poses a threat to those
not part of it, and this leads to the formation of other protocoalitions, in a manner reminiscent of John K. Galbraith's
"theory of countervailing power." Side payments may include (1) threats of reprisal, (2) objects whose value can be
reckoned in money, (3) promises on policy, (4) promises

[31]*Ibid.*, pp. 88–89.

about subsequent decisions, and (5) payments of emotional satisfaction. Clearly, interpersonal comparisons of the utility of such a variety of payments is out of the question. That assumption is not made, and Riker avoids the need to compare utilities by assuming only that the payments made to those joining the coalition are adequately satisfying—formally a weakness in the argument, though again acceptable if the results prove useful.

Can a strategy be formulated that will guarantee or maximize the possibility of success in the transformation of a protocoalition into a winning coalition? The Shapley value for n-person games,[32] which depends on the number of times an individual occupies a pivotal position in coalition formation, is rejected because it does not incorporate information acquired during the course of play. "Pivoting" is less important to those trying to choose among protocoalitions than the ultimate chance of success of the coalition. The general strategic consideration which Riker proposes is weak, largely because he is aware of the importance of unique events in coalition formation on the potential to win of protocoalitions:

If at some jth stage . . . some proto-coalitions can form a minimal winning coalition and others cannot, those that can may have a strategic advantage. This advantage consists simply in the fact that those who can form a minimal winning coalition may be able to agree on a more profitable arrangement of payoffs. Among rational players, this advantage is sufficient to guarantee that any coalition so situated in the [penultimate] stage will belong to a winning coalition at the [ultimate] stage.[33]

This proposition is then formalized for conditions in which there are no more than five protocoalitions, assuming that members may not resign from coalitions already joined and that payments to followers may not be lowered without their

[32]See L. S. Shapley and M. Shubik, "A Method for Evaluating the Distribution of Power in a Committee System," in Shubik, *op. cit.*
[33]Riker, "A New Proof of the Size Principle," pp. 126–27.

consent. What emerges, very weakly, is the suggestion that one protocoalition *will have* strategic advantages at some stage in the play of the game and that these advantages can be exploited to achieve a winning coalition. Curiously enough, the advantage does not always lie with the largest coalition, and the analysis even suggests that in some cases the largest coalition (not yet large enough to win) will do well to divest itself of some of its members in order to increase its strategic advantage.

From the assumption of strategic advantage, it follows that the model is biased toward decision, that is, that it is unstable and lacking equilibrium and, indeed, tends to upset any temporary equilibrium achieved before a winning coalition is formed. This is the third of Riker's major propositions, the "disequilibrium principle." It is applicable only to zero-sum conditions, not to the whole of society, of course; but as Riker points out, it amounts to a denial of the common assumption that rational politics is inherently stable in all circumstances. An examination of the principles of equilibrium postulated by Morton A. Kaplan leads to the suggestion that the rules themselves contain precisely the inherent disposition to instability that the "disequilibrium principle requires." No "balance-of-power system," if Riker is correct, can guarantee stability. This leads to a discussion of the means of maintaining equilibrium (moral restraint and institutional control) and the sources of disequilibrium (changes in the weight or power of two or more of the elements in an equilibrium and a willingness on the part of the winner to set high stakes), and an examination of the exogenous and endogenous factors that influence them. The conclusion, though weak, is formidable in its implications:

[W]hat is the relative importance of exogenous and endogenous factors? To this question I can give no certain answer, except to say that my subjective impression is that the endogenous factors count most. In the fall of leaders, men and nations alike, it seems to me that the miscalculations of leaders themselves, their overspending, their restless search, as Hobbes put it, for power after power, is the primary factor in the change of weights [power]. And if this is so, then the decision-making system is in disequilibrium unavoidably and absolutely.[34]

Although the list of applications of game theory to political phenomena remains comparatively small, it is growing; and as the examples chosen here demonstrate, it can be very suggestive indeed, though it is not useful as a normative theory in the way that Morton A. Kaplan employs it. What the future is likely to bring depends as much on developments within the formal theory of games as on the attitude of political scientists. If, for example, Schelling's suggestions could be incorporated in a formalized structure, the result would be a very powerful analytic tool with both explanatory and normative implications for political science. Already, it is a conceptual framework that students of political thought (or theory) need to familiarize themselves with, since they will be called upon to examine critically empirical studies in which game theory is employed. Happily, the necessary formal material is being produced that will make this possible. Luce and Raiffa's volume, read in conjunction with Rapoport's study of two-person games (and, hopefully, a promised volume on n-person games), will go a long way toward satisfying the basic needs of the student of theory. Shubik's collection of applications is equally valuable. If to these three books we add Schelling's *Strategy of Conflict*, the student should be reasonably well prepared to deal with applications of game theory as they arise. Finally, it should be noted that developments in gaming and simulation offer a natural corollary to game theory, suggesting both modification of the theory and applications that might otherwise escape notice. The discussion of simulation that appears below should indicate some of those associations and connections.

[34]*Ibid.*, p. 210.

INFORMATION THEORY AND CYBERNETICS

"Information theory" and "cybernetics," like game theory, are formal mathematical systems, though many of the concepts they employ have found their way into popular use. Although both systems have influenced the social sciences, that influence has been indirect and conceptual; I have found no example of the use of the formal mathematical structure in social inquiry. The reason is not hard to find. In both cases, though more particularly in the case of information theory, the formal structure is too limited and the assumptions are too restrictive to be of much use in social science.

Information theory was developed independently by Claude E. Shannon and Norbert Wiener shortly after World War II, in an effort to solve certain problems in electrical communication.[35] Wiener was concerned with the problem of separating one symbol from a background containing many signals; Shannon was interested mainly in encoding messages efficiently and transmitting them with minimum error at the highest rate possible over channels containing noise. Now, although this problem sounds very much like the general political problem "How does the ruler of country A ensure that those who rule country B understand his meaning or intentions?" they are in fact quite dissimilar. In the case of the political question the problem is comprehension or understanding—even if the "message" is transmitted from A to B without distortion, it may be "misinterpreted." Shannon's problem has nothing to do with comprehension; had that been the case, he could not have solved it mathematically.

The reason why Shannon could not have solved the general problem of transmitting knowledge rather than "infor-

[35] A good nontechnical discussion of Shannon's work and of the development of communications theory can be found in J. R. Pierce, *Symbols, Signals, and Noise: The Nature and Process of Communication* (Harper & Row, Publishers, 1961).

mation" in the limited sense in which that term is defined in information theory is very important. When the problem of "meaning in context" is approached in its wider sense, the carrier of meaning is the sentence and not the letter of the alphabet, combination of letters, or word. The number of possible sentences in the English language is simply enormous; it has been estimated at 10^{50} by one authority. No formal mathematical structure could possibly handle that order of complexity.[36] Mortimer Taube makes the point very strongly in a scathing attack on those who claim to be developing electronic equipment that can be used for mechanical translation of languages.

What Shannon and Wiener did was solve certain limited problems arising in a very limited class of communications—specifically, the most efficient means of decoding and transmitting messages from sources that are "stationary" and "ergodic," using a random, probabilistic, stochastic process as a model. The meaning of "stationary" is highly restrictive: "If we can find a way of assigning probabilities to the various starting conditions used in forming the ensemble of sequences of characters which we allow the source to produce, probabilities such that any statistic obtained by averaging over the ensemble doesn't depend on the distance from the start which we take as average, then the source is said to be stationary."[37] Essentially, "stationary" means that what appears at one point in a message is like what has gone before, an assumption that a physicist might make (but does not need), but one that is hardly applicable to human messages if they are examined with reference to content. One way of eluding the problem, of course, is to examine a message as a sequence of *letters of the alphabet*, in which case it has been found that the frequency of occurrence of the letters is roughly the same for all sources. But letters do not carry

[36]Estimate by V. H. Yngve; cited in Mortimer Taube, *Computers and Common Sense* (McGraw-Hill Book Co., Inc., 1961), p. 29.
[37]Pierce, *op. cit.*, p. 58.

knowledge; hence a study of messages that is limited to the frequency of occurrence of the different letters would be worse than useless for social scientists.

An ergodic source has certain unvarying statistical properties, specifically, "every possible ensemble average [of letters, digrams, trigrams, etc.] is equal to the corresponding time average," which means essentially that the frequency of occurrence of elements in the message does not vary with the length of the message, and the statistical description of the source obtained from the study of one message is applicable to *every message coming from that source.* Again, the assumption hardly seems possible with regard to human communication if the unit of meaning is taken as the sentence; certainly it would be impossible to produce the necessary calculations even if the mathematical structure were available. Even if it could be demonstrated that all human messages approximate ergodic sources when they are considered as collections of letters of the alphabet, that would not suffice to deal with the communication of knowledge, and no one has even suggested that humans are ergodic sources when messages are construed as successive sentences. Formal communication theory, therefore, seems unlikely to be of any great use in social science in the immediate future.

Cybernetics, though it begins with formal communication theory, purports to be far more general in its applications.[38] The term was derived by Wiener from the Greek word for "steersman" and was used to designate a vast field of inquiry which included not only Shannon's version of information

---

[38]The initial volume on cybernetics was Norbert Wiener's *Cybernetics* (John Wiley & Sons, Inc., 1948), a highly technical volume. In 1950, Wiener published *The Human Use of Human Beings: Cybernetics and Society* (Doubleday & Co., Inc., 1950), a popular exposition of his mathematical structure. His most faithful follower has been W. Ross Ashby, whose principal works are invaluable as an introduction to the field: *Design for a Brain: The Origin of Adaptive Behavior* (2d ed.; John Wiley & Sons, Inc., 1960) was published first in 1952; *An Introduction to Cybernetics* (John Wiley & Sons, Inc., 1963) first appeared in 1956.

theory but the theory of games, self-controlling machines, computers, and the physiology of the nervous system. Indeed, in some of Wiener's statements, it is clear that he is thinking in terms of recasting the whole of scientific inquiry into the cybernetic mold, that he regards the cybernetic conceptual structure as adequate for the investigation for any kind of phenomena—indeed, as necessary for the investigation of any phenomena. The program envisaged for the social sciences is concise: "It is the thesis of this book that society can only be understood through a study of the messages and the communication facilities which belong to it . . . ."[39] Or in W. Ross Ashby's terms: "[Cybernetics] offers the hope of providing the essential methods by which to attack the ills—psychological, social, economic—which at present are defeating us by their intrinsic complexity. Part III of this book does not pretend to offer such methods perfected, but it attempts to offer a foundation on which such methods can be constructed, and a start in the right direction."[40] The cyberneticists are not particularly modest.

Leaving applications aside for the moment, what is cybernetics all about? Essentially, it is concerned with the regulation and control of machines—any machine. It combines, in effect, a way of looking at machines, information theory, and a conception of control and regulation. From another point of view, it is concerned with dynamic systems and their processes. Have the cyberneticists managed to formalize so massive a field? No! In fact, it is very difficult to say with any precision just how much of cybernetics is mathematical and how much is informal, though mathematical notation is frequently used. A brief look at the formal basis of cybernetics that Ashby provides will suggest some of the difficulties.

The basic formal unit in cybernetics in the *transformation,*

---

[39]Wiener, *The Human Use of Human Beings: Cybernetics and Society,* p. 16.

[40]Ashby, *An Introduction to Cybernetics,* p. 6.

which is held to be an exact formal parallel to real-life machines and systems. The unit is built in this way: an operator (*O*), acting on an operand (*OP*) produces a change; this is called a *transition*. To use Ashby's example, the sun (*O*), acting on human skin (*OP*), produces a dark skin. A transformation is a list of the transitions produced by a given operator. Now, that produces real problems for social scientists, since it is rarely possible to say what the full effects of any given "operator" may be. Ashby's assertion that cybernetics is not concerned with the "why" of phenomena but only with the "what" loses its force when he adds: "[W]hat we *must* know is how it acts on the operands; that is, we must know the transformation that it [the operator = cause?] effects."[41] Further, a very restricted type of transformation is used as a base for the formal structure—what are called *closed* transformations, defined as sets of transformations that contain no *new* element. That is, a transformation is closed if the operator interacting with a set of operands produces only those effects already contained among the operands. If the effect of an operator is to change *A's* to *B's*, *B's* to *C's*, and *C's* to *A's*, then the transformation is closed, whatever the meaning of *A*, *B*, and *C*. The restriction is of the greatest importance, for cybernetics has formalized most completely the behavior of a *determinate machine* which is defined "that which behaves in the same way as does a closed, single-valued transformation."[42] The determinate machine has roughly the same status in cybernetics as the two-person, zero-sum game in any game theory. Because the machine is "single-valued," it can move to one and only one state; if the circumstances and state of a machine can be fixed, the next state to which it will move is then uniquely determined. That is the reason why the transformation that represents the machine must be *closed*. Otherwise,

[41] *Ibid.*, p. 11.
[42] *Ibid.*, p. 24.

it would be impossible to formalize the operation of the machine or system.

As the formal structure expands, some inviting neologisms appear to tempt the unwary. A machine that can be represented by a formal structure becomes a *transducer,* the inputs to the machine turn into *parameters,* the elements in a system become *coupled;* and when the coupling acts in both directions, *mirabile dictu,* we have *feedback.* The sarcasm is not misplaced. "Feedback," for example, has become the common property of every "systems theorist" in social science; yet, as Ashby himself points out:

[The] concept of "feedback" is nowhere important. The fact is that the concept of "feedback," so simple and natural in certain elementary cases, becomes artificial and of little use when the interconnexions between the parts become more complex. When there are only two parts joined so that each affects the other, the properties of the feedback give important and useful information about the properties of the whole. But when the parties rise to even as few as four, if every one affects the other three, then twenty circuits can be traced through them; and knowing the properties of all twenty circuits does *not* give complete information about the system. Such complex systems cannot be treated as an interlaced set of more or less independent feedback circuits, but only as a whole.[43]

A similar warning is issued against misuse of the concept of "stability":

As a shorthand, when the phenomena are suitably simple, such words as equilibrium and stability are of great value and convenience. Nevertheless, it should be always borne in mind that they are mere shorthand, and that the phenomena will not always have the simplicity that these words presuppose. At all times, the user should be prepared to delete them and to substitute the actual facts, in terms of states and transformations and trajectories, to which they refer.[44]

Such warnings are not always heeded, of course. The concept

[43]*Ibid.,* p. 54.
[44]*Ibid.,* p. 85.

of feedback is casually applied to whole societies, and the search for specific feedback circuits in such complex wholes is sometimes urged as the best strategy for the advancement of our knowledge of a system, even in quite sophisticated applications of the conceptual apparatus of cybernetics.

In its simplest form, cybernetics appears as a method for examining the logical properties of certain classes of systems called determinate machines. By extension, systems whose behavior is open to statistical description can be examined, less precisely, using the same tools. The behavior of the structure must in all cases be sufficiently regular or repetitive to permit prediction of its future states, either in absolute or in statistical terms. Cybernetics stands in relation to its structures in precisely the same way as game theory relates to the systems to which it can be applied. Indeed, the "theory of regulation and control" used in cybernetics makes use of a "table of outcomes" that is *identical with* the "payoff matrix" used in game theory.[45] Regulation and control, in other words, are defined in formal terms only. Before the apparatus of cybernetics can be applied, the essential variables in the system to be regulated must be known, and the states of the system that are necessary for continued existence must be given: "[B]efore any regulation can be undertaken or even discussed, we must know what is important and what is wanted."[46] This much given, cybernetics can demonstrate that for systems of the type that it can explore, certain relations must hold if the system is to be regulated. When system states cannot be defined determinately, the mathematics of cybernetics or information theory becomes more complex, and the results are less precise, though still useful. In an indeterminate or probabilistic system the transformations become "stochastic processes," and the sequences of states are known as "Markov chains." "Markovian ma-

[45]*Ibid.*, p. 241.
[46]*Ibid.*, p. 219.

chines" have many of the properties of determinate machines, but the behavior of a Markovian system is apt to be
quite different from the behavior of a determinate system,
and it is extremely important that the two forms be kept
distinct.

Neither cybernetics nor information theory has had any
great direct influence on political scientists, though studies
of the communication process are quite plentiful.* One of
the few books by political scientists to make any use whatever of information theory and cybernetics is Karl W.
Deutsch's *The Nerves of Government: Models of Political
Communication and Control;* and even in this case, it is not
really accurate to say that Deutsch has sought to apply them
in any formal sense. Rather, Deutsch has made use of some
of the concepts used in cybernetics and information theory
(feedback, entropy, channel, etc.); but the precise definitions
employed in the formal mathematical structures have been
alloyed with everyday usage, and much of their accuracy
is lost. What Deutsch has done, in effect, is to combine sets
of concepts borrowed from Wiener, from the MIT elec-
tronics-neurology specialist Warren S. McCulloch, and from
Talcott Parsons in a not altogether systematic way, producing a volume that is at once suggestive and exasperating.
For example, the concept of feedback is used to build a

---

*See Richard R. Fagen, *Politics and Communication* (Little, Brown &
Co., 1966), especially chaps. i and ii, for a brief survey of the uses of the
concept in political science. For an example of communications studies in
the immediate post-World War II period, see Bernard Berelson and Morris
Janowitz, *Reader in Public Opinion and Communication* (Free Press, 1950).
For some more recent examples, see Wilbur Schramm, *Mass Media and National Development: The Role of Information in the Developing Countries*
(Stanford University Press, 1964); or W. Phillips Davison, *International
Political Communication* (Frederick A. Praeger, Inc., 1965). Schramm's
book contains an extensive bibliography. None of these volumes so much
as mentions the work of Wiener or Shannon. The principal emphasis in
political science has quite properly been placed on the *content* of communication, not on its logical form or structure. See the excellent introductory chapter in Bernard Berelson, *Content Analysis in Communications
Research* (Free Press, 1952).

"model" that suggests a number of interesting questions about the performance of governments but offers very little help in answering them: What is the *load* placed upon the decision-making apparatus in the state? How much *lag* is there between the emergence of a new challenge to government and its response? How effectively can government predict and anticipate new problems? It is doubtful that questions of such generality could be stated in terms that would permit a meaningful answer; it is certain that nothing in either information theory or cybernetics would in any way assist us to answer them. They are interesting and doubtless important; and we may, perhaps, credit cybernetics with raising them. But the fact remains that Deutsch is still a very long way from making effective use of the formal structure embodied in cybernetics and in information theory.

MODELS AND SIMULATIONS

Models are not always derived from mathematics or borrowed from economics; they can also be made to order for the task at hand. As an engineer builds a model of an aircraft, so the political scientist may build a model of some aspect of politics. Often, they do so far the same reasons. In recent years, model building, long popular in economics, has begun to catch on in political science. The trend, as might be expected, has been ignored by many, hailed as the dawn of a new era by some, and denounced as the work of fools by a few. Clearly, models are not useless; their value as instruments of conceptual clarification alone justifies their use. However, those who build and manipulate models claim more for their intellectual offspring than mere clarification. No general rule can be provided for evaluating such claims; they must be examined *in situ* and pragmatically.

Simulations and models are here considered identities. That is, a simulation is simply a model by another name. It is true that those engaged in simulation sometimes distinguish between the two forms, particularly when the simulation involves the use of live subjects in an experimental situation. However, the distinction seems to depend more on the *formality* or logical structure of the model than on any other factor. There is no reason why any model must be completely formalized, though we have concerned ourselves here primarily with formal models. When a simulation employs a live "decision maker" to represent the government of a nation in an international simulation, the system is left open and incomplete, and an element of uncertainty or unpredictability is built into the model. On the other hand, some simulations are carried out wholly with computers, in which case they are necessarily formal and complete; yet the title "simulation" is not denied them. In the remainder of this chapter, we shall examine two recent attempts at model construction in political science, the first formal and deductive, the second a simulation involving live participants.

Anthony Downs

Anthony Downs's widely discussed model of democratic politics is a classic illustration of model building as it is practiced by economists. A two-element model (voters, parties) is used to explore the effects of uncertainty and "information cost" on the behavior of the model. The findings are summarized as a set of "testable propositions," which may lead to "nonobvious conclusions about the actions and development of parties, thus adding to our knowledge of reality."[47] In this case the model is being used primarily as an aid to theory construction and not only as a clarifying device. Leaving aside the question whether Downs's derivations are logically secure, it provides a good example of both the uses and the limitations of this kind of model.

[47]Downs, *An Economic Theory of Democracy*, p. 33.

The fundamental postulate in Downs's model is the *rationality* of all of the actors or elements, defined in the following way:

1. The actor can always decide when faced with alternatives.
2. Alternatives are ranked in order of preference.
3. The ranking is transitive.
4. He always chooses the alternative with the highest preference ranking.
5. The decision will be identical under identical circumstances on every occasion.[48]

The economist's "rational man" is here transposed to the political arena. The application of the concept is limited, however, to the means chosen for achieving goals; the goals themselves are not evaluated.

The environment in which the actors function is "democratic," defined as follows:

1. A single party or coalition is chosen by popular election to run the government.
2. Periodic elections must be faced by the party in power (which cannot change their timing).
3. All adults who meet minimal legal requirements may vote.
4. Each voter casts one vote only.
5. The party that receives a majority of the votes acquires control of governmental power until the next election.
6. The losing parties do not resort to extralegal means of acquiring power.
7. The party in power never attempts to restrict the political activity of citizens or other parties so long as they act legally.
8. Two or more parties compete in each election.[49]

The principles of behavior followed by individual or collective actors are simple and restrictive. Parties are, in effect, defined as individual persons (a team of men seeking office through election who agree on *all* of their goals); their goal is election (power) or, when the party is in power, reelec-

48*Ibid.*, p. 6.
49*Ibid.*, pp. 23–24 (paraphrased).

tion. The important principle here is that every individual is both rational and selfish; thus, party members seek office only in order to hold office, not for altruistic or other purposes. (Downs could, of course, have avoided that assumption.) The assumption of rationality has the interesting consequence of making social policies an accidental by-product of the individual pursuit of selfish ends. Only the "invisible hand of God" is needed to complete the parallel to Adam Smith's free market.

The individual voter, like the political party, acts rationally in the pursuit of selfish ends. He "calculates," on the basis of the value *to him* in terms of his own preference scales, the effect of a victory by one party or another, using all of the information available to him (past performances, promises, etc.). Since the voter is also a realist, he knows that no political party delivers all of its promises; hence, he "handicaps" the competitors for office according to past performance, etc. The importance of uncertainty and lack of information is here evident. Though falsehood is excluded from the model, Downs's examination of the consequences of uncertainty on the behavior of the actors in the political system is perhaps the most valuable part of the book.

The government, which is also selfish, seeks votes. Downs postulates a "master plan" for governing that is modified by "marginal alterations" rather than full-scale policy changes.[50] Two situations are considered, one with full information, the other including uncertainty. In the first case, assuming two political parties, known utility functions for all voters, and full information for everyone, the only possible policy for government is to take a hypothetical poll on each issue and follow the majority principle. This will guarantee reelection except in those cases where the opposition proposes exactly the same policy but commands more support from the voters

[50]Compare Aaron Wildavsky, *The Politics of the Budgetary Process* (Little, Brown & Co., 1964).

on the basis of previous experience, or cases where the preferences of the individual voters are divided in such a manner that the opposition can obtain a majority by supporting minorities on particular issues—the so-called "Arrow problem."[51] When there is a strong consensus, a "passionate majority," the majority principle will guarantee success; it must be abandoned when the consensus is weak or lacking altogether. Downs suggests, in other words, that majority rule is possible only when there is a consensus of "intensity" as well as a consensus of views.[52]

The consequences of uncertainty for the model can only be summarized since they constitute a major portion of the book. Uncertainty affects voters differentially and not equally, thus making persuasion possible; this generates competition for influence based on persuasion. The differential development of influence forces government to regard some voters as more important than others. The parties seeking office can no longer depend on the voter's ability to relate party policy to personal preferences; in consequence, they develop appealing principles (ideologies) designed to influence the voter in nonrational ways and thus obtain his vote. In a two-party system the parties tend to converge on a position that is roughly but not perfectly central; in multiparty systems, emphasis is placed on uniqueness rather than similarity, since the conditions that generate multiparty systems also tend to their perpetuation. Similarly, the cost of information has differential effects on the population, disenfranchising some, stimulating others to vote, leading others to abstain. The reader is strongly urged to examine the course of the argument for himself; the aim here is only to provide the bare bones of the model and suggest its fruitfulness for the discipline. For that purpose an examination of some of the testable propositions that Downs has derived

---

[51]See Arrow, *Social Choice and Individual Values* (John Wiley & Sons, Inc., 1951), especially chap. v.
[52]Downs, *op. cit.*, p. 67.

from his two-axiom model (political parties in a democracy plan their policies so as to maximize votes; every citizen seeks to maximize his utility income, including that portion derived from government) will serve best.

Some of Downs's propositions are political commonplaces, though that should not devalue their significance, since they are derived from the model and a model that can generate commonplaces (among other things) is clearly on the right track. Among the commonplaces, we may include:

Proposition 2: Both parties in a two-party system agree on issues that a majority of citizens strongly favor.

Proposition 4: Coalition governments are less effective than single-party governments.

Proposition 6: Democratic governments tend to redistribute income from rich to poor.

Proposition 11: Many citizens who vote and consider voting important are not well-informed on the issues in elections.

Proposition 12: The incentive to vote is small for most citizens.

Proposition 13: A large percentage of voters do not become well-informed, even on significant issues.

It should probably be added that these "commonplaces" may very well have acquired that status largely as a result of recent inquiry into voting behavior, particularly in the United States. Further, though commonplace, they are not unimportant—consider proposition 6.

Other propositions on Downs's list are neither commonplace nor trivial; some are well worth further inquiry. For example:

Proposition 7: Democratic governments tend to favor producers more than consumers in their actions.

Proposition 23: Political parties tend to carry out as many of their promises as they can whenever they are elected.

Proposition 25: In systems usually governed by coalitions, most citizens do not vote as though elections were government-selecting mechanisms.

Downs's book is one of the best demonstrations available

of the power and richness of a relatively simple set of assumptions; the "heuristic value" of the model is very great. The propositions, of course, are true only of the model; their validity for the empirical world is a matter for inquiry, as Downs states very clearly. But let us suppose, first of all, that all of the propositions that Downs lists are formal or deductive inferences that can be drawn from the model (in some cases, that is not completely certain), and suppose further that in every case the propositions can be verified empirically. What are the uses and limitations of the model in those circumstances?

The first thing to be noted is that the model, qua model, has in no way been *validated* as a "model of reality" because the propositions drawn from the model coincide with empirical data. Indeed, there are good prima facie grounds for supposing that the two axioms with which Downs begins are false. However the truth or falsity of the basic assumptions of the model is clearly not decisive for all purposes; the results obtained from an examination of the model have proved useful. The empirical evidence validates only the results, not the model from which the results are obtained. Downs's model, in short, is a predictor; it does not suggest an explanation. His propositions deal with expectations, but not with the reasons why those expectations should be entertained. The reason why we derive certain expectations from the model is relevant *to the model* and not necessarily to empirical reality. That is, we can answer the question "Why do these conditions obtain?" only with reference to the model.

If a model is to be used to suggest why certain expectations are reasonable under given conditions, then the predictive power of the model is not a sufficient index of its value. We must also be able to relate the variables employed in the model to the variables found in the empirical situation to which the model is applied. Downs quotes with approval Milton Friedman's assertion that models should be tested primarily by the accuracy of their predictions rather than by the reality of their assumptions; but that criterion is only valid for particular uses of models, not for all of their uses. A model is a structure that is *in some ways* isomorphic to empirical reality. Predictive models are isomorphic only with regard to outputs or behavior; a model may be quite useful as a predictor yet not in the least isomorphic to the phenomena in other respects. The nature and the extent of the isomorphism between model and reality determine the use that can be made of any given model. Now, every model can make some kinds of predictions, just as every theory necessarily involves predictions. But the capacity to predict does not necessarily involve the capacity to explain, in models or in theories; the two functions must be kept separate. To be useful in the development of theory (or explanation), a model must go beyond the capacity to predict so that an explanation of a phenomenon (a prediction) in terms of the model will suggest an explanation that will hold in the empirical world as well as in the model. A system that will grind out hypotheses is simply not enough. Downs's model may have considerable heuristic value; its value as an aid to explanation is limited. The prime importance of the purpose for which a model is used can hardly be overemphasized when the time comes for evaluation.

Simulation

The Inter-Nation Simulation (INS) developed at Northwestern University by Harold Guetzkow and his associates for teaching and training in international relations offers an interesting and suggestive contrast to Downs's economic model. The antecedents are quite different; traditional military war games, decision theory, and group dynamics provided the impetus for Guetzkow's work.[53] The model is informal, though some procedures in the simulations are for-

[53]Harold Guetzkow *et al.*, *Simulation in International Relations: Developments for Research and Training* (Prentice-Hall, Inc., 1963). See also William D. Coplin, "Inter-Nation Simulation and Contemporary Theories of International Relations," *American Political Science Review*, Vol. LX, No. 3, for a friendly review of the accomplishments of INS.

malized. The developers are of course hopeful that it will lead to a more formal structure and perhaps provide a means for testing theoretical constructions in international relations, though the prime concern has been heuristic. The value of the model as a teaching instrument seems reasonably well established, even if the accounts given by those with an interest at stake are discounted. Whether it will develop further into a viable device for theory testing and theory generation remains to be seen.

The model consists of five national "units," each governed by a "decision maker" who seeks to remain in power through his choice of policies. An aspirant to office stands ready to take his place if he loses favor, according to stipulated rules, with his "validators" (his constituency). Each nation has at its disposal a basic supply of resources, military and other, which can be augmented by negotiation and alliance. The decision maker must keep the validators' support by providing adequate internal consumption and national security, each judged by a fixed rule. Satisfaction with regard to internal consumption is determined by the ratio of units of resources left in the nation and a minimum consumption standard set arbitrarily by the investigators. Security is measured by comparing the force capability of the nation and its allies with the strongest nation or alliance of nations not allied with the home nation. The degree of dependence of the decision maker on the validators varies on a "decision-latitude scale" which helps distinguish, presumably, between democratic and authoritarian political structures.

Within each nation the internal organization is determined largely by the participants; in some cases, multiple decision makers are employed in a single nation to simulate administrative difficulties. The aspirant for office may seek the support of the decision makers by offering alternative policies and by issuing policy statements. Provision is included both for orderly transitions and for revolution within the system.

A communication system is provided in two ways. Nations communicate with one another directly, and a "world newspaper" is published containing statements made by members of the system. Aspiring decision makers are not allowed to communicate externally. Complex rules govern message transmission, and they provide an important source of information about the outcome of play. The rules of play effectively exclude propaganda statements to the home population; that is, the validators are construed as rational actors who simply calculate the relationship between resources available and satisfaction obtained from them and use the results to judge the efficiency of the rulers—the format resembles in a number of ways the set of assumptions that Downs employs in his model.

The rules governing the interactions of nations in the simulation are quite limited. Nations may trade, provide aid for one another, make agreements, or make war. Occupations are permitted to the victors in war; revolutions may be launched against the occupying nation; reparations may be exacted and used to bolster the domestic resource capability.

The simulation is "played out" during a fixed time period. Since the aim of each decision maker is to remain in office rather than to achieve any fixed goal in international affairs, success is measured in terms of domestic rather than international achievement; or more precisely, international relations become an accidental by-product of policies that are essentially guided by internal considerations, just as Downs's model has the effect of making domestic policy an accidental outcome of the clash of selfish interests. The emphasis is somewhat biased in the direction of military security, and the rules of the game force the decision maker to calculate the desirability of all possible choices in terms of two value scales—consumption satisfaction and security. Various criticisms can be made of the degree of "realism" achieved in the model: There is no active opposition within the nation; past history has little constraining influence on the decision maker; geographic restraints are ignored; communications are limited, and propaganda is ruled out. The designers are of course well aware of these limitations, and the state of the simulation at any given time (it is developing constantly) is a compromise between optimal and possible accuracy and its complexity for the performers.

A model like INS can have two fundamental uses. First, it can serve as a training ground or teaching device for students, providing them with an opportunity to test their knowledge, serving as an interest generator, providing insight into the problems that face decision makers in international relations, and otherwise facilitating comprehension. Second, it does provide some base for testing hypotheses about the functioning of the international system.[54] Some insight into the influence of resource inequality and power on policy can certainly be gained through such experimental studies. By controlling different variables in the basic model (communications channels, amount of misinformation, penalties, linkage between population and decision makers, etc.), it ought to be possible to produce some interesting comparative studies, particularly since replication of a fairly precise sort is readily achieved.[55]

EXPLANATION: A FOOTNOTE

The quality of the explanations that political scientists provide is not very impressive. To make the point in another way, political theory is presently in a very undeveloped state. The conceptual frameworks examined in Chapters 3, 4, and 5 are uniformly loose, vague, and ambiguous; their applications reflect that looseness. In explanation, as in purse mak-

---

[54]See Chadwick F. Alger, "Use of the Inter-Nation Simulation in Undergraduate Teaching," in Guetzkow *et al., op. cit.*

[55]A somewhat different simulation, inspired by the INS model, can be found in Andrew M. Scott, William A. Lucas, and Trudi M. Lucas, *Simulation and National Development* (John Wiley & Sons, Inc., 1966).

ing, sow's ears do not make silk purses. But some few aspects of the contemporary scene justify sanguinity. There has been a steady growth of self-consciousness about the need to explain systematically, and that is an essential first step. Further, the conceptual frameworks now being used in political science are not inherently faulty and beyond correction. Functionalism, field theory, and the various models and simulations now employed in inquiry show promise of developing into reasonably powerful explanatory tools.

The weakness of political explanations is hardly surprising. Methodological sophistication is still uncommon within the field, though that situation is improving. More important, it would be wrong to exaggerate the amount of explanation that political scientists actually undertake. For the most part, political science is still concerned mainly with adequate description rather than explanation, and with the search for concepts that can be used to further description and provide a basis for useful generalizations. Political "analysis," in other words, is really static classification and description rather than explanation in all but a small number of cases.

In this regard, the impact of behavioralism on the discipline is often seriously misconstrued. The traditional or institutional approach to politics concentrated on descriptions of institutions and certain overt processes. The behavioralist complaint against institutionalism rightly stressed the need to go beyond the institutional facade to see what "really happened" in an organization. Behavioralism changed the focus of attention in the field. But it did not change the mode of inquiry. Most behavioral studies are still descriptions, though the phenomena being described are different. Further, behavioralism remained focused on the operation of the political system, ignoring its consequences for other systems. The behavioralist asked: "How does the system actually operate?" but he did not ask: "What does the system do?" Here, we may expect functionalism to be of major assistance, for it does tend to concentrate inquiry on the *consequences* of particular elements in a system rather than on processes that go on within the system. Both aspects of systems are important, certainly, but their development in political science has been grossly unequal.

To put the matter in a nutshell, political science tends to deal with the static rather than the dynamic aspect of politics. One of the more significant books to appear in recent years—Robert A. Dahl's *Who Governs?*—exemplifies that tendency beautifully; the question is a request for a description and not a request for an explanation. As someone has suggested, "Who cares who governs?" is in many ways a far more interesting question. And it can be answered, incidentally, without answering the question that Dahl posed. The point is that explanations arise in answer to questions that begin "why" or "how"; and so long as political science remains enamored of traditional concepts like party, Congress, executives, or courts, it is very difficult to formulate meaningful requests for explanations. One does not ask "Why is a political party?" or "How is a Congress?" Explanations are concerned with dynamics; they account for movement and change over time. They require differentiation (and to that extent the claim of the comparative government specialists that their investigations are fundamental to the development of political theory has some substance). Political phenomena, in order to be explicable rather than merely subject to description, must be housed in concepts that emphasize dynamic rather than static properties.

An illustration may clarify the point. Assuming that governments are devices for mobilizing and allocating resources, the *flow* of resources into and out of government provides a focal point for study that is almost painfully obvious. By adding the question "Why?" to Harold D. Lasswell's classic formulation of politics—*Who Gets What, When, How*—the request for an explanation is obvious and not forced, and the nature of the phenomena that require explanation is reasonably clear. It is unfortunate that the allocative function of government has for so long been ignored by political scientists, perhaps on the mistaken view that allocation lies in the economist's domain. It could provide a very useful focus for examining political dynamics. In any case, if the need for explanation should become the dominant concern of the discipline, it might force the kind of reconceptualization that is needed to change the direction of its development. And in passing, it would serve to eliminate or at least reduce attempts to produce general theories and vast classification schemes.

PART III

Political Evaluation

THERE IS no better argument for the view that systematic and responsible inquiry into political and social evaluation is urgently needed than the grossly inadequate normative judgments of society and politics that are presently being foisted off on the reading public. It is ironic that an era which has produced more academics than ever before in human history should allow the most significant of all forms of intellectual activity to go by default to a motley collection of interests lying almost wholly outside the main current of contemporary intellectual life. Yet so it is. The professional moral philosophers have, with some few exceptions, retreated into the new scholasticism, concentrating on the validity of their syntax and the grammatical properties of their word usage and ignoring the moral problems that arise in everyday life, individual or social.[1] Political scientists and

---

[1] A splendid example of the manner in which moral philosophers burke the problems of evaluation can be found in Richard T. De George (ed.), *Ethics and Society: Original Essays on Contemporary Moral Problems* (Anchor Books, 1966). The titles of the essays are revealing: "Morality and Politics," "Love and Justice," "Responsibility and Freedom," "The Mental Health Ethic," "Respect for Persons," "Ethics and Revolution," and so on. The treatment is almost uniformly literary, historical, grammatical, and syntactical.

351

sociologists, who might presumably be more conscious of the desperate need for a careful restudy of moral argument, seem to have divided into those who seek primarily after "scientific" status and those who concentrate on criticism and evaluation. The level of communication between the two schools is extremely low. For the most part, evaluation has been left to the Platonists and the Aristotelians, the idealists, the Marxists, the Freudians and neo-Freudians, the Thomists, the existentialists, and, of course, the quacks and the purveyors of utopian panaceas.

Neglect or aloofness on the part of social scientists would be excusable if evaluation were an insignificant problem, which hardly seems a tenable position, or if nothing useful or important could be said about it, which is also patently not the case. Granted that moral principles cannot be decided by logical-empirical argument, such principles are not applied in a vacuum, and political scientists should have a great deal to say about the kinds of assumptions that are needed to apply moral principles to society. The very inadequacy of political evaluation underlines one of the more glaring weaknesses in political science—its failure to deal adequately with the consequences of politics for society as a whole and for individual members of society. We know a great deal about the factors that lead to political action and about the machinery that is used for making political decisions, but we are abysmally ignorant of the consequences of politics—the "outputs" of the system—for different parts of the political system. And it is precisely at this point that much of political valuation is concentrated. If we are to evaluate normative judgments adequately and create normative judgments that can be defended, we need to know far more than we now do about the effect of politics on the social, physical, and psychological aspects of human life.

At this point the political scientist is likely to protest that the indictment is too strong, that political scientists and sociologists *do* evaluate phenomena and do criticize such evaluations. Indeed, it may appear that I am raising once again that decaying red herring, "value-free" social science, that is, the question whether *any* study of human society can be wholly free of values, since the student must choose and select from among the phenomena available for inspection, and choosing and selecting means evaluating. That problem can be settled summarily. When a Talcott Parsons or a David Easton chooses to study the factors in society that make orderly coexistence among human beings possible, does that choice automatically introduce a bias into the study? The answer, quite simply, is no. The results of such studies are not necessarily normative assertions; more commonly, they lead to technical judgments to the effect that "If you wish to achieve condition X, you must do Y." That is quite different from asserting that you *ought* to achieve condition X and that therefore the choice should be Y. The latter proposition is normative; the former is not. The purely "normative" implications of man's need to choose and select his phenomena are trivial. I study X rather than Y because I believe, for whatever reason, that X is more important than Y or because I find it more interesting. My choice, at this level, has implications only for me. If I try to convince others that I have chosen correctly then, of course, I am faced with the problem of justifying a normative judgment. But so long as I pursue my studies on the basis of my own judgment, I may be normative with reference to myself, but the consequences are trivial. To call such choices "moral" judgments is to stretch the meaning of the term unconscionably. Further, it forces us to seek some absolute standard of selection, some way of deciding what is *really* important, and the search for such standards can only be a consequence of profound ignorance of the nature of the scientific enterprise.

Political scientists do make evaluations of politics and criticize evaluations made by others, but the meaning of what they do depends on the kinds of evaluations they make.

There are three distinct kinds of activity that can be called evaluation: (1) technical criticisms of the means used to achieve agreed objectives, (2) application of normative principles to concrete situations, (3) discussions of the justification for particular normative principles. By tradition, the problem of justifying normative principles falls to political and/or moral philosophy. Without disparaging the importance of the question, it tends to lead into a bottomless morass. We can avoid that impasse by restricting the discussion to the *application* of normative principles to concrete situations, leaving aside the question how moral principles are determined and how they may be justified. That is, moral philosophy and political philosophy, in the traditional sense of the term, are treated in the same way as mathematics or statistics; they are relevant, useful, and even necessary to political study, but they are not identical to political study. We use them, but they do not constitute the focus of our inquiries.

The most important contribution of political science to normative discussion relates to the process we call technical evaluation, the selection of ways and means of achieving goals. Such problems are not, strictly speaking, normative; they are empirical questions that call for explanations and predictions rather than normative judgments.[2] In addition, there are endless discussions among political scientists and political philosophers about the normative principles that ought to be used in political valuation—what are essentially arguments about moral philosophy rather than arguments about politics. Political science has little to say about these matters. There are fierce conflicts among traditional political philosophers and political scientists, but the discussion tends to flow at two nonintersecting levels and accomplishes very

[2]For example, Scott Greer, *Urban Renewal and American Cities* (Bobbs-Merrill Co., Inc., 1965); or Norton E. Long, *The Polity* (Rand McNally & Co., 1962).

little.[3] Finally, there is a small but extremely useful body of writing that attacks normative judgment on analytic grounds, examining both the concepts employed in evaluation and the propositions in which they appear.[4] More work of this kind is very badly needed, of course, but it must be said that the task of demolition appears almost hopeless—new misconstructions are produced far more rapidly than they can be reduced to rubble. Worse, those who misuse the concepts seem little influenced by the criticism. Most of the normative discussion in political science, then, is either technical evaluation or is really moral philosophy in disguise rather than applied moral philosophy.

This way of treating political evaluation may seem to exclude traditional political philosophy from the study of contemporary political thought in an arbitrary and unwarranted manner. Why, for example, is a discussion of the "great questions" of political philosophy—liberty, freedom, justice, equality, etc.—any less worthy of study than the validity of a functional explanation? Two things need to be made clear on this point. First, discussion of the great questions of politics all too often turns into a semantic squabble simply

[3]See, for example, the discussion of Christian Bay's *Structure of Freedom* (Stanford University Press, 1958) in the journals, notably Walter Berns, "The Behavioral Sciences and the Study of Political Things: The Case of Christian Bay's 'The Structure of Freedom,'" *American Political Science Review*, Vol. LV (September, 1961); or Felix Oppenheim, *Dimensions of Freedom* (St. Martin's Press, 1961). Another illustration of the breakdown of communication between two disparate schools of political scientists can be found in the comparison of Herbert J. Storing (ed.), *Essays on the Scientific Study of Politics* (Holt, Rinehart & Winston, Inc., 1962), and the reviews by Sheldon S. Wolin and John H. Schaar in *American Political Science Review*, Vol. LVII (1963). Whatever the merits of the argument, the dogmatic attitude of those who consider themselves the custodians of tradition in normative political philosophy is most annoying.

[4]For example, T. D. Weldon, *The Vocabulary of Politics* (Penguin Books, Inc., 1953); Robert A. Dahl, *A Preface to Democratic Theory* (University of Chicago Press, 1956); Thomas L. Thorson, *The Logic of Democracy* (Holt, Rinehart & Winston, Inc., 1962); or even Raymond Aron, *The Opium of the Intellectuals*, trans. Terence Kilmartin (W. W. Norton & Co., Inc., 1962; first published in 1955).

because there are no concrete referents to anchor the argument. Second, moral philosophy is not excluded from discussion but is considered in a different context. When normative principles are applied or justified with reference to empirical situations, the discussion will almost certainly lead to argument about concepts such as liberty, equality, or freedom. But the great value of the change of emphasis is that it keeps the student face to face with the concrete applications of the principle he is supporting or applying. At the very least, the principle must be stated in terms that permit application, and the possibility of indulging in sterile symbol manipulation is thereby much reduced.

The point is that if moral principles are to serve as guides to human conduct, in politics or elsewhere, then their consequences in concrete situations are necessarily a major element in the argument for or against them. The pragmatist is on firm ground when he claims that principles which have no consequences are not worth considering. It is therefore of the utmost importance to determine what those consequences actually are, and there seems no better way to do so than to examine the applications of the principle. In short, it is possible to come to grips with the problems of moral philosophy just as readily and much more accurately by considering applications. Furthermore, the emphasis on application helps to eliminate from argument the misleading references to imaginary cases that make up so much of the grist for the modern philosopher's mill. Objections or illustrations that are conjured up from the imagination are sometimes treated as though they were forceful, as though the imaginary case were evidence. But that is impossible. No principle, in physical science or in philosophy, could survive under those circumstances. The case must be real. Finally, this mode of treating evaluation avoids the heavy burden of philosophic tradition and forces the student to examine each problem for himself. Tradition can be helpful, of course, but it can also hinder. The traditional questions may well turn out to be the best men can ask, and traditional answers may prove more satisfactory than any alternative men can create; but there can be no harm, and there may be much potential benefit, from requiring all arguments to compete on their merits rather than their pedigree.

CHAPTER SIX

POLITICAL AND SOCIAL EVALUATION

W HEN we move from the study of descriptions and explanations to the study of political and social evaluations, the
change in the intellectual milieu is radical and fundamental.
Empirical or scientific philosophy draws its inspiration almost wholly from the present century, and in particular
from the accomplishments of modern science. The outlook
is rational-empirical; logical coherence and well-established
relations among concepts and generalizations and empirical
data serve as the prime criteria of meaning and validity.
Clarity, accuracy, and consistency with the facts are valued
above literary merit, tradition, or metaphysical values. In
the world of normative philosophy, the value structure is
quite different. The primacy of epistemology, virtually taken
for granted in empirical philosophy, is rejected by moralists
in favor of religious experience, ontology, and metaphysics.
The limits of empiricism and rationalism, rather than their
merits, are most frequently attended, particularly by those
who assert that inquiry into human society is wholly different
in kind from inquiry into the physical universe. It is here, in
the contrast between explanatory and normative inquiry,
that we find C. P. Snow's "two cultures" exemplified. To
those who live and work in the empirical-rational world of
explanation, normative inquiry appears as a dark and murky

terrain in which it is difficult or even impossible to find land-
marks; to those concerned primarily with the normative, explanatory inquiry seems barren and devoid of interest.

Yet, whatever the epistemological and other philosophic
barriers that separate those seeking explanations from those
seeking normative judgments, the two are intimately and
necessarily related through the phenomena to which they
refer. Every evaluation involves an explanation of some kind,
and there are various points in evaluation where the criteria
of adequate explanation are relevant and useful. That is not
to say that the sole criterion of adequacy in normative judgment is the acceptability of the explanations it employs; but
normative judgments that rest on an inadequate explanatory
foundation are less compelling, less entitled to our support,
than those which are firmly grounded. It may be possible,
therefore, to rule out certain kinds of evaluations on rational-
empirical grounds, although there are bound to remain broad
areas where it is possible to do no more than clarify the
principles on which normative judgments rest.

The objectives of this chapter must therefore be somewhat
diverse. The study of political evaluation has an intrinsic
importance for students of political thought or, for that matter, students of politics; hence, even simple exposition of the
main trends in contemporary political evaluation has some
merit. In addition, it seems possible to indicate some of the
criticisms that will hold against particular modes of evaluation and suggest some of the consequences that follow from
the use of particular approaches to normative judgment or
the application of particular normative principles. Finally,
a careful study of the questions raised in normative discussions is of positive value to political science to the degree
that it reveals aspects of social and political life that have
hitherto been neglected by those concerned mainly with the
search for explanations. In one sense, an inadequate normative judgment is usually a good sign of an inadequacy in
political inquiry as a whole.

The political and social evaluations found in contemporary thought are remarkably numerous and diverse, yet they display a fundamental thematic unity. The critics agree to a surprising extent on the aspects of the human situation that stand in need of correction. There are profound differences in the explanations offered for these dilemmas and in the solutions proposed for them. Some observers are optimistic and even chiliastic; others are pessimistic to the edge of morbidity. Some are radical and others conservative. Some are religious, and others are secular. Some define the human situation in subjective or psychic terms, relying heavily on concepts like anomie, alienation, identity, or anxiety; others prefer to deal with abstract properties of social relations like order, equality, or liberty. They are as one, however, in their denunciations of the social order presently dominant in the Western world. And they tend to agree on the characteristics of modern society that require denunciation.

The central theme that unites the critics is the inadequacy of the scientific outlook. In effect, they have produced a litany on the collapse of rationalism and the liberal value system that it supported. It is taken as a matter of course that to be "scientific" automatically precludes consideration and concern for the "higher" aspects of human life—esthetic and normative matters. In most, though not all cases, it is assumed that scientific inquiry into human affairs (as distinct from material things) is a contradiction in terms. While there is no agreement on the alternatives, the attack on science and its concomitants—technology, rationalization, etc.— serves to concentrate social criticism to a remarkable degree.

The similarity among the social critics is heightened by their tendency to rely upon roughly the same method of approaching the problems of evaluation. Both evaluations and explanations, of course, relate to phenomena, and each can be taken as an answer to some question about phenomena. But the form of the question and the kinds of answers that are considered acceptable differ radically from one to the other. Requests for explanations, questions that ask how or why particular events or sequences of events occur, are answered by the use of generalizations that may already be at hand or may be generated specifically for the case in question. Those at hand, moreover, were generated earlier in response to other, similar phenomena. We have explanations ready-made because we are born into an ongoing enterprise; established generalizations are part of our intellectual heritage, in science and social science alike. Similarly, the concepts used in such generalizations must have linkages connecting them to particular sets of phenomena; they, too, are created from the ground up, as it were, beginning with observation. It is a serious error, though not uncommon, to suppose that the task of science is to seek concepts or theories that will serve all purposes, to search for a conceptual framework without some specific task in mind. In principle, we might expect evaluations to be generated in the same way, but the fact is that moral judgments are rarely produced *ad hoc* in response to particular situations. In most cases, evaluations are made by generating universal principles, ignoring the case at hand. That is, moral philosophy tends to search for principles that are universal in scope and applicable to all situations; it works deductively rather than inductively. Perhaps there is no choice in the matter, but the contrast is striking.

In effect, I am arguing that normative judgments are usually made by comparing the world as perceived with a predetermined conception of the world as it ought to be. The difference between explanation and evaluation, considered as modes of inquiry, lies fundamentally in the relation between the conceptual apparatus and the empirical data to which it is applied. In explanation the conceptual framework is built from an empirical base; in evaluation, it is created full-blown and then applied. The importance of the distinction emerges when we examine the form of argument employed in the two kinds of inquiry. In explanation, attention focuses on the relation between concept and data as well as among concepts; in evaluation, argument concentrates on the relation between concept and normative principle. Evaluations often leave a curious impression of unreality with the reader simply because the discussion seems wholly removed from anything in human experience. Moreover, both the meaning and the validity of an evaluation depend on the terms of the conceptual framework; hence, when the framework in which normative argument is deployed is almost completely divorced from the conceptual structure in which we habitually think and observe, criticism becomes exceptionally difficult. It is easy, too easy, to assume that a normative argument is wholly meaningless. And it is tedious and time-consuming, and sometimes impossible, to transpose an argument from one conceptual framework to another.

THE CONCEPTUAL FRAMEWORK

Normative conceptions of the world, definitions of the world as it ought to be, arise in answer to the question "What constitutes the good life for man?" Philosophers have been answering that question for a very long time. In most cases, they have advised the elimination of evil (specified with varying degrees of precision) and not the positive creation of good. It is always easier to see what is wrong than to suggest what is right. That trend has continued in contemporary thought, though positive proposals for reforming society are made from time to time. Whether or not the social critic chooses to prescribe for society's illness, he must have a frame of reference in which the disease can be identified and a remedy suggested. Any number of different conceptual frameworks can be found in contemporary political thought; but by the mid-1950's, one such structure, combining elements from G. W. F. Hegel, Karl Marx, and Sigmund Freud, was clearly predominant among the social critics. That structure, identified here as the *subjectivist* conceptual framework, will serve as a focus for the discussion of evaluation in contemporary thought.

The distinctive characteristic of the subjectivist conceptual framework is the practice of defining the good life in terms of individual self-realization. Self-realization, in turn, is usually defined in terms of subjective or psychic states. While the concept of self-realization can probably be traced to antiquity, the contemporary formulation of its meaning derives most clearly from the work of Hegel, Marx, particularly in his "early" period, and Freud.[1] Without pretending to make a detailed historical study of the development of the conceptual structure, we can best illustrate the meaning of the concepts it employs, the kinds of normative problems it defines, and the solutions offered for those problems by sketching its origins.

The basic formulation of the problem of self-realization is found in Hegel's discussion of the master-slave relationship. The point of departure is self-conscious, existential man, a conscious self that cannot "exist for itself," that is, a man aware of himself as a man and unable to live in isolation. The self must be "realized," meaning that it must be created through experiencing; by creating itself, the self creates the world in which it lives.[2] This is done in two ways: first, by transforming the natural environment and creating "things," meaning essentially transformation through work; second, by developing adequate relations with others, relations in which the self understands the behavior of others, and in which the behavior of the self, as reflected by others, is understood by the self. Much the same statement of the problems of social adjustment and self-realization can be

[1] The development of the subjectivist conceptual framework can be seen most clearly in Herbert Marcuse, *Reason and Revolution: Hegel and the Rise of Social Theory* (Oxford University Press, 1941), and *Eros and Civilization: A Philosophical Inquiry into Freud* (Beacon Press, 1955).

[2] G. W. F. Hegel, *The Phenomenology of the Mind*, trans. J. J. B. Baillie (2 vols.; Macmillan Co., 1910).

found in the social psychology of George H. Mead or John Dewey. In this context the key to adequate social relations lies in the degree of congruence between the value systems of the individual and of society (or others). In Hegelian language the self that has not been realized (Hegel, a teleologist, considered man as a body of unrealized potential) is not free. The self that is self-conscious and aware that it is not free is unhappy. If the objects in the environment are strange and unfamiliar (a sign that the self has not been fully realized), then the self is "alienated" from them. Since the self is a reflection of the environment, alienation from the environment amounts to alienation from the self. The happy self, on the other hand, is self-conscious but lives in an environment in which material objects are familiar (presumably self-created or made by processes that the self grasps or understands), and relations with others involve no strain or stress. Self-realization, in Hegel, can only be achieved by transforming the environment and the self, by fulfilling a predetermined pattern.

The critical points in Hegel's statement of the problem of self-realization are (1) the emphasis on self-consciousness and awareness, (2) the definition of self-realization in terms of subjective states rather than rational-legal terms, (3) the use of the concept of alienation to designate a lack of understanding on the part of the self of either the physical or the social environment, and (4) the suggestion, later expanded by Marx, that work directed at nature is an important element in self-realization. By focusing on subjectivity and emotion, Hegel attacked the tendency of Enlightenment rationalists to define social problems in terms of abstract principles, rational-legal relations, or types of social machinery, and in effect ruled out the possibility of solving the problem by employing these concepts. The change is highly significant. Western moral philosophers, following the classic Greeks, had assumed as a matter of course that morality is essentially the subordination of passion to reason. David Hume had broken the pattern by demonstrating that abstract reasoning could not establish value judgments and hence that they must in fact be derived from the passions. Hegel now provided a framework in which the focus shifted from reason to history and, by implication, to theology.

That is, by assuming a pattern to human history, Hegel was able to provide a solution to the problem of self-realization that is still very powerful in normative philosophy. Not until Friedrich Nietzsche did modern philosophy face the problem of creating a moral system in which all values came from man and not from objective studies of history or from religious insight. According to Hegel, man realizes himself and becomes "free" by taking his proper place in the community. As in Jean Jacques Rousseau, freedom consists of doing what is required by the community, acting according to the universal or general will—the will of the community when it is willing properly. The individual achieves self-realization by internalizing the moral precepts of the community and making them his own. The self will then be "at home" and satisfied, for it will do what society requires *because* it wishes to act in that way, not because it is coerced. The actions of the self will then be recognized by others and will produce expected reactions from others. The resemblance to Talcott Parsons' solution to the problem of social order is striking.[3]

Hegel's solution to the problem of self-realization, then, was immersion of the self in the community, and the community was defined in terms of the state—the highest form of social development in Hegel's philosophy. The communal form of self-realization, though it satisfied some subjectivists,

---

[3]Probably the clearest statement of the reasoning that lies behind Hegel's construction of freedom can be found in F. H. Bradley's "My Station and Its Duties," *Ethical Studies* (Liberal Arts Press, Inc., 1951). For two interesting examples of the direction taken by those under Hegel's influence, see Benedetto Croce, *Politics and Morals*, trans. Salvatore J. Castiglione (Philosophical Library, Inc., 1945); and A. J. M. Milne, *The Social Philosophy of English Idealism* (Allen and Unwin, 1962).

could not suffice either for those whose highest values were religious or for the secular individualists. SÃ¸ren Kierkegaard, the Danish mystic and theologian, though he joined Hegel in attacking the absence of concern with passion, feeling, and moral commitment in his age (which he ascribed to the pernicious influence of Enlightenment rationalism), proposed self-realization through individual action—a leap into a subjective relationship with God, as a means of escaping from the terror and dread that was the subjective lot of the person contemplating an environment in which everything was strange and communication was virtually impossible. Moral values are still derived from a source external to the person, but the state of social relations is in Kierkegaard wholly irrelevant. The solution is unassailable, like any other form of mysticism; whether or not it is convincing is another matter.

Nietzsche followed Hegel by concentrating on self-awareness and immediate experience, by posing the problem of values in terms of the individual's self-conscious search for identity or self-realization. But Nietzsche eliminated both the order of history and the teleological direction of God from the universe by announcing that God was dead and that the problem facing the individual was to work out his values without assistance from anyone. Self-realization, in Nietzsche, could be achieved only through the exercise of will, the affirmation of the self, the imposition of the self on the environment. Society contributed nothing to the individual, since it restricted his affirmation of will. Only the superman, the man able to impose his own values on society, could really be free within society. The "herd" counted for nothing. Nietzsche's morality is for the few, and it is achieved at the expense of the many. Contemporary existentialism takes as its point of departure the Nietzschean conception of the human predicament; Heidegger's strictures on the "unauthentic" quality of human life and Edmund Husserl's phenomenology serve as a bridge to connect them.[4]

Marx's influence on contemporary social criticism is so pervasive that it would be impossible to detail every phase of it. His contribution to the conceptual framework we are trying to outline here, however, is more limited and specific. Two points are particularly important: first, the linkage that Marx provided between social structure, particularly the mode of economic organization, and the achievement of self-realization; second, his extension of the concept of alienation, particularly in the early philosophic works written while Marx was still under the influence of Hegel. The differences between those like Georg Lukács and Herbert Marcuse, who interpret Marx in terms of Hegelian philosophy, and "Marxist humanists" like Erich Fromm, who insist that his work is *sui generis*, are in this context largely irrelevant.[5]

According to Marx, individual consciousness, what the person thinks, is determined by the individual's social existence, by the social environment. By making a distinction

[4]The best single volume of Søren Kierkegaard's work, for our purposes, is *Concluding Unscientific Postscript*, trans. David F. Swenson (Princeton University Press, 1941). Friedrich Nietzsche's main works are *Thus Spake Zarathustra*, trans. Thomas Common (Modern Library, Inc.); *Beyond Good and Evil*, trans. Marianne Cowan (Henry Regnery Co., 1955); and *The Birth of Tragedy and the Genealogy of Morals*, trans. Francis Golffing (Doubleday & Co., Inc., 1956). For a good summation of the links between Kierkegaard, Nietzsche, and the existentialist movement, see F. H. Heinemann, *Existentialism and the Modern Predicament* (Harper & Bros., 1953); or William Barrett, *Irrational Man* (Doubleday & Co., Inc., 1958).

[5]See particularly T. B. Bottomore (ed. and trans.), *Karl Marx: Early Writings* (McGraw-Hill Book Co., Inc., 1964). Interpretations of these writings differ considerably. Compare Herbert Marcuse, *Reason and Revolution: Hegel and the Rise of Social Theory* with Erich Fromm, *Marx's Concept of Man* (Frederick Ungar Publishing Co., Inc., 1961); Erich Fromm (ed.), *Socialist Humanism: An International Symposium* (Anchor Books, 1966); or R. C. Tucker, *Philosophy and Myth in Karl Marx* (Cambridge University Press, 1961). For a quite different interpretation, see Sidney Hook, *From Hegel to Marx: Studies in the Intellectual Development of Karl Marx* (University of Michigan Press, 1962). Not all of the social critics accept the "humanist" version of Marx by any means. See C. Wright Mills, *The Marxists* (Dell Publishing Co., Inc., 1962), for example.

between the content of human consciousness and the content of objective reality, Marx was able to argue that much of what lies in consciousness is in fact false ideology and rationalization, not truth. These notions were examined extensively, and developed further, in the work of Max Weber and Karl Mannheim.[6] Now, if Marx is correct, if consciousness is a social product, and if self-realization depends upon the content of consciousness, then major changes in consciousness, and self-realization, depend upon changes in the social structure. Human consciousness, in other words, originates in the material relations between man and his environment (Marx is curiously evasive about human society and social relations), and self-realization depends on the manipulation of those relations. Unfortunately, the social structure prevents man from seeing his own "true" needs, particularly under capitalism. Therefore an "interpretation" is needed; man must be shown what he really needs and disabused of his illusions. In Fromm's words: "The task of the analyst of society is precisely to awaken man so that he can become aware of the illusory false needs and of the reality of his true needs."[7] The content of these "true" needs must be derived from the nature of man; that is, the human potential must be stipulated.

The second point that is crucial in Marx is the centrality of work in the process of self-realization. In early Marx, labor is taken as the prime form of self-expression; it is the creation of self through the manipulation of nature, as in Hegel. Restrictions on man's capacity to express himself, to unfold

[6]Max Weber's *The Protestant Ethic and the Spirit of Capitalism*, trans. Talcott Parsons (Charles Scribner's Sons, 1958), was written in an attempt to invert the Marxist position on the relationship between ideas and social structure. See also Reinhard Bendix, *Max Weber: An Intellectual Portrait* (Anchor Books, 1962), chaps. ii and iii. Karl Mannheim, *Ideology and Utopia: An Introduction to the Sociology of Knowledge*, trans. Louis Wirth and Edward Shils (Harcourt, Brace & Co., first published in 1936), attempts to build upon Marx's assumption that belief is socially conditioned. See above, Chapter 2.

[7]Fromm, *Marx's Concept of Man*, p. 63.

his capacity through work, particularly when they are embodied in the social structure and in the mode of production
established in society, lead to alienation—estrangement from
the products of labor and eventually from the self. The concept of alienation actually serves Marx as a springboard for
attacking the capitalist system, since the prime factors in the
creation of alienation among the working class are all properties of capitalist production—the division of labor, specialization, rationalization, the growth of bureaucracies,
and so on. Private property becomes, in the terms of Marx's
definitions, the product of alienated labor. Alienation from
the products of labor leads first to self-alienation and
ultimately to the destruction or distortion of all social values.
In particular, workers become oriented to meaningless consumption, to meaningless work, and to meaningless lives;
they become instruments in the work of others—in Immanuel
Kant's terms, men serve as means rather than ends. Marx
believed that the most alienated class in society was the
working class, but most contemporary social critics point to
the "white-collar" workers as the principal sufferers under
the existing system.[8]

Marx's solution to the problem of self-realization,
like Hegel's, is communal and optimistic. Marxian Com-
munism purportedly eliminates restrictions on self-
realization through labor by restoring a productive relation
between man and nature. But Marx deals entirely in nega-
tives; he seeks his ends by eliminating what he considered
the primary source of alienation and repression—capitalism
and its concomitants. Historical determinism, operating
through an inexorable Hegelian dialectic, eventuates in
utopia.

Both Hegel and Marx, then, define the central problem of
moral philosophy in terms of individual self-realization, in

[8]For example, C. Wright Mills, *White Collar* (Oxford University Press,
1951).

subjective terms. Self-realization requires a productive relation to the natural environment through work and an adequate relation to the social environment, established through the organization of the economic system in Marx, and through subjection to communal values in Hegel. Both solve the problem by postulating utopian communities, though the nature of the community is quite different in each case. The uselessness of the traditional dichotomy between conservative and radical could hardly be demonstrated better. Hegel is usually considered an archconservative; Marx epitomizes the radical. Yet they differ chiefly in the importance that Marx attached to the organization of production in society. Other 19th-century solutions to the problem of self-realization were individualistic rather than communal. Kierkegaard opted for individualism oriented to religious insight. Nietzsche chose individual egoism in an indeterminate universe in which each person creates his own values. It remained for Arthur Schopenhauer to suggest that self-realization is only an illusion, that frustration is the lot of man, individually and collectively. He commended quietism and asceticism, and annihilation of the will, lightened occasionally by brief periods of esthetic satisfaction.

Freud's work in psychoanalysis fitted beautifully into the subjectivist conceptual framework in all respects save one. He underscored the limits of rationality in human behavior in a way that satisfied even the more ardent critics of rationalism. By rooting human behavior in the irrational unconscious, Freud supported Marx's thesis that repressed humans could not be aware of their own repressions. The characterology in Freud served to connect the development of self-expression with the social structure in which the self developed. But Freud's social philosophy is profoundly pessimistic, and he is hardly concerned with the social environment in which the individual functions. Freud is much closer to Schopenhauer than to utopian optimists like Marx or religious mystics like Kierkegaard. Even Nietzsche's superman, given the Freudian pattern, cannot achieve self-realization, for however much he might dominate others, he would have to repress his own unconscious desires in some degree or perish. The problem of self-realization for Freud was really a problem of learning to live without fulfillment. Repression was an unavoidable consequence of being alive and of being a civilized person.

Social critics have evaded the horns of the Freudian dilemma either by reinterpreting Freud, as in the case of Herbert Marcuse, or by going to the neo-Freudians and the ego psychologists. Very few rely directly on Freud. In most cases the characterology found in Erich Fromm, or more recently in Erik H. Erikson, serves the same purpose—linking personal fulfillment and social structure—without including Freud's pessimism. The use of "anxiety" and "identity crisis" as signs of social malaise is widespread. Unlike Freudian repression, these concepts are defined in terms that permit meliorism to flourish; the causes of anxiety can be eliminated, and identity crises can be overcome.[9]

The "subjectivist" conceptual framework resembles in a number of important respects what is sometimes called the "Romantic" outlook. Assuming that there are certain temperamental proclivities inherent in man that play a significant role in the development of the personality, the collection of these biases usually labeled Romantic comes very close to the world view implied in the subjectivist conceptual scheme. W. T. Jones, for example, in a detailed analysis of Romanticism, defines the "Romantic syndrome" by the use of seven preference continua. Other things being equal, the Romantic is a person who prefers disorder to order, dynamic to static situations, continuity and flow to discreteness, inner experience to outer experience, a soft rather than a hard "focus" in his perception of the world,

---

[9]It would be redundant to detail the conceptual machinery that psychoanalysts use to link personality, character, and social structure. See Chapter 4, especially pp. 228–32, 251–57.

novelty and risk to lawfulness and stability, and other times and places to the here and now.[10] Similar temperamental characteristics have been suggested by Nietzsche, Ruth Benedict, and many others.

Although Jones's definition of a Romantic is similar to the definition of a social critic who uses the subjectivist conceptual framework, the parallel is not perfect, and the typology is different. The subjectivist is defined in terms of the concepts he uses rather than his subjective preferences. Further, terms like "Romantic" tend to cut across certain lines of association or similarity in a way that is quite misleading. Both Hegel and Nietzsche are Romantics, for example; but there are profound differences between them that need to be underscored: One is an individualist who conceives the universe in nondirective terms, the other a communalist whose universe is ordered by the logic of the "spirit." Even the term "neo-humanist," which might serve to identify those concerned with the normative aspects of contemporary society, would not be informative or helpful. Our purpose in defining the subjectivist conceptual framework is to facilitate generalized criticism and thus anticipate problems that appear when the framework is applied to particular situations.

Critique

There are three points in any political evaluation that require special attention from the student of political thought: the adequacy of the definition of the situation provided by a conceptual framework, including the amount of bias that it introduces; the adequacy of the technical evaluations on which the normative judgment depends; and the terms of the justification, if any, offered to support the normative judgment. The justification of normative judgments depends on the particular case, usually, but it is possible to deal

[10]W. T. Jones, *The Romantic Syndrome* (Nijhoff, 1961), p. 35.

generally with both the definition of the situation that a conceptual framework permits or enforces and the technical evaluations that the conceptual structure implies.

The first point that needs to be made with reference to the subjectivist conceptual framework is that the concepts, as we might expect, are extremely loose and ambiguous and hard to relate firmly to empirical data. The crucial concepts in the framework—alienation, anxiety, loss of identity, etc.—refer to subjective or psychic states, and the definition of the situation produced by using them is often difficult if not impossible to verify. The problem is compounded by the practice of omitting the indicators that are needed to determine the presence or absence of the condition designated by the concept. Actually, there have not been very many attempts to operationalize such concepts. Robert K. Merton, in a lengthy article on anomie, cites only two cases; and Rollo May, in an essay on the importance of anxiety in the contemporary world, cites only one empirical reference— the Middletown studies—and even in this case, he relies on assertion without discussing indicators.[11] To complicate matters, concepts like anomie, alienation, mass society, etc., are used differently by different social critics. In most cases the social critics have a disturbing habit of using the terms as though they were well established, citing one another as evidence. Both C. Wright Mills and Erich Fromm, for

[11]Robert K. Merton, *Social Theory and Social Structure* (rev. ed.; Free Press, 1957), pp. 164–66. Rollo May, "Centrality of the Problem of Anxiety in Our Day," in Maurice Stein, Arthur Vidich, and David M. White (eds.), *Identity and Anxiety: Survival of the Person in Mass Society* (Free Press, 1960). See also Marvin B. Scott, "The Social Sources of Alienation," and Ephraim H. Mizruchi, "Alienation and Anomie: Theoretical and Empirical Perspectives," both in Irving Louis Horowitz (ed.), *The New Sociology* (Oxford University Press, 1964); Sebastian de Grazia, *The Political Community: A Study of Anomie* (University of Chicago Press, 1948); Lewis Feuer, "What Is Alienation? The Career of a Concept," in Maurice Stein and Arthur Vidich (eds.), *Sociology on Trial* (Prentice-Hall, Inc., 1963). In every case, there are few if any references to empirical evidence of the presence of anomie or alienation and little or no discussion of the kinds of indicators that might be employed to answer the question. Usually, the existence of anomie is simply asserted without argument.

example, are frequently cited as authority for statements about the incidence of alienation in American society, yet neither of these writers provides any real evidence to substantiate that claim.

In view of the importance of the point, a somewhat extended example may prove useful. In a discussion of social attitudes and political life, Robert E. Lane asserts (following Elton Mayo) that anomie, or social disintegration, is a prime factor in much of American political life. He then goes on to say: "This is not without its danger, for anomic individuals, however many there are, may attempt to reintegrate with the society, ideologically and socially, through some totalitarian movement." Now, that is a very strong statement, and Lane supports it by citing Erich Fromm's *Sane Society*. But Lane's reference is to an 88-page segment of the book, and it is quite impossible to say what part of the rather discursive argument he finds convincing. Certainly Fromm cites no concrete evidence to support the generalization. It is taken from an earlier book, *Escape from Freedom;* but there is no concrete evidence of the influence of anomie on behavior in that work, either. At first, Lane uses the material cautiously, stuffing his propositions with "may" and "apparently," but the remainder of his treatment of the topic is somewhat less restrained.

The principal part of the discussion depends on an article by Leo Srole (also cited by Robert K. Merton) that seeks to define and measure anomie, using a five-question interview. The questions are:

1. The individual's sense of the unresponsiveness to his lot and to his needs shown by community leadership: "Most public officials (people in office) are not really interested in the problems of the average man. In general, do you agree or disagree?"
2. The individual's perception of the social order as essentially fickle, unpredictable, and orderless, giving rise to the feeling that he could do little to direct his life with any degree of time perspective or planning ahead: "Nowadays a

person has to live pretty much for today and let tomorrow take care of itself."

3. Loss of faith in the doctrine of progress as applied to the self: "In spite of what some people say, the lot (situation, condition) of the average man is getting worse, not better."

4. Deflation or loss of meaning of internalized group norms, values, and goals, resulting in extreme form in the individual's sense of the meaningless and futility of life itself: "It's hardly fair to bring children into the world with the way things look for the future."

5. The individual's sense that the framework of immediate personal relationships, the very rock of his social existence, was no longer predictive or supportive: "These days a person doesn't really know whom he can count on."[12]

Leaving aside the question whether or not the kinds of inferences between remarks in interviews and social conditions implied in these five questions can legitimately be made, it is clear that the questions can only indicate the presence of anomie in society if there is some theoretical structure that links the answers to the psychic state or condition being examined. Certainly that cannot be assumed. Yet Lane's response to Srole's treatment of the concept is to assert that a study of automotive workers carried out by William Kornhauser and others brought to light "certain properties of the anomie complex in America." But that is to make the same mistake as assuming that intelligence tests tell us something about "intelligence." Furthermore, Lane goes on to make some strong statements about the relation between anomic attitudes and political behavior; for example, he claims anomic persons are likely to be politically apathetic and politically deviant. The chain of reasoning by which he links studies of anomie to political behavior is astonishing in a reputable and responsible scholar:

The student who believes that government officials are not interested in the average man, i.e., oneself, also tends to believe that

[12]Robert E. Lane, *Political Life: Why and How People Get Involved in Politics* (Free Press, 1959), pp. 167–68 (grammatical errors in original).

instructors are not interested in their students. And lying behind this general attitude, there lurks the childhood experience of parents who were not interested in their children, the experience of emotional abandonment. These experiences are likely to produce separation anxiety in the child, and if this anxiety turns to hopelessness, it is a state of mind which leads away from political participation, not back to politics. Here, as so often in the analysis of politics, the original theories of government as an extension of the family, both historically and functionally, turn out to have psychological validity.[13]

Lane has built a mountain of argument on the head of a pin. Nowhere, for example, is there any attempt to separate mistaken beliefs from true beliefs, and surely it matters greatly whether the student's assessment of the situation is correct. Nor does Lane provide any evidence to justify the inference from childhood experience to adult behavior. Such inferential gymnastics are possible only by assuming the validity of a concept and postulating the existence of a theoretical connection between concept and behavior.

Now, let us be perfectly clear about my intentions. It would be absurd to impugn the value of an excellent and interesting study on the basis of one tiny segment of the whole. My quarrel is not with Lane's book but with the manner in which a concept can spread on faith and authority rather than the merits of argument. One of the more unfortunate consequences of the subjectivist conceptual framework is a tendency to use fuzzily defined psychic concepts and build on them houses of straw that gain credence through repetition. The assertion that certain psychic states are causally linked to the growth of totalitarianism provides a good example of the kind of conceptual looseness that permeates social evaluation. Concern with the question "How was Hitler possible?" is understandable, particularly in the years immediately following World War II, but answers to the question that depend on inferences from psychic states are

[13]Ibid., pp. 168–69.

extremely suspect. An examination of the works most generally cited by those who accept and use such explanations is not encouraging. Erich Fromm's *Escape from Freedom,* Hannah Arendt's *Origins of Totalitarianism,* and other volumes in the same genre are so woolly and imprecise that the argument is totally beyond verification or even testing. They are literary exercises rather than essays in social science.

The illustration from Lane can also be used to highlight a second area of weakness in the subjectivist conceptual framework—the technical explanations that it employs. When indicators cannot be supplied for the key concepts in an explanation, the explanation is necessarily weak. Even more important, however, as we have seen in Chapter 4, the psychologist's ability to relate psychic states and behavior is extremely limited. We simply do not have the kind of theories that would be needed to give credence to such explanations. Indeed, even the generalizations used in explanation lack empirical foundations. When the subjective states used in explanation are located in the unconscious rather than consciousness, so that the reports of the person on his own subjective states cannot be used as evidence, then the whole apparatus totters. If the fact that Jones and Smith do not feel alienated does not mean that they are not alienated, how on earth is one to decide whether or not alienation is a meaningful concept?

The simple answer to that rather awkward question, of course, is that one cannot really decide—on empirical grounds. And the fact is that social critics do not really make such decisions. But if that is the case, how do they arrive at the propositions they assert? The answer, I believe, lies in a curious practice of inferring from principles and not generalizing from experience. Arguments that make use of the subjectivist conceptual framework tend to be verbal and not empirical; indeed, in one very important sense, empirical data are wholly irrelevant. For example, it is often said that the entire social-political-cultural-economic structure in the

United States and elsewhere must be abolished and replaced. On what grounds? Not the empirical consequences of the operation of the system. The evaluation is in fact an inference from a set of assumptions that are taken as given—neo-scholasticism is not limited to the universities by any means. For example, when Erich Fromm asserts that men need to enter into "productive" relations with others, his argument does not depend on evidence that shows that people whose relations with others are "productive" are happier, more useful, or more interesting. The argument depends on the fact that Fromm has so defined his terms that the conclusion follows from his premises. He *asserts* that relations among men are unproductive. His frame of reference *defines* unproductive relations as normatively improper. It follows that relations should be productive. At no point in the argument does he depend on observation. Such "arguments" are in fact no more than word manipulations. There is no way they can be criticized empirically, any more than we can criticize the axioms of geometry on empirical grounds. They are wholly abstract.

Given the weakness of explanations in contemporary psychology, and particularly in the psychoanalytic branch of the discipline, the least that can be expected of those who use them responsibly is caution in drawing conclusions and making recommendations. But among the social critics the imperative and the categorical are normal modes of expression. One of the major shortcomings of contemporary social critics is that they use arguments that at best seem to justify a need for further inquiry as a basis for demanding wholesale revision of the social structure. It is hard to escape the conclusion that the prescription is arrived at quite independently of the argument that supposedly supports it.

The rebuttal to this point, of course, is that if the tools are faulty, then the user cannot be blamed. But that is not quite true. Social scientists, even those who are concerned with explanation rather than evaluation, tend to assume all too often that because certain kinds of inquiry are obviously important, they are therefore worth carrying out, whatever the quality of the results. That proposition is not altogether convincing. Every science must forgo certain lines of inquiry simply because the tools needed for it are not available; the moon cannot be explored in an airplane. Impatience is understandable, but the first order of business may well be the need to construct an adequate foundation, however exasperating it may be to devote time that might be spent on direct inquiry to what appears as "nonproductive" work. Perhaps I am guilty of gross methodological conservatism, but what is impossible cannot be done, and self-delusion is a poor basis for constructing a discipline.

The subjectivist conceptual framework suffers from gross conceptual ambiguity and vagueness, and its capacity to explain is very weak. In addition, it involves a definite normative bias. That is, phenomena defined by the terms of the framework are evaluated automatically. The central normative principle of the subjectivists, the belief that the goal of human life is self-realization, is literally built into the conceptual framework. Alienation, by definition, inhibits self-realization; it is automatically evaluated negatively by those who use the conceptual framework. By extension, any factor or condition that leads to alienation—capitalism, rationalization, specialization, etc.—is also evaluated negatively. In such cases, evaluation has nothing to do with weighing or judging; it follows automatically from the application of the conceptual structure.

In effect, the use of a biased conceptual framework involves the application of a utopian ideal to concrete situations. The basic normative assumption that the goal of life is self-realization is beyond criticism. That is true of every normative principle. But in this particular case the result is utopian or at least highly optimistic. The subjectivist conceptual framework becomes a device for criticizing what is the case in terms of what ought to be the case. Empirical data are evaluated automatically in terms of congruence with the ideal. But that ignores two vital questions. First, are the conditions observed subject to change? If they are not, criticism is surely pointless. Second, are the consequences of altering the social structure to conform to the ideal going to produce the desired results? Will alienation really cease if the mode of production is changed? And are there any unforeseen and undesirable consequences likely to follow from the change? Social critics seldom concern themselves with such questions, yet they are highly relevant to normative judgment. If, for example, some degree of alienation is inescapable, as Freud would insist, then the meaning of self-realization must be altered accordingly. Is the cure for alienation likely to produce an even less desirable social condition? In that case, some modification of intention seems desirable. It is pointless to cure cancer by killing the patient. It is one thing, in other words, to have an ideal; it is quite another matter to insist that society conform to the ideal. Further, it is one thing to suggest that certain conditions should be changed and quite another to specify the actions that will produce that change—and no other. The social critic who assumes that certain changes in social structure will produce the results he wishes is in fact claiming a level of capacity to forecast that is presently far beyond what even the most powerful of the physical sciences possesses.

The criticisms made of the subjectivist conceptual framework apply equally well to other conceptual structures used in normative judgment. It is no easier to find an indicator for equality than for alienation, and those who extol the value of property or religion must rely on prophesy and not on predictions based on adequate explanations, even as the subjectivist. Finally, the atheist is regarded evaluatively by the conservative in precisely the same way the Marxist evaluates the capitalist and the worker. The weaknesses encountered in our examination of the subjectivist conceptual framework are endemic to the whole class of conceptual frameworks employed in evaluation. The principles of evaluation are different; they will emerge more clearly in the detailed discussion that occupies the remainder of this chapter. The concepts through which those principles are applied are surprisingly similar.

THE HUMAN CONDITION

The picture of advanced industrial society that emerges from the writings of the contemporary social critics is familiar. Society is large and complex and heavily organized. It tends to be ordered on "rational" principles, in Max Weber's sense of the term; productive efficiency is the prime criterion of organization. Because of the sheer scale of social organization, relations among members tend to be formal, conducted in terms of status rather than person, abstract, and remarkably similar throughout the society. Society is relatively affluent; the output of goods is enormous, and scarcity is more a problem of distribution than production. Work has become increasingly specialized; division of labor has been carried to the nth degree. Social norms have been adjusted to the needs of large-scale production, and life is increasingly molded and directed by forces beyond the control of the individual—both private and public organizations. Rationality has extended to the school system, higher education, the communications and transportation systems, and so on through almost every phase of human life. Urbanization, mass housing facilities, and a decline in privacy follow from population increase and concentration of living sites. Primary ties are loosening, and the importance of the family is declining as compared to the influence of peer groups and public authorities. Political organization tends to democracy and egalitarianism, but it tends also to centralism and the destruction of secondary-group formations. International tensions act to increase the stress on society, to augment the power of the political system, and to facilitate regimentation. The picture of "mass society" has been painted often and in livid colors.

What is to be made of these developments? What are the consequences of social and political life in the mid-20th century? Clearly, they bear close examination, for there is no denying their relevance and importance. One of the major contributions of the social critics has been to call attention to this aspect of the human condition by denouncing its alleged consequences. Granted that the consequences are often difficult to stipulate and that empirical information is very often lacking, the attempt can still be useful. The portraits of society painted by the social critics are sometimes highly abstract and often unrecognizable, particularly to those unaccustomed to the genre in which the painting appears. Paintings are not photographs; they are interpretations. And a good painting can call attention to aspects of a scene that the camera fails to emphasize by altering, emphasizing, simplifying, and restructuring. By avoiding the two extremes of studying the painting alone and ignoring the referent or complaining bitterly that the painting too faintly resembles reality, the analogy becomes a very useful tool for social analysis.

Modern industrial society, to continue the analogy, sits as a model for the social critic as artist. What kind of portrait has been produced? In fact, there is not one portrait but many. Some artists focus on society as a whole, others on elements of society. We have studies and sketches of elites and workers, intellectuals and engineers, men observed from outside and men seen from within. The variety is endless. But there are some few definitions of the human situation that recur more frequently than others, certain major themes that channel and direct the output of the social critics. There is the portrait of (1) man alone and unaided, searching desperately within himself for a value system; (2) man alienated and estranged, from himself and from society; (3) man repressed and suffocating; and (4) man strayed

from the path of truth and right. On these we shall concentrate.

Man Alone and Unaided

Nietzsche had portrayed man alone in the universe, unable to derive values from sources outside himself. In the
aftermath of World War II, that portrayal served as a point
of departure for the existentialists. The principal figure
in existentialism, Jean-Paul Sartre, was a French intellectual,
playwright, and man of letters. He was supported, in the
early postwar years, by Albert Camus and Christian philosophers like Karl Jaspers and Gabriel Marcel. By 1950, they
separated: Sartre turned increasingly to Marxism, Camus
became a critic of extremism, Jaspers and Marcel moved
in other directions. There was never much of a "movement,"
and it cannot be said that the existentialists succeeded in
their purpose, but they did produce some interesting and
very influential work.

The problem, particularly for the secular existentialists,
was to find some basis for human values within the human
condition itself, avoiding both religious authority and the
appeal to historicism. The answer was sought in terms of
emotion, feeling, immediate experience. In a sense, existentialism was a reaction against scientific rationalism, deper-
sonalization, totalitarianism, system, and dogma—all assumed to be connected. Philosophically, the existentialists
followed Edmund Husserl into phenomenology; they used
Cartesian methods to attack the influence of Cartesian rationalism. Husserl, like René Descartes before him, sought
certainty. He found it in feeling rather than in thought.
The fundamental "given" in phenomenology is immediate
experience or existence. On that base, Husserl, Sartre, and
others constructed a complex, abstruse, and at least partially obscure philosophy. A. J. Ayer's remark that existentialism consists mainly of an exercise in the art of misusing
the verb "to be" is not entirely misplaced. For our purposes

the important point in the formal philosophy is the attack on positivism and empiricism.

The human predicament is defined by the existentialists in purely subjective terms. "Existence precedes essence." Man is born into the world as a body of possibilities; what he is at any moment in time is what he has experienced. Man defines himself by experiencing and by acting; he creates his values by living and by choosing. Even the Christian existentialists did not, in the early postwar years, rely upon the Supreme Being for moral values. Man must be self-sustaining, creating his own moral system, accepting responsibility for his own actions. That is the basic existentialist thesis.[14] The existentialists have by no means been clear about the positive means for achieving that goal, but they have usually been quite explicit in their attack on the conditions that impede its achievement.

Jean-Paul Sartre.[*]   Sartre begins in abstract technical

[14]See Karl Jaspers, *Existentialism and Humanism* (Russell F. Moore, 1952); and Gabriel Marcel, *The Philosophy of Existence* (Philosophical Library, Inc., 1949).

[*]The more important primary sources of Jean-Paul Sartre's thought are *Being and Nothingness: An Essay on Phenomenological Ontology,* trans. Hazel Barnes (Philosophical Library, Inc., 1956), part of which appears under the title *Existential Psychoanalysis,* trans. Hazel Barnes (Henry Regnery Co., 1962); and *Critique de la raison dialectique (précédé de question de méthode),* Tome I (Gallimard, 1960), of which the Introduction has appeared in English as *Search for a Method,* trans. Hazel Barnes (Alfred A. Knopf, Inc., 1963). See also the essay "Materialism and Revolution," which appears in *Literary and Philosophical Essays,* trans. Annette Michelson (Collier, Inc., 1962); and the collection published as *Existentialism and Human Emotions,* particularly the lecture on "Existentialism," trans. Bernard Frechtman (Philosophical Library, Inc., 1957). Maurice Cranston's *Jean-Paul Sartre* (Grove Press, 1962) is a useful short summation of Sartre's work. Wilfred Desan, *The Marxism of Jean-Paul Sartre* (Anchor Books, 1966) is vital.

Some of the better secondary sources, for Sartre as well as the other existentialists, are Roy Pierce, *Contemporary French Political Thought* (Oxford University Press, 1966); F. H. Heinemann, *Existentialism and the Modern Predicament* (Harper & Bros., 1953); Edward A. Tiryakian, *Sociologism and Existentialism* (Prentice-Hall, Inc., 1962); Hazel Barnes, *The Literature of Possibility* (University of Nebraska Press, 1959); Henri Peyre, *The Contemporary French Novel* (Oxford University Press, 1955); Joseph Chiari, *The Contemporary French Theatre* (Rockliff, 1958); E. L.

philosophy and ends in a philosophy of commitment that has brought him increasingly closer to the French Communist party in everyday politics. His social philosophy rests on two fundamental concepts, freedom and responsibility, neither very clearly defined. Man, in Sartre's terms, is completely free to choose his own actions; yet he is responsible for those actions, to himself and to others. Oddly enough, though Sartre denies Kant's assertion that men should be treated as ends, not means, since he holds that men always seek to impose themselves on others and that conflict is unavoidable, his view that men should choose their values as though all other men were observing the choice sounds remarkably like Kant. The human dilemma, in this formulation, centers on the fact that while men seek freedom through their own actions, freedom is always conditional on the response of others. That is the central thesis of the play *No Exit*—"Hell is others." One possible escape from the dilemma, quietism, is specifically rejected. Is man, then, free to choose anything? No, for that leads to nihilism. Man's choice is "conditioned by his situation." In that case, how is the situation defined? Sartre faces a dilemma. There is nothing in his philosophy to suggest that man *must* involve himself in social life; that is only a postulate. And even if commitment is essential, what form is the commitment to take? Sartre solves the problem by his celebrated "leap" to commitment and his equally celebrated commitment first to Marxism and more recently to the French Communist party. By defining the situation in terms that are essentially Marxist, he produced a philosophy of revolu-

Allen, *Existentialism from Within* (Routledge and Kegan Paul, 1953); James Collins, *The Existentialists* (Henry Regnery Co., 1952); Wilfred Desan, *The Tragic Finale* (Harvard University Press, 1954).

Finally, one should read some of the literary and theatrical works of Jean-Paul Sartre and Albert Camus, particularly Sartre's *Dirty Hands, No Exit, Nausea,* and *The Flies;* and Camus' *The Stranger, The Plague,* and *The Fall.* They provide more of the flavor of existential writing than the more formal works.

tion that bridges the gap between the need to choose and the absence of rules of choice in nature, history, or theology.

His principle of choice, enunciated as early as 1946, is to choose so as to set men free, to liberate men from oppression. And oppression, as revealed in the life situation of man, is defined in Marxist terms. It is the man of the working class who is the victim of present-day oppression and seeks to transcend it. Behind the solution lies the conception of *solidarity*, the model of human relations which Sartre collates roughly with the position of those who took part in the French resistance movement during World War II. Participation in common work, which links man and nature, also provides the best basis for linking man and man. The revolutionary, then, defines the situation in terms of the conditions of the working class, and he chooses the action that will serve to liberate them from their oppressors. That necessarily involves a rejection of bourgeois morality and the rules of conduct that the ruling class has erected to protect its privileged position. The whole fabric of society must change so as to exclude all privilege; Sartre is an egalitarian and a leveler, and the roots in Hegel and Marx are clearly marked.

How to become a revolutionary? That requires a moment of transcendence, a recognition of the condition of man—an action that much resembles Camus' conception of "revolt." The task of social philosophy is to explain the possibility of transcendence to the members of the working class. Like Marx, Sartre provides no blueprint for the future; values are only established by achieving them in action, not by abstract discussion. The liberation of man can only be achieved by liberating man. Does that mean that Sartre, like Marx, would find himself redundant following a successful revolution, or forced to postulate endless successions of revolutions, blindly seeking liberation but unable to recognize liberation if it was achieved? It is hard to say. Certainly Sartre seems to feel that liberation cannot be achieved for everyone, that it remains as an ideal that can inspire men for the indefinite future. For a time, Sartre seemed to consider the possibility that revolution might be directed by noncommunist Marxists; but in the 1950's, he was increasingly led to the view that the working class could not hope to achieve liberation without an alliance with the Communist party.[15]

Albert Camus. Albert Camus begins at roughly the same point as Sartre, though he poses the question in a different way. He is equally opposed to system and abstraction, but he is far more sympathetic than Sartre to naturalism and humanism. Camus took the most radical possible approach to the solution of the problem of values given a universe without God or historical direction. In *The Myth of Sisyphus,* he asks quite simply: If God is dead and man must create his own values, are there any values at all? Given the absurdity (lack of purpose) of the world, should one die voluntarily—commit suicide? The answer is no! And interestingly enough, his argument is basically naturalistic: "The body's judgment is as good as the mind's, and the body shrinks from annihilation."[16] Suicide rejected, life has value, for to reject one is to affirm the other. The fact that life has no intrinsic meaning is viewed as an asset and not a liability, an opportunity and not a restriction. To revolt against absurdity is not to accept suicide but to give life value, to restore freedom of action to the individual, to make the individual aware of life. "Being aware of one's life, one's revolt, one's freedom, and to the maximum, is living, and to the maximum."[17]

[15]See Wilfred Desan, *The Marxism of Jean-Paul Sartre* (Anchor Books, 1966), especially chaps. i and ii; and Iris Murdoch's sympathetic study, *Sartre: Romantic Rationalist* (Yale University Press, 1953).

[16]Albert Camus, *The Myth of Sisyphus and Other Essays,* trans. Justin O'Brien (Alfred A. Knopf, Inc., 1955; first published in 1942), p. 6.

[17]*Ibid.,* p. 46. Camus' other important works are *The Rebel,* trans. Anthony Bower (Random House, 1956; first published in 1951); *Notebooks, 1942–1952,* trans. Justin O'Brien (Alfred A. Knopf, Inc., 1965);

Though it may not seem much, Camus has in fact asserted that there are at least *some* values in human existence.

In *The Rebel,* the concept of revolt, which was used to define the subjective situation of the actor in the earlier volume, is explored more fully. It serves as a focus for delimiting the kinds of actions that are incompatible with the development of an adequate value system. In one sense, Camus provides an answer to Emile Durkheim's contention that man in a world without predetermined values is prone to anomic behavior and even suicide, and to the Christian thinkers who asserted that in a world where God is dead there can be no values whatever. It remained now to consider in more detail the form that individual revolt might take, and its consequences. The result is one of the more eloquent pleas for moderation and tolerance to appear in this century, a fact that helps explain the enthusiasm of Camus' supporters. Camus may have been naïve at times—too prone to value naturalism above civilization, direct experience above abstraction; too quick to condemn rationalism in absolute terms—but his integrity shines through his work like a beacon for those seeking relief from the dilettante and the poseur.

The ostensible focus of *The Rebel* is murder, but the theme remains the same. In *The Myth of Sisyphus,* suicide was rejected and value affirmed. In *The Rebel,* murder is also rejected, and on the same grounds; human life is asserted as the only necessary good. Nihilism is impossible. "Rebellion is born of the spectacle of irrationality, confronted with an unjust and incomprehensible condition. But its blind impulse is to demand order in the midst of chaos . . . its preoccupation is to transform . . . but to

---

and some earlier essays available in different editions. Some of the better secondary sources are John Cruickshank, *Albert Camus and the Literature of Revolt* (Oxford University Press, 1959); Germaine Brée, *Camus* (Rutgers University Press, 1961); and Philip Thody, *Albert Camus: 1913–1960* (Macmillan Co., 1961).

transform is to act and to act will be, tomorrow, to kill . . . Rebellion engenders exactly the actions it is asked to legitimate."[18] How to avoid the conclusion? The analysis shows, in Camus' view, that rebellion is not an act of egoism; the demand for respect is identified with respect for the community, for others as well as the self. Hence, rebellion, like Sartre's commitment and action, requires principles, and they are to be found in human solidarity—rebellion is a reaction to common suffering, not individual experience. Rebellion therefore asserts human nature, the need to defend something sacred in man.[19]

Most of *The Rebel* is devoted to an examination of the various forms that rebellion has taken in history, considered first as a metaphysical reaction and then as a historical revolution. Camus rejects, in turn, because they are unlimited, what he calls metaphysical rebellion, nihilsm, and historical revolution. The protest against the human condition and the whole of creation that Camus calls metaphysical rebellion leads, he says, to a desire for order, and that desire leads men to resort to crime and murder in an effort to impose themselves on their situation. Nihilism, the condition where everything is permitted, has the same result, since if there are no values, murder is a matter of indifference. Revolution, which is different from rebellion (the latter is limited, while the former reintroduces the concept of destiny in the form of history), ends by demanding total control of the world. In brief, Camus is rejecting the Hegelian and Marxist solutions to the problem of values— and this was the prime source of his rupture with Sartre after the publication of *The Rebel*—as well as the nihilist's

---

[18]Camus, *The Rebel*, p. 10.

[19]The parallel to Simone Weil, whom Camus much admired, is striking. "Something in every man expects good, not evil—that is sacred." See Simone Weil, *Selected Essays, 1934–1943*, trans. Richard Rees (Oxford University Press, 1962). He does not, however, follow Weil into the mystic individualism of her later writings.

claim that everything is permissible and possible. Only the Russian terrorists of 1905 are treated with sympathy and consideration, not because of the nature of their acts, but because "in the midst of a world which they deny and which rejects them, they try, man after man, like all the great-hearted ones, to reconstruct a brotherhood of man."[20] They rebelled, they killed, but they doubted, even while they were killing.

Camus rejects absolutism in its metaphysical, historical, and nihilistic forms because they lead to murder and injustice. What has he to offer in their place? The doctrine of rebellion! Rebellion as a limit on absolute freedom, on absolute justice, and on murder. The rebel opposes, with all of his power, servitude, falsehood, and terror. He demands for himself no more freedom than he demands for others, and in no case can he demand the right to destroy the freedom and existence of others. Camus is an optimist, hoping for the future and committing himself to the present in the name of the future, but conditionally and guardedly. Only in these terms can commitment to revolution and violence be justified. Like Oliver Wendell Holmes, Camus believes that the danger should be clear and present, the wager worth the risk. The rebel stands with those who suffer: "The toiling masses, worn out with suffering and death, are masses without God. Our place is henceforth at their side, far from teachers, old or new."[21] The rebel is aware of his ignorance, of the inevitability of suffering and injustice, of the pitiful state of the human condition, and he seeks to transcend it realistically and humanely. "Then we understand that rebellion cannot exist without a strange form of love. Those who find no rest in God or in history are condemned to live for those who, like themselves, cannot live: in fact, for the humiliated."[22] The power of

[20]Camus, *The Rebel*, p. 170.
[21]*Ibid.*, p. 303.
[22]*Ibid.*, p. 305.

the testimonial for moderation, for moral responsibility, for awareness, for willingness to commit the self on behalf of the moral principle while remaining doubtful and uncertain is remarkable.

Camus' faults are the faults of the literary figure deeply immersed in politics. It is very difficult to say what constitutes an act of rebellion in the concrete sense. How does the rebel know injustice when he sees it? Camus provides no ethical theory which can be attacked or defended. The historical illustrations are broad, the concepts hard to operationalize. Against these aspects of his thought, we may balance the absence of cant and self-deception, the refusal to descend to "moralizing" in the worst sense. As Roy Pierce points out, Camus is very much a man of his own age, and he seeks to live with the modern world, not to destroy it. Granting the evidence that convinces the pessimists, he refuses to be pessimistic, but his optimism is conditioned by a fine sense of relevance. *The Rebel* bears reading.

Gabriel Marcel and Karl Jaspers. Although Gabriel Marcel and Karl Jaspers no longer consider themselves existentialists, and though both are considerably removed from the concept of social philosophy that appears in Sartre and Camus, Jaspers is usually considered the founder of existentialism as philosophy, and Marcel accepted the classification until around 1950. They belong to an older generation; Jaspers was born in 1883 and Marcel in 1889, and the differences between their definition of the situation and that of Sartre or Camus is instructive.[23] Marcel is the more obviously Christian in emphasis; Jaspers, particularly in his early works, most clearly influenced by Hegel and Nietzsche.

Both men attack mass society, and Jaspers' *Man in the*

[23]See particularly Gabriel Marcel, *Man against Mass Society*, trans. G. S. Fraser (Henry Regnery Co., 1962; first published in 1952); and Karl Jaspers, *Man in the Modern Age*, trans. E. Paul and C. Paul (Doubleday & Co., Inc., 1957; first published in 1931). Jaspers' *The Future of Mankind*, trans. E. B. Ashton (University of Chicago Press, 1961; first published in 1958), is also interesting.

Modern Age, though it appeared in 1931, anticipates many of the criticisms of mass society now being published. Both celebrate the downfall of science as a philosophic base; Marcel is most concerned with the decline of Christian faith and argues consistently that moral life cannot be achieved outside its bounds. Both attack the "leveling-down" tendency in mass society, Marcel more strongly than Jaspers. Each seeks to "save the few"; neither believes that attempts to raise the standards of the mass as a whole can succeed. Where Marcel asserts that the good life can only be achieved in small Christian communities, Jaspers talks in Hegelian terms of the role of the state when it is serving its "true" purpose and not pandering to the masses; and he assumes that state-directed education, aimed at "true" knowledge, offers the best hope for the future.

In their attack on mass society, Jaspers and Marcel follow the older tradition of Gustav Le Bon and Jose Ortega y Gasset. The masses are described as pleasure-seeking, willing to work only when driven by dire need or the whip, and perpetually craving novelty and amusement.[24] The quality of mass culture is low. Mass culture facilitates the development of bureaucracy, fosters irresponsibility among political leaders ("the scum rises to the top"), and breaks down primary institutions like family and church. The mass becomes, in effect, the principal example of the degradation of modern man. Politically, Jaspers favors democracy, particularly in his later writings, whereas Marcel, who is more pessimistic, seems to support a return to aristocracy. Both urge the need to accept "the transcendent," a return to faith, Marcel perhaps more strongly than Jaspers.

What has all of this to do with existentialism? Very little. The one weak link between Camus and Sartre and Jas-

[24]Compare José Ortega y Gasset, *The Revolt of the Masses* (W. W. Norton & Co., Inc., 1957; first published in 1930); and Gustav Le Bon, *The Crowd: A Study of the Popular Mind* (Ernest Benn, 1952; first published in 1896).

pers and Marcel is concern with the individual in mass society, but the individual that interests Jaspers and Marcel is the unusual man, the artist or creative person, and not the run-of-the-mill citizen. Jaspers and Marcel emerge from these particular works as traditional conservatives, strongly religious, deeply concerned with encroachments on social tradition and older values, and alarmed at the inroads of rationalism on traditional metaphysics and mysticism. They do not search for principles to guide man in an unstructured world; they are disturbed by the manner in which the world is altering its structure away from the pattern they consider desirable.

Though existentialism flourished during the 1950's, its strength declined toward the end of the decade. Camus was killed in an automobile accident; Jaspers and Marcel renounced existentialism; Sartre was driven ever deeper into the fold of the French Communist party. It was not really a movement; the technical philosophy propounded by Sartre in *Being and Nothingness: An Essay on Phenomenological Ontology* was too abstract to become popular and too faulty to gain acceptance—among Anglo-Saxon professional philosophers particularly. Sartre's political commitment is not required by his philosophic principles and may, in fact, be incompatible with them. Camus managed to clear away some of the debris surrounding the search for values without benefit of God or history, but his achievement is chiefly negative. *The Rebel* remains as a testament to moderation, humanity, and personal integrity, but there is little more that commends itself because of its contribution to the development of a viable value system. Much of what seemed best in existentialism has in fact been absorbed into other modes of social criticism. It seems a pity, for the concept of the human condition from which existentialism began its inquiries is important and not too popular in other parts of the world where antireligious sentiment is less radically militant than in France.

Man Alienated and Estranged*

Perhaps the most important theme in the social criticism of the 1960's is the alienation or estrangement of man—from society, from other men, from the product of his work, from himself. A variety of terms is used to identify the condition: alienation, anxiety, rootlessness, loss of community, loss of identity. The gist of their meaning is the same. Man stands alone in a bewildering universe, like the prisoner in Franz Kafka's trial, detached, unhappy, misunderstood and unable to understand, guilty (of unknown crimes), suffering. Through the haze of conceptual obscurity the point emerges, in most discussions of alienation or estrangement, that man lacks fulfillment. The self is not being realized. How did this come about? What are the characteristics of the state? How can the condition be cured? We shall examine next the answers given to these ques-

*The concept of the human situation that views man as estranged, alienated, anxious, and without an identity can be found in any of the works of Erich Fromm, David Riesman, Hannah Arendt, Erik H. Erikson, C. Wright Mills (with some interesting modifications), the so-called neo-Marxists who follow Georg Lukács, and many, many others. For a good introduction to the statement of the problem most commonly met in the 1960's, see Maurice Stein, Arthur Vidich, and David M. White (eds.), *Identity and Anxiety: Survival of the Person in Mass Society* (Free Press, 1960); Maurice Stein and Arthur Vidich (eds.), *Sociology on Trial* (Prentice-Hall, Inc., 1963); Irving Louis Horowitz (ed.), *The New Sociology* (Oxford University Press, 1965); Robert A. Nisbet, *Community and Power* (Oxford University Press, 1962); Erich Kahler, *The Tower and the Abyss* (Jonathan Cape, 1958); Robert Presthus, *The Organizational Society: An Analysis and a Theory* (Alfred A. Knopf, Inc., 1962); Roderick Seidenberg, *Posthistoric Man: An Inquiry* (University of North Carolina Press, 1950); Thomas Molnar, *The Decline of the Intellectual* (World Publishing Co., 1961); Robert C. Angell, *Free Society and Moral Crisis* (University of Michigan Press, 1958); or Kenneth E. Boulding, *The Organizational Revolution: A Study in the Ethics of Economic Organization* (Harper & Bros., 1953), especially the interchange with Reinhold Niebuhr in the discussions; Ernest van den Haag, *Passion and Social Constraint* (Stein and Day, 1963; first published in 1957); Jacques Ellul, *The Technological Society*, trans. John Wilkinson (Alfred A. Knopf, Inc., 1964); William H. Whyte, Jr., *The Organization Man* (Simon and Schuster, Inc., 1956); Maurice Stein, *The Eclipse of Community* (Harper & Bros., 1964); Paul Goodman, *Growing Up Absurd: Problems of Youth in Organizational Society* (Vintage, 1962); William Kornhauser, *The Politics of Mass So-*

tions by some of the more eminent of contemporary social critics.

Those concerned with alienation and estrangement in modern society are seeking to deal normatively with the relation between society and the individual. In the process, of course, they are necessarily involved in technical evaluations, predictions about the future and explanations of the present. They make use of a variety of concepts and terms. The technical evaluations and the concepts tend to be weak, vague, and ambiguous, as we would expect. The evaluations range from the completely pessimistic view of C. Wright Mills, who sees nothing good in present-day society, or Roderick Seidenberg, who foresees something like an ant-colony future for man, to the utopian optimism of Erich Fromm, who believes that a transformation of society

---

ciety (Free Press, 1959); Paul Goodman, *Utopian Essays and Practical Proposals* (Vintage, 1964); Bruno Bettelheim, *The Informed Heart* (Free Press of Glencoe, Inc., 1961).

For purposes of comparison, these same phenomena are treated quite differently by those who do not make use of the subjectivist conceptual framework. See Daniel Bell, *The End of Ideology* (Free Press, 1960); Seymour M. Lipset, *Political Man: The Social Bases of Politics* (Doubleday & Co., Inc., 1960); Daniel Boorstin, *The Genius of American Politics* (University of Chicago Press, 1953); John K. Galbraith, *The Affluent Society* (Houghton Mifflin Co., 1958); John K. Galbraith, *American Capitalism: The Concept of Countervailing Power* (Houghton Mifflin Co., 1956); Adolph A. Berle, Jr., *Power without Property* (Harcourt, Brace & Co., 1959); Adolph A. Berle, Jr., *The Twentieth Century Capitalist Revolution* (Harcourt, Brace & Co., 1954); Karl R. Popper, *The Open Society and Its Enemies* (2 vols.; 4th ed.; Princeton University Press, 1963). In these works, modern industrial society is generally considered to provide opportunity for man, rather than inhibiting and restricting his activities. The effect on politics is, however, causing some concern; witness the growth of interest in the nature of consensus and the sources of democratic stability in recent work in political science. See Robert E. Lane, "The Politics of Consensus in an Age of Affluence," *American Political Science Review*, Vol. LIX, No. 4 (December, 1965); Robert E. Lane, "The Decline of Politics and Ideology in a Knowledgeable Society," *American Sociological Review*, Vol. XXXI, No. 5 (October, 1966); David E. Apter (ed.), *Ideology and Discontent* (Free Press of Glencoe, Inc., 1964); Peter Bachrach, *The Theory of Democratic Elitism: A Critique* (Little, Brown & Co., 1967); or the exchange between Robert A. Dahl and Jack Walker in *American Political Science Review*, Vol. LX, No. 3 (September, 1966).

is possible that will produce a productive, happy, well-adjusted man. Pessimist and optimist agree, however, that the fault lies in the organization of society and not in the individual; here they differ radically from existentialists like Camus or Marcel. It follows that what is needed is a reorganization of society and not a refurbishing of man; society must be adjusted to man, not man to society.

The social critics approach the problem of individual-social relations in two somewhat different ways. One school, for which Erich Fromm is perhaps the best-known spokesman, deals with the problems in terms of the impact of social organization on human personality. The technical evaluations used in the explanation of existing conditions and in predictions of the future depend for their validity on certain assumptions about the relation between character or personality and the structure of society. The second way to approach the problem is to concentrate on the *gemeinschaft-gesselschaft* dichotomy developed by Ferdinand Tönnies and used effectively by social critics like Karl Mannheim.[25] In the first case, social structure is criticized because it produces a personality type that is undesirable; in the second, criticism suggests that society does not permit, or even interdicts, the close interpersonal relations that human beings must have. One of the more persuasive recent spokesmen for the second point of view is Robert A. Nisbet, whose *Community and Power* we shall examine with some care.

Erich Fromm.   Erich Fromm is one of the more prominent of the "Marxist humanists," the group concerned with the Hegelian phase of Marx's early work. He is also noted as a member of the "neo-Freudian" group of psychoanalysts. Finally, he has produced an enormous amount of social criticism since the end of World War II, combining psy-

[25]See Ferdinand Tönnies, *Community and Society*, trans. Charles P. Loomis (Harper & Bros., 1957); Karl Mannheim, *Diagnosis of Our Time* (Oxford University Press, 1944); and Karl Mannheim, *Freedom, Power, and Democratic Planning* (Oxford University Press, 1950).

choanalytic and sociological explanation with very broad kinds of historical generalizations.* In general, he is far more influenced by Marx than Freud; his theory of knowledge is essentialist, in Karl R. Popper's terms (Fromm's favorite phrase, which recurs constantly, is "geting beyond the veiled surface of things to grasp their essence"); and he uses "reason" in the same way as the German *Verstehen* sociologists and not in the Cartesian sense. His approach to social criticism follows the pattern used by psychoanalysts to cure individual patients: Find the source of the disability (in the past history of the individual), make the individual aware of the source of the trouble, and then get the patient to make changes in his own thought structure that will eliminate the problem. Fromm treats society like a patient, an individual with a serious mental illness—and it is here that he uses the notion of society as an entity separate from the individuals that compose it—and he both performs diagnosis and prescribes the cure. His prognosis is generally optimistic.

Fromm's argument depends on certain basic assumptions and practices that require identification. In ethics, he is an essentialist who believes that reason is an inadequate instru-

---

*See above, pp. 251–57. The Fromm bibliography is quite large. Fortunately, there are more books than ideas, and much repetition. For our purposes, *Escape from Freedom* (Rinehart & Co., Inc., 1941); *Man for Himself* (Holt, Rinehart & Winston, Inc., 1947); and *The Sane Society* (Holt, Rinehart & Winston, Inc., 1955) cover most of the important material. Other volumes that are relevant are *The Art of Loving; Sigmund Freud's Mission* (Harper & Bros., 1959); *Beyond the Chains of Illusion;* and *May Man Prevail?* They throw interesting light on Fromm's attitude toward Marx and Freud and toward the place of religion in society. John H. Schaar's *Escape from Authority: The Perspectives of Erich Fromm* (Basic Books, Inc., 1961) is useful, particularly with regard to the validity of technical valuations in Fromm and the operational characteristics of Fromm's concepts. Schaar shows, for example, that Fromm consistently uses the term "society" in two ways: Society is considered *only* as a collection of individuals (see Fromm, *Escape from Freedom*, p. 137) when Fromm is attacking society; but when Fromm is arguing about the relation between character and social structure, society is construed as an entity with its own properties. This kind of ambiguity is common in social criticism.

ment for dealing with normative matters; ethics, in the last analysis, becomes applied psychology. His goal is a "productive" life for man, the unfolding of human powers "according to the laws of nature." The problem of scarcity is, he believes, solved; but in the process, man has become a slave to his machines. The basic explanatory instrument is a characterology that depends on the assumption of a distinct relation between clusters of character traits and social structure.[26] In fact, Fromm postulates a "social character," a structure generated by society to fit its own requirements. The properties of social character can be inferred from the historical development of society. Character traits may be either conscious or unconscious; in effect, the character system is the general form for channeling human activity in society. Beneath character, however, lies a fundamental human nature,[27] which is essentially "good" but is repressed by the social system. Like Thorstein Veblen's "instinct for workmanship," the goodness in man strives for release; man desires a genuinely productive life but is prevented from achieving it by society. The final link between character, human nature, and society is provided by a theory of motivation that resembles fairly closely Leon Festinger's "cognitive dissonance" to the extent that it implies a need on the part of the person to resolve contradictions in his perceptions and actions.

The content of human nature is defined by Fromm as a set of needs. First, man has a need for relatedness to others. That need can be fulfilled in various ways, some desirable and others not. Unproductive relatedness (read undesirable) are based on either submission or dominance, neither of which is satisfactory for either party. Productive relatedness, which is Fromm's ethical goal, is a "loving" relation in which there is no loss of self. The relation is characterized

[26]Fromm, *Man for Himself*, p. 23.
[27]*Ibid.;* Fromm, *The Sane Society,* p. 205.

by care and respect for the other person, a feeling of responsibility for the other person, and adequate knowledge. In context, it is obvious that Fromm attaches far more importance to the need for relatedness than to the other human needs that social life must satisfy. Beyond relatedness, man, according to Fromm, has need for transcendence (creativity), for roots, for a sense of identity, and for a frame of orientation. In effect, these terms define the meaning of alienation, for Fromm uses that term in much broader terms than either Marx or Hegel, or even other contemporary social critics. The alienated person, in Fromm's writing, has not fulfilled any of his basic needs—he lacks roots, a sense of identity, relatedness to others, a frame of orientation, and an outlet for creativity. Since Fromm argues that alienation in modern society is "nearly complete," the next step in the process of analyzing society is clearly to locate the source of the problem, to fix the blame for the failure of man to fulfill his needs.

The key to Fromm's diagnosis lies in the explanation he offers of the relation between social structure and personality or character. Following R. H. Tawney, and to some extent Max Weber and Karl Marx, Fromm asserts that society produces a social character appropriate to its requirements and that social character is the prime determinant of individual character. Fromm's position is profoundly anti-individualistic, for he obviously must assume that the individual has very little control over the development of his own character if individual character is primarily and almost exclusively a function of social character. The point is extremely significant because he goes on to assert that the prime determinant of *social* character is the mode of production in society. That being the case, it is 20th-century capitalism that is responsible for the kinds of individual characters that society is today producing, and there is little or nothing that the individual can do about it (except, presumably, if he happens to be Fromm) unless he attacks the capitalist system. Capitalism, in other words, is conceived as a vast matrix, a mold for shaping a particular kind of social character. Individual character is produced in a master mold defined by the mode of production on which the economic system is based. Fromm does not argue his point on the basis of evidence gathered by him or others, it is simply taken for granted, or perhaps inferred; and at times, it seems no more than a logical consequence of the set of definitions that Fromm chooses to employ. Certainly he is not abashed by evidence. In a brief discussion of the empirical evidence for work satisfaction, in *The Sane Society*, for example, he uses figures from C. Wright Mills's *White Collar* (quite uncritically) and, as John H. Schaar points out, treats them as though only one interpretation were possible, though Schaar is able to produce at least two alternative interpretations of equal persuasiveness.[28] As an example, Fromm cites a study indicating that about 49 percent of American manual workers say that the worker should turn out "as much as he can," while 41 percent of the workers state that the worker should "turn out an average amount." To him, it means that "there is a great deal of conscious, and even more unconscious dissatisfaction with the kind of work which our industrial society offers most of its members."[29] Even if the restriction on output is granted, Fromm's assumption that it is due only to conscious and unconscious work dissatisfaction is quite unwarranted. Anyone familiar with American labor union practices and policies could produce a variety of different reasons to account for the facts.

Given that the mode of production is the prime determinant of social character, what are the salient features of the mode of production that we call capitalism? Fromm cites technological change, concentration of capital, separ-

[28]Fromm, *The Sane Society*, pp. 258–61.
[29]*Ibid.*, p. 260.

ation of ownership and management, the growing importance of the domestic market, the development of bureaucracy and antonomous authority, and the rationalization of production as its principal qualities. His recitation of the facts, which relies heavily on the work of Adolph A. Berle, Jr., and Gardiner C. Means, John K. Galbraith, and others, corresponds roughly to the description found in most other sources. But Fromm's description of the social character that is required by 20th century capitalism is something quite uniquely his own. For it seems to Fromm that the capitalist mode of production necessarily produces alienated men with a "receptive" or consumption-orienated outlook, for whom work is an obsession and conformity a necessity. Man, under capitalism, has come to regard himself in abstract and quantified terms, to see himself as a "thing" to be bought and sold in the marketplace. Under the existing system, it is utterly impossible for man to fulfill the basic needs of his own nature. Capitalism enforces the victory of *animal laborans* that Hannah Arendt deplores in *The Human Condition*; it creates the fractionalized man, alienated from himself, his work, and his community, that Erich Kahler attacks in *The Tower and the Abyss;* it reproduces C. Wright Mills's "happy robot" and David Riesman's "other-directed man." The root of social evil is capitalism.[30]

Fromm's solution to social sickness follows almost automatically from the diagnosis, and Fromm's own task in life becomes clear—he must make the patient aware of the nature of the disease. What can the individual do qua individual? Virtually nothing. The only cure for the disease is to transform society. The aim is not to produce a man who can fulfill a role in society; man must alter society so that he can fulfill his "real" nature within its confines. Given such

[30]For a study of the development of this same attitude toward capitalism among British socialists in the postwar years, see Eugene J. Meehan, *The British Left Wing and Foreign Policy: A Study of the Influence of Ideology* (Rutgers University Press, 1960), especially chap. iii.

a radical interpretation of the causes of individual discontent, Fromm's solution is surprisingly mild and prosaic. In effect, he goes back to the guild socialists, urging that the economic system be organized around production for use rather than production for profit and that worker participation in industry be expanded so that "workers employ capital" rather than capital employing workers. As Schaar quite rightly notes, the solution does not go very far toward fulfilling the conditions set by Fromm himself for adequate social relations. The possibility that a new ruling class might emerge from an attempt to install a new productive system, expounded so eloquently by Milovan Djilas in *The New Class*, is ignored. The economic solution is simplistic and even trite.

In political matters, Fromm urges the restoration of the town meeting and a decentralization of government. He feels that no new normative principles are needed; the content of the philosophic tradition is already adequate to man's purpose. In his later works, religion has occupied an increasingly important part in his ideal scheme of things. But in general, the treatment of social and political organization is hopelessly inadequate. Marcuse's proposal that industry might be automated to the point where individuals spent most of their time in creative action is dismissed as utopian. But the question whether individuals who perform the same work on the same site are improved psychically by merely obtaining a voice in management is badly argued, and none of the studies of nationalized industry that might be germane to the problem are cited. Finally, there is a sense in which the transformation of society Fromm advocates could not possibly eliminate insecurity from human life; man, according to Fromm, must learn to live with insecurity, not transcend it.[31] Nothing is said of the way in which changes in the mode of production might alter the individual's ca-

[31]Fromm, *The Sane Society*, p. 174.

pacity to absorb change and adapt to insecurity. In fact, Fromm does not really indicate the way in which social analysis might proceed. Fromm has faith and a program. He has no argument.

Robert A. Nisbet. *Community and Power* is one of the dozens of suggestive studies of contemporary life that appeared after World War II. Like Fromm, Nisbet begins with alienation, "the state of mind that can find a social order remote, incomprehensible, or fraudulent; beyond real hope or desire; inviting apathy, boredom, or even hostility."[32] But he considers alienation within the context of community, that is, in terms of the individual's relation to social function and social authority. He agrees that alienation is one of the central concerns of the era. He claims that men search avidly for community, for a sense of belonging, that will eliminate alienation. He asserts that alienation makes totalitarianism more likely because the alienated man is attracted to the community that totalitarian movements have to offer. But he rejects Fromm's belief that the cause of alienation lies in capitalism, together with Max Weber's thesis that capitalism is intimately related to the development of Protestantism. Instead, he asserts that the quest for community arises out of certain "profound dislocations in the primary associative areas of society, dislocations that have been created to a great extent by the structure of the Western political state."[33] Human life has been affected by the growth of centralization of power, remoteness of authority, impersonality in social relations. The problem, in fine, lies in the decline of primary groups in society, the reduction of pluralism in the interests of a monolithic state. Nisbet produces a powerful plea for political pluralism as a remedy for the social ills of Western industrial society. The diagnosis is radical, the cure conservative.

[32]Nisbet, *Community and Power* (Oxford University Press, 1962), p. viii.
[33]*Ibid.*, p. 47.

Nisbet's argument is thought-provoking. Like Fromm, he asserts that medieval life was characteristically associational life and that the transformation that produced the modern world in effect released the individual from his ties to older, smaller associations and transferred his loyalties and hopes to the political state. Like Fromm, Nisbet claims that man, loosed from the moral ties that once bound him to society, is confused and a ready prey for totalitarianism. But in Nisbet's argument the source of the difficulty lies in the transfer of function to the state. Associations whose functional usefulness has disappeared soon lose their vitality. When the state performs the functions formerly performed by the family, the role of the family is weakened, and its bonds are loosened. The key to modernization, in these terms, is the conflict between central political authority and the various intervening groups between state and individual. The conflict, needless to say, has usually been decided in favor of the state. In opposition to Weber's and Fromm's theses, Nisbet claims that the functional expansion of the state created the climate of laws that made individual business operations possible and provided shelter for religious persons seeking relief from Catholicism. Clearly, Nisbet does not like the state. Large organizations of this kind, he holds, rest on power and force. Only the smaller organizations in society rest on mutual respect, friendship, and responsibility. Hence, only the small organization allows man the opportunity to exercise his natural propensity for sociability, permits him to develop the ties and links that make possible a happy and stable life. The state is an incubus that "becomes powerful not by virtue of what it takes from the individual but by virtue of what it takes from the spiritual and social associations which compete with it for men's devotion."[34]

Nisbet links modern society to totalitarianism through

[34]*Ibid.*, p. 163.

the concept of "masses." Specifically, totalitarianism is defined, in terms of mass attitudes, as the suppression of all
images not directly related to the central authority in the
political system. Totalitarianism is not, in these terms, irrational; indeed, it is highly rational. Nor is it necessarily evil
incarnate; in most cases, totalitarianism is achieved in the
name of high moral principles. The crucial factor is the
existence of a mass, not just a large number of persons but
persons who have been cut from their moorings and alienated from society. Totalitarianism, he claims, depends on
the psychological premise that the human personality cannot tolerate moral isolation; life apart from membership
in a larger order is unbearable for most people. The totalitarian state therefore proceeds quite rationally by creating
new functions, statuses, and allegiances to replace those
it has destroyed, all centered on itself: "[By] conferring
community . . . the manipulation of the human will [is]
scarcely more than an exercise in scientific social psychology."[35]

Nisbet's solution to the problem of alienation is tame
by the standards of the radical critics. He seeks to maintain
liberal, or conservative, values through social pluralism
and decentralization of administration. He wishes to see
autonomous and meaningful groups created in society on
the ground that they, and they alone, can provide man
with a source of roots, individual strength, and creativity.

The contrast between Nisbet and Fromm is striking. But
is one a conservative, whereas the other is a radical? The
question is almost meaningless. What we need to ask is
whether Nisbet has produced a relevant and significant criticism of contemporary society. It is obvious that he has
indeed done so. And his awareness of the complexity of the
problem under discussion is refreshing. One of the great
errors in contemporary social thought is the confusion of

[35]*Ibid.*, p. 208.

radicalism of the left with social criticism. Too often, it is assumed that what is not radical is necessarily uncritical. In time, the development of adequate social criticism divorced from outdated concepts like liberalism, socialism, left, or right may eliminate that particular bias. Meanwhile, Nisbet's effort can serve as an antidote. And in its own right, it calls attention to an aspect of the relation between human behavior and the larger historical and philosophical issues of the age that is all too readily overlooked by social critics too deeply immersed in psychoanalysis.

Man Repressed

The social critic who relies on orthodox Freudian psychoanalysis seems to face an insuperable difficulty. Freud, particularly in his *Civilization and Its Discontents,* said quite clearly that civilization *is* repression, that civilization cannot be attained without cost to the individual. The result is pessimism toward the human future, for as civilization grows more complex, the cost is presumably greater. Curiously enough, the social critics who rely directly on Freud rather than on socialized psychoanalysis or ego psychology nevertheless manage to fit utopian schemes into the Freudian framework. The transformation is fascinating and ingenious. Freud emerges—through a certain amount of reinterpretation, of course—as an optimist. The central theme of man repressed is retained by both Herbert Marcuse and Norman O. Brown, but the nature of the repression and the possibility of cure have changed radically.[36]

The more interesting thesis belongs to Marcuse. In *Eros and Civilization* he combines Hegel, Freud, and Marx in a

[36]Marcuse, *Eros and Civilization: A Philosophical Inquiry into Freud;* Herbert Marcuse, *One-Dimensional Man* (Beacon Press, 1964); Norman O. Brown, *Life against Death: The Psychoanalytical Meaning of History* (Alfred A. Knopf, Inc., 1959). See also Robert P. Wolff; Barrington Moore, Jr.; and Herbert Marcuse, *A Critique of Pure Tolerance* (Beacon Press, 1965).

truly virtuoso performance. The achievements of repressive civilization, he claims, make possible the elimination of repression by eliminating scarcity. In fact, *all* scarcity is now due to control over distribution aimed only at domination of man by man. Human productivity has eliminated scarcity and, with it, the basis of Freud's belief that repression was inevitable. The pleasure principle, though subject to the reality principle, need no longer be controlled by the special form of the reality principle that Marcuse terms the "performance principle." The "surplus repression" enforced on mankind by those who dominate can be eliminated. The amount of time required for satisfaction of the reality principle can be reduced to a minimum and perhaps ultimately eliminated altogether through automation. Man will "realize himself" by allowing free scope to the pleasure principle—which has suffered most from the surplus repression imposed for purposes of domination.

The connection between Freud and Marx is also established through the performance principle. When work is rationalized through performance, society is stratified according to competitive economic achievement. Alienation of labor is necessarily generated by the effort to structure human behavior in a pattern that will maximize production by distributing output differentially. Alienation spreads to free time so that workers may be better prepared to perform their tasks. Sexual repression, particularly, is extended by tabooing all sexual activity not directed to procreation (which is economically useful under scarcity). Like Marx, Marcuse agrees that the performance principle was useful while industrial civilization was being built and that the life of the individual worker was both sustained and improved by productivity increases. But as man's control over nature improved and productivity expanded, human needs were more and more fulfilled only as a by-product of labor. Indeed, higher productivity actually increased the need for repression; otherwise, the worker might realize that he

need work only a short period of time to fulfill his basic
needs. The root of the problem, for Marcuse as for Marx,
is the capitalist's desire for profit. Marcuse comes very near
a "conspiracy theory" of industrial development. "Civilization has to defend itself against the spectre of a world
that could be free. If society cannot use its growing productivity for reducing repression (because it would alter the
status quo) productivity must be turned *against* individuals; it becomes an instrument of universal control. Totalitarianism spreads over late industrial civilization wherever
the interests of domination prevail upon productivity, ar-
resting and diverting its potentialities."[37]

Rationalization provides Marcuse with another fulcrum
for attacking the existing system. Domination which has
congealed into a system becomes administration—deperson-
alized and rationalized. Division of labor and simplification of function, together with increased rationalization of
other aspects of production, lead to administrative domination. Individuals become commodities; men sell their labor,
their free time, ultimately themselves. Therefore, if mass
production provides man with more free time and a wider
range of choices, that merely diverts attention from the real
issue—man's inability to choose his own work and determine
his own needs and satisfactions. In time (actually, now)
the alienation of labor is complete. The world of work becomes a system of "things," organized according to rational
rules. The essential humanity is lost. And to make matters
worse, the individual does not realize what is happening to
him. He believes that he is happy. In an age of anxiety,
"anxiety has disappeared from expression."[38] Why the absence of expression of unhappiness does not indicate that
the term "age of anxiety" is a mistake Marcuse does not
say. Actually, he is little concerned with empirical studies

[37]Marcuse, *Eros and Civilization,* p. 85 (italics in original).
[38]*Ibid.,* p. 94.

of human attitudes. If men are happy, they are only deluded. If they are unhappy, the thesis is proved. Alienation is an inference from a set of definitions, not an observable state of society or man.

In Marcuse's view, Freud's chief error was to mistake the reality principle of his time (the performance principle) for a timeless rule. The performance principle enforces repression of the pleasure principle; if it is faulty, then repression may not be necessary. The performance principle depends on scarcity; if scarcity is no longer essential, the performance principle can be dropped. At that point the pleasure principle can be safely liberated; society is mature. The inversion of Freud is complete. Under another form of civilization, different from the one that Freud generalized, repression is not necessary. When society is fully mature and scarcity has been conquered, nonrepressive civilization is possible. It follows that nonrepressive civilization is possible *now*. The play impulses can be set free, the esthetic dimension can be freed. The world can be transformed. Nature will then be experienced primarily as contemplation. Violent and explosive attempts at domination will cease. Man will be actively engaged in display, in the "free manifestation of potentialities."[39] The individual himself will be responsible for harmonizing relations between himself and others: "In a truly free civilization, all laws are self-given by the individuals."[40] Time is overcome, for only thus can civilization be truly nonrepressive. Marcuse quotes Friedrich Schiller: The liberating play impulse abolishes "time in time," reconciles being and becoming, change and identity—whatever that means. "In this task culminates the progress of mankind to a higher form of culture." Labor has been transformed into play, productivity into display; sensuousness has replaced reason as the prime factor in hu-

[39]*Ibid.*, p. 173.
[40]*Ibid.*, p. 174.

man life; time has been conquered so far as it affects lasting gratification. In Marcuse's utopia, rationality has the function of organizing the productive system in a way that requires the least amount of time from the members of society to produce their own necessities.

Marcuse has sketched a utopia, but he believes that it can be achieved. And he means to have it. For he asserts that his utopia is a form of "objective truth," that "there *is* an objective truth which can be discovered, ascertained only in learning and comprehending that which is and that which can be and ought to be done for the sake of improving the lot of mankind."[41] What is needed is revolution, the development of a "subversive majority," which can seek out this objective truth for themselves. "This means that the ways should not be blocked on which a subversive majority could develop, and if they are blocked by organized repression, their reopening may require apparently undemocratic means. They would include the withdrawal of toleration of speech and assembly from groups and movements which promote aggressive policies, armanent . . . or which oppose the extension of public services, social security, medical care, etc."[42] Further, teaching and related practices in educational institutions may have to be controlled, a set of policies that Marcuse calls "liberating tolerance," which means "intolerance against movements from the right and toleration of movements from the left."[43] Tolerance that serves to preserve repressive society (as defined by Marcuse, presumably) is perverted. Tolerance should be withdrawn from "regressive" movements *before* they can become active; the danger is too great to allow them to act. What were formerly "neutral, value-free, formal" aspects of learning must become political: "Unless the student learns to think in

[41]"Repressive Tolerance," in Wolff, Moore, and Marcuse, *op. cit.*, p. 89.
[42]*Ibid.*, p. 100.
[43]*Ibid.*, p. 109.

the opposite direction, he will be inclined to place the facts into the predominant framework of values." Finally, oppressed minorities have a "natural right" to use extralegal means when legal means prove inadequate; and no third person, and least of all the educator and intellectual, has the right to preach them abstention."[44] Marcuse has come a long way from the revolutionaries whom Camus admired. They acted, and they committed murder; but even as they acted, they doubted. Marcuse does not doubt.

Man Strayed from the Path

There remains to be examined the conception of the human condition which assumes that the present age is deficient because it fails to appreciate the value of what it already possesses. The conservative outlook is a powerful force in every society, though it varies greatly in focus, intensity, and tone. At the extremes the radical conservative is far closer in outlook to the extreme left than to his more moderate counterpart. Some conservatives concentrate on economic matters almost to the conclusion of other concerns; others are so deeply involved in religion that it comes to occupy a central position in their thinking. Moderate conservatism, which takes its inspiration chiefly from Edmund Burke, tends to avoid dogmatism in both areas—Nisbet's treatment of community is representative of this point of view. In this section, we examine briefly the evaluation of present-day society found in the work of Russell Kirk, perhaps the most articulate of American spokesmen for the Burkean view. Kirk paints an interesting picture, even if we agree with Clinton Rossiter that he has the sound of a man born a century and a half too late.*

[44]*Ibid.*, p. 117.

*The literature of conservatism is endless. Frank S. Meyer has edited a useful collection of essays by American conservatives entitled *What Is Conservatism* (Holt, Rinehart & Winston, Inc., 1964). The flavor of that peculiar brand of economic liberalism that often passes for conservatism in

Kirk, needless to say, does not employ the subjectivist conceptual framework outlined at the beginning of this chapter. Yet his frame of reference includes most of the phenomena that attract the attention of other social critics. He is concerned with the loneliness of Riesman's "crowd," though he interprets the sources of that loneliness differently. He dislikes the blaring publicity of Madison Avenue, the mechanization of human life, the social boredom that is evident in the human misuse of leisure, the materialism of the age. He is neither a simplistic economic liberal nor a fanatical churchman. "The enlightened conservative does not believe that the end or aim of life is competition; or success; or enjoyment; or longevity; or power; or possessions. He believes, instead, that the object of life is Love." How that life can be achieved, and to what degree, is the problem he seeks to answer.[45]

Kirk's enumeration of "the most urgent problems of the age" is instructive:

1. Redeeming the intellect from the uniformity of the mass age
2. The resuscitation of spirit and conscience
3. How to give meaning to human life in an industrialized and standarized society
4. Restoration of community (in Nisbet's sense) without collectivism
5. Social justice which limits avarice

America can be had from Milton Friedman's *Capitalism and Freedom* (University of Chicago Press, 1962); F. A. Hayek, *The Road to Serfdom* (University of Chicago Press, 1944); Ludwig von Mises, *Omnipotent Government* (Yale University Press, 1944); or John Chamberlain, *The Roots of Capitalism* (Princeton University Press, 1961). The work of Peter Drucker, particularly *The New Society*, has been quite influential with thoughtful conservatives. See also Henry Hazlitt, *The Foundations of Morality* (Van Nostrand Co., Inc., 1964); Wilhelm Röpke, *A Humane Economy* (Henry Regnery Co., 1960); Michael Oakeshott, *Rationalism in Politics* (Methuen & Co., Ltd., 1962); and the writings of Reinhold Niebuhr and Jacques Maritain (for the Protestant and Catholic outlooks, respectively).

[45]Russell Kirk, *Prospects for Conservatives* (Henry Regnery Co., 1956), p. 19.

6. Satisfaction of just desires and limitation of unjust desires
7. Maintenance of order without loss of variety
8. Control of power in the interests of justice
9. The revival of loyalty to country and tradition
10. The maintenance of links between the generations

The chief source of the difficulty, in Kirk's view, is the development of personal ambition, of ideals of social efficiency and control over nature, and of an appetite for social reform, all without an adequate purpose. The solution cannot be purely rational and intellectual; man must draw on all of his resources—by which Kirk means using what tradition has to offer.

The core principles in Kirk's conservatism, the normative assumptions from which his solutions to these problems are derived, differ sharply from those held by the social critics considered earlier. Belief in God, in the existence of a supreme order, is prime; men are *placed* on earth, they do not simply find themselves there. There is a human nature, then, though quite different from Erich Fromm's: Men are, if anything, inclined to evil and in need of restraint. Kirk's problem is to determine the essential restrictions, not to eliminate all restrictions; to do the latter, given his view of man, would only lead to chaos. Beyond these fundamentals, there are certain basic choices that Kirk has made; his value hierarchy is ordered in a particular way. He values liberty above equality or security, since he does not feel that men are equal in capacity, and he conceives of justice as reward according to merit. He fears power and therefore he seeks to control it in a way that will prevent abuse rather than looking for ways to use it for good ends. He rejects the possibility of perfection in this world; politics becomes a matter of restraining evil and not seeking positively defined goals. In brief, Kirk's conception of society is directed toward self-fulfillment, but through acts of individual initiative. The degree of self-fulfillment depends primarily on the innate capacities of the person. Private property is for Kirk the prime agency through which the individual achieves self-realization. The rule of inheritance, which is logically incompatible with this view, is nevertheless maintained as a necessary requisite for the preservation of the "natural" family.

The prescription for society's ills flows from the diagnosis and the assumptions. If man is lonely, it is because he has been separated from God and the concept of higher purpose; that purpose must be restored. Social boredom and the absence of purpose are due to the declining importance of traditional sources of drive and initiative—religious faith, emulation of peers, concern for the family, desire for self-advantage, and desire for liberty. The social power of concepts like honor and dignity must be revived, and internalized values must be changed; adjustments of external conditions are always inadequate. By maintaining private property rights, rewarding ability and diligence, and teaching men to feel responsible to both past and future, it might be possible to alleviate the plight of the proletariat. Success, in Kirk's view, is problematic but worth the effort. A restoration of community, in terms very close to those used by Nisbet, can also perform a vital function for society. This, too, is largely a matter of internalized values rather than external manipulations. Fundamentally, Kirk asserts that the crux of the difficulty lies in the principles that men are acculturated to apply, not in the external machinery of society.

In economic affairs, Kirk agrees that a major aim ought to be the elimination of drudgery from human life, but he holds that man cannot appreciate leisure unless he has learned the meaning of work. Similarly, the economy ought not to neglect the dignity of man; yet a free economy is essential—it is prerequisite to all other freedoms. Kirk is extremely vague about the manner in which these seemingly contradictory goals might be achieved. And in view of the later discussions of class and status, where he argues that men ought to do the work for which they are best suited and to recognize for themselves their station in life and take pride in it, it seems unlikely that he attaches any great importance to the point. His view is strongly antimaterialist, and he makes much of the desirability of the simple life and of the tendency for wealth to enervate. The possibility of achieving "general luxuriousness" through expansion of production he regards very suspiciously, apparently on the view that men are ill-equipped to handle the time and opportunity that might thereby be provided them.

In political matters, Kirk's central precepts are the control of power, chiefly through dispersion, the inculcation of loyalty, and a harmonious arrangement of classes and functions based on the spirit of duty, honor, respect. He bewails the decline of mutual trust, the lack of respect for the law, the increase of crime, and other signs of disorder. His solution to the problem seems to be the development of a class of natural leaders, honored, respected and obeyed by the population. Government is necessary, but it is a necessary evil. The only principle that can be applied to problems of government is the rule of parsimony; allow government no more power than is necessary. How that amount is to be determined Kirk does not say.

REPRISE

The quality of normative discussion of politics in contemporary thought is deplorable. Leaving aside the acceptability of the normative principles being applied to society, the attempts made to apply them are for the most part wholly unconvincing. The conceptual apparatus is so loose that the definition of the situation is either undecipherable or patently in error. Much of what passes for reasoned evaluation is merely the result of bias built into a conceptual scheme. And the technical evaluations used to either account for the human situation or suggest a remedy for its undesirable aspects are hopelessly inadequate. No sane person

could believe that a "sane society" might be achieved by
following Fromm's prescriptions. The inadequacy of tradition seems empirically confirmed; Kirk's own argument
would not really be necessary had not tradition come under
attack. As for the arguments produced by Herbert Marcuse
and his followers, to paraphrase Bertrand Russell, I can find
nothing in either the universe or Marcuse's writings that
would lead me to accept what he has to say. As a normative
principle, "The left is always right" is only a bore.

The principal fault in normative inquiry as today practiced—in my opinion, at least—is the determined separation
of reason and ethics, or science and normative discourse,
that the moralists and the social critics propose. First of all,
it seems to me to increase greatly the dangers of ethical
absolutism. As Morris Ginsberg, one of the most humane
and tolerant of men, has said: "If my analysis is right, it
follows that the different forms of totalitarianism have this
in common: they all involved the subordination of ethics to
politics and the removal of morals from the sphere of reason."[46] Human reason is certainly fallible, and man cannot
live his life by reason alone, but that is not an argument for
eliminating reason entirely from moral affairs. Second, the
assumption or assertion that political science can add little
or nothing to normative judgment can only stem from a
gross misunderstanding of the nature of normative judgments. Evaluations necessarily depend on descriptive and
explanatory propositions, and to the extent that they have
been established in political science, they are relevant to
any normative judgment that involves their use. At the very
least, those who indulge in normative arguments must make
use of what political science has to offer—normative discussion of the ethics of jumping off tall buildings cannot ignore
the law of gravity. Third, the repression of reason and exalta-

---

[46]Morris Ginsberg, *On the Diversity of Morals* (Macmillan Co., 1957),
p. 33.

tion of emotion and passion necessarily lead to an excessive exaggeration of the importance of the subjective aspect of human life and a consequent neglect of its objective or social aspects. I would probably agree that emphasis upon the subjective consequences of social life is the most important dimension added to ethics since Plato and Aristotle, but that does not mean that an adequate ethic can be formulated solely in terms of subjective states. The subjective and objective must somehow be combined. Indeed, that seems one of the major priorities in moral philosophy at the present time.

Whatever their faults, the value of normative criticisms of contemporary society seems undisputable. For one thing, they are very definitely relevant to the human situation in some sense of the term. Granting conceptual fuzziness and explanatory weakness, the fact remains that human society *is* growing larger, more complex, and more rational; that men *do* seem concerned with the inadequacy of traditional values; and that tradition, Russell Kirk notwithstanding, has not proved adequate for contemporary man. I am not sure that the sight of contemporary man hunched down in front of his "idiot box" watching morality plays starring cowboys and Indians, or soap-opera heroes and heroines, is any more disturbing than the mental image conjured up by medieval life—millions of humans chained to the earth, rude, ignorant, barely more than animals in many respects, toiling endlessly for a paltry living and an early grave. The "noble savage" was a decidedly unpleasant fellow, so far as I can tell, and his contemporary counterpart is a definite improvement. Nevertheless, contemporary man does have more time to spend, more choices to make, and, apparently, very little in the way of adequate guidelines. Marcuse's facile assumption that the problem of scarcity is solved for humanity is too preposterous to take seriously; but for some segments of some communities, that is almost the case; and it is in these limited segments, if anywhere, that we find some inklings of things to come—doubtless on a much grander scale. It is wise to take heed of them.

The central problem facing industrialized societies, I believe, has to do with the development of adequate and realistic sets of aspirations for the men and women who live in them. Under what circumstances can a mature man living a half century from now look back on his life with some measure of contentment? Certainly the day when a woman's life was considered well spent if it eventuated in a brood of brats who somehow reached maturity is gone—and good riddance. Similarly, the "good provider" of the early 20th century is no longer the young maiden's dream, even if she hasn't attended Smith or Vassar. What direction ought men to choose when they allocate their one irreplaceable commodity—time? I suspect very strongly, though a full inquiry will have to await another occasion, that the principal obstacle to adequate discussion of this problem is the set of normative principles inherited from the Enlightenment and from 19th-century socialism—in particular, the principle of equality and the dogma of private property. But the question can only be settled, or argued adequately, if those principles are discussed in terms of present-day society, its exigencies, and its potentialities. In brief, we may make some progress, or at least achieve some clarification, by bringing political science and normative inquiry into a reasonable working relation.

The intransigence of the radical social critics and of the conservative diehards will doubtless prove a substantial obstacle in the path of any proposed fusion of scientific inquiry and normative judgment. What is really dismaying, however, is to see how very little political science or the other social sciences, as presently constituted, can contribute to the discussion of normative problems—in practice and not merely in principle. What *are* the effects of government on social organization? Is Nisbet correct when he claims that intermediate social organizations are being gobbled up by the state? Can the situation be alleviated in the way he suggests? At what cost? What is the relationship between the organization of the economic system and the character of those who earn their livelihood in that system? How different would things actually be if social production were organized around some principle other than the profit motive? What are the psychological consequences of worker control in industry? Large-scale bureaucracy? What can government do —and how—to alleviate psychic maladjustment? These are not questions that require normative answers; they are strictly empirical. And political science is unable to answer any of them adequately. Yet, until they are answered, the normative judgments we make in these and related areas cannot be very meaningful.

The remoteness of the questions that political scientists tend to study from the kinds of problems raised by the social critics is truly striking. The December, 1966, issue of the *American Political Science Review* contains the following major articles: "Political Theory and Political Science," "Transaction Flows in the International System," "Political Aspects of Mobility in China's Urban Development," "Discerning a Causal Pattern among Data on Voting Behavior," "The Governor and His Legislative Party," and "Some Effects of Interest Group Strength in State Politics." Is it any wonder that those who believe—rightly, in my judgment— that in the last analysis the most important thing about any political system is its consequences for the members of society abandon hope of obtaining anything useful from the profession most directly concerned with the study of politics? Perhaps these problems are really meant for sociology or anthropology? Utter nonsense. If political science is concerned with politics, it must be concerned with the effect of politics as well as its machinery. What else is there to be concerned with? When there is widespread agreement on the inadequacy of some of the basic conditions of human life, why are those conditions not a part of the definition of the situation employed by the political scientist? In an era when governments spend enormous sums on community rehabilitation, social welfare, and education, are not welfare, education, and community rehabilitation political problems? Is not a government in some sense a device for fulfilling human needs and desires and for creating them? And if that is so, is not the student of politics concerned directly and immediately with the nature of human needs and desires and with the conditions of their fulfillment? If political scientists are to leave the discussion of such urgent and pressing problems to people in other fields while they pursue the goals set by unexamined tradition with an air of detachment, then the discipline will surely perish—and it will deserve its fate. I exaggerate, perhaps, but not very much.

If it is any consolation to political scientists, both political philosophers and moral philosophers, those who earn their keep by taking an interest in normative affairs, are equally remote and detached from everyday life. Much of their work is mere gloss, endless exegesis of texts. I have yet to see a normative principle examined by a political philosopher in terms of its relevance for the empirical present. Apparently, "purity" can only be maintained by total dissociation from the here and now, for nothing else would account for the tendency for political philosophy to proceed in such a vacuum. I have argued that along with the discussion of man's feelings, we must have discussion of more abstract and general questions like "liberty" or "equality," but that discussion must be carried out in terms of the facts of political and social life. How can they be separated? How can the validity of a normative argument be established independently of the circumstances to which it is applied?

The quality of normative discourse is poor. Vast improvement is possible, even with the weak tools now available. Evaluation must be tied to reliable knowledge. More knowledge is needed in certain areas crucial for evaluation that have hitherto remained untouched by political science.

ᴨere does responsibility lie for these matters? We can, perhaps, insist that those who make evaluations and seek to attract others to them should steep themselves in the lore of the discipline; but clearly, they have no intention of doing so, and they could in any case reply that at present the discipline would not provide much help. Alternatively, we can concentrate on the present, on contemporary problems, seeking to intrude political science into political valuation in a meaningful way. That would have the dual advantage of introducing what is already available in the form of knowledge of politics into an area of discourse where it is badly needed and at the same time calling attention to areas that need further exploration. Curiously enough, the American federal government may eventually generate precisely this outcome through sponsored research in areas where it is planning to intervene. It is a fact that more relevant and significant data about the urban community have been produced since the national government took an interest in urban affairs, and supported its interest with funds, than ever before in history. The same situation seems to appear in other disciplines—psychology, sociology, etc.; the Yale studies in mass communication are a good illustration of the point. That trend is not without its dangers, but it is an interesting commentary on the state of the discipline that direction of research is so easily achieved on monetary grounds and so hard to procure through reasoned argument. In the phrases of the social critics, political science seems all too often to have become a success channel for the upward-mobile and the other-directed rather than a communal enterprise of persons with a lasting interest in a particular set of phenomena.

CHAPTER SEVEN

CONCLUDING REMARKS

EVERY age is in some respects a period of transition; our own is no exception. And nowhere are the signs of change more readily perceived than in academic life, and perhaps even in political science. In a transitional period the interested observer finds it difficult to avoid imposing his own outlook on the events he records. If he is pessimistic, those events tend to appear as a harbinger of a disastrous future. If he is optimistic, the same events appear as a remnant of a departing age. In those circumstances, there is a powerful temptation to straddle the fence, cleaving strongly to the present and neither bewailing the past nor hoping too much for the future. That choice minimizes risk. But it will not really do. The future is in some respects conditional upon the present, and no survey of the present can avoid all implications for the future. Since the survey just completed led to some rather dismal conclusions about the present state of political thought, the reader is entitled to ask whether the pessimistic or the optimistic outlook is more appropriate to the situation. And the author, I believe, is obliged to reply. Both parties must, certainly, keep the nature of the enterprise firmly in view and avoid unwarranted or exaggerated emphasis on what is necessarily a hazardous undertaking.

I believe that the present state of political thought is the tag end of a dying tradition and not a portent of things to come. My reason for believing this is simply that most of the really gross inadequacies in present-day political thought can be traced quite clearly to an earlier period, and most of the changes that have taken place in the past decade or two seem to me to be changes for the better. Here, I must hasten to say that I do not mean that "behavioralism" is good and "traditionalism" is bad. In fact, I shall argue shortly that behavioralism could well turn into a serious handicap for the discipline if it persists in supporting a tradition that is now losing its force in other areas of intellectual inquiry.

To be specific, the conceptual apparatus that political science employs in description and explanation—the terms, the concepts, the criteria of significance—date almost without exception to the period between World War I and World War II. The conceptual framework used in evaluation, as I have tried to demonstrate, goes back even further in time. The bias to static analysis that is still a major handicap in the field is clearly traceable to the institutionalism of the 19th and early 20th centuries. The lack of methodological sophistication among political scientists is not unique; it is even more pronounced among historians. Political scientists have been exasperatingly slow to learn. It would be pointless to spin out the indictment in great detail. The simplest way to make the point is to note that John Locke, or even Aristotle, would have understood perfectly well what political scientists were saying until very recently. Indeed, they would still feel quite at home with much if not most of the work that political scientists are producing. I am not here mounting an argument in favor of technical jargon or the use of logical and mathematical symbols (thought I believe that in time social scientists will read pages of such symbols quite as easily as they now read pages of written text). It is not archaic to write clear

English. It may even be necessary to retain concepts whose history reaches back to the pre-Christian era. But it is also the case that the development of a technical vocabulary is to some extent unavoidable as a discipline gains power and precision, and the rate of development of new concepts in political science has been extremely slow until quite recently. At the very least, that is cause for thought. So much for the negative side of the argument.

In positive terms, there can be no doubt that the rate of change in political science has accelerated greatly since World War II. Is that a sign of rebirth or the last flutterings of decadence? Surely the former. To be specific again, it seems to me beyond argument that the conceptual apparatus now coming into use in political science is immeasurably superior to what is being abandoned. With all their shortcomings, functionalism, formalism, and even psychological explanations are far superior to conceptual frameworks based on power, law, institutions, or mechanical analysis. Current investigations of the socialization process, group interaction, and the relation between culture and personality, to mention only three major areas, indicate a basic modification in the way politics is being conceived. The level of methodological sophistication has improved greatly in the 1960's; there are more courses, more texts, and of better quality than we thought possible even a decade ago. Methodological competence is not, of course, a panacea; but without the kind of self-consciousness that acquaintance with methodology brings, progress toward better explanations is likely to be slow. More important, of course, is the fact that concern with methodology is a clear indication of the degree of interest in the quality of political knowledge on the part of members of the profession. Other signs of vitality and new life are readily perceived: the determined effort to achieve quantification of data, the search for new concepts, new aspects of political life that require investigation, the extension of political inquiry into related fields, the heightened interest in theory. There is much that seems hopeful on the contemporary scene.

Having taken a position on the side of the angels, I may perhaps be allowed to serve also as devil's advocate and offer a word of warning or caution. The principal sources of much of what is new and encouraging in political science, speaking very broadly, have been in the philosophic tradition known variously as logical empiricism, logical positivism, or analytic philosophy and the more recent offshoot of that philosophy—philosophy of science. In most cases, their influence has reached political science only indirectly, through sociology or psychology and not directly from philosophy. In fact, political "philosophers" are notable for their skill in avoiding the influence of what was surely the dominant trend in English-speaking philosophy in the first half of this century. The confluence of native pragmatism, cultural approbation for the scientific outlook, and philosophic attitude produced a trend in political science that has gathered momentum at an astonishing rate since around 1950. By the 1960's, it was the dominant influence in political science, certainly with the younger generation, which is another way of saying that political scientists were increasingly motivated to follow the scientific pattern in their inquiries. The quest for "hard" data, for logical relations among data, for "empirical theories," and so on reflects that concern. So does the sharp separation of empirical and normative inquiry.

Now, I have myself argued very strongly that political science could benefit enormously from judicious borrowing from the physical sciences, logical empiricism, and philosophy of science. There seems no reason to alter that position. But there is, I believe, a real need to point out the dangers of overcommitment. Analytic philosophy and philosophy of science have had a profound impact on contemporary thought; their influence, for the most part, has been salutary. But carried to extremes, both are self-defeating, and there are already signs of that overextension in philosophy. Logical empiricism has, I believe, done its work; certainly the beachhead is secure, and what is going on now is mopping-up rather than massive attack. As befits decline, criticism increases. One of the major latent effects of logical empiricism was the near elimination of moral philosophy from the English-speaking world; metaethics is not a substitute for normative philosophy, however beneficial it might be. Dissatisfaction with the current state of philosophy is becoming louder and more frequent. Marx thought that philosophy should change the world rather than seek to understand it; logical empiricism reversed the relation. It is becoming increasingly clear that philosophy can legitimately concern itself with both points. Similarly, philosophers of science, the real heritors of strict logical positivism, pressed formalism and logic to the point where no juice could be had from the cabbage. It is clear already that the reconstructed formal logic on which philosophy of science relied so heavily bears too little relation to the working logic that scientists employ, and that formal logic must be conditioned by historical and empirical study. As the generation that dominated postwar philosophy of science (and spent its professional life exorcising the empiricist devil—metaphysics—from philosophy) dies away, major changes should appear in that discipline as well. The old arguments continue, of course, in philosophy as in philosophy of science, but much of the vitality is gone and seems unlikely to return. Such changes are neither regrettable nor a source of gratification. Logical empiricism did yeoman work in philosophy, and no one would seek to eliminate what has been accomplished under its aegis. The task of consolidation goes on and will doubtless continue for years. But its accomplishments lie in the past and should be treated accordingly.

Of course, the scientific outlook is still a very long way from achieving the position of dominance in political science that logical empiricism enjoys in philosophy. But if historical patterns recur, political scientists can expect to find themselves a decade from now arguing fiercely about philosophic matters long since abandoned by the philosophers. It is pointless to dehydrate a discipline only to find that the water must be restored—usually at great cost in both time and anguish. With restraint, that outcome can be avoided. Let us by all means milk the empiricist cow, but let us not permit it to become sacred. Let us pay our respects to Lord Logic without becoming his slaves. Let us measure where we can but avoid trying to measure the immeasurable and under no circumstances limit ourselves to what measurement can produce. Inquiry need not be black or white; various shades of gray are useful. Tolerance does not mean a loss of integrity. Concern with values need not imply a loss of "scientific" status. Speculation is not a crime against nature.

The signs of malaise are unmistakable. It is painful to see political scientists coming to maturity with little knowledge of and even less interest in history, with too much regard for technique and too little understanding of judgment, with too much respect for the quality of data and too little concern for their significance. In the wider context of the intellectual revolution that is presently under way, such trends may appear as minor consequences of a major upheaval. Where the wider movement will lead no one can say with assurance; but in the day-to-day activities of those caught in its sweep, the need for integrity, tolerance, and moderation could hardly be greater. The record of the moderates in the great revolutions of the past is not conducive to optimism.

The division of political science into traditionalists and "scientists" is commonplace; powerful forces on each side press toward dogmatic intolerance with alarming consequences. The reward mechanisms in the discipline tend to be controlled by one side or the other, and there is no machinery for mediating between them and no standard that might be used to judge their respective claims. Both the great journals and the university departments serve as instruments for propagating a particular point of view or as battlegrounds where different points of view vie for domination. Here, in the day-to-day life of the discipline, we find the major obstacles to the development of an adequate study of political thought. In the long run, I have no doubt that the "scientific" outlook will survive. What we must avoid at all costs is a transformation of that outlook into rigorous orthodoxy.

INDEX OF CITATIONS

429

INDEX OF SUBJECT MATTER

433

*This book has been set in 11 point Cale-
donia, leaded 2 points, and 10 point
Caledonia, leaded 1 point. Part numbers
and titles are in 30 point News Gothic Condensed. Chapter numbers are in 10 point
News Gothic Condensed Bold and chapter
titles are in 18 point News Gothic Condensed. The size of the type page is 24 by
39½ picas.*